SUNSETS

Sunsets into Sunrises

Received through the Inner Word
by Jakob Lorber

Lorber Verlag D-7120 Bietigheim
Germany

Translated from the German by Violet Ozols
German title: ,,Bischof Martin"

ISBN 3-87495-307-6
©Copyright 1987 by Lorber Verlag
D-7120 Bietigheim Germany

*"Thou hast turned our
sunsets into sunrises."*

Clement of Alexandria

PREFACE

WHY DO we live on this earth, enter this life, and have to leave it again after a longer or shorter term? This is one of the most profound questions of our existence. To comprehend the problem of "whence", "whither" and "why" means spiritual integrity and making true use of the powers of mind and reason inherent in man as a spiritual being from eternity.

A spiritual rift runs through our era which was predicted in ancient prophecies as the coming "separation of the spirits". Part of mankind has become enslaved by soul destroying materialism which, by denying God, is also denying the eternal continuance of life. In physical death it sees the final extinction and, consequently, all its aspirations are directed towards the transient apparent values of life. By accepting only that as a reality which can be grasped with the senses, it sees in the passing of all material forms of life nothing but destruction and extinction instead of recognizing the liberation of the living core in order to progress to higher forms of manifestation of the spirit.

Countless millions, however, did not lose the knowledge of the eternal worth of man. Had this not been so, all religious feeling would have died on earth and mankind would have lost its last support. Especially in our present time there is much searching for truth in the souls of those who are not satisfied with what the churches or philosophic systems of today have to offer. Hence, for generations, truth-seekers have reached for the powerful works of the New Revelation received and written down by the God-inspired Styrian mystic Jakob Lorber, who during twenty-four years — from 1840 to 1864 — served the Inner Word, the voice of the Divine Spirit dictating to him large volumes about the secrets of creation and life, which are without equal.

Among the works dealing in particular with the states of existence in which man finds himself after death and his development in the beyond to his spiritual perfection, this one plays an important part. Here we see a man, after breathing his last breath on earth, pass through the "big gate" into the beyond. We see how in the other world his "sphere" begins to take shape, initially like a dream-life still reflecting all his earthly errors, notions and desires. We accompany him on his various progresses and regresses on the path to cognition and see how numerous higher spiritual beings and angels join him and, through purifying and instructive experiences, prepare him for a true understanding of God.

We see how realization dawns in the soul of the former bishop, and how his spiritual awakening eventually leads him into realms of the celestial spheres. His ever-growing love enables him to recognize the deity in Jesus as the Father of Eternity, and thus he enters into the state of his perfection — as a child of God, with all its freedom, creative power, and bliss. Comparing the initial scenes of this work of education in the beyond with the attained goal, we realize how the human spirit can fight its way through from sphere to sphere up to the highest spiritual altitudes.

For the uninhibited reader this book gives witness of the loving and wise guidance man receives after his temporal life. In Martin's discussions and encounters with perfected spirits, as the disciples Peter and John, and finally the Lord Himself, the seeker will find a vast amount of answers to questions about his existence. And he senses the immensity of the great idea of creation but, at the same time, also the majesty of man who has attained to the sonship of God and matured to the crown of creation.

The Lorber Publishers

THESE REVELATIONS end with an admonition to the reader by the Lord. We bring this already at the outset as it may help to better understand this work.

The Lorber Publishers
Germany

* * *

"He who will read these scenes from the beyond with an open mind and in good faith will easily understand what happens to man in the world of spirits after he has left his physical body, and he will be able to use this knowledge to his advantage. The materialist, however, will reject this book, as he does the Scriptures, claiming it to be the foolish product of a brainless would-be writer. This, of course, is of no importance, for sooner or later he himself will arrive in that world where no one but I will be able to help him!

"In case one or the other poetically or philosophically inclined reader should take offense at some of Martin's talk as sounding too earthly, filthy and profane, let him realize that 'where there is a cadaver, the eagles flock together.' The human spirit is the same in his misery, be it on earth or in the beyond; only when purified will he also talk like a pure spirit.

"Although these revelations give a comprehensive picture of the spirit world and the guidance of souls in the beyond, you should not regard this as a general but only as an individual case of guidance, aiming solely at the perfection of Martin. Still, the scene around Martin must be regarded as a self-contained whole.

"Accept these revelations in good faith, and your paths in the other world will be easier than those of thousands, who in their spiritual darkness have not even an inkling of life in the beyond.

"My grace, blessing and love be with all of you!

Amen."

THE END OF OLD BISHOP MARTIN'S TEMPORAL EXISTENCE, AND HIS ARRIVAL IN THE BEYOND.

1. A bishop who had always been very conscious of his dignity as well as his dogma fell ill for the last time.

2. He, who even still as an assistant priest, had been wont to paint the joys of heaven in the oddest colors and to describe the delights and bliss in the realm of the angels with great enthusiasm, not forgetting to mention hell and purgatory, did not yet desire, even as an old man of almost eighty, to take possession of his much praised heaven. He would have preferred another thousand years on this earth to a future heaven with all its delights and bliss.

3. Therefore, our sick bishop did everything in his power to restore his health. He had to be surrounded by the best physicians. Powerful masses had to be celebrated in all the churches of his diocese; all the sheep of his flock were asked to pray for his life. In his sick-room an altar had been erected at which mass had to be celebrated three times every morning to help restore his health, whereas, in the afternoon, three of the most pious monks had to keep praying the breviary in front of the consecrated host.

4. He himself kept uttering: "Oh, Lord, have mercy upon me! Holy Mary, beloved mother, help me! Have mercy upon my dignity and grace as prince-bishop for your Son's glory! Oh, do not forsake your most faithful servant, you helper in need, you sole support of the afflicted."

5. But all this did not help. Our man fell into a coma from which he did not awaken again in this world.

6. You know of the "highly important" ceremonial for a deceased bishop, and we need not waste any time with its description. Instead, let us look around in the spirit world to see what our man will be doing there.

7. Look, here we are — and there our man can be seen still lying on his bed; while the heart is still warm the angel does not sever the soul from the body. This warmth constitutes the nerve spirit which has to be wholly absorbed by the soul before complete severance can be undertaken.

8. At last this man's soul has completely absorbed the nerve spirit

and the angel is severing it from bis body with the words: "Ephetha — arise thou soul, but thou dust revert to thy decomposition through the kingdom of vermin and decay. *Amen.*"

9. Already you see our bishop rising in his full bishop's robes, just as during his lifetime, and he opens his eyes. He looks around in astonishment, not seeing anybody, not even the angel who awakened him. The surroundings are visible only in a fading light, as of late dusk, and the ground seems to be covered with dry alpine moss.

10. Our man is not a little astonished at this unusual situation, and says to himself: "What is this? Where am I? Am I still alive, or have I died? I must have been seriously ill, and it is quite possible that I am already among the deceased! Oh, for God's sake, this must be so! Oh, Holy Mary, St. Joseph, St. Ann — you, my three most powerful helpers, come and help me into the Kingdom of Heaven!"

11. He waits for a while, looking around carefully to see from which direction the three will be coming, but they do not come.

12. He calls once more, this time louder, and waits; but still nobody approaches.

13. For the third time he calls, louder still, but again in vain.

14. Now our man begins to feel very scared. He realizes his desperate situation and says: "Oh, for God's sake, Lord, help me! (This is only his habitual phrase.) What does this mean? I have called three times and no response!

15. Am I damned? How can that be, for I do not see any fire nor any devil?

16. Oh, Oh, Oh [trembling]. It is truly terrible! So alone! Oh, God, if one of these devils turned up now while I'm without a consecrated font or crucifix — what will I do?

17. And the devil is said to be particularly keen on bishops! Oh, what a desperate situation! I believe the 'howling and gnashing of teeth' is already upon me!'

18. I will discard my bishop's robe so the devil will not recognize me. But maybe that would give him even more power over me? Oh, what a terrible thing death is!

19. If at least I were quite dead, then I wouldn't be afraid; but this being alive after death is so terrible!

20. "I wonder what would happen if I walked on? No, no, I'd rather stay here. What consequences a step in the dark might have only God knows. Therefore, I would rather remain here until Doomsday, in the name of God and the Blessed Virgin!"

BISHOP MARTIN'S BOREDOM IN HIS ISOLATION. HE IS CONSIDERING A CHANGE.

1. After having stood in the same spot for some hours without anything happening, time (also in the natural sphere of the spirit world there exists something like our notion of time) seems to be dragging, and our man once more starts a monologue:

2. "How odd, now I've been standing here for half an eternity and nothing has changed. Nothing is moving — neither the moss nor a hair on my head or my robe! Whatever is going to happen?

3. Could it be possible that I am condemned to remain here forever? No, no, that just couldn't be! It would be hell! And if this were the case, the ghastly clock of hell would be visible with its terrifying pendulum calling with every swing — 'ever' and then again, 'never.' Oh, how terrible!

4. Thank God that I do not see this awful thing! Or, maybe it appears only after Doomsday. I wonder whether the sign of the Son of Man will be appearing on the horizon? How many millions of years have I been standing here, and how much longer will I have to stand waiting for Doomsday?

5. In the world nothing was pointing to the approach of Doomsday, and here in the spirit world there is even less evidence! If my faith were not so firm, I might begin to doubt the coming of Doomsday and, altogether, the truth of the whole Gospel!

6. Isn't it odd that all the old prophets seemed to be saying very much the same as the Oracle of Delphi, that is, that these prophecies can be understood one way or another, and interpreted as required. And the Holy Ghost of the Gospel must be a rare bird, for it hasn't been seen since the time of the disciples!

7. My faith is still very firm, but whether it will remains so under the present circumstances, I honestly can't say.

8. There even seems to be something wrong with the much praised Mary of my Church, as well as the saints! Otherwise, Mary would have answered my prayers. I have the feeling as if some millions of years have passed since my physical death, and there is not a trace of the Mother of God, nor of her Son or any of the saints. Fine helpers in need they are!

9. If I didn't have such a strong faith I wouldn't be still standing here in this forsaken spot; only my faith is keeping me here. But not for much longer! I would be a fool if I kept standing here for another million years. Sufficient that I've been a fool on earth, and it is time I made an end to this fruitless comedy!

10. On earth I was at least well paid, and it was worth my while to play the fool there. However, as my experience of millions of years has now revealed, there is nothing to the whole thing, and I will renounce all this nonsense."

11. Look, now he is going to leave this spot, after the angel has given him the feeling as if the few hours spent here have been millions of years. He is still standing firmly in the one spot, looking around timidly as if to choose the best way. Looking towards the west, it appears to him as if something were moving in the distance, and he says to himself:

12. "What is it that I'm seeing there in the distance for the first time since my being here for several millions of years? This is most alarming, for maybe some sort of judgment is in preparation.

13. Should I risk walking in that direction? It might be the end of me! But then, it could also be my salvation!

14. However, for one like myself, who has spent millions of years rooted to a spot, it doesn't really matter what happens now. Nothing worse could happen to an honest man having been rooted to a spot like a statue for millions of years — a true damnation.

15. Therefore, I'll now say to myself, good luck, and risk it! The result couldn't be worse than eternal death, which I would only welcome. An eternal non-existence is much preferable to an existence like my present one.

16. No more hesitating! Let happen what will! No! This is still unknown territory for me. I shall not say any more until I know what my feet are standing on.

17. The thing out there seems to be moving more now; almost like a little tree in the wind. Courage, my long disused feet! Let's see whether we can still walk.

18. I have been told on earth once that a spirit has only to think and finds himself already in the place where he wanted to go. But there does seem to be something wrong with the spirituality of my person for I do have feet, hands, a head, eyes, nose, mouth — in short, everything I had on earth — even a stomach which has had a fast worthy of a cardinal. If there hadn't been plenty of moss all

12

around me, with a lot of dew, I might already have shrunk to the size of an atom. Maybe I'll even find something better for my stomach over there?

19. So, once more, good luck! At least there'll be a change from my present state. Therefore, in God's name!"

BISHOP MARTIN IN THE COMPANY OF AN APPARENT COLLEAGUE. — THE GOOD SUGGESTIONS OF THE GUIDE.

1. Look! Our man now starts walking carefully, step by step, towards the moving object . . . .

2. Soon he has reached the spot, and is not a little surprised to see a man like himself under the tree, a bishop with all the trappings — that is, so it appears to him. In reality, it is the angel that had accompanied him, invisibly, all the time. This angel is the spirit of the disciple Peter.

3. Listen now how our man addresses his presumed colleague:

4. "Do I see right? A colleague, a co-worker in the Lord's vineyard? What a great joy after millions of years to meet a human being, and even a colleague, in this desert of deserts.

5. I greet you, dear brother! Tell me, how did you get here? Could it be that you, too, have reached my age in this beautiful spirit world — about five million years in one spot?"

6. The angel, as presumed a bishop, speaks: "First of all, I am your brother in the Lord and, of course, an old worker in His vineyard. However, as regards my age, I am older than you measured by time and activity, but much younger measured by your imagination.

7. For, five million earth years is quite a considerable time for a created spirit, although it is very little for God, since His Being is not measured by time and space, but is eternal and unlimited.

8. Therefore, being a newcomer to the unlimited spirit world, you are quite wrong. For, if you had been in this place for five million years, you would be wearing a very different garb, as during that time the mountains of the earth would have been levelled, its

valleys filled, its seas, lakes, rivers, and swamps dried. And a completely new creation would then exist on earth, for which today not even a seed has been placed in the furrows.

9. But so that you, dear brother, may see for yourself that your supposed age is only a product of your own imagination, due to your notions of time and space which are considerably spiced with hellish elements, turn around and you will still see your body which died only three hours ago."

10. Our man turns round quickly and discovers his corpse lying in state in the cathedral, surrounded by numerous tapers and even more sightseers. The sight of this spectacle annoys him very much, and he says:

11. (The bishop): "Dearest brother, what can I do about it? Oh, what terrible nonsense! From pure boredom, minutes turn to eternities for me, and still it is I who dwelt in this body. I am desperate for hunger and lack of light, and these fools worship my fleshly garment. Shouldn't I now, as a spirit, have the power to tear up this junk and scatter it? Oh, you stupid devils! Do you think you are doing this stinking dirt a favor?"

12. (Says the angel): "Turn back to me now and don't excite yourself; for didn't you do the same while you were still in the natural world? Let the dead bury the dead, but you turn your back on all this and follow me, so that you might find life."

13. (The bishop asks): "Whither should I follow you? Are you, by any chance, my name's patron, St. Boniface, that you seem so concerned with my welfare?"

14. (Says the angel): "I tell you, in the name of the Lord Jesus, follow me to Jesus! He is the right Boniface for all men. But your Boniface is nothing, nor am I what you think I am.

15. But if you follow me — that is, do what I tell you — you will understand everything that has happened to you so far . . . the how and the why. Besides, you will immediately find yourself on better ground and also will get to know the Lord as concerns His person, through Him the path to heaven and, at the same time, also me, your brother."

16. (The bishop): "Oh, do speak, I would rather fly than walk from this desolate spot!"

17. (Says the angel): "Listen! Take off your ridiculous raiment and dress yourself in these common peasant clothes."

18. (The bishop): "It is with pleasure that I'll exchange this irksome robe for the most common rag!"

19. (The angel): "Right — you are already clothed in peasant's garb. Now follow me!"

BISHOP MARTIN'S ANNOYANCE AT THE SIGHT OF A LUTHERAN CHURCH, AND THE ANGEL'S COMMENTS. — HIS READINESS TO SERVE AS A SHEPHERD.

1. They follow a road in a southerly direction and come upon a farmhouse, in front of which there is a small, obviously Lutheran, church. Noticing this, the bishop stops and begins to cross himself repeatedly, uttering: *"Mea culpa, mea culpa, mea maxima culpa."*

2. But the angel asks him: "Brother, what is it? Is anything worrying you? Why aren't you proceeding?"

3. (Says the bishop): "Don't you see the Lutheran church which is of the devil? How can a Christian go near such a d--- — I'd rather not say it — place?

4. Or, maybe you are a devil in disguise! Oh, oh, if that were true, then clear out, you abominable fiend!"

5. (Says the angel): "Would you like to repeat your experience of the five to ten million years, in an even darker and more desolate spot of the spirit world? If you prefer that, just let me know. Look, your old bishop's robe is ready for you! But this time, you might have to wait ten times as long until somebody will come to your aid.

6. Don't you see me still walking around in a bishop's robe? And you used to believe that the devil could disguise himself as an angel of light, but could never appear in the disguise of a bishop who is filled with the Holy Ghost. If you do not want to condemn your own belief, how then can you take me for a devil? (The bishop almost collapses, but crosses himself and says: 'God help us!')

7. But if you do condemn your dogmatic belief that the rock of St. Peter is invincible to the gates of hell, you repeal all that Rome teaches. And then I couldn't understand how, as an opponent of Rome, this little building which you take for an evangelical church can annoy you. Don't you see that your whole attitude at this

moment does not show the least trace of moral or religious consistency?"

8. (Says the bishop): "I regret to say you are quite right, but if you are a real bishop, you should know that Rome demands absolute faith and blind obedience of every true believer. And where the mind is kept captive in strong shackles, how can you expect consistency in thought and deed?

9. We say, a man should take care not to fathom the essence of religion; to know nothing, but believe blindly and firmly. It is better for him to enter heaven as a simpleton than hell as an enlightened person. God should be feared because of hell and loved because of heaven. If this is the basis of our teaching, how then can you expect consistency on my part?"

10. (The angel): "Unfortunately, I am only too well aware as to the state of things with your Babel's teachings, and that they clearly contradict the Gospel, wherein it says, 'Judge not, that ye be not judged!' However, you keep judging and condemning everybody who does not bend under Babel's scepter.

11. Tell me, are you really Christ's followers when you do not follow His gentle teaching at all? Does not His teaching comprise the greatest and most sublime order and consistency, as is the case in all creation? Does not every word of the Gospel emanate the Holy Spirit in its fullness? But have you not always opposed the Holy Spirit in word and deed, quite consciously acting contrary to the Lord's purest teaching full of the Holy Spirit, which the latter rendered to the Apostles and disciples forever to remain?

12. From this you can see how damnable the ground is on which you are standing, how ripe for hell. But the Lord is willing to show mercy, and that is why He sent me to you to help rescue you from your old Babylonian captivity.

13. For this reason, the Lord wants you to make your peace with your greatest cause for vexation, that is, if you do want to take advantage of His mercy. If you, however, prefer to stick by your Babel's teaching, you will drive yourself to hell, from whence you will not have much chance of being rescued by a friend of the Lord Jesus."

14. (Says the bishop): "You are right, dearest friend, and for the first time I feel something like consistency emerging! Do have patience with me. I will do what you ask, in God's name, but do not speak to me of that terrible hell! Let us go on!"

16

15. (The angel): "For the time being we have reached our destination. You will serve this Lutheran farmer and bishop, which is I, as a shepherd. Faithful performance of your duties will provide bread for you and gradual advancement. Should you, however, attend to your duties in a morose or judicial way, you will do great harm to yourself and diminish your food and advancement. If you do want to be a faithful servant, forget about your temporal existence, but think that you have to start with the lowest service if you want to get ahead.

16. Do not forget one thing: To advance here means to stand back, waiting to be the last and least of all. For no one can come to the Lord before he has abased himself to the lowest possible degree. Now you know what you need for this present situation, so follow me into this house in the right spirit."

17. The bishop follows him without protest, convinced that his guide does mean him well.

IN THE HUT OF THE ANGEL PETER. — AN ENLIGHTENING WORD FROM THE ANGEL ABOUT LUTHER. — MARTIN'S EMPLOYMENT AS A SHEPHERD IN THE BEYOND.

1. When the angel and Martin entered the house, which was furnished very simply, our bishop noticed on a small, triangular table, a Lutheran Bible containing both the Old and New Testaments. This causes him obvious embarrassment.

2. (The angel, Peter, notices it and says): "Whatever could Luther have done to you that you not only despise him but, at the same time, also his faithful Bible translation, which contains nothing but the pure Word of God?

3. Even if Luther was not in every respect a man of whom one could say, 'He was a man according to God's own heart,' he was still very much better than many from your church who claim to be the most righteous and good men, but are in reality exactly the contrary! He alone had the courage in the midst of the darkest night of Babel

to restore to mankind the pure Word of God, thus leading it back into the right path to the Lord.

4. Notwithstanding a few errors also on this path as a result of the closeness of Babel [Rome], his teaching of the pure Word of the Lord, compared with Rome's false doctrine, was like the midday sun against the dim light of a will-o'-the-wisp on a dark night!

5. If Luther has achieved this in the name of the Lord, tell me, what reason could you possibly have to abuse and despise this worthy man?"

6. (Says the bishop): "I do not actually despise him, but you know how it is when one has been a slave of a party for a long time. Gradually an artificial hate is fostered against a person whom your party has constantly cursed and damned. This has also happened to me. However, I hope and expect of God to help me get rid of all the foolishness I have brought with me from my temporal life. Therefore, do not lose patience, I do hope things will improve with me soon."

7. (Says the angel Peter): "Oh, brother, it is not I who needs the patience, but you will! You do not know all that you will be faced with as yet, but I do. Therefore, I have to handle you in such a way that will help to fortify you in truth and resistance to the numerous temptations that will confront you on your way to the Lord.

8. Look out the window! Do you see the thousands of sheep and lambs running and frisking about?

9. Here is a book recording all their names. Take it and call their names. If they recognize the voice of the true shepherd, they will come hurrying to you. If, however, they hear only the voice of a hireling, they will scatter and flee from you. Should that happen, then do not grumble but know that you are a hireling; then another shepherd will come and teach you the right way to call and tend the sheep and lambs.

10. Now then, take this book and do as I have advised you!"

BISHOP MARTIN'S PLEASANT BUT DANGEROUS SURPRISE. THE FLOCK — A HOST OF BEAUTIFUL MAIDENS.

1. Our man, in his peasant's clothes and with the thick book under his arm, goes outside to where the flock had been pointed out to him. In the spiritual distance it had appeared as a flock of sheep and lambs, but seen from up close, these turned out to be pious and gentle people, mainly female spirits who had led godly lives on earth but had thought higher of the Roman clergy than of Me, the Lord. They did not know Me then, nor have they come to know Me here, as yet. This is the reason why, seen from a certain spiritual distance, they still appear as animals, though of the gentlest kind.

2. Martin, in a happy mood, sits down on a moss-covered rock and looks around for the sheep. But instead of sheep, he sees only a crowd of the most beautiful maidens running to and fro in a vast meadow, picking flowers and winding pretty garlands.

3. At this sight, our man starts wondering: "Isn't it strange? It is the same meadow in which I just saw the sheep and lambs. Now the flock has vanished and, instead, there are now thousands of the sweetest maidens, one lovelier than the next. Honestly speaking, if this is not some sort of delusion, I'd by far prefer this type of flock. However, in this world, one can never trust his senses — in a moment everything may have changed!

4. Oh, now they are all coming in my direction, even before I have called their names! But never mind; now I'll be able to have a close look at these fair children to my heart's delight and, maybe, I'll even have a chance of cuddling one or the other. In that case, it wouldn't be so bad at all to be a shepherd of such a wonderfully changed flock in all eternity.

5. The closer they approach, the more beautiful they appear. There is one in front — oh, isn't she a beauty! Oh, my moral strength, don't forsake me now! It is as well that silly celibacy doesn't count here, otherwise one could only too easily commit a deadly sin.

6. I was told to call them by their names from the book. However, I'd better not do that, for they might then run away. Therefore, my thick register of names shall not be opened for this flock.

7. They are coming nearer and nearer, and have almost reached me, the sweet little angels!"

8. Look, the "sweet little angels" surround our man, asking him what he is doing there.

BISHOP MARTIN'S TEMPTATION AND THE ADVICE RECEIVED FROM THE ANGEL PETER.

1. Our man, quite overwhelmed by all this beauty and his own feelings, says in a trembling voice: "Oh, you heavenly little angels, you lovely little angels of the Lord, I — I am supposed to be your shepherd, but, as you can see, my sweet little angels, I am too stupid for that!"

2. The most beautiful of the maidens now sits down close beside our man, and the others follow her example. Then she says to the shepherd: "You dear man, you are too modest; I find you very handsome, and, if you are willing, I would be only too happy to be yours forever. Look at me — don't you like me?"

3. Our man is so enamored that he can but utter, "Oh . . . oh . . . oh!", for the lovely head with the golden curls, the friendly, large blue eyes, the beautifully shaped mouth, the delicate full bosom, the beautiful hands and feet drive our man almost out of his wits.

4. The little angel, seeing the shepherd's great agitation, bends over and kisses him on the forehead.

5. This costs him his last self-control, and he embraces the beautiful maiden passionately, uttering a flood of protestations of love.

6. Then suddenly the whole scene changes. The "little angels" vanish, and the angel, Peter, is standing beside our man, saying:

7. "But, brother, how are you tending your sheep? Was this the advice I gave you? If you handle the sheep and lambs entrusted to you in this way, it will take very long for you to reach the goal of eternal life! Why didn't you make use of the book?"

8. (Says the bishop): "Why didn't you tell me that the sheep and lambs seen from your house are really the most beautiful maidens, to

whom only a stone could remain indifferent? As you see, the whole thing was a hoax, so why make a lot of fuss about it?"

9. (Says the angel): "But what about your celibacy? Haven't you broken that as well as your vow of chastity?"

10. (Says the bishop): "Never mind celibacy and vow! I am now altogether on Lutheran ground, where both are abolished! And, anyway, to an angel like that maiden, I would, even on earth, have sacrificed my celibacy and turned Lutheran to please her! But where have the beautiful maidens got to now, especially that one? Oh, if I could only see her once again!"

11. (Says the angel): "Friend, you will see her again very soon with all the others; but you will not be allowed to speak to her, nor approach her. However, if she tries to follow you, raise your hand and say: 'Return to the right order, in the name of the Lord, and do not tempt me, but follow the voice of order!'

12. Should, however, the flock disregard your words, then open the book and read aloud the names in it. The flock will then either scatter immediately or — if it detects a sound arising from the power of the Lord in you — follow you! In that case, you will lead it onto that hill in the south, where I shall meet you again.

13. But what has just happened, you should sacrifice in your heart to the Lord Jesus, for He allowed you to fall, and in your fall to cast off your tenacious celibacy.

14. But now make sure that you do not fall again, for that might have disastrous consequences for you, and could cost you hundreds of earth years to overcome. Therefore, be watchful and wise! Once you are purified, you will meet much greater beauties in the realms of heaven, but not before you have uprooted all your earthly foolishness.

15. Now wait here and do as advised, and that will mean a pleasant path for you in the name of the Lord."

16. Immediately after these words, the angel Peter vanishes so as to give the bishop no opportunity to come out with any of his burlesque remarks or to contradict him.

BISHOP MARTIN'S CRITICAL SOLILOQUY AND CONFESSION.

1. All by himself in the meadow, he begins the following soliloquy:

2. (Bishop Martin): "Where has he got to now, my guide? A fine guide he is! Vanishes just when one needs him most! But when one makes a mistake — he appears right away! This I don't like at all! If he doesn't stay with me to lead me on these insecure roads in the spirit world, he may as well clear out for good rather than come to me when I have already sinned in some way or another.

3. If he wants to lead me to salvation, he must stay with me visibly, otherwise his guidance is of no use whatsoever. Well, wait, you Lutheran hide-and-seek patron of a guide, you will find me a hard enough case and soon lose your patience! What worse could happen to me now? I am already a Lutheran — quite ripe for hell by Rome's standards! Maybe, even in hell already without having realized it.

4. Therefore, let the lovely lambs only return to me. I shall not be a wolf in sheep's clothing to them, but an ardent lover. I shall never raise my hand against them, nor read their names from this book, so as not to make them flee from me. I will not forget myself to such an extent with one or the other as I did before; but I will definitely not raise my hand or read their names! And should my guide then reappear from some hiding place, I will show him how a bishop from earth can speak, if he wishes to!

5. I wonder what could be keeping the dear little angels? Not a trace of them anywhere! As for me, I now feel much bolder. Just come along, you darling little angels, and you'll find the right man in me now, no longer a coward, but a hero! And what a hero!

6. But where could they be? It is quite a while since my guide left me, and still no sign of anyone. What could that mean? Is it possible that my guide has fooled me again? It almost looks like it! I have again the feeling as if scores of years have passed since he left me — maybe they'll even grow into millions.

7. Life in this spirit world is really beastly. Everything looks hazy, no proper light. And things are not what they pretend to be. Even the rock on which I am seated awaiting the sheep and lambs is

probably not a rock at all. And who knows what the dear little angels are in reality? Most likely — nothing! Otherwise, they would be here by now. Oh, yes, nothing is what it seems, not even my guide, or he couldn't vanish into nothingness so suddenly.

8. This reminds me very much of dream life. How often I have dreamt of all sorts of silly things, of various transformations. And what were they really? Nothing but pictures created by the fanciful imaginative power of the soul. In the same way also, this life is nothing but an idle, empty, probably eternal, dream. Only my contemplations seem to have a real content, everything else is imagination. Now I must have been waiting for the lambs and sheep for nearly two hundred years, and no trace of them.

9. What still strikes me as odd is that in this world of imagination the book here, my peasant's clothes, and the whole landscape, including the Lutheran house and church, have remained unchanged. There must be something in this whole business, but the question remains — what?

10. Could it be that I was wrong in not following his advice right away? But if he is a real guide, he should have reprimanded me immediately instead of vanishing. Didn't he say that if I fell again, it would do me much harm and might cost me several hundreds of earth years? But have I actually fallen? With my thoughts and will, of course, but not with deeds, which is impossible since certain little angels haven't appeared at all.

11. Perhaps they do not appear *because* of my thoughts and will. That could easily be the case. If I could only rid myself of such thoughts. Why did the little angels have to be so attractive? Now I have really got myself into trouble. I shall just have to bide my time until my foolish thoughts and inclinations subside.

12. I do understand that if this is meant as a trial concerning my greatest weakness, I shall be in a most difficult position, for in this particular point I have been a beast in my temporal life. Whenever I saw a buxom girl . . . *taceas* [hush] ! And all the lovely young nuns I have . . . *taceas de rebus praeteritis* [do not talk about things of the past]! Oh, those blissful times — but now *taceas*!

13. How strict I was in the confessional with the penitents and how lax against myself! Most regrettable and very wrong! But who, except God, has the strength to resist the urge of nature?

14. If it weren't for the silly celibacy, then a bishop could be the husband of a good wife which, as far as I know, St. Peter ex-

pressly demanded. Then the fight against the flesh would surely have been so much easier.

15. Oh, blast! But then, things are this way and who can change them? The Creator, naturally, if He wishes, but without His aid, man, especially my kind, will at all times remain just a beast.

16. Lord, have mercy upon me! I do realize that if You do not help, I haven't a chance, for I am a beast — and my guide a stubborn wretch, maybe even the spirit of Luther! Patience, do not forsake me. I must have spent another thousand years in one spot."

17. At last he falls silent, waiting for the sheep and lambs.

FURTHER PATIENCE TEST FOR BISHOP MARTIN AND HIS GRIM HUMOR.

1. He looks around expectantly, but still no trace of the sheep and lambs.

2. Now he starts calling, but also in vain. After having waited a bit longer and nothing happens, he rises impatiently, takes his book, and says:

3. "Now I have really had it! Another million years must have passed, at least it seems like it, and still no change. But now I will no longer be fooled by you, my fine guide. Being an honest chap, I shall put the silly book in your Lutheran house and start on my way, wherever it may lead me. I must assume that this particular world has some sort of boundary where one will be able to say, 'Huc usque et non plus ultra!' [This far and no farther!]

4. And if at such a point I'll have to spend billions of years here, at least I'll know why! Rather than play the fool here for no apparent reason! It is always easier to bear the consequences of one's own mistakes than to be pushed around by a conceited dunce. I am so angry with this Lutheran scoundrel that I might lay hands on him if I should meet him now!

5. Could there be anything more boring and tormenting than to have to wait for something that has been promised and then does

not come? What a terribly long time I have been waiting here, and apparently for no reason. This story about the sheep and lambs is obviously not true.

6. If I could only meet someone of my own kind, wouldn't that be wonderful! How we could, together, abuse this wretched spirit world. It would be sheer enjoyment! But now — on my way! I shouldn't waste any more time here.

7. Now where has that unfortunate book got to? Has it taken itself home to save me the trouble? But I *do* find this a bit awkward; all the time it has been lying here and now, when I want to pick it up, it has vanished.

8. How terribly stupid this spirit world is set up – quite incomprehensible for the human mind. A book vanishes because of some justified criticism!

9. I suppose I'll have to ask the forgiveness of this rock for having rested my unworthy person on it for such a lengthy period, otherwise it, too, might vanish. And since I intend to march through these beautiful fields of mist and moss, with their will-o'-the-wisp lighting, I might have to ask the moss permission to tread on it!

10. Oh, this d --- — *stop*, I mustn't swear! Now look, even the Lutheran house with the church has taken its leave! Only the rock is still there . . . that is, I think it is. But I'd better make sure. There you are, Mr. Rock too has taken his leave!

11. It is high time I left too. But where will I go? There isn't much choice here, so I'll walk straight ahead — follow my nose, if I've still got one after having been led by it for the second time in a million years. However, thank God I still have my nose, and so I shall follow this only guide I have here in this fine spirit world."

12. Look, he now starts to walk with the angel Peter invisibly behind him. "To walk" in the spirit world, however, means "to change one's inclination," and to the extent that this changes, also the surroundings appear to change. We shall soon see where our man is now going.

BISHOP MARTIN GOING ASTRAY. — HINTS FROM THE LORD ABOUT SPIRITUAL CONDITIONS AND THEIR CONSEQUENCES.

1. Whoever is familiar with the spiritual compass will soon notice that our man, instead of turning toward noon, is walking straight toward evening. He marches boldly along, but sees nothing except the fairly level ground, covered by sparse moss and a greyish light where the horizon seems to be getting darker the farther he proceeds toward evening.

2. This growing darkness begins to puzzle him, but it does not keep him from walking on in that direction because his cognition and faith are practically nil, and what is left is some false reasoning against the pure Word of the Gospel, a clearly antichristian attitude, and a hatred of sects hidden behind a humorous mask.

3. Therefore, the bishop's walk toward evening and the sparsely moss-covered ground signifies the dryness and meagerness of My Word in his heart. And the ever-growing darkness is due to the fact that the little respected and even less heeded Word of God (to which bishops of this kind, in red and golden robes, bow merely for the sake of appearance) in him never developed that warmth of life which could generate the glorious light of the eternal morning for the soul.

4. In the spirit world, people of this type must be faced with the greatest apparent destitution and the darkest night; only then does it become possible to change them. Difficult as it would be, already in this world, to lead such a bishop onto the path of a true disciple, in the other world it is even harder, for there, as a spirit, he cannot be influenced from the outside whilst in him there is only error, false reasoning, and lust for power.

5. However, My mercy can achieve what normally would be impossible. Therefore, let us look at this man and see where his inclinations would lead him, but what My mercy can do if the worst comes to the worst, without interfering with his spiritual freedom. This mercy will be extended to him because, at one stage, he asked Me to help and hold him. But the force of My mercy cannot take hold of him until he has rid himself of the junk of false ideas and hidden evil within him, which is becoming apparent in the utter darkness that will surround him.

6. So now let us watch our wanderer. He is proceeding with slow and careful steps, scanning the ground to make sure it is firm enough to carry him; for the ground is gradually turning boggy which means that his fundamentally false concepts will soon be flowing into an unfathomable sea of secrecy. Therefore, various smaller swamps of secrecy are already becoming apparent — a state which on earth often becomes manifest when people do not want to listen to talk about life of the spirit in the hereafter, claiming that such talk only confuses and worries them, and that brooding over such things could easily cause a person to become mentally unbalanced.

7. This reluctance only shows that the spirit has stepped onto very boggy ground, where no one has the courage to measure the uncertain depths of such swamps with his much too short measure of cognition for fear of sinking into the unfathomable.

8. Look, the ground carrying our man is beginning to show more and more pools of water, with only narrow strips of apparent soil between them. This corresponds to the fanciful drivel of a spiritually ignorant person confessing God with his mouth only, whilst in his heart he is actually an atheist.

9. This is the ground on which our man is walking, and so are many millions! The strips of firm soil between the pools are growing narrower and the latter deeper and deeper and desperately unfathomable for his cognition. He is already swaying like a person balancing over a narrow plank bridge across a torrent. Still he does not stop; a sort of deceptive curiosity leads him on, looking for an imaginary end of the spirit world on the one hand but, secretly, also hoping to find the beautiful sheep and lambs which are still on his mind.

10. Everything that might remind him of them has been removed; the book, the meadow, the rock (representing a stumbling block), and the sheep and lambs, which latter had a lot of attraction for him in the world supplying amusement and diversion. That is also why the angel Peter produced them with a view to revealing his weakness to him.

11. This shows us what is driving our man until he will reach the endless sea, where it will become apparent: "This far and no farther your blindness, ignorance, and utter foolishness will lead you!"

12. So let him stagger on to the extreme land spit of his drivel, which is not far away. There we shall overhear all the follies he will be ejecting into the sea of his spiritual night.

13. And let each of you search into his own secret foolish in-

clinations to prevent him from entering upon the desolate path of this wanderer!

THE WANDERER IN A DIFFICULT SITUATION. HIS FURTHER SOLILIQUY, AND ABUSIVE LANGUAGE.

1. Now look! Our man has already reached the sea; no spit of land is any longer visible in this endless sea, having its origin in the boundless folly of this man, which it illustrates. It also shows a mental state in which a man becomes incapable of any concept, showing a total lack of understanding like a complete fool whose ideas all flow together into a sea of nonsense.

2. Sullen and very annoyed, he is now standing on the edge of the sea, that is, on the verge of his last concept. He is still aware of himself, everything else has turned into a dark sea in which huge sinister monsters are swimming blindly and silently, surrounding our man threateningly as if to swallow him. It is pitch dark, and the place is damp and cold, and only from a faint shimmer on the waves and their ghastly, muffled gurgling does he realize that he is standing on the edge of an endless ocean.

3. But listen to his foolish talk! This will demonstrate to you how not only this man fares, but also a great number of others, who have everything in their heads they imagine in their stupidity, but nothing, or very little, in their hearts. Now listen to him.

4. (Bishop Martin): "So here I am! Oh, damn this wretched life! For at least ten millions of earth years I had to wander about as a poor soul in this night and utter darkness, and instead of reaching the longed-for good destination, I have come to this sea which will swallow me for the whole of eternity.

5. That would be a nice *Requiescant in pace, et lux perpetua luceat eis!* (May they rest in peace and the eternal light shine upon them!) On earth they have probably sung this beautiful hymn for me. I suppose for the world I am resting eternally and the sun might shine on my ashes. But what about me, my ego? What has become of me?

6. I am still quite the same man I used to be, but where have I got to? Here I am, standing on the farthest edge of a spit of land, and all around me is the blackest night and an endless, unfathomable sea.

7. Oh men — you who are still privileged to live in your physical bodies (provided that the world still exists) — how fortunate you are and how very rich compared with me; even you who, clad in rags, have to ask kind people for a charity! Unfortunately, my lot — if not a worse one — is waiting for you here!

8. Therefore, everyone on earth should seek to save himself; either by sticking to God's commandments or by becoming stoics with body and soul, which would be preferable. Everything else is of no use. Had I done the one or the other, I would be much happier now; but thus I am standing like a complete fool facing this sea which will probably swallow me up, although it cannot kill me since I must now be immortal.

9. If anything in this silly spirit world could kill me, it would most likely be the terrible hunger that has been torturing me for millions of years.

10. Should this sea swallow me, how will I fare in the vast fish world? How many sharks and other monsters will devour me and cause me terrible pain without being able to kill me? Oh, what prospects for my future in eternity!

11. Perhaps those sheep and lambs were some kind of spiritual sirens drawing me invisibly to this place in order to devour me. I can scarcely imagine having really seen them millions of earth years ago, but nothing would be impossible in this silly spirit world, where one can spend thousands of years without seeing or recognizing anything whatsoever, except oneself, carrying on fruitless soliloquies like a complete fool in the mortal world.

12. Just one thing I don't understand: that this my desperate situation does not scare me more. I am more furious than scared; but since I have nobody on whom I can vent my anger, I just have to swallow it down.

13. Still, I have the feeling that even if God (should He exist at all) came to meet me now, my anger would flare up again. I could then really lay hands on such a mock God, if He exists, who adorned the transient world with so much splendor, while this immortal world was treated worse than a tyrannical step-father would provide for his hated step-children.

14. Wouldn't it be a pleasure to vent one's anger on such a God, if He existed! But unfortunately, there is no God, and there can never have been one. For, if some higher being had existed, you would have expected it to be wiser than we, its creatures; but as things are, there is not even a trace of wisdom noticeable.

15. Even a blind person would understand that everything that exists and happens must have some purpose; and I, too, am something that exists and is, innocently, subjected to happenings. I live, think, feel, smell, see, and hear; I have hands to work with, feet for walking, a mouth with a tongue and teeth and — a very empty stomach! But let this God tell me what for! Why should I be equipped with all this which cannot be used ever?

16. Therefore, let this so very unwise God — if He does exist — come forward and face me so that He might learn some wisdom from me. But I could challenge Him forever and He wouldn't come, since He doesn't exist."

BISHOP MARTIN IN A DEADLOCK. RESCUE BY THE LONGED-FOR SHIP. MARTIN'S ADDRESS OF THANKS TO THE SKIPPER, WHO IS THE LORD HIMSELF.

1. After having waited for the boldly challenged deity, with some misgivings for quite a while, he begins another gloomy soliloquy:

2. (Bishop Martin): "Nothing, absolutely nothing! I could challenge and grossly abuse whomsoever I want to, but since there is nobody, I cannot be heard. I seem to be here alone, as if I were the sole living being, conscious of itself, in the whole of infinity!

3. However, how could I possibly be alone? Where have the thousands of millions of people, who — like myself — were born, lived, and died on earth, got to? Have they ceased to exist or are they isolated from each other at different points of infinity, sharing my silly lot? This is probably the case, for my guide and the lovely sheep and lambs are surely proof that there must be other human beings in this endless world. But where can they be?

4. Beyond that vast sea, there is not likely to exist any life, but

it might be at a great distance behind me. If I could only retrace my steps, I could try and find them. Unfortunately, I am surrounded by water to such an extent that to turn back seems practically impossible.

5. My feet are still on dry soil, even though it is very loosely packed. I wonder what would happen if I set a foot backward or forward? Most probably I would sink into an unfathomable abyss in this vast grave of water. So I'll have to remain here forever, which I shall find most entertaining.

6. Oh, if I only had a small, but safe, ship which I could board safely and steer on whatever course I wanted to. What bliss that would be for me, poor de- - -, oh, no — that name should never pass my lips! Probably Satan is quite as unreal as the deity, but the concept is so disgusting that it makes an honest man shudder.

7. What is it that I see on the surface quite close by? Is it a monster? Or could it perhaps be a ship? It is coming closer and closer! By God, it is really a ship, with sails and a rudder. If it comes to me, I shall have to believe in a God again, for it would be too striking a proof against all the things I have uttered. Yes, it *is* coming here! There might by somebody on board who might hear me if I called out.

8. (Shouting): "You there! Help! An unhappy bishop has been waiting here for ages — one who played a great man on earth but who, in this world of spirits, has sunk into utter wretchedness and cannot find his way out! Oh, God, my great, almighty God, if You do exist, help me — help me!"

9. Now look, the ship is fast approaching the spot where our man is standing. On board you see a skilled skipper who is I Myself, and behind the bishop, the angel Peter, who is quickly boarding the ship, together with him.

10. The bishop, however, can see only Me as the skipper, not the angel who is all the time keeping behind him. He now walks straight towards Me in the friendliest manner, and says:

11. "What God or other blessed spirit has made you steer your boat to this shore where I have been waiting for salvation for an endlessly long time? Are you, perhaps, a pilot in this spirit world, or some sort of rescuer? People like you must be extremely scarce here, for I haven't seen a trace of any man for an infinitely long time.

12. Oh, you wonderful and dearest friend! You seem to be a much better man than one who, a very long time ago, imposed him-

self upon me as a guide to lead me onto the right path. But that was a fine guide for you! May the Lord forgive him, for he guided me only for a short time and then only towards a lot of evil.

13. First, I had to discard my bishop's robe, which I had some-how brought with me from the world, and don this peasant's garb, which must be of very good material or it wouldn't have lasted for millions of earth years.

14. This wouldn't have been so bad since I was hoping for a better fate. But what did this heroic guide do then? He engaged me as a shepherd for his sheep and lambs, with lots of moral maxims.

15. I willingly entered his service — although on Lutheran terri-tory — and walked outside with a thick volume containing the names of his flock, intending to do as he had told me. But then the flock turned into a crowd of lovely maidens, and there was then no trace of the sheep or the lambs.

16. I should have read their names from the book, but in the whole area there weren't any of the animals I had clearly seen from the house of this Lutheran guide.

17. But the beautiful maidens flocked around me without wait-ing to be called by name. They joked and even kissed me, and one — the loveliest of all — even embraced me with both arms, pressing me to her tender bosom to such an extent that I was overwhelmed by feelings as never before experienced by me in the world.

18. It wouldn't have been so bad, since I was new in this world and I couldn't have possibly known that instead of sheep and lambs, I was expected to tend such maidens.

19. But my guide suddenly appeared like a flash of lightning, giving me a sermon that would have done credit to Martin Luther. Then he gave me new instructions, accompanied by plenty of admoni-tions, which seemed even sillier than the previous ones and which I was to follow strictly, eventually driving all the sheep and lambs up a certain mountain.

20. Of course, I wasn't very happy with this unusual commis-sion, but then, neither the guide nor the flock appeared, although I waited for millions of years — but all in vain. Eventually, I wanted to return the book to the house of my fine employer, but it disappeared — probably being some sort of spiritual automaton, and so did the whole landscape. So I also took my leave and came to this spot, where I couldn't proceed any further. I was very angry and abusive

for a while and then despaired completely, as for such an infinitely long time there wasn't a trace of any rescue.

21. But at last you arrived, a true angel of salvation, and took me into your safe vessel. Accept my deepest gratitude for this! If I had anything with which I could repay you, it would be a pleasure to my eternally grateful heart! But as you can see, I am here the poorest imaginable creature and do not own anything except myself. Therefore, I can repay your friendship only with my gratitude and with myself, if I could serve you in any way.

22. O God, o God, how calmly, safely, and quickly your boat is riding the stormy waves of this endless sea, and what a pleasant sensation! You dear, divine friend, now my past conceited guide should be here! It would really be worth my while to introduce you to him and show him what a true guide and savior should be like. I myself was a guide, or leader, in the world once, but I'd rather be silent on that subject. Thank you, oh, thank you! How wonderfully smooth this little ship is sailing!"

13

THE DIVINE SKIPPER'S WORDS ABOUT THE BENEFITS OF SOLITUDE. — A CONFESSION REFLECTOR FOR THE ADVANCEMENT OF SELF-REALIZATION.

1. Now I, as the kindly skipper, speak: "It may be disagreeable to be on your own for quite a long period; however, such a prolonged solitude is really most beneficial. It gives one plenty of time to reflect on one's follies, to detect them, and rid oneself of them altogether. And this is of greater value than the most distinguished company, where you find at all times more foolishness and evil than wisdom and goodness.

2. Although the situation appears even more desperate when, in your solitude, your life seems threatened, this is still a thousand times better than the most glamorous and best company. If your life is threatened, you can still be saved; but many real dangers threaten a person in glamorous company, each one serious enough to destroy his soul and send him to hell, from where he will find it almost im-

possible to escape. Therefore, your state of loneliness, though most unpleasant, was actually beneficial for your character.

3. For, the Lord of all beings looked after you and showed great patience with you. I am quite aware of the fact that in the world you were a Roman bishop and that, although in your heart you didn't care about them, you attended to your heathenish, idolatrous duties with pedantic strictness. However, how could this be of any value since, as you know, God looks only at the heart? Besides, you were arrogant and tyrannical and, notwithstanding your vows of celibacy, you were too fond of the flesh of women. Can you imagine that God would look kindly on acts like those?

4. You were also quite busy looking into the affairs of monasteries and loved to visit nunneries, where you could find many attractive novices. You enjoyed it when they threw themselves at your feet and you could submit them to all sorts of morality tests, some of which were plain lewd. Do you think your moral zeal could have found favor with the Lord?

5. Think of the considerable riches you possessed in the world, contrary to what Christ demanded of His disciples. Your table was laden with selected dishes, you owned a splendid carriage, and the most elaborate bishop's insignia adorned you in your lust for power.

6. Pretending to be a messenger of God, you swore false oaths, cursing yourself if this or that were not true (which you never believed, anyhow!

7. How often you committed self-abuse, but in the confessional you were inexorably hard with the poor and unimportant people, whilst persons of standing were treated with utmost leniency.

8. Do you think that the Lord, who abominates the Roman Babel anyway, would approve of this?

9. Did you ever say in your heart: 'Let the little ones come to me'? Oh, no! Only the great personages counted with you!

10. Or did you ever take into your home a destitute child in the Lord's name, and clothed or fed it? How many naked did you clothe? How many hungry did you feed? How many prisoners did you free? . . . . I do not know of any! However, I do know of thousands whom you imprisoned spiritually; and you often deeply wounded the poor by your curses and damnation. At the same time, you gave dispense upon dispense to the great and rich — for money, of course! And only in exceptional cases was it free of charge — to the very important people, to impress them. Do you seriously believe

that God could look with favor upon such acts and that after your physical death, you would be admitted to heaven right away?

11. I am not telling you all this in order to judge you, but merely to convince you that the Lord did not wrong you if He apparently withdrew from you here; and that only His mercy saved you from being thrust into hell immediately after your death, much as you deserved it.

12. Think this over and do not abuse your guide, but realize, in all humility, that you do not deserve the Lord's mercy at all. For, if even the most faithful servants are to consider themselves bad and useless, how much more this applies to you, who has never done a thing in accordance with God's will!"

14

BISHOP MARTIN'S SINCERE REPENTANCE AND HIS WILLINGNESS TO BETTER HIMSELF.

1. (Bishop Martin): "Oh, my rescuer whom I owe so much gratitude, all I can say is, *Mea culpa, mea quam maxima culpa!* (my guilt, my greatest possible guilt.) It is all absolutely true, but what could I now do about it?

2. I now feel the deepest contrition about all I did, but it can never be undone, and thus my guilt and sin remain as the seed and root of death. How could I in my sin find mercy with the Lord?

3. I realize that I am ripe for hell, and there is nothing I can do about it, except that, perhaps, the Lord would grant me another life on earth where I could make up for my wrongdoings as much as possible. Or, since I am so terribly afraid of hell, maybe the Lord could place me as the very least being in some corner for all eternity where, as a farmer, I could make a meager living with my own two hands. I would not expect to attain to any higher degree of beatitude, being aware that I am much too unworthy for even the lowest sphere of heaven.

4. This is how I feel about it. In the world it might be rather hopeless as the general trend is evil all through, making it almost impossible to be good, as you have to battle against the current like a swimmer.

5. The governments just please themselves, and religion is used merely as an opiate for the common people, in order to make them more easily manageable. Even if the Pope himself endeavored to give religion a purely spiritual meaning, his declared infallibility would be attacked from all sides. This only shows how difficult it is, particularly for a bishop, to keep on the true path of the Word of God, as he is spied upon by a legion of secret observers.

6. Although you still retain your free will, action is made difficult, often even impossible.

7. It might seem good and beneficial for these times to become a martyr for the Word of God. However, what could it help? If you only criticize the misuse of religion, you would be put away somewhere and ordered to hold your tongue, or you might even be done away with secretly.

8. Therefore, what use could it be to swim against the current, reveal the truth, and sacrifice yourself for poor, blind mankind?

9. Knowing this from experience, it is only understandable if you say to yourself: *Mundus vult decipi — ergo decipiatur!* (The world wants to be deceived, so let it be deceived!).

10. I am convinced that the Lord endeavors to save every human being; but if man does prefer hell to heaven, even He, the Almighty, cannot prevent him from going down into the bottomless pit.

11. I have no intention of minimizing my guilt, but I just want to point out that in the world you are rather a compulsory than a voluntary sinner, which is surely taken into consideration by the Lord.

12. Not that I mean He should consider my guilt less serious, but the fact that the world is what it is, and that you cannot help it even if you would like to and, therefore, eventually cease trying, should carry some weight?

13. My dearest rescuer, do not be cross with me for what I have said, as this is the way I have seen things until now. Judging from your words, you are full of divine wisdom and will be able to tell me what I should do to, at least, save myself from hell.

14. I assure you that, as demanded by you, I forgive my former guide with all my heart! For I was only annoyed with him because I couldn't understand what he actually planned to do with me. If he came along now, I would, for your sake, embrace him like a son would embrace his long-lost father."

THE DIVINE SKIPPER'S PENITENTIAL SERMON TO BISHOP MARTIN.

1. Now I speak again as the skipper: "Listen carefully to what I shall tell you!

2. I know very well what the world is like, and if it had not always been like that, the Lord would not have been crucified. Therefore, the Lord's words, as quoted in the Gospel, have once and for all to be applied where the world is concerned, namely:

3. In these days, that is, the time of this world — the kingdom of heaven needs force; only those who apply force will possess it. However, you, my friend, have never applied this moral force where the kingdom of heaven is concerned. Therefore, do not accuse the world too much, for I know that you were at all times more concerned with the world than with the spirit. In this respect, you were one of the chief opponents of enlightenment, an enemy of the Protestants whom you persecuted for alleged heresy with bitter hatred.

4. Your slogan was never *Si mundus vult decipi!* — but just a merciless, *Mundus decipi debet!* (the world must be deceived) — and that *sine exceptione* (without exception)! I can tell you that the world is nowhere as bad as in the sphere of you and the likes of you who have, at all times, been enemies of the light. There were even times when you burnt at the stakes those who were only a little more enlightened in their thinking.

5. You were one of those who spread darkness in the nations, not the worldly rulers whom you excommunicated if they dared to think with more enlightenment than suited your darkest tyrannical despotism. If some rulers are ignorant, they are your work; but never the other way round.

6. I am quite aware of the fact that in some countries it would be particularly difficult to promote enlightenment; but for this, nobody can be blamed but your church.

7. Who told you to erect idolatrous temples and altars? Who directed you to establish your so-called divine service in Latin? Who invented the indulgence? Who banned the Scriptures and substituted the most absurd and untrue legends of the so-called saints? Who invented the relics? Who invented the millions of holy images? Not an

emperor or prince, but your church, which at all times has spread darkness to increase its power.

8. Most princes are obedient believers in your doctrine, but what faith did *you* have, being well versed in the Scriptures? And whom did *you* obey, or how often did *you* pray without being paid for it?

9. Since you had a bad influence on the world around you, and not the world on you, how can you expect any consideration from the Lord?

10. And as to the martyrdom you have mentioned, you would much rather have been crucified for your tyrannical love for the darkness than for the pure light of God. You would have had little to fear from the princes, even less from their overseers, for I know only too well how you dealt with the princes if they opposed your absurd and degrading demands.

11. I know only of very few cases where truly enlightened priests, teaching the pure Word of God, were jailed or even put to death as per your very grave accusations. However, I know of numerous people who suffered thus from you because they dared live in accordance with the Word of God.

12. Do you think the old God has weakened since the time of the disciples, and cannot help him who is "clever as a serpent and as harmless as a dove", should he be threatened by the world?

13. Look, I could name many brothers, besides Luther, who, in the darkest of times, still had the courage to own up to the true Word of God before all the world. The princes of the world did not behead any of them, but if they fell into your hands, they fared badly enough.

14. I do hope you will understand that in this world nothing counts but pure truth combined with eternal love, and all your excuses are futile except your *Mea quam maxima culpa* (my greatest possible guilt). You must admit that God alone knows the world in its minutest detail from eternity. Therefore, it is absurd of you to try and describe the world to the Lord, in defense of your attitude, for His consideration, without realizing that you were one of those mainly responsible for the world's deterioration.

15. To what extent you, as a prisoner of the world, deserve consideration, it will be afforded you. What the world owes you before God will be only a minor account. However, *your* debt will not be so negligible unless you repent and confess that you — who have

always been bad — can do absolutely nothing, but the Lord alone can redeem and forgive you.

16. You have a great fear of hell because your conscience tells you that this is where you belong, and you think God will throw you into hell like a stone into a chasm. But you do not realize that you fear only your imagined hell, whilst you enjoy being inside the real one.

17. Behold, all your thoughts so far represented were more or less hell literally. For wherever there is a spark of egotism, arrogance, and blaming of others, there is hell; where carnal desire has not been dispelled voluntarily, there is still hell. As all this is still part of you, you are still very much in hell. Do you see how idle your fear is?

18. The Lord, who has mercy with all beings, wants to save you from this hell and not condemn you deeper into it — as per your Roman maxim. Therefore, don't claim the Lord may say to those who want to go to hell: 'If you insist on going to hell, let it be so!'

19. This is a sacrilegious claim! Though you do not wish to renounce hell, when did you ever hear the Lord condemn you to it?

20. Ponder over these, my words, and change your attitude accordingly and I will pilot this boat that it will take you away from your hell into the realm of life. So be it!"

BISHOP MARTIN'S CONFESSION OF GUILT. — HIS RESOLVE TO STAY WITH THE PILOT, HIS RESCUER. — AND THE ANGEL PETER AS THE THIRD ALLY.

1. (Bishop Martin): "Oh, my dear friend, I must admit to my regret that you are right in every detail and I do see now that I have no excuse whatsoever and am alone responsible for everything that has happened. But I would like to learn from you where you are taking me and what my lot will be for eternity."

2. (The skipper): "Ask your heart, your love! What does it say? What does it desire? When your love will have given a definite answer to your query, your lot will have been decided within you. For everyone is judged by his own love or desire."

3. (Bishop Martin): "Oh, friend, if I were judged by my love, only God knows where I would get to! For my mind is still like that of a fashion-crazy woman who has a choice of hundreds of dress materials and is unable to make up her mind which to take.

4. An innermost feeling draws me towards God, my Creator. But then my numerous great sins get in the way and make the realization of this wish seem impossible.

5. Then I remember those sheep and lambs of this world, and that it wouldn't be unpleasant at all to live with such sheep in eternity. But an inner voice warns me that it would never bring me nearer to God, it would rather take me farther away. Thus, also, this pet idea of mine sinks into this fathomless sea.

6. Once more the thought comes to my mind that I could live as a simple farmer in some corner of this eternal spirit world and maybe once be granted the favor of seeing Jesus, even if only for a moment. But then my conscience again reminds me that I am not worthy of such a great honor — and I sink back into my sinful insignificance before Him, the Most Holy!

7. Only one idea seems to me the least difficult to realize, and I must admit it has now turned out to be my pet idea — namely, to stay with you through all eternity, wherever you may go. Although, in the world I could not stand those at all who dared face me with the truth, I have come to love you very much, as you have told the truth to my face like a wise but mild judge. To this pet idea of mine I would stick in eternity!"

8. (The skipper): "Alright, if that is your main love, of which you will still have to convince yourself, this can be realized immediately. We are not far off the shore now and quite near the hut where I live. You are aware of my trade by now — that I am a pilot in the truest sense of the word. You can take part in my business and in my little plot of land, which we shall work diligently in our free time to provide our livelihood. And if you now look, you will find somebody beside you who will stick to us faithfully."

9. For the first time on this voyage, the bishop turns round and immediately recognizes the angel Peter. He embraces him, asking his forgiveness for insulting him.

10. Peter reciprocates with the same love and praises the choice the bishop's heart has made.

11. The boat has meanwhile reached the shore, is tied to a post, and the three enter the hut.

IN THE PILOT'S HUT. — THE BLESSED BREAKFAST, AND MARTIN'S THANKS. — HIS NEW JOB WITH THE FISHERMEN.

1. So far it has been rather dark. Inside the hut, the light seems to increase and a pleasant dawn gradually banishes the darkness of night. This, of course, takes place only before the eyes of the bishop, as it is always the brightest, everlasting and unchangeable day for the Lord, as well as for the angel Peter.

2. The reason why it begins to dawn also for the bishop, is that love began to emerge in his heart because, through My mercy, he had, of his own free will, thrown out a lot of worldly filth and was still continuing the process.

3. After he will have had My bread of life as refreshment, I shall instruct him in his duties. However, it is understandable that this man must be very hungry, since he has never before tasted of this truly nourishing food.

4. Look how he eats one piece of bread after another, moved to tears!

5. (Bishop Martin): "Oh, my dearest friend and from now on my employer, how good it is to be with you. Accept my deepest gratitude, and pass it on through your pure heart to God, the Lord. For my tongue is ever unworthy of giving thanks to the Lord, being much too great a sinner before Him.

6. Thinking of the endless time of my hunger, thirst, and uninterrupted night, I want to thank the Lord with all my heart, that He allowed you to rescue and feed me so that I now feel like re-born. And look, it is getting lighter and lighter, like a morning in spring with the sun beginning to rise! Oh, how marvelous this place has now become!

7. My dear friend, and you too, my first guide, do give me some work now so that I might express my great love for you, at least with the work of my hands!"

8. (The Pilot): "Step outside the hut with us and there will be plenty of work for you. We are once more out of doors and on the seashore. Over there are the fishing nets. Go with the brother and bring them here to the boat. The sea is calm today and we shall have a good catch."

9. The two hurriedly fetch the nets and put them into the boat, and the bishop says happily: "What a pleasant job! I do like the sea like this, but it did look so terribly different when I was waiting on the crumbling shore of my failure.

10. But are there also fish in the spirit world? I never imagined this on earth!"

11. (The Pilot): "And what fish! You will be surprised, and the more so, because we are supposed to catch all the fish from this sea. But don't despair, we'll manage it. It is just a matter of patience and courage and great manly perseverance.

12. There will be many perils to overcome and often you will fear you are lost. In such moments, however, look at Me and do what I do, and everything will turn out in your favor. For every worthwhile act needs effort, patience and steady work! Now, let us untie the boat and put out to sea."

13. The two untie the vessel and an easterly wind carries it as swiftly as an arrow out to sea.

14. (Bishop Martin): "Oh, friends, it must be terribly deep here. The water looks quite black! Whatever would happen to us if the ship sank?"

HUNTING FOR FISH.

1. (The skipper): "Friend, don't be scared, for we are here on the water for a good purpose. Be it as deep as it may, we have nothing to fear. Now, take care! Throw the drag-net out! Where you see the water heaving, there is a huge fish. Quick, don't let us lose it!"

2. The two throw out the net and the moment it has spread out in the water, a monster of a fish rushes in. Unable to break the strong net, it drags the boat away with it, not relaxing for a moment, but with ever growing fury.

3. (The bishop, terrified, exclaims): "For God's sake, now we are lost! The monster is so huge that it fills the net with half of its head! Only God knows how deep its body reaches into the water. It may

be three times the size of our boat! Even if we managed to kill it, what would we do with it? Oh, oh, it is dragging the boat with ever increasing fury and speed!''

4. (Peter): ''Don't be childish! Let the fish rush wherever and as long as it likes! While its head is in the net, it cannot go under; that I know, as an experienced fisherman. And after a while, it will calm down. Then it will be easy enough for us to tow it to the shore. Look, the fish is rushing straight towards the shore, which will soon stop it bolting!

5. And have you forgotten what our beloved Master has told us? Look at Him, He is so calm. So we should be the same! But when He says, 'Follow Me; get to work,' then we'll have to get busy as directed by Him. For there is no greater Master than He in the art of fishing. But now watch out, we shall have to act in a moment!''

6. (Now I speak): ''Peter, take the big hook and thrust it behind the fish's gill. And you, Martin, jump out onto the shore, take the rope, and pull the boat onto the sand; tie it quickly to the existing pole, board the vessel again, take the second boat-hook and do what Peter did, for the monster is now worn out and will not give any trouble. But be quick!''

7. The bishop hurries to carry out the instructions and having forcefully thrust the hook behind the other gill, the monster is fastened securely.

8. (And now the Lord orders): ''You two go and get the big rope with the heavy and sharp throwing-hook from the shore. It is lying in readiness near the hut. Meanwhile, I shall drag the fish closer to the shore, where you will hurl the hook at the monster's head. And you, Martin, mustn't be afraid if the fish should struggle mightily. With the necessary courage and perseverance, everything will work out satisfactorily! Hand Me the two shafts of the boat-hooks and then do as I have instructed.''

9. Everything is carried out as required, but when the heavy and sharp throwing-hook penetrates into its head, the fish starts twisting and struggling terrifyingly (for Bishop Martin), lashing up the water, throwing mighty waves onto the shore, which now and then cover up our new fisherman, Martin, who is all the more scared by the monster's huge jaws, with a thousand sharp teeth sometimes snapping at him dangerously close to where he is holding the rope. He is very frightened, but now even more for My sake, seeing that the fish

with its mighty tail keeps lifting the boat out of the water and flinging it back again.

10. (Peter says to the bishop): "Hold fast, brother! Gather all your strength or the monster might drag us down into the depths!"

11. (The bishop): "Oh, brother, if I only were behind you! That beast keeps snapping at me, and the Master seems to be pushing it right under my nose. Every time it closes its mighty jaws with a snap, it discharges at least a hundred buckets full of water right into my face!

12. This is a desperately hard and dangerous task! It would be too much even for galley slaves! Oh, m-m-m-brr-ah-ah, another full load of water into my face! I'm going to drown if this happens a few more times! Look, the jaws are opening up again. No! I can't stand it any longer! The water is so terribly cold and I'm frozen stiff as if I were lying naked on ice! In a moment the jaws will shut again!"

13. (Peter): "There, take the spreader and prop up its jaws so that it cannot shut them."

14. (The bishop): "Let's have it! Fine! Now this is the end of your snapping, you beast! That was a good idea, but you should have had it a bit sooner. However, it's all right now."

15. (Now I speak from the boat): "Good, now fasten the hook-rope to a pole and board the ship. This fish is ours and won't get away. But we'll have to put out to sea without delay. Maybe we'll soon make another, even better catch."

16. The two do as ordered, although Bishop Martin scratches his head for he has had quite enough with his first experience of fishing; however, he does as instructed.

17. Both have boarded the ship, which is sailing out to sea as swiftly as an arrow.

18. (Meanwhile, I remark to Bishop Martin): "Friend, you should never allow things to annoy you here. The man who tackles a task morosely, seldom succeeds. Therefore, patience, courage, and perseverance; joy will come after an accomplished task.

19. Yes, my dear friend, in the spirit world, your *Requiescant in pace* (May they rest in peace), often rattled off in the world, doesn't count; but instead, 'Work while it is day! It is sufficient to rest during the night when nobody can work!' When it was night for you, you had no job; but since the day has dawned for you, you also have

to work, for the realm of God is one of work and not one for idlers and breviary-worshippers. Therefore, take heart!

20. Look towards the north where the twilight is still heavy on the waters. There the sea is heaving heavily, although there is no wind anywhere. Consequently, there must be some big fish there. So let's hurry and get busy; this fish shall be worth our efforts."

21. (Bishop Martin): "Oh, friend, this fish might finish us off, with the help of the devil! But what are these big fish for in the spirit world? Is there a fast when only fish may be eaten? Or could it be that here, too, the flesh and fat of fish is traded?"

22. (Say I): "Quickly now, take a sword, each of you, for this is a ten-headed hydra! The monster has noticed us and is heading straight for us! You, Peter, already know how this type of fish is caught. But you, Martin, do as the brother does. As soon as the hydra bends its serpent-heads into the boat, you start cutting the heads off until all ten have been severed from its long serpent-body, and I shall do the rest."

23. Look, Peter, with his sharp sword, cuts one head after another from the black scaly body of the terrifying monster, or rather off its necks, for out of the body grow ten necks, each holding a head. But our bishop is somewhat at a loss as to where to hit because sheer terror has his eyes more closed than open.

24. Peter has just severed the tenth head from its neck, and streams of blood are gushing from the monster. The sea around is red from blood and heaving wildly from the ravings of the headless serpent, whose body appears to the bishop to measure over a hundred fathoms in length, as well as in girth!

25. (I again address the two): "Peter, put the sword back in its place and pass Me the big boat-hook, which I shall thrust into the monster's body to drag it toward us. And you, Martin, take the rudder, set it at the seventh degree east, and we shall soon have reached the shore with this excellent haul."

26. Everything is carried out as directed and the boat, with its catch in tow, is soon swiftly sailing toward the familiar shore.

27. As the shore is approaching, the bishop scans it for the first big fish, but to his astonishment, he can't see a trace of it.

28. (Bishop Martin): "But what has happened? After all the trouble we had catching it and getting it here, we have now lost it! I did have a feeling as if we hadn't secured it safely enough.

29. Oh, what disappointment! Now we have nothing to show

for all the danger and trouble we went through! Dear friends, we'll have to fasten this new catch more securely, otherwise we might lose it too if we put out to sea again."

30. (Peter): "Don't worry! The first fish has been taken care of. You see, there are more workers here who know exactly what to do with our hauls. Since we have now reached the shore, jump out and fasten the boat, and I and the Master will pull our spoil onto the shore."

31. Bishop Martin, somewhat bewildered, does what he has been told, while we do, before his eyes, as Peter has said.

32. When the second haul has been secured, I speak: "Since this catch has been so successful, we have accomplished one of our main tasks. So, let us now lift the smaller fish from the water with the drag-net and put them on the shore. We have hunted down the two big monsters, of which species there are no more in these waters. Therefore, we can now get on with the lighter work. Let's board the ship again and try our luck with the smaller fish."

33. As directed by Me, the two lower the drag-nets into the water and I steer the boat. The work progresses well, and after every pull the fish from the nets are flung onto the shore. However, the moment they hit the shore, they disappear.

19

BISHOP MARTIN'S DOUBTS ABOUT THE FUTILE TASK. — PETER'S GOOD REPLY, POINTING OUT THE IDLE, SENSELESS PERFORMANCES OF A ROMAN BISHOP.

1. This vanishing of the fish gradually gets on Bishop Martin's nerves, and he mutters angrily: "What a stupid job! I am almost exhausted from all the lifting out and throwing onto the shore of these fish, and all in vain, as they all melt like butter in the sun!

2. `I must watch carefully to see where the fish are getting to. Hmm, I can't see a thing! Another throw by my colleague and nothing is left in this realm of immortality! A nice immortality — this! On earth, not much is left of the things that have been, but here — nothing at all!

3.   I have been looking forward to a hot, cooked salmon or other fish, but I haven't much hope now. I am not really hungry, but even thinking of hot, cooked salmon makes my mouth water.

4.   'Of course, it is a million times better here than where I was before, but I don't fancy this breezy fisherman's work for all eternity. It is also strange how it has been dawning here for a considerable time, yet there is still no trace of a rising sun.

5.   What a strange world! What a strange existence! Whichever way you look at it, it doesn't make any sense. These, my only friends, are wise enough in their speech, but all the more stupid in their actions. If you take this senseless fishing, what a silly, un-rewarding work it is; yet still these two go about it as if eternal salvation depended on it. But what can I do? I cannot expect anything better, and so I must be satisfied in God's name; I'll just have to carry on with this fishing; maybe later on something else will happen."

6. (Peter asks the bishop): "What are you mumbling about? Could you already be tired?"

7. (The bishop): "I'm not exactly tired, friend. But I must admit that I find this work rather funny, although I have no doubts that you and the Master are very wise men.

8.   'Look, we have been laboring for quite some time now, and all for nothing! The first big fish is gone, and I cannot see a trace of the second one! The small fish vanish into the air before they even hit the ground! Tell me, what can such idle work be good for?

9.   I do know you as wise men, and most likely this work will have some wise purpose too. But could you tell me *why* we are doing all this and what it is good for?"

10. (Peter): "Now look here, dear brother, when you were a bishop on earth, how much even idler work did *you* perform? Would anyone have been allowed to question your actions' real value and importance? Take for instance, the baptism of a bell, the consecration of an organ, or the various so-called priestly vestments.

11.   What significance and efficacy would all the different vestments have? Or the various monk's cowls? Why is one image of Mary more miraculous than another? Why is Florian for fire, and Johan Nepomuk for water, since both were thrown into the water -- one in Austria into the Danube near Linz, the other one in Bohemia, into the Moldavia in Prague?

12.   Why is Jesus not found among the fourteen helpers in need?

And why does the holy supplication-litany appeal to God's mercy first, when in the following the saints are appealed to for their intercession? Is it in order to induce God to listen to the saints? But if God listens, why then appeal to the saints at all?

13. Why is Mary addressed with the Lord's Prayer ten times in the so-called Rosary, but God only once? Why does a church hold such a great number of large and small, wooden and metal crucifixes, and at least as many different images of Mary?

14. What is the difference between Solemn Mass and an ordinary low Mass for the spirit? When did Christ, St. Peter, or St. Paul institute the so-called unbloody sacrifice with different rates of fees? What must God's heart be like, that it can watch with goodwill the millionfold daily slaughter of His Son?

15. Look, my dear friend, in the world you performed countless futile and absolutely senseless rituals without believing in them at all! And still, with such futile actions, you didn't even ask yourself to what purpose. You were paid for it, you will say. Well, you will not have to work for nothing here either. What more do you want?

16. But I can tell you that this work is not half as futile as your work on earth. Therefore, refrain from mumbling to yourself in future. Tell us frankly what worries you and our futile fishing will soon come to an end. However, as long as you play the Roman mystery-monger, we'll have to go on fishing, and our catches will keep coming to nothing, exactly like our advice in your heart. Try to understand this! Now take the net and resume your work patiently."

THE SPIRITUAL CORRESPONDENCE OF THE FISHING. — THE COMPOSITION OF THE SOUL. — MARTIN'S EXCUSES, AND THE LORD'S REPRIMAND.

1. The bishop does as told, and says: "I do feel a bit better since I have now, at least, an idea why I am doing this and what this seemingly futile work is good for.

2. As I see it now, these fish illustrate my follies: the big ones my cardinal follies, and the smaller ones my countless minor

blunders. But how my follies and various shabby tricks managed to turn into big and small fish in this sea, I cannot figure out.

3. Most probably this sea has its origin in the deluge, whose waters absorbed the bulk of man's mortal sins, including mine in advance. This is the only explanation that seems to make any sense to me.

4. However, why the sins present themselves as fish in this deluge of water is beyond me! Only the Almighty, Who has stored away these waters from the ancient deluge for the spirit world in this endless basin, knows the reason why.

5. Therefore, I shall not ask any more questions, but carry on with the fishing in order to remove my share of sins as soon as possible."

6. (Now I speak): "That is right! Work diligently, friend! Rome was not built in a day. With patience, all difficulties can be overcome. This is not Noah's flood, nor are the fish we are removing from the water your anticipated sins. But this sea is nevertheless a deluge, though not of anticipated sins, but of *all* the sins you committed in the world.

7. The reason why your sins appear in the shape of fish and sea monsters in different sizes is that every sin causes incompetence of the soul, which then disperses its countless mangled constituents, **originating in the water and perfected in the fire of love of God in the human heart, resulting in the attainment of God's image.**

8. As a child you were endowed with a physically complete soul in your body. However, by not living according to God's order and only to bestial order from the elements of which the soul is originally composed, you lost a lot of your soul's components. And now, in order to make your soul plastically complete, we have to lift all that was lost from the sea of your sins. Only after this has been accomplished can we take care of your spirit and its unification with your soul. Therefore, be diligent and patient, and you will soon understand what a good pilot is supposed to do here.

9. As these sea monsters here represent your sinful actions, they must disappear the moment they are lifted out, to face the light of God, which results in the manifestation of which it is written:

10. 'The kingdom of heaven is like unto a net, that was cast into the sea, and gathered of every kind: which, when it was full, they drew to shore, and gathered the good into vessels, but cast the bad away.'

11. We have already lifted out quite a number of your deeds in the form of various fish, but, as you can see, they do not last in the light of God. And why? Because your ruined soul consumes them in order to regain its full shape.

12. When will there be deeds in your sea that last? Seek to fill your heart and awaken its love. There is still going to be a lot of futile work for your hands before you experience love of God in your heart.

13. If you realize this and understand what you have to achieve, you will keep working in true remorse, humility, and patience, until you succeed in your aspiration, thus gaining a clear vision as to your own proper judgment — and from this the mercy of God. So be it!"

14. Bishop Martin ponders over these words, but keeps working. After a while, he again turns to Me and says: "Dearest Master, you seem to be able to see through my life on earth like a jeweler does through a diamond, and although I find you most kind, in your justified reprimand you are as relentless as the barest truth itself.

15. It is true that all my actions must be an abomination before the Lord, due to the fact that all my life on earth I moved in false-hood and, to a certain degree, was forced to do it. Consequently, my actions couldn't possibly be anything but bad, which I now see clearly. But even if you were an angel yourself, you must admit that man cannot be blamed for all his shortcomings and faults, consider-ing that he did not create himself with all his various inclinations.

16. If I had created and educated myself, I alone would be the cause of everything I did and should, of course, be held responsible for all my actions, and be condemned accordingly. However, to con-demn all my actions and brand them as deadly sins because I com-mitted them, seems, if not exactly unfair, at least too severe.

17. If the son of a robber becomes a robber, too, having had no other background than robbery and murder, could he justly be blamed for his horrible deeds?

18. Or can the tiger be condemned because he is cruel and bloodthirsty? Who equipped the viper with his lethal poison?

19. Can you blame a cannibal in darkest Africa for eating men if he can hunt them successfully? Why doesn't an angel or other good spirit descend from heaven to teach him what is right? Or should God really have created millions of people merely for damnation? This would indeed be cruel tyranny.

20. My opinion is therefore: To everyone his due, but he

shouldn't be condemned for what is not his, and he cannot be blamed for."

21. (I reply): "Friend, you do a great injustice to Me with your words. Don't you see that we are helping you with this work because I am quite familiar with your stoical principles of justice?

22. Whatever you blame on your alleged neglected education, Brother Peter has taken upon himself. And all the things you blame on your Creator, I Myself have shouldered.

23. Do you really believe that you are quite guiltless where your own part is concerned? Can you honestly assert this? Were you not taught God's commandments, as well as the laws of the civil code? Didn't you, in many instances, know exactly that you were planning to commit a sin?

24. And when your conscience warned you, did you not ignore it, but did evil against it's loud voice? Do you blame that too on your education, or on the Creator?

25. Although your parents were paragons of generosity, you were hard-hearted toward the poor. Do you blame that, too, on your upbringing?

26. Since you became more tyrannical than an eagle whilst your parents were humble in their hearts, as demanded by the Word of God, was that, too, the fault of your upbringing or even the Creator?

27. Do you see now how wrong it is of you to blame your Creator? It is better to realize this and be humble, for none of your excuses will have any weight with God. But if you love God above all and love your brothers, you will find justice. So be it!"

21

BISHOP MARTIN'S PHILOSOPHICALLY SILLY EXCUSE. — A KINDLY AND DIVINELY EARNEST CONSCIENCE REFLECTOR.

1. (Bishop Martin): "It would be quite alright to love God above all else, and your neighbor as yourself, if only one knew how to do it. For shouldn't God be loved with the purest love, which most likely applies also to the love of your neighbor; but how can we awaken such a love in ourselves?

2. I am familiar with the feeling of friendship and with love for women. I also know the selfish love of children for their parents. But parental love I do not know. The love of God could not possibly be like any of these types of love, which, being directed toward other creatures, are based on self-interest.

3. I even claim that man, as God's creature, is incapable of loving his Creator. This might be possible only with absolute divine freedom, which maybe the archangels enjoy. But man finds himself only on the lowest spiritual level, far removed from God's holiness and absolute divine freedom.

4. God should be satisfied to be loved by His creatures as they love each other; as children love their parents, or as a young man loves his girl, or as one brother loves another; or also as a poor man loves his unselfish benefactor, or a ruler his throne, or like every man loves himself.

5. But for such love, there is no object — not even the ability to visualize such a sublime object. What does God look like? What man has ever set eyes on God? Who has spoken to Him? How is it possible to love a being which you cannot even imagine? A being which is not even known historically, only mythically, with poetical embellishments interspersed with ideas from the severe ancient Hebrew moral code."

6. (Now I speak): "Friend, with this absurd rubbish, you couldn't even cleanse a single thread of your filthy garment! You had plenty of objects in the world. There were the many poor, the widows, orphans, and countless other needy people. Why did you not love them although you had plenty of love for yourself?

7. You loved your own parents only for the sake of their gifts to you. And if you thought they had not given you enough, you wished they would die so that you could inherit from them.

8. You loved your subordinate priests if they supplied you with rich sacrifices; if the latter stopped coming in, you became their relentless tyrant.

9. You blessed the rich sheep who sacrificed abundantly, whilst the poor were threatened with hell.

10. You loved the widows well enough if they were young, pretty and rich, and willing to please you; and the same applied to the well-developed orphan girls between the ages of sixteen and twenty years.

11. With a love toward these types of objects it is, naturally, im-

possible to exalt oneself in contemplation and love of the supreme and most lovable object.

12. Since the Gospel, the most sublime teaching of Jesus the Christ, was the main subject in your education, why didn't you at least *once* in your lifetime try to practice even *one* of the texts in order to find out who inspired it?

13. Is it not written, 'He that hath My commandments, and keepeth them, he it is that loveth Me and I will manifest Myself to him.'?

14. If you had tried out in practice but one of the texts, you would soon have convinced yourself that this teaching is of God and, besides, God's objectivity would have become imaginable as it has become to many thousands of simpler people than you are.

15. It is further written: 'Ask, and it shall be given you; seek, and ye shall find; knock, and it shall be opened unto you.' Did you ever do any of these?

16. As you never tried any of these, you could not possibly acquire a spiritual image of God. Therefore, it is absurd of you to say you cannot love God because He has never become an object for you; whilst this would have happened if you had done anything at all towards this aim.

17. Tell me, what image of God could your impure love have evoked that might have drawn some sparks from your hardened heart? You are silent, but I will describe it for you.

18. God would either have to be a beautiful female, or endow you with the greatest possible power and glory, and besides, allow you to sleep with the most beautiful maidens without your virility ever lessening. He would have to allow you everything your imagination might consider enjoyable, even pass His divine nature to you, so that you could use the universe for your own pleasure.

19. Such a God you might find lovable, but the image of a poor crucified Jesus would make the concept of divinity unbearable, even contemptible for you.

20. No wonder that, under these circumstances, you have to ask how God can be loved with pure, worthy love. The reason is obvious: you never wanted to apprehend God and, consequently, love Him! You were afraid a better spirit might take possession of you and guide you to meekness, love of your neighbor, and eventually, to true cognition and love of God.

21. This is the actual reason why you have asked how God

could and should be loved. But since you do not love your brothers whom you see and still do not want to love, how could you love God Whom you do not see and do not want to see?

22. We two are now your best friends and brothers, but in your heart you continuously despise us, although we want to help you. Therefore, change your heart! Begin with loving your benefactors and you will find the way to the heart of God without your stupid philosophy. So be it!"

23. (Bishop Martin): "Oh, yes, you are quite right, and I do love and respect both of you very much, in your wisdom, your strength, love, patience, and perseverance. But if you, my dearest friend, wouldn't keep reminding me of my accursedness, stressing its severity, I would love you far more deeply. However, the penetrating sharpness of your words fills me with fear rather than with love for you and your friend, Peter. Let your words be more considerate, and I shall love you with all my heart."

24. (Say I): "Friend, what do you expect of Me? Do you consider a flatterer a true friend, one who is afraid to tell the truth to somebody's face? You deceive yourself!

25. There is not a good word to be said for you! Not one noble deed of love on your part! If ever you did something that appeared noble to the world, it was really evil. For all your actions were just policy hiding some secret tyrannical scheme.

26. Of any occasional miserly charity, just about the whole world had to be notified. Is that in accordance with the Gospel which teaches that the right hand should not know what the left is doing?

27. When you gave somebody advice in your capacity as a cleric, there would always be some profit for you in it.

28. When you appeared affable, it was meant to show all around you how high you actually were.

29. When your voice sounded mild, you merely sought to achieve what the sirens did with their songs or the hyenas with their cries. You were always a greedy beast of prey!

30. In short, there was no redeeming feature about you, and you were practically already over head and ears in hell. But the Lord had mercy with you, took hold of you, and wants to free you from the shackles of hell. Do you really think this could be possible without showing you what you are like?

31. Or have you never seen what a watchmaker on earth does

with a watch that is out of order? He takes it apart, examines and cleans every one of its parts carefully, straightens out what is bent, files where necessary, adds what might be missing, and then puts the whole movement together again. Could a watchmaker make a faulty watch go if he just polished it on the outside but left the movement as it was?

32. You are like a watch movement which is completely out of order; and you can only be bettered if your corrupt nature is completely dissected. Everything has to be exposed to the light of eternal incorruptible truth so that you might have a good look at yourself and see everything that is totally corrupt within you.

33. Only after you have recognized all your faults, can work be commenced to once more make of you a man in accordance with the order of God. But it must be a completely *new* man, for your present one is absolutely useless!

34. Since I am doing all this for you, don't I deserve your love?"

22

BISHOP MARTIN'S HUMBLE REPENTANCE AND THE AWAKENING OF HIS LOVE. — THE CHANGED LANDSCAPE, AND THE PALACE AND ITS DIRTY INTERIOR.

1. (Bishop Martin): "You are quite right, dearest friend. Only now do I seem to understand! I also feel love within me — yes, I now love you with all my heart! Oh, let me embrace you, for I now see how terribly stupid I have been and how truly noble your intentions are. Oh, you wonderful friend, and also you, my first guide, do forgive me my gross blindness!

2. But what is this? The sea has vanished and so has our boat. Everything is dry, beautiful land! What lovely meadows, and that beautiful garden and over there where the hut once stood, now stands a magnificent palace! How did this happen?"

3. (Say I): "Look, brother, a tiny spark of true love for us, your brothers and friends, created all this. It dried out the sea of your sins with all its evil effects, and it converted the mire of your heart into fertile land. The poor hut of your cognition was turned into a palace by that spark of love.

4. However, notwithstanding the beauty of all this, no ripe, eatable fruit can be found anywhere. Everything is still very much like the fig tree which bore no fruit at a time when the Lord was hungry for its fruit.

5. Therefore, it is now important to become active and let the newly awakened love have its way; as a result, these trees will soon bear fruit. As in the world everything grows and ripens in the light and warmth of the sun, here it does the same in the light of the love of a human heart. Man's heart is forever the sun of this world!

6. Soon many opportunities will present themselves to keep your heart active, expand and increase its strength. The more kind acts you let it perform, the greater will be the blessings you will notice in this area.

7. But now let us enter the palace, where we shall discuss the details of your present state. There you will also find many opportunities to occupy your heart. So be it!"

8. We are already inside the palace, where it does not look by far as magnificent as it did from the outside. Bishop Martin is also rather struck by what he sees, and cannot refrain from making a satirical remark:

9. Appearances are deceptive! Whoever built this palace has planned badly. It looks as if the interior of this building has not been completed at all, but just superficially done up for appearance's sake.

10. Dear friends, I must admit that I would prefer the former hut a million times to this. Look at all the dirt here. I couldn't bear to stay here for very long.

11. I beg you, dear friends, let us go outside again where it is so beautiful. In these filthy rooms I wouldn't be capable of one good thought. I find these rooms singularly repugnant!"

12. (Now I speak again): "I can see that you do not like the interior of this palace, dear friend. But you will understand that the interior of your heart, which corresponds to this palace in every detail, is quite as offensive to the Lord as these filthy rooms are to your eyes.

13. In the world, you surely heard the fable about Hercules, who had to perform twelve hard tasks in order to be admitted into the community of the gods. One of those tasks was the famous cleaning of the stable.

14. And what did Hercules do? He diverted a whole river

through the stable, and all the manure was lifted and washed away in the shortest time.

15. In the same way, you should conduct a whole stream of love through the sin-filled chambers of your heart, to quickly clear away all the dirt.

16. While we were still at sea — the sea that arose from the deluge of your sins — a tiny spark of true love was sufficient to dry it up and change the mud into fertile soil.

17. This little spark, the result of My words, an outward stimulant, could only stir up the surface of your heart and purify it, but the core remained unchanged, a regular Augean stable, which only you yourself can clean up. And, as already said, this can be done by means of a stream of true love for us, your brothers and greatest friends, as well as for those whom you will soon be meeting and who will be needing you.

18. Look out through this window. What do you see in the distance, towards the north?"

23

BISHOP MARTIN'S FIRST DEED OF CHARITY TOWARDS THE POOR NEW ARRIVALS.

1. (Bishop Martin): "I see a number of ragged people limping along very slowly. They seem to have no shelter. Most likely, they are also hungry and miserable.

2. Friend, I pity those wretched wanderers. Allow me to go to them and lead them to this place to give them shelter and look after them as best I can. Though these rooms are dirty, they will serve them better than those rough, frozen paths leading in the familiar direction where, as I know, conditions are getting worse."

3. (Say I): "That is all right! Go and do as your heart dictates. But don't be discouraged when you find the travelers to be Lutherans!"

4. (Bishop Martin): "I don't like the idea very much. But then, I don't seem to care really whether they are Lutheran , Mohammedan, Jewish, or Chinese! Every man who needs help, should have it!"

5. Bishop Martin, still in his peasant clothes, hurries after the travelers, shouting at them to wait for him. This they do, in order to hear what he wants of them. They have only just arrived in the spirit world from earth, and they do not know what to do.

6. Having reached the group, the bishop addresses it in a very friendly voice: "Dear friends, where to are you heading? For heaven's sake, turn back and follow me or you will all perish! The path that you are following leads dead straight to an abyss which will swallow you forever!

7. I, however, have been in this area, together with two dear friends, for quite a while, and thus am able to warn you.

8. Look towards the south, and you will see a palace there. Although its interior is by far not as good as it looks on the outside, it will provide shelter and a piece of bread, which in any case would be much preferable to continuing on your dangerous path. Therefore, don't hesitate, but return with me and, by God, you will not regret it!"

9. One of the wanderers speaks: "All right, we will follow you, but be sure not to take us to a Catholic house! There we wouldn't stay, for we find nothing as disgusting as Roman Catholicism, the Pope, his bishops, and the most evil monasticism of the Roman whore!"

10. (Bishop Martin): "Rubbish! Pope, bishop, monk, Luther, Calvin, Mohammed, Moses, Brahma, Zoroaster — all that counts only on the silly earth; here in the spirit world, all these earthly differences cease to exist. Here, there is only one thing that counts, and that is *LOVE!* This alone can help us to get ahead; everything else is only of minor importance.

11. On earth I was a Roman bishop, and very proud of it; but when I arrived here, I soon learned that it does not make any difference whatsoever what one had been on earth. All that counts here is what one has done.

12. Therefore, forget about Luther or Calvin, but follow me! You will not regret it! However, should you not like it here, you can still continue on this road."

13. (The leader of the party): "You seem to be quite a sensible man and, therefore, we shall follow you to your house. But one thing we must ask of you beforehand — that there will be no discussions about religion between us, for we detest anything that is called 'religion'!"

14. (Bishop Martin): "As you wish! Discuss whatever you want to! I hope that we shall get to know each other better and that you will never find anything about my person that might offend you. So let us go and establish ourselves in the house which is mine and also my friends ."

15. Bishop Martin leads the way, and the whole party of thirty follows him. He leads them straight into the palace where I and Peter are waiting and addresses Me joyfully:

15. (Bishop Martin): "Look, my dear friend and brother in the Lord, I brought them all safely here. Would you be good enough and show me where we could put them up. And then I must ask you for some bread, for they will no doubt be very hungry."

17. (Say I): "The door over there to the east leads to a large and well furnished room. There they will find everything they require. But you come back immediately, as an important task is waiting for us which cannot be delayed."

18. Bishop Martin does as instructed by Me, and the party is very pleased with the well-equipped room. Then the bishop returns and asks where the new task may be found.

24

A NEW TASK FOR THE BISHOP. — PUTTING OUT A FIRE AND SAVING LIVES. — THE FIRE VICTIMS ARE TAKEN IN AND FITTED OUT WITH CLOTHES.

1. (And I say): "Look to the north! Do you see the fire? We must hurry there and stop the fire, or the whole area here might suffer. A fire of evil in the spirit world spreads much faster than a fire in the natural world."

2. We hurry toward the fire and have already reached it. A very poor village is enveloped in flames, and we see a crowd of wretched, totally naked villagers fleeing from their burning huts. In the center of the village, however, we see a better-type house with a balcony, on which there are five people pitifully shouting for help. The flames have almost reached them and could devour them in a moment!

3. (Bishop Martin, seeing this, shouts): "Friends, for heaven's

sake, where could we find a ladder so that I might climb up to them and possibly save them, with your help?"

4. (Say I): "Look, there is something like that lying at our feet. Take it and follow your heart!"

5. Bishop Martin grabs the ladder and rushes to the house with the balcony. The house is already completely enveloped in flames. He leans the ladder against the balcony, climbs up fearlessly, takes two of the people who had already collapsed on his shoulders, and carries them to safety, while the three stronger ones follow behind him. Thus he has saved the soul-lives of five in a minute's time.

6. After completion of this task, the bishop returns to Me and says: "Oh, thank God that I succeeded in this rescue! I thought already that my zeal had got me into serious trouble.

7. Oh, friends, what heat! My hair must be all singed! But it doesn't matter as long as these poor people are safe! Two were already near death, and it was high time to rescue them from the flames. But they are quite revived now, and this gives me more happiness than if I had gained the beatitudes of the three or seven heavens.

8. And, brothers and friends, let us take the poor people whom I rescued and all the homeless ones crouching along the fence, naked and lamenting, to our place. Oh, dear brothers, do allow me this joy."

9. (Say I): "Of course, we'll do it! That is mainly why we did come here. But first, we have to put out the fire, and after that we can take the poor things home with us! So let us fight the fire!"

10. (Bishop Martin): "That would be all right if we had a little ocean on hand. But I cannot see a drop of water anywhere. How are we going to fight the fire without water?"

11. (Say I): "See that staff on the ground, similar to the one Moses carried? Take it up and thrust it into the ground. If you do that full of faith, we shall have plenty of water. For this area here is quite swampy. So do it!"

12. Bishop Martin does as I suggest, and a spring gushes from the ground. The bishop says: "That is fine! Now we'll have to get some vessels to carry the water."

13. (Say I): "Friend, that will do! The water will do its part by itself, for this mighty spring will soon quench the flames. Therefore, we can now take the rescued people home with us, have some rest and refreshment so that we can tackle a new task. Go now and bring them all to Me!"

60

14. Bishop Martin, in the best of spirits, goes to fetch the poor fire victims, and we all enter the palace where the guests are accommodated in another spacious room.

15. And there, since they are still naked, the bishop takes off his peasant smock and puts it around the shoulders of the one he considers to be the poorest and weakest of all. And his vest he gives to another one who seems just as pitiful; whereupon everybody praises his attitude.

16. But he, like an upright man, says: "My dear, poor friends and brothers, do not praise me, but rather praise God and my two friends here! For I myself have been taken in by them only recently and they have done so much for me. I am only a poor servant of these friends, but your rescue has given me great joy, and that is my best reward!"

17. (Say I): "So it is right, beloved brother! You have changed from a Saul into a Paul! If you continue in this way, you will soon be a real helper for Me and My friend and brother. But let us now go to our apartment!"

25

DIFFERENT THINKING ON EARTH AND IN THE BEYOND — INTRODUCTION TO THE LIVING SCIENCE OF CORRESPONDENCES. MARTIN'S THIRST FOR ACTION AND FATIGUE OF KNOWLEDGE.

1. We now enter our apartment, which is nicely furnished, but without luxury.

2. Bishop Martin is astonished at this unexpected change, and says: "But, dear friends and brothers, whoever has cleaned up and decorated this room so beautifully during our absence? It was poorer before than the most ordinary peasant's dwelling. Now, even the windows seem larger and the tables and chairs are so clean and attractive! Oh, tell me, how has this been achieved?"

3. (Say I): "Dear brother, the explanation is simple enough! On earth, if someone wants to redecorate his house, he plans it in his

head and then engages various craftsmen and artists to carry out the actual work in accordance with his plans.

4. However, on earth, due to the inertia of matter which has to be overcome, this takes much longer than it does here. Here, this obstacle does not exist and thus such a plan becomes a completed task immediately. For what a perfect spirit thinks and wills, is already completed as intended.

5. Naturally, in this eternal realm of spirits, the thinking differs considerably from that on earth. There, thinking consists of ideas and pictures taken from worldly notions and the changes they are subjected to. But here, the thinking arises out of the spirit's God-given abilities, awakened by him through active love for God and his neighbor, and enlightened by the Divine Light.

6. This apartment is solely the result of your charity toward your fellowmen. But it is still simple, though attractive, because the Divine Light has not yet taken root in you and filled your life. When this happens, you will be fully conscious of the fact and will understand all this. You are still lacking the right cognition of God essential for this, but if your love continues to grow, you will soon have achieved it. Let us now sit down at the table where some refreshment is already waiting for us. So be it!"

7. (Bishop Martin): "Yes, yes, so it is! Everything is miraculous here, like a magic table; one has to get used to it, the same as on earth one has to get used to the wonders of nature. It does not worry you if you don't understand them — you just get used to them. The same will probably apply here.

8. Anyway, I don't mind not understanding God's miracles. As long as I am kept busy and get some rest and refreshment now and then, as is the case at present, and with you two as company, I could not think of anything better for all eternity.

9. I now comprehend God as a real Person Who dwells in an eternally inaccessible light and Who is holy, most holy, almighty and infinitely wise. To know more about Him, the Eternal, I would even consider a deadly sin, and we should just accept with gratitude whatever His kindness provides for us!"

10. (Say I): "All right, My dear brother, let us now sit down to our bread and you, Peter, go and fetch the wine-filled cup from over there!"

26

BISHOP MARTIN'S MODESTY AND MEEKNESS. THE BLESSED LOVE-FEAST AT THE LORD'S TABLE.

1. We now sit down at the table and Peter brings the wine and a toga (old Roman outer garment) for Bishop Martin, and says: "There, brother, since you gave your coat and vest to the poor, put on this somewhat better garment for the meal."

2. Bishop Martin looks at the beautiful light-blue robe with deep red trimming, and says: "Ah, but this is much too beautiful for the likes of me! How can you suggest that I, a poor sinner, should wear a robe similar to the one our Savior Jesus, the worthiest of all men, used to wear on earth? That would be a mockery!

3. No, I shall not do that! Although Jesus was not exactly the God ignorant people like to make Him, He was still the wisest and best of men that ever walked on earth, the perfect man without sin, deserving the highest goodwill of the Lord; whereas I am and was a great sinner. Therefore, I cannot wear this robe!

4. I would rather not eat a morsel of bread, nor have a drop of wine, than put on this Jesus-robe in the truest sense, being as unworthy as I am. Give me any rag suitable for me! It is quite enough that in the world I wore the robes of Melchisedec, which folly caused me enough suffering here; for the future, I hope to be wiser with the help of God!"

5. (Say I): "As you wish! There is absolutely no coercion here. Have your meal without a coat. So be it!"

6. (Bishop Martin): "I am glad about that — no luxury for me! But now, dear brothers, I do have a request. Although I am quite hungry and thirsty by now, I am sure our poor protégés are much worse off. Therefore, do grant me permission to give them my share and let me take it to them personally. The joy of having fed these poor ones shall be the main satisfaction of my heart!"

7. (Say I): "Dearest brother, this wish from your heart makes Me very happy! However, this time your wish is sufficient, as your protégés have been well provided for. Therefore, come and sit down with Me and eat and drink to your heart's content. After the meal, we shall go and visit them and see whether we find some suitable occupation for them. So be it!"

8. (Peter speaks): "Lord and Master, do administer the bread and wine, for it tastes so much better when You do it, than if I help myself. Please do this for us, dearest Lord and Master!"

9. (Say I): "Yes, my dear brother, it will be My pleasure, if only our dear friend and brother here does not mind."

10. (Bishop Martin): "Not at all, dear friends. I do know the sect of the so-called bread-breakers; you probably belonged to it on earth. This, of course, does not make any difference in the spirit-world, but if somebody enjoys such human pious memories, let him do it. But I have had my fill of ceremonies in the world, so that I can do very well without them here.

11. Therefore, I do not care whether you break or cut or saw up the bread, as long as there is something to chew when it is needed! But I quite agree that the master of the house should distribute the bread to his servants; you feel more free and easy eating bread that has been handed to you, than if you had helped yourself."

12. (Say I): "Quite right! So, since you do not mind, I shall break the bread, bless it, and give it to you!"

13. I now break the bread, bless it, and give it to them.

14. Peter is close to tears with joy, but Bishop Martin puts his arm around him and says: "What a dear, good soul you are! The breaking of bread must have reminded you of the scene with the two disciples on their way to Emmaus, which might have been real, but most likely was a pious invention. I must admit, I was often moved to tears by it myself.

15. For this scene is not only of deep significance, it also makes you wish it had really taken place. Weak and short-sighted men just love to hear and dream of miracles, especially in ancient times, when God Himself played a part, unrecognized by the people involved. A miracle like that happening during their own lifetime would seem much more incredible.

16. Dearest master and friend, do break the bread any time, as I, too, like this pious custom!

17. What wonderfully-tasting bread! And the wine — I have never tasted better wine on earth, I'm sure! Is this wine, maybe, also of a spiritual nature? Although it doesn't really matter where it has come from as long as it tastes good. God be praised in eternity for this delicious meal! Now I can tackle the next job even if it is hard work."

18. (Say I): "I am glad that you both have enjoyed this meal.

May it be blessed for you! But let us now go and see how our poor are getting on."

27

BISHOP MARTIN'S PECULIAR EXPERIENCE WITH HIS PROTÉGES. — HE WANTS TO ENLIGHTEN BUT IS HIMSELF BEING ENLIGHTENED.

1. We now go to the first thirty people whom Bishop Martin had brought to the palace. As we enter, they prostrate themselves, crying: "O Lord, o Lord, almighty God in Jesus Christ, do not come to us, for we are great sinners, unworthy of any mercy! Your nearness, Most Holy, is too overwhelming for us!"

2. Bishop Martin looks around to all sides, wondering where the thirty might have seen Jesus. But, still not seeing anything, he asks Me: "Dear friend, whatever is the matter with these poor people? Are they out of their minds? Or did they, maybe, have some wine, fell asleep, and are now having either a Lutheran or a Roman nightmare?"

3. (Say I): "Oh, no, nothing of the kind. They are taking Me for Him, and that is why they are crying like that!"

4. (Bishop Martin): "So it is a sort of mental weakness after all. But, in my opinion, they are quite right to praise you, their present greatest benefactor, as representing the Most High. For, as I see it, every benefactor like you has in him a considerable portion of the actual deity, and by praising him, the deity in him is also praised. What should be done now with these poor people?"

5. (Say I): "We shall honor their wish. We'll leave them to their notion and go and see the others. For if they, at this stage, believe not to be able to bear My nearness, we should not torture them. Eventually, things will come right!"

6. (Bishop Martin): "I'm sure that will be the best! Such things should not be rushed. So let us go quickly to the ones we saved from the fire. I am looking forward to seeing them."

7. We now quickly go to the others. At the door, I say to the bishop: "Brother, do go in first and tell them that I and Peter are

coming. If they want to see Me, I shall go inside, but if they don't, which you will soon gather from their words, come back without delay and we shall turn to some other task."

8. Bishop Martin does as directed by Me, goes to the fire victims and addresses them with a somewhat pathetic air, like that of an official: "Dear friends, the Lord and Master of this house is willing to visit you if it suits you. If it shouldn't suit you just now, let me know and he will not come. But I, as your friend, would like to point out that he is a very good and mild master, and you should really want to see him. However, you are free to decide for yourselves. So, let me know what you think."

9. The fire victims, however, ask the bishop: "Do you know at all who the master of this house is?"

10. (Bishop Martin): "Not really, but this is not necessary in the spirit-world. I know from experience that he is an exceptionally good and wise man. To want to learn more would be foolish. Therefore, you, too, should be satisfied with what I have truthfully told you. And now let me know what you want to do."

11. (One of the victims): "But friend, why are you so insidious and want to hold back from us the Most Holy and Highest?

12. For behold, the Lord and Master of this house is also the sole Lord, Creator and eternal Master of the heavens and all the solar systems of the whole of infinity, as well as of all men and angels in Jesus Christ!

13. How then can you say you don't know Him? Are you blind that you have not noticed His pierced hands and feet, which we saw at the first glance?

14. Behold His mild earnestness, His great love and wisdom, and lay your hand in His pierced side; surely you will then understand, even clearer than we, what is behind your Lord and Master!

15. As if we didn't wish in our hearts that He, the Most Sublime and Most Holy would come to us in this chamber of His mercy. But we are all such great sinners and absolutely unworthy of His visit! We are his lowest creatures who, in the world, so often disregarded His love and patience!

16. Therefore, you most fortunate friend of your God and Lord, Whom you do not know, or do not want to know, tell Him our hearts are always yearning for Him but our sins have rendered us so ugly, filthy, and naked, that we cannot even wish He would come to us.

17. We are already ashamed and humiliated to find ourselves in this house where He is staying, and where He bestowed His mercy upon us sinners. But where could we hide if He actually came to us?

18. Therefore, you most fortunate man, ask Him to spare us unworthy creatures. However, His most holy will, and not ours, be done!"

BISHOP MARTIN, AS A BLIND RATIONALIST, IS IN A FIX.

1. (Bishop Martin): "Oh, what are you talking about? God, the Most High Eternal Being, dwelling in the forever inaccessible light, filling infinity with His might and power, should ever manifest in a man and work with His hands as we do?

2. God does fill such men and spirits with the light of His grace — some more, some less. But there will always remain an immense gulf between God and man.

3. Jesus, although filled with more of God's power than other men, was still no more a god than we are. No sensible man or spirit could assume that, for if so, one would also have to believe that the small planet earth is the center of all creation, which assumption would be very foolish.

4. Therefore, let us be more sensible in this eternal realm of spirits. We have been foolish enough in the world, taking bread, wine and sometimes even carved images for deities, forgetting about the sun as the most magnificent image of God.

5. Take me and my two dearest and best friends for what we really are and you will not suffer from such unreasonable fear.

6. I am quite aware that the lord and master of this house is mightier and wiser than all of us put together. And he might even be that Jesus who gave us the wisest teaching, but you must not take him for *God*, only what he really is: the best, the wisest and most godinspired man on earth.

7. You know how he was put to death on earth. Could you seriously believe that God, as the primordial source of life, would let Himself be killed by wretched men?

8. What would happen to a house if its foundations were destroyed? It would no doubt collapse very soon.

9. And what would happen to God's house, the whole of creation, the moment God Himself were annihilated? Would not, through His death, all life and being have been destroyed long ago? Therefore, my dearest friends, do be sensible here in the realm of the spirits."

10. (Says one of the party): "Friend, even though your words appear wise, you are still much farther from the goal than we are — notwithstanding the fact that you enjoy the constant presence of the Lord, whilst we poor sinners must fear to face Him.

11. And I, as a sinner, must tell you that you have not even made the first grade in wisdom, yet you want to judge God's inner wisdom! Naturally, if you judge God only by volume, Jesus must seem far too small to you. But if you take into consideration that God created not only suns and planets, but also the gnats, you might understand that He concerns Himself quite as much with the tiniest things as He does with the biggest, and that He would be able to show Himself as a man to teach and guide men onto the right path. And He, as the Sun of suns, no doubt guides also the solar systems.

12. But since we can understand only a human being, we conceive God through the man Jesus. The suns and their God would be inconceivable for us without Jesus.

13. This is as I see it. Go now and find out more about the Master of this house, and then return to us and tell us whether I was wrong."

THE LORD MAKES HIMSELF KNOWN AS JESUS TO THE BLIND BISHOP MARTIN.

1. (Back with Me, Bishop Martin says): "My beloved lord, master, friend, and brother — what a dilemma my innate stupidity has got me into! Now I really do not know whether I am the fool or are those behind that door!

2. They fear you even more than the others do, and they, in all seriousness, take you not only for Jesus, founder of the Christian faith, but even for the Supreme Godhead in person, basing their con-

victions on a sort of logical philosophy which it is not exactly easy to prove wrong.

3. Do tell me, dearest friend, what makes all these souls and spirits have such a peculiar notion about you? I now do notice the well-known stigmata on your hands and feet, and am practically positive that you are the Savior Jesus; — but *God*? Jesus and God at the same time? That, if I may say so, is overdoing it!

4. And still those spirits boldly maintain this! What gave them such an idea? Could it be that they are right after all? That would be too much for a poor soul like me. If that were true, although I could not comprehend it, I would be terrified. Oh, dear friend, do reassure me on this matter."

5. (Say I): "Friend and brother, you yourself, as a bishop on earth, preached Jesus the Crucified, and proved His deity to be present even in the smallest particles of the Host. And behold, all those whom we saved from the flames and who are now here with us, are sheep from your diocese and followers of your teaching.

6. Why then did you teach them this in the world if you now claim it to be nonsense? If it is nonsense, we must ask: Whose nonsense is it? If it is the truth, we must ask: What honor is there in it for their former teacher if he is now fighting his own doctrine in his students?

7. As a matter of fact, I *am* Jesus the Crucified, and in this brother here, I introduce to you the real old Peter, on whose assumed chair the Roman bishops are sitting and ruling. Of course, this is not being done according to the order of the real Peter, but only the one they themselves have invented to be used to their best advantage. So, now you know who I and your first guide, Peter, are. Your own followers will give you further details.

8. I once said that the children of the world are more prudent than those of the light. Since you, like an emperor of China, consider yourself a son of the light, go to your followers, who are genuine children of the world, and let them teach you at least good sense if you have no relish for their wisdom."

9. (Bishop Martin): "Oh, friend, although you are the Jesus who made himself known as the Son of the Most High, where then is the Most High, the almighty eternal Father? And where is the Holy Ghost coming forth from the Son and the Father — since we are now reverting to the dogma, disregarding the light of pure reason?"

10. (Say I): "How is it written in the Gospel? Behold, it says:

'I and My Father are one; who sees Me, sees also the Father!' If you do believe, why do you still ask, seeing Me? If you do not believe, why do you ask at all? Stay the way you are and I shall stay as I am and, I think, there is no reason for us to argue.

11. In that room there are your followers. Go to them and learn My teaching from them again. Then come back so that I may interpret it for you!

12. For I, the true Savior, am telling you here in My eternal kingdom that you are a foolish spirit in not recognizing My great love for you. I have treated you with the greatest consideration, and you are still deaf and blind. I gave you the bread of life, and you devoured it like a polyp, paying no attention to the sudden spiritual effect it had on these sinners.

13. With open eyes and ears you neither see nor hear! I cause the strangest things to happen around you, and you do not even ask, 'Who is He Whom the seas and winds obey?'

14. So return once more to your followers and learn from them how to recognize Him Whom you have all the time considered your equal. So be it!"

30

DISCUSSION BETWEEN THE RATIONALIST MARTIN AND THE WISE AND BEAUTIFUL SPIRIT ABOUT THE DEITY OF JESUS.

1. Bishop Martin looks even more puzzled, but does as earnestly advised by Me.

2. On his return to the fire victims, he is astonished to see them considerably changed in appearance. Their faces look younger and nobler, and their heretofore almost naked bodies are clothed in blue robes, their ample folds held together by purple girdles. Among the party, he notices the outstanding figure of a man with a shining white hat on his head, from under which his hair falls halfway down his back in rich golden curls.

3. This handsome man immediately approaches Bishop Martin and says: "Friend, it did not take you long to return to us. Did you find in the sublime Master and Lord of this house that to which we

drew your attention? Is He Jesus, Lord of the heavens and earth in a natural and spiritual, as well as a temporal and eternal sense?''

4. (Bishop Martin): "Oh, yes, he is Jesus all right, but as to his deity — that point has not been quite clarified as yet. In my opinion, one should be a bit more careful with an assumption that Jesus could also be God. For if it turns out that he isn't God after all, the Supreme Being might resent this assumption and the result could be our damnation, as has happened to many peoples of ancient times who dared believe in other gods besides Him.

5. For, according to Moses, it says once and for all: 'You shall believe in one God only, not worship any graven image, but praise Me alone. For I am the one Lord and God, Who made heaven and earth with all that is upon it or in it, that lives and breathes!'

6. Although Moses alludes mysteriously to a Savior Who is going to liberate the nations from the hard yoke of the old bondage, it does not say anywhere that Jehovah Himself would descend to earth in this Savior. Therefore, I consider this assumption of yours too rash and think it should be examined most carefully.

7. If you compare Moses with Jesus, you will find the God of Moses practically irreconcilable with the Godhead within Jesus. Moses, at God's bidding, had to institute the death sentence for blasphemous actions, like sacrificing to a graven image or making a sorcerer, a prophet, or some hero, one's God. This was one of the reasons that brought Jesus to the cross, although he used to express himself about his alleged divine mission in most obscure metaphors in the presence of the scribes.

8. Besides, it is hard to understand why God should have founded a church through Moses with so much heavenly pomp, if the same church was later abolished through Jesus, who represented the same God, contrary to His promise.

9. In view of all this, dear friends, your rash assumption of the deity of Jesus is a risky matter in this realm of spirits.

10. It is obvious that in this house of Jesus your belief has improved your condition, thanks to some minor miracle. But you may rest assured that I do not envy you this as my principle is: 'He laughs best who laughs last.' ''

11. (Says the tall man with the shining hat): "Friend, I am quite as familiar as you with all the things you have just mentioned, but I pity you for your blindness and am afraid that you haven't a chance of 'laughing last.' I, and the whole of this party, think as follows:

12. Jesus Whose advent all the prophets predicted and of Whom David sings 'The Lord said unto My Lord' or 'The Lord said unto Himself: Sit thou at My right hand, until I make thine enemies thy footstool!' and, 'Lift up your heads, o ye gates; and be ye lifted up ye everlasting doors; and the King of glory shall come in.'

13. Jesus Whose birth, according to all the evangelists, was accompanied by many miracles, and Whose whole life represented a miracle.

14. Jesus Whose teaching revealed only too often Who He really was in His innermost Being, and Who asked one of the ten cleansed who came back to praise Him: 'Where are the other nine that they did not return to praise God?'

15. Jesus Who, of His own power, rose from the tomb on the third day and walked on earth for another forty days to instruct His disciples, then ascended to heaven before the eyes of many of His followers, and soon after that sent the Spirit of eternal strength, might, love, and wisdom from the heavens down to His disciples.

16. Jesus, about Whom John gives the most sublime evidence, both in his Gospel and his Revelation.

17. Tell me, friend, are you still capable of taking this man of all men to be just an ordinary sage of the world?

18. Look, friend, I will tell you something foolish, which, however, appears to be wiser than your words: If God the Lord had not assumed human form in order that we, His creatures, could see Him, why would He have created us at all? Not for Himself, surely! For what could that give Him if we never could see or love Him? And what good would a life without a comprehensible God be for us? Think this over! Maybe it will help you to some enlightenment!"

19. (Bishop Martin): "Leave me alone for a while so that I can ponder over your words."

20. After quite a while, the bishop speaks again: "Friend, I have weighed your words carefully and can still see only the contrary of what you have maintained. However, I am not stubborn, and I will assent to your views with all my heart if you could give me satisfactory answers to some questions."

31

BISHOP MARTIN'S CRITICAL QUESTIONS AND THE WISE MAN'S ANSWERS.

1. (Says the wise man of the party): "Ask and I will answer, but it will be immaterial to me whether you find my answers convincing and satisfactory or not."

2. (Bishop Martin): "Why has the earth only one highest mountain? And does the Godhead in its fullness reside in or above it because it is the one highest mountain on earth?"

3. (The wise man): "The earth has, it is true, one mountain that is higher than any other known mountain. However, that does not make it God of all the mountains. God knew why He set a highest mountain upon this planet. Probably to provide a general dividing point for the winds. For that same reason, the highest mountains are to be found in the tropical regions near the equator, as in those regions the winds, due to the earth's rotation, must be the strongest. There, the effect of the centrifugal force is the most violent and, consequently, the rotation circles farthest removed from the center or axis of the earth.

4. If the Lord had not erected such high wind-regulators in these regions, they would probably be forever uninhabitable. In those areas — mostly in the largest continents, especially in Asia — where the air flows together in a main current, we find the highest mountains. Therefore, the highest mountain of all has to be in Asia, it being the largest of all continents. Are you satisfied with that answer?"

5. (Bishop Martin): "Perfectly — as far as that goes! But now a further question: Why is the Amazon in America the largest river on earth? Does it, perhaps for the same reason, hold the Godhead in its fullness?"

6. (The wise man): "Friend, I understand what you are aiming at, but I will still answer this extremely silly question as thoroughly as possible.

7. Look, America is a much younger continent, with very considerable mountain ranges in the Cordilleras, as well as the Andes.

8. These ranges are situated very close to the greatest ocean of the world and, consequently, their subterraneous bases contain a vast

amount of water, incessantly welling up through the innumerable pores and the many larger veins and channels. On the other hand, especially South America, as a very young continent, having been above sea level for just a few thousand years, has many vast plains of loose sand, just slightly above sea level.

9. And in a region where extensive mountain ranges draw vast amounts of water, which then accumulates in the great plains, spreads unimpeded, and then flows towards the ocean only very slowly, there needs must be the largest and widest river. Naturally, this need not contain more of the Godhead than a raindrop! Tell me, does this answer satisfy you?"

10. (Bishop Martin). "Perfectly, as far as that goes! Your answer is quite satisfactory, but let us continue.

11. Tell me, why is the diamond the most precious gem and gold the most precious metal?"

12. (The wise man): "Because man made it what it is. And the reason he did it is that these minerals are less frequently found than others. If there were as many diamonds as pebbles and as much gold as iron, diamonds would be used in road-making and gold as mountings on cart-wheels.

13. However, the Lord knows best why these two minerals are rarer than others. Probably because they poison man's mind with hellish elements. In view of that, you wouldn't expect them to hold any considerable portion of the Godhead? Are you satisfied with this answer?"

14. (Bishop Martin): "I cannot raise any objections to your explanations, and so have to be satisfied! But I did not find in your answers what I really expected to find, namely: genuine proof for the deity of Jesus.

15. For there are on earth, as most likely on every planet, in all things, beings and men culminations which are unique and forever unequalled. Thus, there has to be some largest sun, a largest planet, and on it a number of unequalled things. However, can a sage claim these to be deities because they are unequalled? Only the heathens did that ages ago, and the result was polytheism.

16. No doubt there has been, at some time or other, a most intelligent ape, dog, or donkey, like the one of Bileam, or the most beautiful and courageous horse, like Bucephalus, or a most beautiful woman, like the Venus of Medici, or an Apollo, a wisest heroine, Minerva, and a most jealous Juno.

17. The heathens deified all these high-ranking personalities; that cannot be denied. And if the inhabitants of a planet did this with superior things and beings from all the realms of nature, it is no wonder that man raised the wisest teacher and the greatest magus to their supreme Godhead — erected altars to him and are still worshipping him to this day — some with genuine piety, but the majority, for reasons of policy, in order to keep the others in the dark.

18. But because men did that to their wisest fellowman, would that be sufficient reason to completely deify him? Or did we ever see or hear higher beings that had come to earth to prove and confirm the deity of Jesus?

19. There do exist tales of miraculous happenings at his birth — that angels descended visibly to earth and told mankind of his divinity. But have *we* seen any of this? Not I! You, perhaps?

20. Such stories have been fabled in the tedious and selfish dreams of monks and nuns, but if you investigate the truth, you will find only human desire to know more and better than your fellowman, although deep in his heart, everyone knows that he is blind and his knowledge is based solely on habitual, indifferent belief.

21. Where a man accepts another man's authority as proof, we cannot speak of genuine conviction. But since one has never heard anything from the real God except through men, where else could one expect to find any living evidence?

22. Thus, a revelation is no more than the work of man. This is obvious, as we have never had a revelation that did not show human influence and imagination.

23. Therefore, dearest friend, I have to verify everything and cannot be convinced. Your proofs are insufficient for me! A man's desire for cognition of God can only be satisfied by God Himself, never by men; and I believe that we shall have to go through many and varied experiences in His spaces of creation before we are ready for a true divine revelation!

24. Everything that we have experienced so far is just an elementary school to prepare us for future great divine lessons. However, if you are in a position to reply to my arguments with something better, purer, truer, and more divine, I shall listen to you patiently and attentively."

32

CONTINUATION OF THE TALK ABOUT THE DEITY OF JESUS.

1. (Says the wise man): "Friend, I must admit that I am unable to cope with your arguments, although you have not removed an atom from the unique deity of Jesus the Lord with their help. On the contrary, you have made me see even clearer that God must be also man, the highest and most perfect man, of course. Otherwise, we could not possibly be human, nor could we love God, if He were not the most perfect man.

2. Love is our most sublime possession, our life, our beatitude! Why then would it exist at all if we could not love God in a human form?

3. Do now whatever you want — but do not expect any more wisdom from me. I gave you all I had!"

4. Bishop Martin ponders the words of the wise man of the party, and after a while, speaks rather to himself than to the other: "Basically you are right, for if the pentateuch of Moses is correct, God had to be a man or He could not have made Adam in His own image, which presupposes also the same nature.

5. Although a watchmaker need not be a watch himself to be able to make one, he must have the concept of the watch in him.

6. But there is a snag again! If a man can have a concept of something quite different and separate from himself, no doubt God would be capable of it.

7. Consequently, the text of the pentateuch could read: 'God created man in the image of His idea', i.e., in exact accordance with His idea!

8. If this interpretation were correct, which is quite likely, it would not mean at all that God created man in His shape, or that He would have to have a limited shape to form a man. Since every idea as such is formless, God Himself, as the fundamental principle or idea, may also be formless.

9. Assuming that God would have to have a human shape in order to create human beings, if He wanted to make a bear, a shark, or any of the innumerable beings, He either would have to be able to change into the shape of all these or He would have to be part of all

these beings, once and for all, so that all things and beings would have in him a permanent archetype.

10. To assume this would be the barest sophistry! Therefore, God needs no form to be able to create men as human beings. And least of all does He need to be human Himself! This supposition would be totally contrary to the idea of complete divine freedom. For how could you imagine complete freedom if there were limitation through shape?

11. Considering this, complete freedom must be formless, which also agrees with the text of the pentateuch, where Jehovah forbids Moses to form any kind of image of Him.

12. Yes, my dearest friend, from the viewpoint of pure reason, I am probably right, whilst you 'walk by faith,' according to Paul! That, of course, is also a sort of life, but one without discernment or opinion. I do not want to take it away from you nor make a proselyte of you. However, I have to show you clearly that a former bishop cannot be turned inside out like a hare's skin, and particularly not by those who used to be his sheep on earth!"

13. (The wise man): "I see now in what quarter the wind is! If you are the bishop who died only a few weeks ago, then it is easy enough to understand why you cannot comprehend the deity of Jesus. *Ex trunco non fit Mercurius*! (A tree-trunk cannot become a Mercury).

14. I am the bookseller of the same town where you were bishop. I know only too well what you were like: outwardly a religious fanatic, but deep inside the sheerest atheist who used to read Kant, Hegel and Strauss with the greatest enthusiasm. And instead of the Vulgata, you had Voltaire, Rousseau and Helvetius on your desk — all the great minds you used to condemn from the pulpit and in your pastoral letters, but in your heart you greatly preferred them to Jesus!

15. I am well aware of all this because I had to supply these books to you, and you used to confide in me. But I was not influenced by you, and secretly pursued my own line by studying Swedenborg, whom you rejected as unsuitable for your Roman treadmill. Good that I know this now, for we might find some things to talk about!"

16. (Bishop Martin, in a startled voice): "That does it! Why the deuce did you have to turn up here?"

17. (To himself): "This bookseller chap knows of quite a lot of

my tricks. Now there is going to be some washing of dirty linen in the spirit-world!

18. I only hope Jesus, who no doubt is the master of this house, doesn't come in now. It would be most awkward for he has already uncovered some of my dirty tricks and has given me a piece of his mind.

19. But if this man with the shiny hat should start revealing some of my most secret rascalities, I may not fare too well. I might find myself once more in a terrible ocean or on a seashore for a million years. Oh, oh, how terrible that would be!

20. Whatever can I do to avoid this calamity? Ha! Well, I might do it some way. And if I don't succeed, I'll just have to spend all eternity fishing from some seashore! But I don't care any more, by God! Why did I have to meet this chap here? However, it has happened, and I shall have to think of some way out."

21.(Here the bookseller interrupts him and says): "If you could share my well-founded belief, it would help you out of your dilemma. And do not take me for an informer, but rather for your friend whom you saved from the fire of his blind zeal, and whom you clothed when he was naked!

22. Believe me, Jesus the Lord does not need us for spies and informers. For He knows our innermost thoughts even before we have become conscious of them ourselves.

23. Look, brother, why shouldn't it be possible for Jesus to be the Lord of Heaven and all creation? Why couldn't He be God the Eternal, the Almighty?

24. Since God created all beings, limited by time and space, should not He be capable out of His love for us, His creatures, His children, to confine Himself in time and space without loss of His omnipotence, considering that time and space have gone forth from Him?

25. Or, should a painter or sculptor who reproduces a thousand forms and shapes in colors or formed matter, not be able to paint his own portrait or sculpt his own image? If a man can do that, though not in a perfect sense, why should we consider it impossible for God to do it?

26. Or, could God be the highest and most independent Being if there were anything at all He could not bring about? With your Hegelian principles, you only limit Him, making Him a prisoner of infinity, capable of creating primordial central suns with planets, men and

beasts, but Who could not possibly have anything to do with infusoria. These, too, have life manifesting through their ingeniously devised organisms, but are much too insignificant for Him to be concerned with, the same as man until he has reached something like the size of a central sun. But how could he achieve this? Even Hegel and Strauss would be silent on that subject!

27. I, your friend, hope you will now understand and no longer object to giving Jesus the honor due to Him for ever and ever; all the more since He has repeatedly shown you great mercy!"

28. (Bishop Martin): "Brother, friend, I saved you from the flames, but you have now awakened in me a different flame — one of the most powerful light! Thanks be to Him and to you! But allow me first to collect myself, for this new thought is too overwhelming!"

33

BISHOP MARTIN RECOGNIZES THE LORD IN JESUS. — THE SINNER'S FEAR. — BISHOP MARTIN'S ENLIGHTENMENT.

1. (After a while, Bishop Martin speaks again): "Yes, dearest brother, from whatever side I look at the points you made, I find them sound. The Master of this house is also the Master of Infinity. He is beyond doubt the Son of the Most High also known as the Father! But where then is the Holy Ghost — or so to speak, the third divine person?"

2. (The wise bookseller): "Friend, just refer to the Gospel. Here you have a Bible with the New Testament. Read what John says, namely: 'In the beginning was the Word, and the Word was with God and the Word was God; . . . and the Word was made flesh and dwelt among us [in Jesus Christ] . . . .'

3. Another passage says: 'In Him dwelleth all the fulness of the Godhead bodily'; and another: 'He that hath seen Me hath seen the Father; for I and my Father are one; I am in the Father and the Father is in me'; and many similar passages.

4. If you meditate on such passages, and altogether the whole of the Old and New Testaments, you will become more and more convinced that Jesus is the sole Lord and Creator of Heaven and earth.

5. When one of His disciples asked Him to show them the Father, since He had told them so much about Him, Jesus said: 'Have I been so long a time with you and yet hast thou not known me? He that hath seen me hath seen the Father; and how sayest thou then, shew us the Father?'

6. And you are now asking the same kind of questions the disciples asked the Lord when they were still spiritually blind!"

7. (Bishop Martin): "You are absolutely right! Now I am really convinced! He is the one and only Lord, God, Creator, and Father of Heaven and the myriads of angels, as well as the suns, earths, and all men. He will surely have His reasons why He chose our earth, and I hope one day to understand this, too.

8. But now, brother, the more I think about all this, the more I begin to understand the significance of the fact that the Master of this house, Jesus, is God Himself, the more afraid I am of having to face Him!

9. For what a terrible sinner I am — that you know only too well! And so does the almighty God! And the result will most probably be eternal damnation. Maybe this did not happen until now because I had not recognized the most just Judge. But now that I have recognized Him, the terrible, without doubt I am sure I haven't a chance!

10. Knowing Who He is, we shall have to address Him: 'Lord, Lord!' But He Himself once said on earth: 'Not every one that saith unto me, Lord, Lord, shall enter into the kingdom of heaven; but he that doeth the will of my Father which is in heaven.' Tell me, friend, have we ever done His will? So heaven is quite out of the question for us!

11. But what else is there besides heaven? Nothing but hell! Barest hell! Oh, I can already picture the flames enveloping me and the devils! Oh, dear brother, a terrible fear has taken hold of me!

12. Whatever can we say if He, the almighty God, the most severe and merciless Judge, should come to us now with His damnation, driving us away into the eternal fire which has been prepared for all the devils?

13. Oh, how terrible! I can already almost hear the thunder of His judgment. What an unutterably dreadful experience that would be! Only I cannot understand how you can be so calm, whilst I am almost fainting from fright."

14. (The wise bookseller): "Pull yourself together, brother, and

rest assured that the Lord is better than described by Rome's popes and clergy. However, while we are so foolishly frightened of Him, He will most likely stay away and come to us only when our fear has been converted to love.

15. Just imagine, what pleasure could it give you to take revenge on a gnat which offended you? Wouldn't such a revenge be senseless, worthy only of a fool? How then could you expect anything like that of Divine Wisdom? What are we compared with God? Aren't we in comparison to Him what a gnat would be to us?

16. We must realize that we are nothing before Him. Why should He take revenge on us? Whereto, friend, whereto? Contain yourself! I am convinced that things will not be as bad for us as you imagine. Quiet! I think He is coming! There He is!"

34

A SUBLIME SCENE OF REDEMPTION: MARTIN AT THE LORD'S HEART.

1. When I enter with Peter, Bishop Martin collapses as in a swoon and all of the party, except the bookseller, cry: "Woe betide us!"

2. Only the bookseller goes down on his knees and says: "Lord, Father, hallowed be Thy name. Thy will be done! We are all of us great and gross sinners, not in the least worthy of Your mercy! But we all love You with all our hearts. Therefore, if it is Your will, show mercy to us! What are we without Your mercy, Your love, Your compassion?

3. You are everlasting, infinitely wise, and Your might is unlimited! We have no excuses before You. Or could anyone in the whole of infinity oppose Your might? For You could destroy him even before he conceived such an idea.

4. I, and all of us, recognize and acknowledge that You alone are the Lord of Heaven and all creation and that we are nothing before You and Your boundless might. Your holy will be done; but remember our weakness and show us Your mercy."

5. (Say I): "Rise, all of you, and do not lament like delinquents on earth. If I come to you, it means that you have already attained

salvation, for the unredeemed souls flee from Me and never want Me to come and save them. Therefore, your fear of Me is pointless and faint is the light of your intellect.

6. Shed all that is useless in My house, in My Kingdom, which is wherever I am and is the innermost and highest part of heaven. This heaven is not one of idleness and eternal inactivity, but one of full action, as you will now be taught. Every one of you will be active in the things for which he showed a talent already on earth. So be it!"

7. They all rise happily, thanking Me for such boundless mercy. Only Bishop Martin is still lying in his swoon, neither hearing nor seeing what is going on around him.

8. At a sign from Me, Peter walks over to the bishop, shakes him, and says: "But Martin, what are you doing here? We have been waiting for you outside for quite a while, but you did not return. You have been chatting here, making us wait for you like a prudish bride her bridegroom while she is adorning herself for the wedding feast. Don't you know that there are some most important and urgent matters we have to attend to?"

9. (After a pause, Bishop Martin speaks again): "Oh, yes, of course, it is you! This time I set out on a very important and distant voyage of discovery, and it takes some time to return from such a voyage. Although I have discovered something most important, this has not made me happy, but only extremely frightened.

10. I have now discovered irrefutibly that our host and master is God, Lord of Infinity! Of this I am now positive! But, just imagine me, the greatest sinner — and God, the Almighty, Omniscient, the Most Wise, Most Just, Most Holy, Who must damn me because of His justice and holiness!

11. My friend over there with the shiny hat has done his best to console and reassure me, but until I have the reassurance from Him, Who can send me to hell for eternity, it does not do me any good."

12. (Peter): "Better rise to your feet and do not be silly! The Lord Jesus, of Whom you are so afraid, is waiting for you with open arms. Does He look as if He were going to condemn you?"

13. Bishop Martin glances at Me and sees My great kindness. This encourages him to lift himself from the ground, and he says, with tears in his eyes: "Oh, no, this mildness does not consider condemnation. Oh, Lord and Father, how good You must be to look so kindly upon a sinner like me!

14. Oh, Jesus, I cannot bear it any longer! My heart burns like a

82

central sun, with newly awakened love for You; let me at least caress Your feet to give vent to my love! Then, Lord, do with me what You will!"

15. (Say I): "Come to Me, you stubborn brother, your sins are forgiven. And do not give vent to your love at My feet, but at My heart!"

16. Following these words, Martin rushes into the embrace of the Lord, Whom to recognize took him so long.

17. After he has had a good cry at My heart, I ask him: "How do you like this descent into hell? Am I really the tyrant I have been made by your church?"

18. (Bishop Martin): "Oh, Lord, I lack the words to confess to You before all these dear brothers how clearly I now see all my faults and errors. But allow me to collect myself a bit in this newly found unutterable bliss, and then I will make a true confession to You, my sweetest, kindest, most merciful Lord Jesus.

19. O Lord, o Jesus, I must love You above everything, You Most Holy, Whose essence is supreme love and boundless patience!"

20. (Say I): "Well, it is this love that I saw in you that made Me attend to you Myself, and which made Me have so much patience with you. Now you are so full of bliss, for you will be wherever I Myself am. But beatitude is never founded on idleness; on the contrary, it consists in the greatest activity, for which there is at all times much scope here.

21. But let us now go to the other thirty people whom you brought here. You go in first and try to lead them to Me. If you succeed in this first task in your state of beatitude, we shall guide them also to their eternal destination. So let us go there, and you will enter their apartment alone. So be it!"

35

BISHOP MARTIN'S FIRST MISSION AND HIS EXPERIENCES. — AN APPARENT MENAGERIE. — "WITHOUT ME YE CAN DO NOTHING."

1. Bishop Martin gladly walks toward the apartment, accompanied by Me, Peter, and the wise bookseller, the latter following

respectfully behind us. At the door, Bishop Martin leaves us behind to join the thirty people within.

2. It must be pointed out that our bishop is now no longer in his own, but in My purest divine light, of which, however, for very good reasons, he is not yet quite consciously aware. In this light, everything looks different from what it looks like in natural light, thus also the souls or departed spirits.

3. N.B. — "Departed" must not be confused with "deceased" in this case. Here, "departed" denotes a state of condemnation as the consequence of various sins (defects of the soul) after leaving the physical body.

4. Due to this order, Bishop Martin, on entering the apartment, is faced with mainly animal shapes instead of humans; not wild beasts though, but rather the timid and stupid kind. Only a few have a crippled human shape, covered with tumors. Most of them look like hunted hares, starved asses or oxen, and some like stunted, mangy sheep.

5. When our bishop finds this peculiar crowd, instead of the thirty Protestants he had expected to find, hiding from him in the corners, he is for a moment petrified. Then he takes a deep breath and says to himself: "What is this infernal spook in the Kingdom of Heaven, the house of the Lord? What a sight! Maybe there are also rats and mice here, and maybe lots of smaller pests!

6. What a sight! Really! And how does that go together with the Holy Scriptures, where it says that nothing impure can enter the Kingdom of God? That couple of mangy sheep over there, those five cretins covered with horrible tumors, all those dirty, emaciated oxen and asses, and some extremely shabby hares — what an exquisite party for the first or highest heaven! This would be some company to enjoy the delights of heaven with!

7. It is my bad luck to be used as April Fools' Day messenger, that is if the month of April does exist at all in heaven!

8. This is too crazy! Whatever will I do with this good-natured menagerie? And where are the thirty Protestants I brought here? Have they, perhaps, been turned into these animals? That would be really funny, considering that this is the center of the highest heaven.

9. The Lord *is* the Lord, indeed — this is now my deepest conviction. My love for Him tells me that. But why has He played this practical joke on me? He knows best. Is it possible that He wants to

84

fatten these animals? That would not be a very promising enterprise.

10. But what am I twaddling like Ass No. 31 of this party? I'd better return to where I came from. So long, my dears, I shall be glad to see you again!"

11. After this laconic address, the bishop returns to us with a puzzled expression on his face. But I ask him immediately where the thirty are.

12. (Bishop Martin replies): "O Lord, surely You know that better than I. Those in there couldn't be the thirty, but if they are, such a metamorphosis wouldn't be at all fitting for the first and highest heaven.

13. Without speaking the language of cattle, if they have a language, I do not think much could be done with the inmates of that room. You, of course, understand the stones and can speak to the elements and command them. But what can I do?

14. Therefore, oh Lord, since You must have been aware of what I would find in that room, You probably set a trap for my stupidity!"

15. (Say I): "Not at all, friend! You set that trap yourself. Don't you know that every new servant must get instructions from his master before he sets out on an errand?

16. It is not enough if I say to you: 'Go there!' and you go, and I say: 'Come here!' and you come. The important thing is the 'why' and the 'how'.

17. Isn't it written: 'Without Me ye can do nothing'? Therefore, when I sent you to that apartment, you should have confessed to Me: 'Lord, without You I can do nothing!', and I would have given this matter quite a different turn. However, you entered the room right away with a sort of self-confidence. Consequently, you had to find out for yourself how little one can do without Me.

18. In the world there are, unfortunately, as many independent performers of actions as there are men, and as many different minds as there are heads. But here it is quite different! For here, there is only *one* self-reliance, which is the one in Me — and only *one* mind and *one* cognition also in Me and through Me! And where this is not the case, there is nothing but self-deception.

19. May this be your guiding principle for the future! But, now let us all go into that room and see what we can do with your would-be heavenly menagerie, and whether these animals will understand My language. So be it!"

36

BISHOP MARTIN'S SECOND VISIT TO THE MENAGERIE UNDER THE DIRECTION OF THE DIVINE MASTER. — HIS MISSIONARY ADDRESS AND DELIVERANCE OF THE LOST.

1. We now enter the same room and find the thirty still crouching in the corners, still in their animal shapes.

2. (Peter calls out to them): "Followers of Calvin, turn around for the Lord is waiting for you! You should not confess to Luther, nor to Calvin, nor the Bible, nor Peter, Paul, or John, but only to *Jesus,* the Crucified! For He alone is the Lord of heaven and earth, and besides Him there is no other lord, god, or life.

3. Our Lord Jesus, Who alone is the true Christ in eternity, is here and prepared to accept you — if you are willing — so that you may all be saved in His holy name!"

4. (One of the party, with the appearance of an ass, speaks): "Who are you that you dare come to me with that old Jesus-fable in this enlightened era? Don't you see my treasures which, I hope, shall last me through all eternity? I am perfectly happy with the state I am in. What do I want with that mythical Jesus, Who never was, nor is, nor will be? When will the ancient mythical sages be abandoned at last and replaced by the really wise men of our present time?

5. Why should Homer still be considered the greatest poet, Orpheus practically a god of sounds, Appeles the first painter, Apollodorus the first sculptor, Genghis-Khan the greatest hero and conqueror, Socrates, Plato and Aristotle the greatest philosophers, the Pharaohs Ramses and Sesostris the greatest builder-kings, Ptolomaeus the first astronomer, Moses the greatest and wisest lawgiver, David and Solomon the wisest kings, and at last, Jesus, the greatest and wisest moralist?

6. Haven't we got a great number of men who stand high above these ancients? And still sacrificial altars are built for the latter, whilst the wise men of our present times are often allowed to die of starvation!"

7. (Peter): "I am who I am — sometimes Simon Jona and at other times just Peter. Your times of enlightenment are not too impressive! Obviously, the ancient Jesus-fable is worth more than the treasures of your donkey-skin. The ancient sages were also worth more than the present-day fops, for they knew what they were doing. That is

why they became teachers of the nations of all times, while the scholars of the present time think a lot of their learning, but do not know what they are doing. They do not know themselves nor their fellowmen, and least of all the purely divine nature and significance of the Lord Jesus Christ. This is the reason why, in the presence of the Lord, they appear in the shape of asses, oxen, hunted hares and mangy sheep.

8. Turn around and look at yourselves, and the truth of my words will become apparent! Why were you so frightened of Jesus a while ago, and asked not to have to face Him? Look at Him now that He has come to you, the merely mythical being!"

9. The donkey-man is now silent, but Bishop Martin says: "Oh, Lord, how great Your patience is and how boundless Your love! But I would enjoy giving this ass a hiding. Oh, what a real ass he is! The Catholics are stupid enough, but I have never met anyone quite as stupid as this Calvinistic ass!"

10. (Say I): "My dear friend and brother Martin, don't you know what I once said to our brother Peter, when he cut off the ear of one of the high priest's servants, Malchus, with his sword? The same applies here. And where love, with meekness and patience, has no influence, there is nothing a sword or any other kind of force can achieve.

11. Omnipotence can condemn and destroy as the result of judgment. But only love, combined with meekness and patience, can help, comfort, preserve life, return what was lost, free a spirit from the strongest shackles. Where there is no love, there is nothing but death and destruction.

12. We do not want anyone to perish, and all who believe in Me shall have eternal life. Therefore, it is up to us in each individual case to use the right means by which someone can be helped.

13. Try your hand at these headstrong, scholarly Calvinists and see what you, as a former bishop, can accomplish with them."

14. (Bishop Martin): "Oh, dearest Lord, my beloved God and Father Jesus, whatever could I accomplish, if even the most worthy Peter does not seem to have much success with them, at least not without performing a miracle?

15. Since You, o Lord, are present in person in Your fullest divine essence, with unlimited resources at Your disposal, it would be unforgivable if I, a nothing before You, tried to act here. Therefore, I beg You to kindly withdraw this commission."

16. (Say I): "No, My dear brother Martin! You, too, are one of My means. If I personally influenced this half-dead party, it would result in their judgment. They are now quite aware of My presence, and some of them are almost inclined to believe that I am the true Lord.

17. So I now entrust you with this task, for which brother Peter has already prepared the way. He himself is also still too powerful for these infirm. Therefore, somebody who is not too strong himself has to help them at this stage, so as not to crush them. For gnats can and must be nursed only by gnats, and infants could not digest a man's fare, but must be fed on easily-digestible milk. Therefore, do go and carry out the task I have given you concerning these thirty helpless. So be it!"

18. Now I, Peter, and the extremely meek bookseller leave the apartment again, and Bishop Martin stays on his own with the thirty.

19. Bishop Martin looks at the herd for a while and then addresses it with the following words, which are in accordance with the state he is in, as well as that of the herd: "You poor, helpless brothers who appear only as dumb animals in the light of the almighty, eternal God, listen to me!

20. In the world I was a Roman bishop and a fanatical opponent of Protestantism, although I thought less of Rome than of Mohammedanism. And exactly as I had been in the world, I arrived here, a beast, recalcitrant to all that is good and true. There was not *one* good hair on my body, and my heart was like an Augean stable. There was in me not even a trace of what could be called Christian merit!

21. Only sometimes, in my imagination, I used to picture the Lord Jesus as He is described, thinking, 'If I could have Him this way and work together with Him in the conviction that He really is the Supreme Divine Being, that would be bliss, indeed! For this would not only be the highest possible honor, it would also be provision for all eternity, the most powerful protection and, besides, in His company I might behold such wonders as no human mind has been able to imagine.'

22. And this thought, these very vague castles in the air, became the means of my salvation from eternal perdition. They were the expression of my hidden love for God, of which I wasn't even aware myself. And look, dear brothers, hard as it was for me in the beginning, these fantasies of my mind have turned into the most

evident reality — unbelievable as it may still seem to you. I am now with Jesus, the sole Lord of the spiritual and material worlds, and am well provided for in all eternity.

23. Brothers, friends, do not be your own greatest adversaries, but follow my example and you will never regret it! Believe me, it is the Lord Who is in this magnificent house, and His goodness is boundless. Therefore, turn around and have faith and you will see how everything around you will look much brighter. Abandon your wrong surmises, adopt my doctrine of experience, and turn into living tools of the Lord!"

24. Following our bishop's truly unctuous speech, all thirty turn to him and reply almost unanimously: "Friend, we prefer these, your words, quite considerably to your earlier ones, although we must say that we do not like your animal comparisons concerning our personalities. You may call a stupid fellow an ass or an ox, but to try to convince him that he has the actual appearance of an ox or an ass is carrying it a bit too far!"

25. (One of the herd now speaks): "But be that as it may, you have proved with your words that you are quite a good and clever chap, and about your Jesus you might be right, too. But one thing is most peculiar, and that is that one does not see any angels here; the landscape is not exactly one of heavenly beauty; and what about heavenly garments? You are wearing peasant clothes, even without a coat. Your Lord Jesus wears nothing less than a heavenly garment, and Peter looks more scanty than heavenly! Only the bookseller from N--------, whom I know quite well, has a somewhat better coat, although it would still not be the right type of heavenly garment.

26. Look, friend, this makes the whole matter rather dubious. If you can give us a feasible explanation, we shall believe whatever you tell us and follow your suggestions."

27. Here, Martin hesitates for a moment, for during his spiritual progress, he had not thought of these things at all. But then he pulls himself together, and says: "Friends, believe me, this is mainly a matter of how one wants it to be. So far, I haven't wanted it any different, but if I did, things would change immediately.

28. Indeed, I haven't seen any angels as yet, but what are all the angels and heavenly splendor as long as you have the Lord of all the angels and heavenly magnificence? He can, so to say, conjure up, in a moment, everything that might be missing. Anyway, I haven't felt in

me any desire for such things, not even for a better garment, for now the Lord is all things to me.

29. When you reach my level, you will think and feel the same way. Eternity is still so long, and there is still so much to behold and experience at the side of the Master of Infinity. That is my profound conviction.

30. And I can only say what I feel in my heart as a living truth: 'Lord, if I have You, I do not ask for all the other splendors. For the Lord, our Lord Jesus, is and shall forever be the glory of glories. Praised be the Lord; He has all my love for ever and ever! Amen.' "

31. Following these words, the whole herd, already in human shape, rises as from a cloud of dust, and shouts: "Amen! Brother, you are right! We all believe you now! Your words have been truly wise and have kindled a light in our hearts that will never go out. We thank the Lord Jesus, your eternal God, and now also ours!"

32. At this moment, I enter the room with My two companions and they all fall at My feet and shout: "O Lord Jesus, You Most Holy Father, You Trinitarian God, have mercy upon us poor sinners! Praise be to You alone in eternity!"

33. (I say): "Rise My children and see your Father come to you with the greatest love, and not with judgment. And since you accepted Him into your hearts, He is now taking you to His eternal Father's heart. Come unto Me all of you who are weary and over-burdened, and I will give you rest."

34. Here they all rise and try to embrace Me, and they weep for the first time tears of overwhelming joy; then they all follow Me to the large dining hall where Peter has already sent the previous party.

37

THE CELESTIAL FEAST. — BLESSING OF THE NEWLY RE-DEEMED AND THEIR CELESTIAL HOME.

1. We now enter a large hall facing mainly the east and decorated in true celestial splendor.

2. In its center there is a large round table of purest transparent

gold resting on twelve feet made of a variety of gems. Around the table are as many chairs of pure gold as there are now guests in this hall. The floor is as white as new snow, and from the light-blue ceiling bright stars are shining. A glorious light enters the hall through its twenty-four windows, each of which is twelve feet high and seven feet wide, and through each window a magnificent and lovely landscape can be seen. On the table are seven loaves of bread and a beautiful large goblet filled with the most delicious wine.

3. The unexpected magnificence of this hall has an overwhelming effect on all who have just entered. The party, led by the bookseller, is quite overawed, and the thirty, who only a while ago had complained about the lack of heavenly splendor, are speechless.

4. Only our *Martin* is unperturbed, and says, pointing to Me: "Dear brothers, what makes you so amazed at the magnificence of this hall? I personally don't care about it, and I wouldn't give a rotten orange for it if our Lord and Father were not with us in this hall. He alone is everything to me, and nothing else counts without Him!

5. If He were with me in a simple hut, I would be much happier than if I were alone in this magnificent hall. He alone, Who is our Father, Lord and God, deserves our respect, love, admiration, and worship, for all this great splendor is His work! Of course, you are all free to do and think whatever you want, but this is as I see it!"

6. (Say I): "Martin, you are doing well and have now become a real Paul. But watch out that you do not, at some time or other, weaken again and say, 'But if the Lord would not constantly be with me!' However, even then I would not leave you. Now, let us all sit down at the table and eat and drink, for great tasks are already waiting for us. So be it!"

7. They all follow My invitation and I break the bread and give it to them. They eat the true bread of eternal life with great love and thankful hearts, and then drink the living wine of cognition, all from the same goblet, feeling cheerful and vigorous. For after drinking the wine, they are filled to such an extent with sublime, heavenly-wise understanding, that they are overwhelmed with joy and are unable to find words to express their love for Me and their boundless bliss.

8. However, I bless them all, and appoint them true workers and servants for My Eternal Kingdom.

9. After this has been done, Bishop Martin rises, and says: "Lord, I have noticed something, namely, that I, too, might have to

leave You to carry out some important task. Do whatever You will, but I cannot possibly leave You! Lord, I am nothing without You and I will not leave You ever, because my love for You is now so great!"

10. (Say I):"My dear brother Martin, I can assure you that you will not for a moment be separated from Me. The same applies to all the others here and to everyone of the countless who have apprehended Me and taken Me into their hearts! On the other hand, it is necessary that everyone go where I send him, apparently without Me, for otherwise his joy would be incomplete and his life without purpose.

11. Therefore, each one here must be extremely active in the performance of good works. The greater the activity, the deeper is the happiness which consists solely in working in accordance with My established eternal heavenly order.

12. Look out the window, towards the east. There, in a beautiful large garden, you can see a nice little house, whose interior is much more spacious than it would seem from the outside. Go there and take full possession of it.

13. In one room you will find a shining white, round tablet. Whenever you return home after some task, look at this tablet, for drawn on it you will, from now on — always — find My will, which will guide you in all your actions. If you will at all times carry out conscientiously what My will requires of you, you shall soon be given greater responsibilities; if the contrary is the case, you will have lesser responsibilities, dependent on your will-power.

14. If there is anything that you do not understand, come to this place and you will be instructed. Whenever in your house you call Me, I shall be with you. Now I have told you what you have to know at this stage. Go, therefore, to your little house where you will get all necessary instructions, which you have to observe in all detail."

15. What I have told you just now I am at the same time telling everyone in this party. Look outside, all of you, and each one will own the house he sees. Go there and do as I have just told brother Martin, for every one of you will find the same arrangement in his house. So be it!"

16. Bishop Martin scratches his head, but then goes where I have sent him, although he still thinks that he will not have nor see Me there. The others of the party, who are still too overwhelmed by My

presence, go with easier minds to rest from the great emotions they have experienced.

38

BISHOP MARTIN IN HIS CELESTIAL HOME. — THE FIRST SURPRISE. — INTERIOR OF THE HOME.

1. On entering his little house, Bishop Martin is very surprised to find Me already awaiting him at the threshold to show him around; for the others, this is done by angels, for their feelings for Me consist still more of awe than of love. With Bishop Martin, the contrary is the case, which is the reason why he did not like the idea at all of having to part from Me.

2. However, when he sees Me in his house, waiting for him at the threshold, he is overjoyed.

3. (Bishop Martin): "Ah, yes — this way I like it even better than in the hall of splendor in Your house! As long as You are with me, my beloved Lord Jesus, the smallest hut is the most glorious heaven for me!

4. But how did You get here so quickly without my noticing it? That is another miracle, my dearest Lord Jesus, as everything about You is miraculous. Only I am still too stupid to comprehend it! But it is peculiar that You arrived here before me, considering that I left You behind at Your house!"

5. (Say I): "Do not worry about these things, My dear brother Martin, for if I were not the First and the Last and All in all everywhere, things would not be too good in all infinity. But you may turn wherever you want to and you will find Me.

6. Let us now inspect this little house, so that I Myself may instruct you in the correct use of all that you will see therein. Come with Me into your home which, though small, contains more than the whole world, even more than a solar system in the sphere of the natural world, as you will soon realize. So be it!"

7. Bishop Martin follows Me in astonishment, for instead of the expected small room, we enter a huge hall. The longer and more attentive he looks around, the more it expands, displaying everything that he is able to imagine.

8. In the center of this spacious hall, a large, shining white, round disc is displayed on a golden stand. Behind it, on a bronze stand, is the most perfect, artificial globe, showing everything — from the largest to the smallest — that the real earth contains, from its center to its surface, including all that is happening there.

9. Behind this globe is a similar artificial display of the whole planetary system of the earth's sun, also showing every detail and peculiarity of the planets and the sun.

10. The floor of this hall appears to be of pure sapphire, the high walls of emerald, the ceiling of lapis lazuli, with numerous stars. A glorious purple light enters through the large windows and shines on a magnificent gallery of finest jasper, adorning the hall at half its height. Twelve doors lead from the hall into the adjoining rooms. And, in addition to all this, the emerald walls reflect in beautifully colored silhouettes whatever Bishop Martin can think of.

11. After he has gazed at all this for a while in astonishment, he speaks again: "Oh, Lord, what does this trickery mean? From the outside the house looks so tiny, yet inside it looks like a whole world! How is it possible that something is larger inside than out? This I cannot understand; it is quite beyond me!"

12. (Say I): "My beloved brother Martin, you will soon understand all this. In the real, true world of the spirits, everything is the opposite from what it is like in the material world. What is great in the world, is only small here; but whatever is small in the world, is great here. Who in the world is the first, is last here; who is the last, is first here!

13. What is the size of a man in the world? It may be six feet high and two feet wide. But if he is a wise man, imagine what boundless greatness and depths are in his heart! Believe Me, all eternity will not suffice to reveal the wealth of its wonders.

14. In the world, you have often looked at grains of wheat. Although such a grain is so small in its volume, it contains so vast a number of its likes, that it cannot be measured in eternity. The same principle is revealed here before you.

15. The exterior of this house compares with your now very humble outer person: it is, as you are, small! However, the interior is like your inner wisdom, which comprises greater things. Therefore, it also appears larger than the exterior of the house. And the more you grow in true wisdom, resulting from My love, the more it will expand. For in this world everyone lives from his wisdom which

depends on the measure of his love for Me. And this wisdom is the originator of all that you see here and find so miraculous.

16. But behold that shining white, upright tablet; it represents your conscience cleansed through Me. From now on, you will at all times find My will revealed on this tablet and you shall act in accordance with it forthwith.

17. In the world, as a matter of fact, every human being has such a conscience-tablet in his heart which records My will to be followed, but only few take notice of it. And many paint this tablet black with their sins so as not to see My will at all.

18. This shows you how true to life the equipment of your house is, and that there is no trickery involved, as you originally assumed.

19. Behind the tablet is a true image of the world as it is in its essence, and behind that, you see the sun with its planets. If there is anything you do not understand, look at the reverse side of the tablet, facing the earth, and you will find the explanation there. And if you then want to know what you have to do about it, the front of the tablet will show you what My will requires.

20. You also see twelve doors leading from this large hall into smaller rooms, where you will find a variety of dishes still partly covered. Do not eat from them before I have blessed them all for you or they would dull your perception and render you unable to read the writing of My will on this tablet for quite a while. Therefore, whenever you come face to face with such covered dishes, turn your back on them and come to Me, and I shall go and uncover the dishes for you and bless them.

21. Now you know the position; act accordingly and you will continuously grow in beatitude! So be it!"

39

BISHOP MARTIN ON HIS OWN IN THE HALL OF HIS HOUSE.— INSPECTION OF THE EARTH GLOBE AND THE OTHER PLANETS. — MARTIN'S BOREDOM.

1. I now leave Bishop Martin apparently, and he commences the following monologue: "So, so, now I am on my own again at long last! Everything here is truly heavenly and sublime. I have eaten my

fill, have been blessed, and should be supremely happy. But I am still alone, quite alone! Only my own ideas reflect from the walls, swaying and interweaving, but otherwise, there is not even a gnat that might hum to me.

2. I shall have a look at the beautiful globe to pass the time. What a unique work of art! And there I can see the place where I acted as bishop; there is the church, there my residence! And there I can even see the cemetery and my grave with a beautiful monument! What fools men are to erect monuments to the muck and forget about the spirit! If I could destroy this monument with a well-aimed flash of lightning, I would feel much better. But it is up to the Lord to do what is right.

3. Let's turn the globe and see what Australia looks like. Oh dear, oh dear, that does not look too good. What darkness, what slavery, persecution and killing of human beings, physically and spiritually. May the Lord bless you, my dear globe, but I do not think we shall spend much time with each other. I would be an ass if I subjected myself to emotions of anger by looking at you, here in the realm of eternal peace! It makes me furious to see how the more powerful men torture and even kill their weaker brothers in the most cruel fashion, as if they enjoyed it! Away with you, miserable demonstration-machine of earthly horrors, we shall not see much of each other.

4. Look, there is the whole planetary system with the sun! Let's have a look at one of the planets. There is Venus!

5. What do you look like, my dear Venus, whose splendid light, like the morning or evening star, I have often enjoyed in the dark world? Let's now have a close look at you. Ah, mm, quite different from what I imagined. You resemble the earth on which I lived; not quite as large areas of ocean though, but a great number of smaller seas and very high mountains!

6. I wonder what the vegetation is like and by what type of creatures this planet is inhabited? I would like to see it somewhat enlarged or be given a sort of spiritual microscope, otherwise I would not be able to see much more than before, since the whole planet is only the size of a hen's egg in the world. To think what the infusoria would be like on this scale!

7. I really should look at the white tablet now; there may already be something written on it. Well, there is nothing on this side. Actually, I am glad of it, for I must admit that it fills me with

awe. There isn't anything on the other side either, which is even better! And now back to my planetary system!

8. There is the Venus once more, but not any bigger yet. All right, since you don't want to enlarge, my beautiful star, there is nothing more I want with you. So push along, my star!

9. Ah, there is little Mercury; quite a neat little world, the size of a hazelnut. Seems to have no seas, but all the more mountains instead — if those pin-head-size roughnesses can be honored with the term 'mountain.' My dear Mercury, we have already finished with each other, so take off!

10. And what does this coppery chap represent? It wouldn't be the earth again? Oh, I've got it — you fiery hero are Mars! In the world, I had quite a different notion of you — imagined you to be tumultuous and stormy, but you seem to be exactly the contrary, judging by your flat surface which shows only few mountains. Since I cannot see any more details, push along, too!

11. Now I can see about seven tiny globules, probably planets, too. Off with you; you wouldn't be of any use to me either!

12. There is already the great Jupiter moving towards me! What a fine planet, and with four satellites — most impressive! And what do you look like? Good gracious, what a lot of water! Only in equatorial areas can I see lots of islands; all the rest just water. There are a few mountains, but they do not appear to be high; What about the vegetation and life on this planet? Although it is a few thousand times larger than the previous planets I saw here, I cannot discern any vegetation on you either. The surface seems to be somewhat rough, but to see what it consists of one would require quite different eyes.

13. And there are also Saturn and Uranus, and in the background a very large planet with ten moons — three quite big ones and some smaller ones! Could those be moons of moons? Now I can see also numerous comets in the background.

14. It is a beautiful sight, but if there is nothing but some oceans and high mountains discernible on these good planets, they will not afford much fun for the whole of eternity! I am already through with them; and in view of the small scale, I shall not have much use for them in future.

15. There, in the center, is still the Sun. It is no doubt a big lump, but what's the use if its size compares with the real sun like a grain of sand with the whole of the earth? I wouldn't be able to dis-

cern anything on it. Therefore, my dear Sun, you, too, are of no use to me; so farewell!

16. I am already through with the inspection of the unique heavenly art-curios adorning my hall. What now? There is no writing on the tablet; I have nothing more to look at on the planets; the globe of the earth I would rather have outside than in here! So what will I do now? If I went across to the Lord? But that would not be the proper thing for me to do just yet.

17. Hmm, isn't it an awkward business that a blessed spirit must suffer from boredom in heaven when he is close to the Lord of Glory? There is probably some good in it, but boredom is boredom in heaven just as it is on earth.

18. On earth, if the worst comes to the worst, you can console yourself with dear death, which puts an end to everything, at least as far as earth is concerned. But here — eternal thanks to the Lord for this — there is no death and everything assumes an eternal character which fact, unfortunately, makes one fear that such a state might remain permanent. As a result, every experience of monotony makes boredom a thousand times worse than on earth, where everything has an end.

19. What shall I do? There is nothing visible on the tablet as yet. Probably the Lord is not too anxious for my services, otherwise He would have given me something to do.

20. Ah, ah, it can be extremely boring here in heaven! I wonder whether I shall have to stay forever in this heavenly art museum? Oh, what a prospect! "

40

THE TWELVE SMALL CABINETS WITH THE COVERED AS YET UNBLESSED SPIRITUAL DISHES. — THE FLOCK OF LOVELY MAIDENS, THE BEAUTIFUL MERCURIAN, THE PERFECTLY SHAPED NAKED VENUSIANS. — THE IMPORTANCE OF THE LORD'S BLESSING.

1. (Bishop Martin): "But now I remember that adjoining this hall there are still twelve cabinets into which the twelve doors lead. And there will be the somewhat ominous covered dishes. These cabinets

I must inspect. So, in the name of the Lord, good luck, for who knows what these secret cabinets might reveal!

2. So, let me open door number one. Oh, oh, just look at this — there is my beautiful flock, shapely as ever! What a surprise; thus, dear eternity will not seem long at all. But now it means 'about turn'! This is already covered dish number one. I had better get on with door number two.

3. There it is! I'll open it carefully, in the name of the Lord, for one never knows what might be behind it. This door does not open as lightly as the previous one, but — thank God — I have opened it at last! In this cabinet, it is darker than in the first one, so I shall have to enter it.

4. Oh, oh, oh! What is this? This room is even larger than the entrance hall. And in the background I can discern a vast crowd of completely naked human beings of both sexes. How beautiful they are, especially the females.

5. Ah, one of them is approaching me. Should I wait for her? Oh, yes, I have to, for this dish is not covered. Oh, no, not a bit!

6. What a breathtaking beauty! The whiteness of the skin, the well-developed figure and bust! It is overwhelming! The softly rounded arms, the divine feet, and this heavenly beautiful face with the tender smile!

7. Oh, oh, I can't bear it! I must leave! But no, I can't, it is impossible, and maybe she wants to tell me something. Here she is already; quiet — she is going to say something!"

8. (The woman speaks): "You must be the owner of this house for whom we have been waiting all this time?"

9. (Bishop Martin): "Oh, yes, but no — not quite! I have only just come to live here. The owner would really be the Lord Jesus, Infinite God. What could I do for you all, and especially for you, you heavenly beauty, who surpasses all beauty of the whole of infinity?"

10. (The woman): "Do not praise me so much, for over there are many of my sex who are incomparably more beautiful than I, and I, as the least beautiful, was sent to meet you so as not to dazzle you too much in the beginning.

11. We are all human beings from the planet Mercury, as you, children of the Almighty, call it. As this is your house, it is up to you to keep us here that we might serve you, or to send us away. But we all beg you to have mercy upon us."

12. (Bishop Martin): "Oh, please, you heavenly, sublime and

sweetest beauty — if there were many thousands of you, I wouldn't think of letting you go. Come to me, you loveliest of all Mercurians, and let me embrace you. Oh dear, you are getting more beautiful every moment, especially when you smile at me so charmingly."

13. (The woman): "You are the master, and I can only be your slave for ever! Therefore, I have to do as you wish, for your will must be sacred to all of us."

14. (Bishop Martin): "But my heavenly beauty, what is all this talk about slaves? From now on, you will be a queen of my heart! Come, oh come, you sweetest beauty! O God, this delight really takes my breath away!"

15. Bishop Martin is just going to embrace the beautiful Mercurian, when I Myself tap him on the shoulder, saying: "Wait, My dear son Martin, this, too, is a covered dish! Only after I have blessed her for you can you embrace her — if you then still feel like it! I suggest an about turn here, too!"

16. (Bishop Martin): "Oh, You, my beloved Lord Jesus! I love You assuredly as much as anyone can love You, but I must tell You honestly that, in this instance, I would have preferred You to arrive a few moments later!"

17. (Say I): "Of this I am quite aware, and already I predicted to you that you would very soon feel like this, although at that moment you did not want to be separated from Me at any cost. However, I never forsake him who has taken Me into his heart. Therefore, follow Me quickly out of this room, then, when the time is right, the reason for this will be revealed to you. And you, woman, withdraw again!"

18. The woman does as told, and Bishop Martin follows Me, with a somewhat long face, but not unwillingly, to door number three.

19. When we come to this door, it opens by itself.

20. Bishop Martin looks inside, full of curiosity, and is amazed when he is faced with quite a new world of splendor, including a crowd of blessed spirits in the most perfect human shape. Their beauty has an almost stunning effect on our bishop.

21. (Only after a while, does Bishop Martin exclaim): "O Lord, You glorious Creator and Master of all things, all beings — human and angelic — this is breathtaking, too superb for human comprehension!

22. What does this mean? Who are these beings? Are they angels or blessed human spirits? Although they are also naked, their sunny white skin, their stature of perfect harmony, a sort of radiance en-

veloping them replaces a thousandfold the most splendid garments. I could not possibly imagine a more beautiful and sublime shape.

23. O Lord, no praise or honor can do You justice! You are holy, holy; heaven and earth are full of Your wonders! Glory be to You in all eternity!

24. I beg of You, let us proceed, for I cannot bear this magnificent sight any longer. Just tell me one thing if You will: What beings are these?"

25. (Say I): "Those are human beings from the planet you call Venus. They are meant to serve you, My children, whenever and wherever you require their services; this is their greatest bliss. Therefore, the more often and wiser you make use of them, the happier they will be.

26. However, these are not the only ones awaiting your orders. There are countless others, from other planets. But you'll have to learn how to use their services in all wisdom. This is all you have to know for the time being; further details will follow later.

27. This will give you an idea of what Paul hinted at when he said: 'Eye hath not seen nor ear heard, neither have entered into the heart of man the things which God hath prepared for them that love Him!'

28. While still on earth, you had no idea why the stars had such a mighty attraction for you. But now you see before you the magnet which so often drew you with magic power and called forth many a sigh of 'Oh, how beautiful!' from your then rather barren soul.

29. Behold, this is already a kind of service on the part of these beings if through their firm and unshaken will they sometimes influence receptive minds of men, turning them toward the stars. That they did also for you, before you knew them. And now they will do this to an even greater extent, since they have seen you, as you have seen them, although not too clearly as yet.

30. But now let us continue to door number four, where you will see something different and even more glorious. So be it!"

31. (Bishop Martin): "But Lord, why are these beautiful beings not allowed to approach us, and why must they first be blessed by You?"

32. (Say I): "My dear son Martin, have you never noticed on earth, when going for a walk along the bank of a river, that there were people doing exactly the same on the opposite bank? Would it have been possible for you, if you had felt like it, to cross over to

them without a bridge or a boat? You'd say, no! But behold, in this world My blessing serves the same purpose a bridge or ship does on earth.

33. Neither on earth nor here in heaven can you do anything without Me! My blessing is My almighty will, My eternal word: 'Let there be!' — by which all that is was made. Therefore, it must also throw a bridge to all these beings to enable you to get to them and them to you without doing any harm. And everything has its right time, which I alone determine, or he to whom I reveal it."

34. (Bishop Martin): "But how was it possible for the lovely Mercurian to come so close to me that I would have embraced her if You had not prevented me, even though, as a covered dish, she had not been blessed by You as yet? What was it that had served *her* as a bridge? Or was that, too, only an illusion?"

35. (Say I): "My dear son Martin, be satisfied to know what I reveal to you, for it was forwardness that caused Adam's fall, and before him the first created and highest angelic spirits! Therefore, if you want to attain perfect bliss, you'll have to follow My guidance completely, without overstepping the mark My love and wisdom have set for you.

36. When the right time comes, you will understand all this. This promise should suffice you, or you might find yourself on another sea which would cause you more trouble than the previous one! For, before you have a heavenly wedding garment, you are not yet a real citizen of heaven, only a poor sinner taken in out of mercy who can become a true citizen of heaven by following certain paths. Therefore, stop asking questions and follow Me to the fourth door. So be it!"

37. Bishop Martin slaps his own face and follows Me, regretting his forward question.

38. (But I comfort him, saying): "Do not be afraid! For every word that I speak to you shall mean eternal life for you, not your judgment! And now we are at door number four, which is opening by itself."

41

THE SPLENDORS OF MARS. — BISHOP MARTIN'S MENTAL FATIGUE AND HIS FOOLISH WISH. — THE LORD'S REPRIMAND.

1. (I continue, saying): "We are already at the open door. What do you see, and how do you like it?"

2. (Bishop Martin, a little subdued): "Lord, I lack the courage and the words to describe this majestic splendor appropriately, but my feeling tells me that all this is getting too much for me. The continuous intensification of celestial beauty, especially that one expressing itself in sublime female shape, has the effect of dulling my senses.

3. How many millions of these beings would such a side cabinet hold, which actually appears to be a world in itself? There are vast crowds, reaching as far as the eye can see and, besides, all the many thousands of neatest little huts, temples, gardens and groves, also hills covered with what looks like beautiful green velvet carpets.

4. It is too much for me, Lord; I cannot comprehend it and **probably never will! Therefore, o Lord, do refrain from showing me any more and greater splendors, for what I have already seen so far** seems to be enough to last me through all eternity.

5. What would I want all this for? If I have You, and perhaps another friend who would live under the same roof with me and stay with me when sometimes You were absent — that would suffice me for the whole of eternity. May those enjoy such sublimities whose consciences tell them that they are pure and worthy of them. I, however, am only too conscious of my unworthiness and would be satisfied with a **thatched cottage and the permission to visit You, o** Lord, in Your house, and obtain from You, my dearest Father, now and then, a little piece of bread and a sip of wine.

6. Therefore, let somebody else have this house of splendor — someone who is worthier than I am and who is capable of owning it! **Do whatever is Your will, Lord, but if I am allowed my free will, I** would rather not continue with the other doors.

7. If I had to make use of the services of all these beings, where would it get me to in my stupidity? So I beg You, Lord, don't lead me any farther in this place. A pigsty like those on earth would make me happier than this house!"

8. (Say I): "Listen, My dear Martin, if you know better what one has to do to become a true citizen of heaven, you may please yourself. But I can assure you that there will be no progress for you in eternity. However, if you rely on Me rather than on your own blindness, then do what I want and not what you would like to do.

9. Do you think I created My children for squatting around in huts, eating bread and drinking wine? There you are absolutely wrong! Have you not read what is written? — 'Be ye therefore perfect, even as your Father which is in heaven is perfect.' Do you believe that the required perfection of My children can be attained in a pigsty?

10. Have you, on earth, never experienced how children of mortal parents would rather be idle and play around than start acquiring knowledge needed for their future trade? Or have you not met lots of people on earth who set idleness above all else?

11. Behold, you are one of those! On the one hand you shy away from all that awaits you here, and on the other hand it is a kind of polite defiance to Me for rebuking you for your silly question.

12. All this is not worthy of one on whom I bestowed already so much compassion, love and mercy, and am still doing it! For you are now experiencing what is not experienced by millions. They are happy in the anticipation of seeing Me at some time, for they are being led only by minor guardian spirits. You, however, are led by Me personally, the eternal God and Father of Infinity, the blessed goal of all angels and spirits! And yet you would prefer a pigsty to what I want to give you, to prepare you for the greatest bliss. Tell Me, how do you now feel about your foolish wish?"

13. (Says Bishop Martin, quite startled): "O Lord, You forever holiest and best Father, have patience with me! I am a stupid beast, unworthy of the tiniest ray of Your mercy! Do lead me wherever You wish, my good Father, and I shall now always follow You without any foolish doubts!"

14. (Say I): "All right, follow Me then from this door of Mars to the door of Jupiter, door number five. So be it!"

SURPRISES BEHIND THE FIFTH DOOR. — THE WONDER WORLD OF JUPITER.

1. We have already reached door number five, which is opening before us, and at the first glance, Bishop Martin throws up his hands in astonishment, and shouts: "For the sake of Your divine name, Lord Jesus, Father — what immensity! The most heavenly world without end! And above it another four globes, all bathed in a light which the most imaginative mortal could not possibly picture. The splendor and majesty of these shining palaces and temples, also the smaller temples, which probably serve the inhabitants as free dwellings.

2. Ah, I can see also lakes, whose water is shining like the most beautifully cut diamonds in the sunlight. But there everything seems to emit light, for I cannot see any particular source of it. O Lord, Father, how unspeakably beautiful and sublime this is! I could almost describe this beauty as holy, if I did not know that You alone are holy.

3. The more I look at it all, the more I see. I can discern already human beings, but they are still too distant for me to see what they are really like. Most likely their beauty will be in accordance with the boundless beauty of their world. It might be better if they did not come too close, for maybe I would not be able to bear the sight of their beauty. I find the sight of this vast, splendid world already overwhelming!

4. But Lord, Father, would it be at all possible for any spirit, besides Yourself, to ever fully grasp the boundless profusion, depth, and magnitude of all this sublimity? This must surely be impossible to even the greatest angel!"

5. (Say I): "Oh no, My dear son Martin, all that you are seeing here, and are still going to see, is but a tiny part of what the wise angels of My Eternal Kingdom fully understand in every detail.

6. For all that you are seeing here, and that which impresses you so deeply, is actually within you; and that you see it as an external manifestation is due only to your spiritual vision. It can be compared to the seeing of regions in your dreams, which appeared to be outside you but actually were in you, and you looked at them

with the eyes of your soul. But the difference here is that it is reality, whilst in dreams such pictures are usually only illusions of the soul. However, do not ask any more questions about all this, for you will understand it in due course.

7. The human beings of this world will not come any closer, for in your present state their beauty would, indeed, be unbearable for you. However, when you have become stronger, you will be able to see everything and enjoy it in blessed purity, which at this stage is impossible for you as you still lack the necessary strength.

8. Let us now proceed to the next door, where even more sublime sights are awaiting you. At this sixth door, however, you have to keep as silent as possible and just listen attentively to what I shall tell you. You must not ask Me why you have to be so quiet, nor shall you ask any questions if you cannot grasp a lot of what I shall tell you, for in due course it will all become clear to you. Let us now proceed to door number six. So be it!"

SATURN, AS THE MOST SPLENDID OF ALL PLANETS. — THE EARTH AS A SCHOOL FOR CHILDREN OF GOD AND THE SCENE OF THE LORD'S INCARNATION.

1. (The Lord): "Here we are, already at the open door, and the magnificent celestial world which you can see clearly: the great rampart which, in the far distance, appears light blue, and above which, in perfect grouping, seven further globes, as if freely suspended, are visible, all this represents in correspondence the planet Saturn, the most beautiful and best of worlds, circling around the sun. Your earth circles it too, but it is the ugliest and last planet in the whole of creation, destined to be a school of meekness and cross for the greatest spirits.

2. The reason for this is as follows: When a great and mighty lord of the world drives or rides through the streets of his residence, the people, being used to him, scarcely turn round to greet and honor him. He, on the other hand, knowing his people like neighbors and aware that they know him, does not expect this at all. However,

if he travels to some distant small place, everybody just about prostrates himself before him, and there he shows who he really is. In his residence, such a display would have no effect, because everybody knows him as a familiar sight.

3. It can also be compared to somebody igniting a small quantity of gunpowder in a very large hall, where the explosion would be quite ineffectual. But if the same amount of gunpowder were ignited in a very confined space, the result would be a loud explosion with a destructive effect.

4. Since the great appears really great when compared to the small, the strong much stronger compared to the weak, and the mighty especially mighty compared to the feeble, — the earth has to be so miserable and modest in everything so that it may serve the greatest and most brilliant spirits, either to learn humility and gain through it a quickening; or judgment and eternal death. For, as already explained to you, the small and insignificant serves towards increasing the characteristics of the great and imposing. And that is already its judgment, for where everything is small and insignificant, the great and important should conform to it and humble itself.

5. If a tall man wants to enter a room through a very low door, he must bend down low or he could not enter it at all. Thus, the earth is a narrow and thorny path and a low and narrow gate to life for all those spirits who were once very great, and who wanted to be even greater.

6. But these spirits rebelled against this path, which they found too humiliating for their pride, and said that this path was too small for them: an elephant could not walk on a hair like a gnat, and a whale could not swim in a drop of water. Consequently, such a path was not wise, and He Who prepared it was without insight or sense.

7. Then I, as the very highest and greatest Spirit in all eternity, took the cross and walked the path as the first. And I demonstrated how this path, which could be walked by the great and almighty Spirit of God, could easily be followed by all the other spirits in order to attain the true, free eternal life.

8. Many have now already followed this path and have achieved the desired goal, namely, to become children of God and inherit eternal life, with the greatest might, power and perfection, enjoying all the creative properties that I possess. This cannot be attained by the spirits from all the other innumerable stars and worlds, just as not all parts of the body can see, hear or feel with the inner mental

perception, which is the actual awareness of one's own, as well as of the other being and the ability to see and know God.

9. Only certain parts of the body have these properties, whilst countless other parts lack them completely; but they are still parts of the same body.

10. The same applies to the rational beings inhabiting all the other stars: they are like individual parts of a body or, in a more perfect sense, of the whole man who is in My own image and that of all the heavens. Therefore, they do not need for their happiness all the divine properties that My children possess. And when My children are blessed, these star-dwellers are the same in and with them, as you, My children, are in and with Me to all eternity.

11. If you enjoy happiness, all these countless spirits enjoy the same in and through you, just as your well-being makes your whole body feel comfortable. In view of this, sacred love makes it My children's highest duty to become as perfect as I Myself am. For, on this perfection depends the happiness of countless spirits, increasing and perfecting yours in turn infinitely.

12. Now you know why I showed you first these planets which are closest to your earth. Ponder on this and follow Me now to door number seven, where you will be instructed in new wisdom. But there, too, you must not ask Me anything. For I alone know the path I have to lead you that you might attain the highest possible beatitude! Let us now proceed. So be it!"

44

THE SEVENTH CABINET. — ABOUT THE NATURE AND PURPOSE OF URANUS AND ITS INHABITANTS. — CREATION WITHIN MAN AND WITHOUT IN ITS CORRELATIONS.

1. (The Lord): "We have already reached the seventh open door. Here, too, you find a new celestial world, though not as vast and as beautiful as the previous one. But instead, here you find buildings of a rare and spectacular style and a vast number of works produced by the inhabitants of this planet, which you call Uranus. You can also see a great number of the most original gardens with an abundance of extraordinary ornaments.

2. A vast crowd of spirits, in perfect human shape and well-clothed, can be seen on the wide smooth paths of those gardens. All eyes are turned towards us, for they suspect that I am near, and so is their future owner and master. Through him, they hope to attain at last complete beatitude, and thus also their full strength and power, as promised.

3. In the background, apparently at a considerable distance, you see five smaller globes. These are satellites of this planet, and quite different, but still in complete harmony with it.

4. The spirits of this planet further the growth of man: in the world physically and here spiritually. However, only as far as concerns the development of the external form in man's physical, as well as in his psychic growth, may this planet influence him.

5. As, naturally, the capacity to grow must exist in man, or he could not grow at all, thus also these spirits, in a corresponding sense, must be present in man in his potential development center. Therefore, all that you are seeing here is within and not outside of you. Of course, this planet, with all it holds, also exists in reality somewhere outside of you; but this you will not be able to see for quite a while yet.

6. When you have attained full maturity in eternal life, then you will also be able to see the great creation outside of you, just as I Myself see it. This is essential, for if I entrust My perfected children with the keeping and guardianship of a whole world, they must be able to see that world in all its detail; for a blind man cannot be a shepherd. However, you will not be ready for that for a long time yet and, therefore, you must be satisfied with what you see now, which is a corresponding living image of reality within you, giving the impression as if it were outside of you.

7. In this inner contemplation, you have to grow and your spirit has to mature and increase its capacity for love of Me and, consequently, also of all your brothers and sisters. Only then will your love become the blessing which I promised you — when you were almost overwhelmed by love for the beautiful Mercurian.

8. This blessing will then last forever and be a true bridge into the endlessly great reality, and on its pillars you will comprehend in all fullness where you are, who you are, and whence you came.

9. Now you know all that is necessary for you to know about what is behind this door. This knowledge you have gained from Me and out of My Self. Do meditate on all this! Now, follow Me

to the eighth door. There we shall get acquainted with yet another, for you, completely new world and its interesting inhabitants. So be it!"

45

THE WORLD OF MIRON, THE SECRET OF THE EIGHTH CABINET. – THE SPIRITUAL AS FIRST CAUSE AND CARRIER OF ALL CREATION.

1. (The Lord): "Behold, we are there! The door is open and you can see through it a new, vast celestial world, bathed in a pale green light. Here, too, you can see tall buildings and mountains of various heights emitting a bluish smoke. These smoking mountains are correspondences of the many fire-emitting mountains of which this planet, the most distant from the sun, with the name of Miron [Neptune], the marvelous, has the greatest number.

2. Behind this planet you can see ten smaller globes — its satellites, which are of quite a different nature from their main planet. On Miron, you see something new every moment: trees floating in the air, and many other things you have never seen before. Even the smoke from the mountains assumes a variety of unusual shapes. The perfectly shaped human beings are mostly well-clothed so that you do not get to see much more than their faces.

3. These men love music and poetry, and as spirits, correspondingly, they influence you, My children, by rendering your hearts, minds, and souls, receptive for these arts. They dwell in the respective human organs, adapting them for the right understanding and reception of music and poetry, toning man to harmony and lifting his imagination and capacity for enthusiasm. All the wonderful and so-called romantic emotions are evoked by this planet in a corresponding sense.

4. Now you know the nature of this planet and what it is good for. Of course, you must not think of the real planet, although its nature is the same, but only of its corresponding image embodied in your spirit. This existed prior to all external, material creation, which was formed in accordance with what had already been present in every perfected spirit for ages. For the spirit existed long before all the world was created, which issued from the spirit, and not vice versa. Therefore, the planet within you is considerably older than

the material one. If it had been absent from the spirit of even one single man, it could never have been formed materially.

5. From this you can conclude that if you learn to know yourself completely, you will also come to know everything outside of you, for nothing can exist outside of you which has not already been present within you. And in the whole of infinity there cannot be anything that has not been within Me in perfect clarity from eternity.

6. Just as I am the primeval source and supporter of all beings, thus now My children in Me are the fundamental substance of everything that is forever filling infinity. The infinite in Me is also present in you through Me, for My children are the crowning of My eternal ideas and great plans.

7. Now you know all you need to know about this door. Therefore, follow Me to the ninth door, where you will see further wonders of My love and wisdom. So be it!"

46

THE NINTH CABINET WITH ITS SAD SECRET. THE SHATTERED WORLD OF THE ASTEROIDS AND ITS HISTORY.

1. (The Lord): "We have reached the ninth door. What do you see here? Now, My dear son Martin, you are again allowed to speak, but only what is necessary. So answer My question."

2. (Bishop Martin): "Lord, I do not see very much, as yet. There are about nine small, bare, shapeless globes floating in this pure celestial air. Except for some scrub, I cannot discern much upon them, although I have the impression as if a vast celestial world were becoming visible in the very far distance. But, due to this distance, it is very vague, and I cannot see what is on it.

3. Four of the globules circling closer to us seem to be inhabited because I notice on them a peculiar type of small buildings, although I cannot see any human beings. These, I assume, would not be very tall, probably a kind of infusorial man. One of these globules is just floating past the door. The only things I can see on it are some stunted shrubs and tiny dwellings, which look rather like ant hills.

But there is no movement, except that of the globule itself. Do tell me, o Lord, whether that, too, is a planet, or what?"

4. (Say I): "Yes, My dear son Martin, that, too, is a planet; however, as you can see, not a whole one, but a badly mangled one. For, in addition to the nine pieces circling irregularly in front of us, there is still a lot of wreckage: some of it scattered on other planets, some floating around in disorderly courses in the endless spaces of creation. Here and there, if they come too close, they are attracted and sort of swallowed by some solid planet or sun.

5. You have now some questions in your mind: 'How and why was this planet shattered? What was it like before? What were its inhabitants like?'

6. "The answer to the 'how' is My omnipotence: It was My will!

7. And why? Behold, this planet was originally destined to what has now become the destination of the earth. For the first fallen spirit had chosen it, with the promise to humble himself and return to Me. Therefore, this planet was meant to become the star of salvation. Here, he promised to be active by himself without ever interfering with the sphere of any of the star's inhabitants, nor those of any other planet.

8. However, he did not keep his promise, but used his freedom to such an evil end that no life could make progress on the planet. As a result, he was banned into the fiery center of the planet, and the destination of that planet was transferred to your earth forthwith.

9. When the earth was ready for human beings and I sowed the seed for the first man, the evil one tore at his prison walls. Out of compassion. I let him do what he wanted, and he tore his earth to pieces and plunged into the chasm of your earth, where, ever since, he has been doing all that is familiar to you.

10. The reason for the destruction of this planet was, as in all things, My compassion. For, while the planet was still whole and inhabited by many powerful nations, the dragon poisoned their hearts with lust for power. As a result, they swore each other continual war and complete annihilation to the last man.

11. There was no other way then but a judgment, and that was the bursting of the planet, whereby many millions of its very tall inhabitants perished. Some were buried under debris, but most of them were flung out into space. Some even fell onto earth, and from that time also dates the pagan myth of the war of the giants.

112

12. But the first human beings died out completely on the remaining pieces of this originally largest planet, because they were unable to find the necessary food. They were eventually replaced by a very small race of men, extremely modest, who represent the hair on the head and the eyebrows of the cosmic man. In the background, you can still see the whole planet as it used to be, preserved for the great day that is going to dawn in the whole of infinity.

13. Now you know also about this door what is necessary for you to know at this stage. In due course, everything else will sprout from the seed I have now placed in your heart. Follow Me now to the tenth door, where new wonders are awaiting you. So be it!"

47

THE SECRET OF THE TENTH CABINET: THE SUN WITH ITS SPLENDOR. — ABOUT THE NATURE OF LIGHT. — THE WONDERS OF THE SOLAR WORLD. — BEAUTY AS THE EXPRESSION OF PERFECTION.

1. (The Lord): "We are standing before the tenth door. Speak now about everything you see here."

2. (Bishop Martin): "Lord, what can I say? My eyes are dazzled by an immense brightness and my ears perceive the most wonderful harmony. That is all I can say so far. I see only the strong light and hear the heavenly harmony, which seems to come from the light.

3. The light appears to fill a boundless space, for wherever I turn my eyes, I see nothing but light. However, it is peculiar that this enormous mass of light doesn't give out more warmth through the open door.

4. What could it be, Lord? Is it, maybe, the light for this house? Or perhaps it is even the sun, a miniature replica of the real sun which gives light to the earth."

5. (Say I): "Yes, that is right! It is the correspondence within you of the real sun. As your eyes adapt themselves to the light, you will discern also other things in this light. Just keep looking for a while, and you will soon start praising the abundance of this light."

6. Bishop Martin tries to penetrate the light with his eyes, in

order to see something else besides the light, but after a while, when he can still see nothing, he says: "Lord Jesus, it seems hopeless! I have strained my eyes to their limit, but still see only that light! Although it is a beautiful sight, it does become monotonous. Not that it really matters, for if I see You, I do not need to see any wonders floating around in this sea of light. But it is peculiar to see only this light — and what a light!

7. My beloved Jesus, what is actually light? In the world, the scientists are still arguing about the nature of light — one has this theory, another one that. But in the end, it becomes clear that none of them knows anything about it. I have read and heard quite a lot about this, but have come to the conclusion that the scientists on earth are on no subject quite as ignorant as they are on the nature of light. Therefore, if it is Your will, could You give me some hints on the subject, please?"

8. (Say I): "Behold, I am the Light everywhere! Because untiring activity is My primary essence, light permeates and envelopes Me. Where the activity is great, there is also much light, for light is actually nothing else but pure manifestation of activity on the part of angels and the better human spirits. The higher their level of activity, the brighter is their light.

9. That is also the reason why the suns shine brighter than the planets, for on them the activity is a millionfold greater than on the latter. Thus, also, the light of an archangel is brighter than that one of some minor, though wise, angel-spirit; for an archangel has to care for whole solar systems, whilst the small wise spirit is only in charge of a small area on earth, or even only on the moon.

10. For the same reason, a diamond shines much brighter than an ordinary sandstone, for in the diamond there is an incomparably greater activity which also renders it so hard. It is obvious that there is more involved in keeping up the cohesion in a diamond than in a sandstone.

11. Anyhow, wherever you notice something to be very bright and shining, you may assume a greater activity in it; for activity is the light and brilliance of all beings and things. The vision of the eye consists in perceiving this activity. If the vision is still imperfect, it will notice only light and brilliance. However, a perfected vision will see the actual activity in its essence. As your vision becomes perfect, you, too, will soon notice activity in this light.

12. Therefore, watch closely, for you will be seeing amazing

things since we now have before us a sun and not a planet! Look at it and then speak!"

13. After gazing into the light for quite a while, our Martin is showing signs of astonishment.

14. When I ask him what it is that he finds so astonishing, he says:

15. (Bishop Martin): "O Lord, o Lord, for the sake of Your most holy name, could this be possible? How is it possible that You can supervise, arrange and guide all these wonders upon wonders? This is above all human, and even angelic, understanding! Oh my God, my God, how inconceivably great You are, and there is no end to your glory and majesty!"

16. (Say I): "But what is it that you are seeing that has caused in you such an ecstasy of devotion? Speak up and tell Me what you see."

17. (Bishop Martin): "O Lord, what shall I say when all this splendor and heavenly beauty and majesty have taken my breath away?

18. It is simply indescribable! The boundless beauty of the human beings is just about the only thing that I know for what it is; everything else is inexpressible! I have never seen anything as sublime; and the most vivid imagination of the wisest men ever, could not have envisaged this! All that I have seen so far has been of great beauty, but compared with what I am seeing now, it becomes quite insignificant!

19. First of all, the great variety here makes it impossible to perceive it all and, besides, new wonders keep developing all the time — every one of them more glorious than the previous one!

20. Only the humans remain unchanged, but their beauty is so breathtaking that I feel like hiding myself in the dust. Everything else keeps changing like in a kaleidoscope.

21. Even the scenery changes. Where the land was first flat, suddenly a high mountain grows out of it, carrying with it big streams which turn the meadows into seas. Then the mountains burst and a number of worlds on fire are hurled from the craters and flee or tumble into endless space, as if driven by a great force. Many again fall back from space and dissolve like snowflakes on a warm ground.

22. Ah, what formidable phenomena! But the beautiful human beings do not seem to take any notice of what is happening around them! They walk in their gardens in an apparently blissful state, admiring the most beautiful flowers which, too, seem to be changing under the gaze of their admirers to more and more glorious shapes.

O Lord, let me watch this for half an eternity! I am sure, even an archangel could not ever take his eyes off this sublime sight!

23. Ah, the unsurpassed beauty of these humans! It is overwhelming! The softness of their perfectly shaped figures, the whiteness, and then the absolutely superb sweetness of their faces! It is too heavenly — I can't bear it!

24. And, oh, some are coming quite close so that I can see their indescribably beautiful features and admire the perfect harmony of their bodies. Now they are close enough for me to talk to them, but I just could not bear it if these heavenly beautiful beings were to speak to me.

25. O Lord, make them go back, for to look at them makes me dizzy. I feel as if I did not exist at all, as if I were in an ecstasy! It is indescribable!

26. O God, You great almighty Creator, how was it possible for You to put such an endless variety and beauty into the human form, which is so simple and basically always much the same? I could picture in my imagination one perfect form, but then all the others would not come up to it. But here, they are innumerable — each one, in its own way, of a supreme beauty. Oh, Lord, this is inconceivable, totally inconceivable!

27. In the world, I had the extremely silly notion that in the celestial realm of spirits all the blessed spirits would resemble each other, like the sparrows on earth. But I can see now that real multiplicity is to be found here, whereas in the world it was too much hidden by the mortal flesh.

28. Ah, ah, more and more splendor! Another couple is approaching! Oh Lord, this paralyzes my brain!

29. Hold me, Lord, that I do not collapse like an empty stocking! Ah, what a female! Oh, my Jesus, what splendor, what unspeakable beauty!

30. Those tender feet, that well-developed figure, the radiance around her, and this unspeakably gentle and friendly expression in a pair of eyes which to describe appropriately, even the archangel Michael would find difficult!

31. I have already gone quite silly — yes, I am a complete fool! I wanted to ask something, but . . . ! Oh, blow the question! I am an ass — yes, a stupid animal! Here I am, staring like an ox at a new gate, almost forgetting that You, Lord, are here with me, compared with

Whom, all these beauties are nothing! You could evoke much greater splendors in a moment, if you wished!

32. Lord, I have now sufficiently enjoyed the sight of these supreme celestial beauties! They are too pure, and too fair for me. Let me see something very ordinary so that I may find myself again and view myself without being shocked at my uglinesss, in comparison with these fair celestial beings.

33. Really, if I look at myself, I appear like an ape compared with these angels! I could spit at my image! Why am I so terribly ugly, although I am a spirit and should look a bit better than a mortal on earth? Why are these humans so beautiful and we, as Your children, look like apes compared with them — especially I?"

34. (Say I): "Because you are My heart, but they are My skin! However, My children, too, are infinitely beautiful when they are perfected. It is only while they are still as imperfect as you, that they do not look too attractive. Therefore, work at perfecting yourself, and you will soon acquire a more celestial appearance.

35. It is My wish that you see these great, pure beauties, so that in their light you may come to know yourself all the sooner and all the easier. Therefore, keep looking into the light a while longer and realize the ugliness of your own soul. This will help to make it pliable and more mature so that your spirit can arise in it and change you into a new being.

36. For, behold, you will not be born again of the spirit for a long time yet. That is why I transferred you to this garden, like into a vast hothouse, to speed up your rebirth. But you must let Me care for you like a precious plant, for conceive this: Thistles and thorns are not grown in the celestial gardens and hothouses! Now, go on looking and tell Me what you see, but do not ask too many questions. So be it!"

BISHOP MARTIN'S FURTHER MARVELOUS DISCOVERIES ON HIS SUN. — THE REASON FOR THE DIFFERENCE IN STATURE OF THE SOLAR PEOPLES. — LOVE AND WISDOM AS THE TRUE MEASURE OF THE SPIRIT. — BISHOP MARTIN'S COMPLAINT ABOUT THE EARTH AND ITS INHABITANTS.

1. Bishop Martin once more turns to the sun and looks at the spectacles and marvels on its shining surface. After a prolonged scrutiny, he speaks again: "Just look, still the same sun, but quite different people. They are also very beautiful, but their beauty is bearable, similar to those seen on the other planets, even to the inhabitants of our earth.

2. I see now several belts around the sun, parallel to each other, and within each of these belts I see humans, some tall, some smaller, some tiny, and — what's that? — there, in the far distance? I can see a giant race of men! They are so huge that the others could live as parasites in their hair like the ones familiar to us!

3. O Lord, forgive me my somewhat dirty remark! I realize it is improper here in the presence of the Sublime, but it slipped out while I was contemplating these giants. Although I have already noticed some very tall humans on the other planets, like Jupiter, Saturn, Uranus, and Miron, who were much taller than the inhabitants of my earth, compared with these giants, they, too, seem only like small parasites.

4. On earth, a giant like this would tower above the highest mountains! Do tell me, my beloved Lord Jesus, my God and Master, why these men are so terribly tall. I was not supposed to ask You a lot of questions, but since I have not asked any yet, will You forgive me this one?"

5. (Say I): "So listen carefully. Think of the different caliber guns, from the lightest to the heaviest, of the armies on earth. What would happen if you put the charge of a very heavy caliber gun into a light caliber? It would tear it to pieces, wouldn't it?

6. What would happen to a planet if it were filled with the sun's power? Behold, if the earth, only for one minute, were submerged in the powerful light of the sun, it would dissolve like a drop of water

falling onto a red-hot iron. In order to be capable of holding the vast power placed in it, with its full activity, the sun has to be of a very large size and matching strength.

7. If you placed a feather on an egg, this would easily hold it, whilst a heavy weight would squash it completely.

8. Could a giant wear the coat of a child? Of course not! But if he did try to wear it, it would, naturally, be torn to shreds.

9. Thus, in the whole of creation, everything has its own measure; the small, in its way, in all its proportions, and so the large.

10. As you now see that there are worlds of different sizes meant to hold corresponding power, thus the spirits on these worlds are of different calibers and, accordingly, their bodies are of different sizes.

11. Not that the true, real caliber of a spirit is measured by his size, but only by his love and wisdom; however, these are still primordial spirits, which, in their free state, fill an entire solar system with their activity. Since they, too, want to participate in the beatitude of My Kingdom, they have to walk the path of the flesh. When they have shed their physical bodies, they will, owing to their gentleness and meekness, be of the same size as we are but, if necessary, also of their former size.

12. Now you know sufficient for this sphere and your present state. So go on looking and speak about your observations, so that we may proceed to the eleventh door. So be it!

13. Bishop Martin once more contemplates the light-filled areas of the sun and soon discerns very large temples and dwellings, also roads and bridges of boldest design . There are majestically high mountains, whose main ranges surround the sun, marking the different belts, each of them with different inhabitants and different ways of life and customs. He also notices that two belts on both sides of the central or main belt seem to be very much alike.

14. He still prefers the humans of the central belt to all the others, to whose beauty he has now got more accustomed, although they must not come too close, especially the women, who seem too enticing. Even the men excite him, for they, too, are so beautiful and have figures of such well-rounded softness which, on earth, could not even be found in the most attractive female figure.

15. After looking around for a while, he notices a building in the middle of the central belt which, in its splendor and ornamentation, by far excels everything our Martin has seen so far. And walking

around this building, he sees people of such beauty that he collapses as if in a swoon, unable to utter a word for quite a while.

16. After some time, Bishop Martin rather moans than speaks, somewhat incoherently: "My God and Lord, who on earth could ever imagine anything like this? The sun is only known as a shining round celestial body, but who could expect this on its surface?

17. What are you, earth, compared with this blessed splendor? What are your wild beasts of men compared with these indescribably beautiful beings, full of celestial glory, beauty, and sweetness?

18. On earth, the more magnificent the palaces in which people live, the softer their skin and the more luxurious their clothes, the more heartless and diabolical they are! Here it is exactly the contrary. Ah, ah, this is unbelievable!

19. Here, the wisest live in unprepossessing huts in the mountains, as I can see. On earth, the dwellings of the top shepherd of Christianity, who imagines himself very wise, are the largest and richest and most luxurious of all, and his clothes are of pure silk adorned with gold and precious gems. Here it is the other way round! Oh, oh, and men on earth are supposed to be children of God! Compared with these pure children of the sun, they are rather children of Satan!

20. The Gospel has never been preached to these, but their nature is pure like the Gospel itself. It probably could not be any different, or this celestial order would be unthinkable. Yes, yes, here I see a living demonstration of the true, most perfect, unadulterated and correctly interpreted Word of God!

21. Consider the lilies of the field: they toil not and reap not, and even Solomon in his glory was not arrayed like the least one of these! There I see many of these lilies; they have no plow, no knife, no scissors, no weaver's loom, and no embroidery frame. But where on the entire earth could a prince be found, or a princess, fit to even approach any of these celestial lilies?

22. O mankind, obscuring and contaminating the earth, who are you and who am I compared with these solar races? O Lord, we are no better than devils and the world is hell itself in its worst form! That is probably also the reason why the stars are so far from the earth: to protect them from being contaminated.

23. O God, You are holy and most sublime! But in Your wrath You must have spat out on some occasion, and from that curse of Yours the earth and its creatures must have originated!

24. Forgive me, Lord, this remark, but I could not help it at the sight of this heaven. Earth and its inhabitants now make me shudder like a poisonous, stinking cadaver does!

25. Send me into endless space, Lord, but never again back to earth, for it is to me like a hell of hells, and its people irredeemable devils with their main object to persecute the few angels among them.

26. O Lord, o Lord, do send a proper judgment over this sole blemish in the whole of Your creation. The more I look at these splendors here, the more I feel that the earth and its mankind are not really Your work, but the work of Satan, the chief of all demons. There is nothing but vice, death, and destruction, of which You, o Lord, could never be the creator!

27. Ah, ah, how magnificent and wonderful it is here, where the eternal order of Your Word is reigning! And how miserable and agonizing it is on earth, a curse emanated from You because it keeps opposing Your order! O Lord, send Your judgment, destroy it, annihilate it forever, for it does not deserve Your mercy!"

28. (Say I): "Calm yourself! Although you have spoken the truth, you do not have the right understanding as yet. Let us now proceed to the eleventh door, where you will see many things clearer and form a different opinion. Therefore, follow Me. So be it!"

A VIEW OF THE MOON THROUGH THE ELEVENTH DOOR. —
BISHOP MARTIN AND THE LUNAR PHILOSOPHER.

1. (The Lord): "Behold, we are at the eleventh door. Look in and then tell Me what you see."

2. Bishop Martin looks inside for a while, and then says, somewhat sulkingly: "What is this crazy world of nonsense? Humans, slightly bigger than rabbits on earth, and the scenery resembling some nice hotbeds. The trees wouldn't be any taller than blackberry or juniper bushes on earth! At least, the mountains, which are extremely high and steep, are notable. I do not notice any seas, but there are lakes, the largest of which might hold about ten thousand

buckets of water. Oh dear, what a difference between door number ten and door number eleven!

3.   But what is that madcap over there with but one foot? That could only be an animal, not a human being. And now I can see a whole herd of a peculiar type of marmot. Anyway, it is strange that so far I haven't seen any animals. And in this crazy world, there appear to be more animals than human beings. Should this actually be an animal world? Yes, it might be, for there I now see a large flock of a kind of sheep. A pity I do not see any oxen or asses to enjoy the company of my own kind! There are also birds; as long as there aren't any too merry birds among them!

4.   There, there, ha, ha, isn't that funny? These humans are grown together, the female sitting like a hump on the shoulders of the male. And there a male is inflating himself like a tree-frog, making a noise with his taut belly like a Turkish regimental drummer on earth. This is extremely funny and ridiculous!

5.   Really, Lord, when creating this little world, You probably did not use too much of Your omnipotence and wisdom, for compared with all that I have previously seen, it is in no way sublime. Now I have to apologize to the earth for speaking so badly of it at door number ten. For, compared with this world, it is a real paradise, except for its mankind. Tell me, o Lord, if You will, what is this world called? It couldn't possibly be within the solar system of our earth."

6. (Say I): "Oh yes, it is, for this is the moon of your earth. And the human beings came originally from the earth, as did the moon itself. It used to be the most inferior part of the earth, but is now much better than the entire earth. Therefore, it has now become a schoolhouse for extremely worldly souls. For a meager, small world with a fertile spirit is preferable to a fertile, big world with a very meager spirit.

7.   Although outwardly these men look miserable enough, you will take quite a while to grow spiritually as fertile as they have already been for a long time.

8.   But in order to convince you of the wisdom of these men, a couple shall approach you and discuss various matters with you. There is already one of these pick-a-back couples; ask them some questions, and rest assured that they will have an answer to everything. So be it!"

9. (Says Bishop Martin): "Oh yes, there is already a couple

approaching us together with their whole world, which appears to be used by them like a ship. Looked at closely, they look rather quaint, especially the little female. However, we seem to be invisible to them, as they are looking around expectantly as if they perceived something but could not see it."

10. (Say I): "You must draw nearer to them and thus establish contact with their little sphere and then they will become aware of you. The inhabitants of all the moons of the planets have the characteristic that they can see spirits from other planets only when they are inside their little spheres. This is due to the fact that the moons are the lowest and most materialistic level of the planets, just as the dirt of animals is their lowest and most materialistic level, but often more useful than beast or man themselves. Now do as I told you, and the couple will be able to see you!"

11. Bishop Martin obeys, and the couple sees him, admiring his height. But Martin immediately starts the following conversation with them: "Are you the real inhabitants of this little world, or are there still others, taller than you and maybe also wiser?"

12. (Say the two): "There is only a certain number of humans like us. But there are many other creatures here, and on the opposite side of this world there are penitents who frequently come to this side, in order to learn the inner wisdom from us. These penitents usually come from another world, probably from the one you come from. They are tall of stature, but their spirituality is very small. You, too, are of a tall build, but the human substance in you is still scarcely visible.

13. And what are you doing, you big men, who have been given so much life? Why do you take so little care of it? When it is time to sow and reap for his temporal life, man toils diligently overcoming all obstacles. He endures heat and cold, rain and storms. He does not spare his physical body and often risks his life to gain a pitiful livelihood. But he does little or nothing to preserve and perfect the true inner life for his real, eternal, divine, great self.

14. What would you think of a gardener who planted fruit trees and as soon as they started to blossom and sprout, he took these first sprouts for the actual fruit, tore all the blossoms and new shoots off the trees and decorated his house with them? Such a gardener would obviously be a great fool, for while his neighbor gathered fruit from his trees, he might have to starve since there would not be any fruit on his own trees.

15. But is not any man an even greater fool if he enjoys already as fruit his temporal life, which is nothing else but blossoms and leaves for the inner, true life? Through this unnatural and immature enjoyment, he only ruins the actual fruit to come, the true, eternal life of the spirit. And only from the inner seed of the ripened fruit can the new, everlasting life develop, but not from the blossoms or the leaves!

16. Thus it is with every man: his body, his senses, and his reason are the blossoms and leaves. From these a mature soul evolves and the proper maturity of the soul will hold a ripe seed. And this seed is the immortal spirit which, when fully matured, will permeate everything with its own immortality, just as perishable flesh, anointed with decay-resisting etheric oils, will also become imperishable.

17. Behold, you big man, this is our wisdom! To achieve this, we follow the recognized order of the supreme Spirit of God, and this makes us fully what we are. You may now argue with me, if you can! I am prepared to put up with anything from you.

18. Our bishop is rather disconcerted and amazed at the enormous wisdom of the moon-couple. After quite a while, he says: "I never expected you moon people to possess such profound wisdom! Who taught you such wisdom, which could not possibly have originated in you?

19. Animals and plants know their natural order by instinct. It is put into them and they must follow it under compulsion. However, man, as a free being, must gain this knowledge through outside instruction, receiving it like an empty vessel. And the Word of God's wisdom must be placed in his heart like a grain of seed into the earth, to enable him to know himself and, consequently, God and His order. If man does not get any instruction at all, he stays more ignorant than an animal and more stupid than a stone.

20. Since you are obviously men with the same divine rights as we are, you must at some time have been taught by God Himself, either directly or indirectly. Otherwise your wisdom would be the greatest wonder I have so far encountered. God must have been the first teacher with all primeval men, or all men would be far below animal level in their intelligence. Where A was blind, who could have given light to B? And if thus, also B had been blind, who could have enlightened C? Since you are a very enlightened man, do tell me, please, how and when the obviously divine light came to you?"

50

DIFFERENT EFFECTS OF EXTERNAL AND INTERNAL TUITION. — THE POTTER'S WORKSHOP.

1. (The moon-dweller): "Friend, you talk and ask as you see it, and I shall answer in my own way. According to you, the Supreme Divine Spirit must have taught you from the outside with a cudgel in His hand. For an inner spiritual tuition you still seem to be much too dull, and so is, most likely, all mankind on your globe.

2. Do you seriously believe that the most supreme, almighty Divine Spirit created man, as His most perfect creature, like an empty bag which has to be filled before it can be expected to contain something? How wrong you are!

3. Man, on whatever globe he lives, has already within him a vast treasure of wisdom! This must only be awakened by some suitable means and then it will bring forth the most splendid fruit, quite by itself! The sublime Spirit of God provides this means.

4. If man does not ignore such means, but makes use of it, the seed in his inner self will sprout and grow and finally begin to ripen. Thus, no outside tuition is needed; it all comes from within!

5. For everything that approaches man from the outside is foreign and cannot give the recipient true, permanent, inherent wisdom; instead it will give a wisdom that is like a parasitic plant, not promoting life but stunting and spoiling it, for, coming from the outside, it will always be inclined to turn to the outside rather than to the inside — the seat of the true eternal life from God, the Supreme Spirit.

6. In this way we attain our wisdom — from the inner and never from an outer source! If your earth-men require external tuition, you must be extremely stubborn beings, most sensual and, therefore, sinful: consequently, opponents of the Divine Order and your own innermost life. In such a case, A — as well as B and C — will be blind and stay so unless awakened by external tuition.

7. Here you have the external answer to your question, for, judging by your question, you still have to go a long way before you'll be ready for the inner one. But you may go on asking questions."

8. During these words of the moon-dweller, Bishop Martin has

pulled quite a long face, realizing that he cannot compete with this man's wisdom. He is now thinking hard how to prove to the moon couple that he, as a mortal from earth, is the wiser man after all. He thinks of this and that, but nothing really clever comes to his mind.

9. Therefore, he turns to Me and says: "Lord, do not let me down. Help me to prevail over this all-too-clever moon-dweller, and let me show him that men on Your earth are worth something, too. He has dealt with me in a way that I have nothing to say and that notwithstanding the fact that I am to be his master and, in due course, the leader of this entire world!

10. What would happen if the inhabitants of all the worlds I have so far been introduced to came to me as their master and proved that I was the most stupid chap in all of creation? To prevent this from happening, they should be shown, through superior wisdom, that one is really their master. This might keep them from treating one like a schoolboy!"

11. (Say I): "Listen, My dear Martin, do you think that weighty arguments on your part would make such a true philosopher shut up? There you are quite wrong! For, as there is only one truth, thus there is also only one wisdom, which stands like an eternal fortress, forever invincible. And since this moon-dweller confronted you with the sole truth, what greater wisdom could you use to beat him with?

12. However, there is quite a different way to make these spirits obliging and submissive. And this way is called love, humility, and great meekness. These three foremost and extremely important characteristics help one to encounter these innumerable star-dwellers most forcibly.

13. Love teaches you to do good to all these beings and to make them as happy as possible. Humility teaches you to be small and consider yourself the least important, and never to raise yourself arrogantly above anybody else, however small and insignificant he may seem. And meekness teaches you to tolerate everyone with unchanged goodwill and endeavor, from the bottom of your heart, to help wherever help is needed. And this should always be done in the gentlest of ways so as not to infringe upon anybody's freedom. If, occasionally, stronger methods have to be applied, the motive behind them must never be the wish to punish, nor a condemning wrath, but always pure, supreme, unselfish love.

14. Those are the aids of celestial mastery! If you acquire them, you will get on much better with the moon-dwellers. Therefore, go

back to the couple and try to handle them in this celestial way and you might find it quite successful. Go now and do this! So be it!"

15. (Bishop Martin once more turns to the moon-couple and says): "My dear great little friend, I have weighed your wise words and see, thanks to the Lord, that you are completely right in everything you say. Nevertheless, I have a further question to put to you — not with a view to testing your wisdom any further, but simply in order to learn from you.

16. You previously declared that all external tuition is useless, and I cannot maintain that you are wrong. However, if all external tuition, including external perception, wherever it may come from and through whichever of his senses man has received it, is bad, useless and thus unacceptable, do explain to me, in your wisdom, why the Creator of all the worlds, human beings, and angels, has given us external senses at all? And why a voice with an outward-directed sound, and why a tongue capable of speaking? What is all this outer form for, all outer appearance of the countless things and beings? Or would it be possible to imagine a being without an exterior? Would not the removal of this put an end to a being? For I cannot imagine any being without an exterior! You will understand my well-founded doubts, so have patience and please clarify these doubts for me!"

17. (The moon-dweller): "Friend, on the one hand you are too superficial, and on the other hand too profound! Thus you will not reach your goal.

18. The Great Spirit has created a multitude of everything. And this multitude can have only external contact in all its parts and, therefore, is only external in its correlation. To enable man to grasp also the external, he has been equipped with external senses. However, he can comprehend it only with the inner senses of his spirit, and never with the outer.

19. Thus man possesses outer senses to grasp external things and inner senses for the comprehension of inner things. And wisdom is part of the inner senses of the spirit. That is why it also has to be developed *within* man and not through external tuition!

20. The inner tuition of the soul is performed solely by the spirit, to which the full truth has been revealed by the Great God about all things that have been created and still will be in eternity.

21. The external language is a means to ascertain the external and then unite it with the internal, and through this union full cog-

nition of the divine order is attained. This cognition is the actual wisdom we should seek, which implies the integral inner strength of the spirit and its effectual life.

22. You will now understand that God has never taught men through external revelations, but always from within, through the spirit. Even if it appeared to be personal, external tuition, this could not have any inner effect before God's animating power had penetrated the innermost spirit of man. Thus, what I have just explained to you will be of no effect until you perceive it within you.

23. If God Himself instructed you externally in all wisdom, as I have now done, this divine tuition would not help you as long as He, the Great God, did not let His most holy spirit teach your own within you.

24. Apprehend this, if you can, as the right answer to your question, and bear in mind that it will not lead to your salvation, but only to your judgment, as long as you do not receive it within yourself. For what is not yours, cannot make you free and will be your judgment until you have made it yours! If you have any further questions, ask, and I shall answer."

25. (Bishop Martin): "Friend, I am all the more convinced that, notwithstanding your smallness, you are a being of truly profound wisdom. I also realize that I am not a match for you by a long way! But even you, as a wise philosopher, will have to admit that if out of great love I instructed someone in matters pertaining to God's order, His might, love and wisdom, such tuition could not possibly be a judgment for a willing disciple, but just a true path to eternal life. I personally do not make too much of wisdom as such, but rather of love. Where there isn't any love, wisdom has no value for me!

26. What do you think of this my opinion? I am quite aware that a man must be born again of the spirit before he can enter into the Kingdom of God. But in order to attain this rebirth, the first direction must be given through external tuition; I cannot imagine inner tuition at the initial stage, especially with children. If I am wrong also in this, tell me how you moon-men instruct your children."

27. (The moon-dweller): "What do you go on asking questions for if you are convinced that your opinion is right? Shortsighted chatterer, is not every external tuition a law that determines how one

128

or the other thing is to be understood? But is not every law or rule a judgment? Where has anybody ever been set free by the law?

28. It is a fact that you make your children prisoners first and then cannot set them free, ever! But we bring up our children the same way a potter makes his vessel, shaping it simultaneously on the inside and outside on his potter's wheel. Otherwise, he would produce a most one-sided pot! So if you want to learn how to educate a human being toward eternal freedom, visit a potter's workshop and recognize your misinterpreted love. Realize this, that there is more wisdom in a potter than as yet in you!"

29. (After this blow, Bishop Martin once more turns to Me and says): "O Lord, there is no getting at this really radical moon-man. For, when I present something in full accordance with Your teaching, he is ahead of me for a good thousand years. The most peculiar thing, however, is that he, as a moon-dweller, has most likely never seen the earth, even as a star, but seems to know it better than even I do. He suggests that I see a potter on earth so that I might study wisdom and, as it were, the secret of love. That is really very funny!

30. What will I do with a potter? Am I supposed to work in this trade here? The fellow goes even so far as to say that You, o Lord, could not help me with Your verbal tuition if such did not come from within me, through my own spirit! That is obviously a gross sin. If it were up to me, I would teach him a lesson about what it means to dispute even the effective power of Your tuition!"

31. (Say I): "Never mind, My dear Martin! If you started an argument with this moon-dweller, you would get the worst of it. He is a very good spirit and does not deserve at all being let down by Me. The reason why he was so blunt towards you was that he discovered in you a sort of very ambitious malice, which these moon-dwellers detest more than anything else. With them, the outer must conform to the inner in every respect.

32. Besides, better heed what you have heard from him, for there will come a time when you'll find it very useful. The potter is an excellent metaphor: from this you can get to know My order in its entirety! For I Myself am a potter, and My work is that of a potter! My order can be compared to a potter's wheel, and My works to a potter's products! How, the future will reveal to you.

33. Let us now proceed to the twelfth door, where some things that you do not understand as yet will become clear to you. So be it!"

51

A GLANCE THROUGH THE TWELFTH DOOR AT THE SMALLEST SOLAR REGION (GALAXY). — MARTIN GETS AN IDEA OF GOD'S GREATNESS AND MERCY. — THE HUMAN FORM AS AN ETERNAL UNIFORM FUNDAMENTAL FORM.

1. (The Lord): "We have reached the twelfth door; like the earlier ones, it is already open. Step to the threshold and then speak about what you see."

2. (Bishop Martin does as told. After an amazed silence, he says): "O God, o God, how endless this is! In vast distances I see innumerable brilliant suns and worlds swarming like on earth the may-flies do a couple of hours before sunset on a summer's day. I wonder how many decillions there might be? And how many eternities would be required to get to know them to some extent?

3. O God, o Lord, the longer I look, the more of them I discern. How can it be possible for You to supervise, guide, and maintain this boundless mass of suns and worlds? It is terrific!

4. The little moon alone would keep me busy enough in eternity! And You, o Lord, just toy with all these countless decillions of suns and worlds; You regulate and maintain them and look even after the very smallest on all these worlds as if it were the only thing in all infinity. O Lord, how can You do it?"

5. (Say I): "No created spirit can fully understand how I can easily do this. However, eternity will teach you many more things which you cannot understand at this stage. Therefore, do not query this any further! If I revealed to you the extent of My almighty love and wisdom, you could not live, for the depths of My Deity are unfathomable for any created spirit!

6. "What you are seeing here is only the smallest solar region, which on earth you have often seen on clear nights. Do not think that this is the only one filling endless infinte space. There is no end of similar, as well as endlessly vaster, richer, and more magnificent solar regions, for My creation is unlimited! Again and again, you will find different and more wonderful arrangements, and forever new forms of unimaginable majesty and splendor.

7. The only constant and uniform form is that of man. The countless inhabitants of the different worlds differ solely in size and

the grade of their love, wisdom and beauty; but all these grades are still based on the unchangeable human form, which is in My own image. The wisest are the most beautiful and those who are filled with love are the most delicate and glorious.

8. However, at this stage, you would not as yet be capable of bearing even the least beauty in human shape of the most insignificant of the worlds you have just seen. Therefore, you have to be satisfied with viewing these suns and worlds from a considerable distance. When your spirit is more mature, you will get a much closer look at the wonders of My creation.

9. But before this is the case, you will have to exercise self-denial, particularly in the lust of the flesh, which is still very strong in you. As long as you do not rid yourself of this, you will not be allowed to contemplate all this beauty which is still inconceivable to you, or you might easily forget Me.

10. To forget Me, however, means to lose life and its celestial freedom, and to expose oneself to judgment, death and hell, from which no spirit is safe that has not been fully reborn in My Spirit.

11. Now you are familiar with your dwelling. I Myself have guided you everywhere to the threshold of eternal life, and now you have to walk by yourself if you want to attain true freedom. I shall now visibly leave you again, but I will send you another companion who will teach you to recognize My will on the white tablet. Ponder faithfully on all you have seen and heard; be calm and reasonable and you will soon make further progress. So be it!''

52

BLESSINGS OF SWEDENBORG'S LIGHT. — THE OLD ADAM IN BISHOP MARTIN. — THE WOMAN'S WISE WARNING, AND BOREM'S SEVERE ADMONITION.

1. After these words, I visibly leave Bishop Martin quite suddenly and another angelic spirit is already standing in My place. It is the bookseller, whom we already know, and who has made great progress at the side of Peter, towards which the inspired writings of Swedenborg have helped him quite considerably.

2. On recognizing the bookseller in My place, Bishop Martin is very surprised and says: "What is this? Are you, by any chance, my future guide? I would rather have believed in death in heaven than have you become my guide! Ah, ah, this is really too much! First the Lord Himself, and now you! That would be like the sun, compared to a backside!

3. Ha, ha, this is ridiculous! You, a bookseller, my guide! A wretched bookseller to make a guide through all the heavens for a fomer bishop, a learned theologian! No, that is quite out of the question! Go back to whence you came, my friend, for I shall not follow you anywhere!

4. 'If the Lord had sent me the first best guttersnipe as a companion and guide, I would not have minded, but *you*, you in particular, who are familiar with all my dirty tricks! No, I will not tolerate it! Either you go or I — it does not matter which! I leave this house of ideas to you! It may not last anyway, as I find its whole set-up suspicious.

5. What this hall contains, you see — that is, if you can see at all what I see, for that much I have already learned in this fantastic world, that two people next to each other see one and the same thing quite differently. Where one sees an ass, his companion sees either an ox or even a philosopher! Or where one sees a light, the other sees but darkness!

6. But a clever chap like me must draw the conclusion from all this that this celestial world, as I now know it, is a very silly and senseless world. It is simply a dreamlike illusion of the senses, absolutely inconsistent!

7. Therefore, I shall just move along, and you, wise bookdust-swallower, may take my place in studying higher astronomy through these twelve doors and, perhaps, fall in love with a beautiful Mercurian, or an even more beautiful sun-dweller, provided that you can see with your eyes what I have seen there. Farewell, and please yourself, while I go looking for a place with more consistency than this astronomical hall."

8. After these words, the bishop turns to leave, but the bookseller prevents him from doing this by the following clever words: "Brother, friend, how foolish you are! Weren't we intimate and close friends on earth? And wasn't I then already quite aware of all your tricks, without ever giving you away? If I didn't do so there, why should I do it here in heaven, where the Lord anway knows you a

million times better than I do, and ever will? Why then are you so annoyed as if the Master of Eternity had made me your guide?

9. There you are quite wrong, for I came to you to keep you company and to serve you in everything. I just want to learn from you, who must have gained so much experience at the side of the Lord, and not that you should learn from me. In view of these facts, why did you flare up like that on seeing me beside you?

10. Just stay here in your property, which is surely more consistent than you think, and take me for what I really am, not what you imagine, which is extremely ungrateful to the Lord. Then we shall, I hope, get on better with each other."

11. Bishop Martin is now silent and at a loss what to reply to the bookseller. He walks over to the door of Mercury to gain time to compose himself.

12. When he arrives at the door, he notices a crowd of Mercurians of both sexes. In the crowd he also sees the beautiful woman who, on the occasion of his first visit to the planet, had already much impressed his eyes as well as his heart. At the sight of her, his companion, whom we now shall call "Borem," is already forgotten, and he walks through the door to meet her.

13. (As he enters her sphere, the fair Mercurian sees him and says): "I know and love you as we all love you as our master. But there is something in you that neither I nor any of us like: it is the fleshly desire in you! Unless you rid yourself of this, you will never be allowed to approach us.

14. I am telling you this because I love you and because I believe that you love me too, and all of us who are hoping to gain beatitude through you when you become as you should be. However, if you do not, we shall be taken away from you and given to a worthier spirit.

15. Therefore, do not let yourself be deluded by my attractiveness, but stay in the order of the Supreme Spirit of God, Whose infinite wisdom has made you and me so beautiful.

16. For you, too, are inconceivably beautiful to me. The true majesty of the supreme Spirit of God is shining from you. But I have to contain myself and avoid you the moment I notice that my image begins to ignite within you.

17. You should do the same until you possess the full divine strength. And when you have achieved this, you will possess me and all of us in divine, celestial delight.

18. But remember this: Whatever you desire here you must flee and you will obtain it. But flee it out of love, not aversion! That is also the reason why I flee you, for I love you very much.

19. Go now and do as suggested, and this heart which is beating for you will express its gratitude in a way the sweetness of which is still quite unknown to you!"

20. After these words, the fair Mercurian steps back, displaying her celestial beauty even more visibly, causing Bishop Martin to collapse from emotion.

21. For a long time he crouches on the ground unable to speak or even think. He stands up again only when Borem bends down to him, taps him on the shoulder, and says:

22. (Borem): "But brother Martin, what has happened to you? Has that beautiful Mercurian cast a spell on you by any chance, and made you weak and faint? Or has something else struck you?"

23. (Bishop Martin, quite vexed): "D--- you, did I call you? If you are my servant and I your master, why do you approach me without being called? Be sure in future only to come when I call you, or you may go back to whence you came!"

24. (Borem): "Listen, friend, this is not the way to talk to me, or the Lord, Whose patience with you has been indescribable, might show you how the one fares who disregards His clemency, as you are doing at this moment. Therefore, follow me in the name of the Lord as well as in the name of that celestial maiden, who has just given you a very wise admonition, or you might soon be very sorry.

25. Think of the boundless mercy the Lord showed you during your last hour on earth, of all the wise precepts you have been taught from all sides! How little effect they have had on you so far! It is now high time for you to change or, as already mentioned, you will have to taste the sharp measures the Lord uses for the very obstinate who trample upon His clemency. For know this: The Lord is not to be trifled with for too long! So, better follow me back to the hall!"

26. (Bishop Martin straightens himself out and says, extremely annoyed): "There, you see, what a fine companion and servant you are! I thank you for such a one! You have been given me as a task-master, and I will not have it! You may stay here and please yourself but I shall be on my way and see whether I can do good also without your help.

27. This is really too much! I, a bishop, consequently an Apostle of Jesus Christ, am to be pushed around and guided by a

lousy bookseller! No, that is unbearable! Get out of my sight or you'll force me to lay hands on you! Unfortunately, I saved you from the flames and was good to you, but now I am sorry to have ever done you good! You are a thorn in my side, being already better than I and having been appointed my taskmaster!

28. There is a lot of talk here about spiritual freedom. That is a fine freedom for me if you aren't even allowed to look through the door of your house without having a taskmaster at your side! You'd better go and make sure you do not lose your heavenly freedom! And threats on top of it all! How charming that you can be disciplined even in heaven!

29. Maybe you have already hidden a cudgel under your celestial toga and are going to start thrashing me in a moment! Go on — try it! You'll soon find out how much you can thrash into a bishop or even out of him!

30. Do you celestial ass really think that I am afraid of any kind of punishment? Just try it, and you will soon see how little I fear it! If the Lord wants to better me through punishment, He may please Himself. But as long as I am allowed my free will, I shall be the way I want to be! I know what it means to defy the Lord, and I know His might. But I deeply admire the greatness of a spirit who has the courage to defy the Lord!"

31. (Borem): "Friend, I came to you on behalf of the Lord, meek as a lamb. I never hurt you in any way, neither in the world, nor here. But you received me as even in the world the lowest slave would not be received by a ruler. Is this attitude wise or loving, as it is supposed to be in heaven? And if the Lord decided to send me to you, are you better and wiser than He Whose order I carried out?

32. The Lord sees the fleshly desire in you, and at the back of it extreme arrogance to anyone who might oppose you in your loathsome lust. Therefore, He sent me to you so that your arrogance should at last reveal itself and with it your ever-growing desire for the flesh of women. However, you receive me like an inmate of hell, apparently not bothering about the Lord Who wants only your beatitude. If you continue like this, the kindness of the Lord will become a judgment for you, the more severe the more you defy Him.

33. I am leaving you now, for I can see that you hate me, although I have not given you any grounds for it. May the Lord do unto you in accordance with His love, mercy, and justice!"

34. As Borem turns to leave, Bishop Martin holds him back in a

friendly manner and asks him to stay as he wishes to make his peace with him and discuss great things. So Borem stays.

35. Borem waits for a while, expecting the bishop to say something. But the latter is trying hard to figure out how he could win Borem for himself concerning the things he intended to discuss.

36. (Borem, however, sees through him, and says): "Friend Martin, I tell you, in the name of the Lord Jesus Christ Who is the sole Lord of Heaven and all creation in infinity, do not go to all this trouble, for I see through you quite clearly.

37. What is in your mind at this moment is in the minds of all purely hellish spirits whom we call 'devils.' Do not dare to come to me with your great things — which to me are disgustingly small — for this plan of yours could be your downfall!

38. Tell me, how long do you intend to defy the Lord in your heart? Tell me this quite openly, so that I can act accordingly. Believe me, although the nature of all that you see here around you is eternal, you could quite suddenly find yourself in a place much less to your liking than this one. For the Lord has instructed me from now on to show you no more indulgence, since the fire of lechery and lust for power has begun to burn in you.

39. Now speak openly and without treachery what you intend to do. But do speak the truth, for I tell you in the name of the Lord: Every deceitful thought in you will be known to me, and your punishment will be that I leave you, and all that is now yours will be taken from you suddenly. Keep this in mind and tell me now, truthfully, what you intend to do — whether you will follow me or not."

53

THE VEXED BISHOP MARTIN. — BOREM'S SHARP WARNING AND DEPARTURE. — THE LONELY MARTIN.

1. Following these severe words, Bishop Martin begins to scratch his head, and says at last in an undertone, as if to himself: "There you are! I knew it, even in heaven you cannot and must not rely on anybody! The Lord has already, so to speak, revealed all the treasures of heaven to me and now this one speaks to me as if I could

land in hell the next moment. What a nice reward! I probably saved him from a little bit of hellish fire, and now he is trying hard to dispatch me to that nice place! Well, if that isn't an unparalleled friendship!"

2. (Bishop Martin, somewhat louder, to Borem): "My dear friend, now you are gradually pulling the mask off your face, showing clearly in what capacity you were sent to me. All right, you do according to your instructions, and I will do what my common sense tells me.

3. It is true that I had a stupid and maybe also evil plan, for I seriously intended to defy the Lord a little bit, just in order to see what would happen to me in such a case; but you saw through me admirably and thwarted my plan.

4. However, you call me a devil and ready for hell, of which the Lord, Who is evidently more than you are, didn't say a thing to me. I shall rely on the Lord, not on you; and shall do what the Lord tells me to do. Only at the white tablet shall I listen to you, since the Lord mentioned that you will teach me how to use it. In all other matters, I shall listen to you if I want to, just as heretofore.

5. And your threats you may keep to yourself, for they don't impress me, as I am not afraid of anything! Even before the Lord, I do not choose my words, but say what I think and feel. Now I am returning to the hall, and you may come too if you want to, or you may please yourself."

6. After these words, Bishop Martin quickly walks into the hall and Borem follows him in a friendly manner.

7. Back in the hall, Bishop Martin notices right away that there is a lot of writing on the tablet. He approaches it and endeavors to read what is written there; but in vain, for he is not familiar with the script, which looks somewhat like hieroglyphs. He begins to lose his temper again, and says:

8. (Bishop Martin): "Why can't the celestial clerks use a script that one can read oneself without having to call for an interpreter? To write to somebody in a script unknown to him is like speaking Chinese to a German. What could this be good for, I wonder?"

9. (Here Borem interrupts him): "For the same thing, friend, for which in the world the dogmatic Latin ritual is good for. There, too, nobody understands it except those who have learned this pagan tongue. But to make sure that nobody, not even those who know Latin, can understand what the Latin ritual of so-called worship con-

tains, a lot of noise is made during mass with organ, drums and trombones, whilst the mass itself is only mumbled. Say, is not that absurd too, although it is pontifical?

10. How then can you, a man who is used to such absurdities, become annoyed if you cannot read this script at first sight? Look more closely at the tablet, maybe you will notice some Latin phrases mystically intermingled with the twelve signs of the zodiac. Look at the top, where I at least can read quite clearly: *'Dies illa, dies irae!'* (That day, the day of wrath)."

11. Now, also, Bishop Martin looks more closely at the tablet, notices the same and asks what it means.

12. (Borem): "You are a scholar of Latin and should be able to translate it. Just go on reading. There are more such phrases at the top. When you are through with reading them, you may then ask."

13. Bishop Martin now concentrates on the tablet and reads the words: *'Requiescant in pace, et lux perpetua luceat eis!'* (May they rest in peace and the eternal light shine on them!). Also: *'Requiem aeternam dona eis, domine!'* (Lord, give them eternal rest!). And then: *'Memento, homo, quia pulvis es et in pulverem reverteris!'* (Remember, man, that you are dust and shall return to dust!). And many other similarly absurd phrases. After having read all of them, he turns to Borem, obviously agitated, and says:

14. (Bishop Martin): "Well, what about all this stuff? What does it mean, and why is it written here? Is it by any chance meant to be a taunt referring to the high office I held on earth?"

15. (Says Borem): "Oh no, friend, not at all! All this was only written on the tablet to point out to you how much foolishness you still have in you. Therefore, you are still in your peasant clothes for which you exchanged your bishop's robe soon after your death. Only your coat is missing, which you voluntarily gave to me when I was naked in the house of the Lord. You remember the occasion. But you can take it back. Look, there it is under the tablet, well cleaned and tidily folded. Take it and put it back on you so that you might find it easier to realize the extent of your folly.

16. Even though the Lord showed you His boundless mercy by relieving you of the poison of evil, you still retained your great foolishness. If you continue feeding it, it may turn into outright wickedness and plunge you into a terrible judgment. For know this: Until you are not fully reborn of the spirit, you are in no way safe from hell. But to help you avoid such a calamity, you are to be

138

shown your great folly to which you are still clinging and from which even the Lord Himself cannot free you without placing you under compulsion."

17. (Says Bishop Martin, thoughtfully): "All right, if this is the case, I shall put on my coat so that I do not look like a porter, but at least like an honest farmer. And then, you super-wise celestial bookseller, you may show me my so-called follies which I am supposed to recognize in the writing on this tablet. However, I don't see how I could recognize them in view of the earnestness and wisdom of these phrases, the authors of which are the sublime early fathers 'whose shoe's latchet we are not worthy to unloose' nor most likely ever will be."

18. (Borem): "Well, then listen! Where and what is the day of wrath or judgment? Who will be full of wrath and hold judgment? Do you believe God is a God of wrath and a God of judgment? Oh, no! God is the purest and highest love personified, and He said of Himself, 'I came not to judge the world, but to save whosoever believeth in Me and loveth Me!'

19. The Lord does speak of a Judgment Day, but this commences for everyone on his physical death. On the other hand, about condemnation the Lord says only that everyone had in him what will condemn him, namely His Word. And if this is what the Lord says, where then is your ominous *Dies irae, dies illa*? This should really be: 'Oh day of my naked folly and my glaring wickedness!' "

20. (Bishop Martin): "If you are conversant with the interpretation of these texts, and in your opinion there is no universal last judgment, how then do you interpret those texts from the Lord's own mouth, which ominously and clearly predict the return of the Lord as a relentless judge? And the Lord Himself names as preceding indications of His coming, great misery, dearth, famine, wars, rebellions, earthquakes, the appearance of the sign of the Son of Man in the sky, the rise and fall of the Antichrist, the darkening of the sun and the moon, and the falling down of all the stars from the sky. After this, He describes the terrible preparations for the Day of Judgment, and finally the latter itself: How the accursed heretics, whoremongers, and adulterers will be dispatched to the devils, accompanied by countless flashes of lightning issuing from the mouths of the chosen and God's angels, as a just curse at all the damnable heretics like yourself.

21. Tell me, you boldly-wise bookseller, how do you explain

this? If I believe in these words of God, am I again stupid, foolish, and malicious?"

22. (Borem): "Hypocrite, how long is it since you reluctantly came to believe in the Deity of Christ, but at the first slight temptation you fall off like dry leaves from a tree? If, during your whole life on earth, you had really believed in these words of Christ, you would now be standing here in quite a different garment! But since you neither believed in the outer, literal meaning of the Gospel, nor in the inner, spiritual meaning, and never tried to practice it, you are standing here in contemplation of all these endless wonders of God and hearing the wisest teaching from His own mouth, but are still the same old, incorrigible fool!

23. Who can understand you and who would want to guide you? For if at long last you show some faith and meekness, you turn the next moment into a being in whom hypocrisy stands for faith and only too obvious arrogance and hatred for meekness and love.

24. As if my teaching would be of any use to you! I know you too well! What good did the wisdom of the little moon-philosopher do you? Notwithstanding the presence of the Lord, your anger grew the wiser the moon-priest, Piramah, talked to you. If I now answered your question which is only nourishing your pride, it would not make you any better, only angrier and, therefore, worse!

25. As long as you continue like this, I shall not teach or instruct you in any way! And in order to avoid vexing you, I shall now leave you in accordance with the Lord's will. You are now free to do whatever you want, but remember this: From here, both paths are open to you — the one to heaven as well as the one to hell, together with the true interpretation of the Gospel's reference to the end of time!"

26. After these words, Borem vanishes, and Bishop Martin is left to his own devices. Now it is of the greatest importance what he does and how he applies all the wise teachings he has received.

27. Bishop Martin calls anxiously for Borem, but in vain. He also calls to the Lord and to Peter, but there is no answer. He runs back to the door of Mercury, through which he can still see the planet but at a considerable distance. He walks over to the door through which he had earlier seen the flock of lambs, but now there is nothing except the rather desolate field on which he had seen that beautiful flock for the first time, when he had the list of their names.

28. He runs from one door to the other, and sees through them the sun, the planets, and the moon, but all at great distances, as they are seen by men on earth. The hall alone is still the same as before — in the center the already familiar tablet and next to it the astronomical mechanism.

29. However, these objects are not to the liking of our bishop, so he goes to the exit, intending to hurry over to the Lord's house, but this, too, has become invisible to him. Since he cannot see this, and since the small garden around his house is rather bare and uninviting, he despondently goes back into his house, where nothing has changed.

30. There he stands for a while, motionless before the white tablet which is blank on one side and on the other side has still the previously mentioned Latin phrases. When he is beginning to get bored, he moves a few steps forward, toward the astronomical mechanism, and begins once more to study the earth. However, he does not dare say anything for he is now beginning to realize that he is in a rather difficult situation.

54

BISHOP MARTIN'S SOLILOQUY. — CRITICISM OF THE CHURCHES. — DISCOVERY OF AN AFTERNOON TEA NOOK.

1. After properly studying the spiritually artistic earth-globe for twelve earthly hours, and when no one has come near him, Bishop Martin begins the following soliloquy:

2. (Bishop Martin): "So, now I have had another good look at the earth and must say it is a shame what is going on there! The fraud, the deceit, the malice, the disgraceful politics, and the unspeakable atrocities that are being committed everywhere! This really surpasses all comprehension!

3. If you look more closely at all this vileness on earth, life appears loathsome. In the midst of the greatest wonders of God, millions seem to have no idea of Him, and their actions are so peculiarly tyrannical as if they expected to live forever in a world upon which the seal of death has been impressed everywhere. How most

peculiar this is! I, too, am still rather a beast, but this is really too crazy!

4. My Roman colleagues sit in conclave and the church councils meet; however, the reason for these meetings is neither the Lord nor the spirit of the teaching of the Gospel, but solely lust for power conferring furtively about the shameful means best suited to achieve its end.

5. The Protestants, too, are endeavoring to conquer the earth with pure reason and to make new laws which would be rather in favor of the legislators than the people.

6. Also the Anglican Church makes every effort, by the foulest of means, to propagate the doctrine of giving among its parishioners. But the Church itself does not give anything at all!

7. In short, conditions on earth are such that even in hell it could not be any worse. Away with you, shameless world! Even to look at you would make a person evil! How much more this must be the case when one has been a Roman bishop for fifty years.

8. I am really a low scoundrel of a spirit in this illusory kingdom of heaven; but what can I do? Maybe my wickedness will peter out in about two thousand years when everything earthly in me may have evaporated. Oh, what a beast I am!"

9. After this soliloquy, Bishop Martin is again silent, pondering on what he can do now, but unable to think of anything worthwhile.

10. Quite a while passes before he remembers that he has not yet inspected the beautiful galleries of his house. So he starts looking for the stairs leading up to them, but without success, for they are hidden. He goes outside, looks around, but sees no trace of them there either.

11. He finds it altogether most peculiar and incomprehensible that his house consists of a very large hall inside, yet from the outside it does not look any bigger or more impressive than a small hermitage on earth. He also wonders why he cannot find any trace of the twelve cabinets on the outside of his house, when they play such an important role on the inside.

12. Having been outside his house for some time and unable to find what he has been looking for so eagerly, our bishop starts walking around in his little garden. There he finds some small berries, a few of which he eats, as he is beginning to feel hungry. But this fare is not much to his liking, so he does not eat much of it. For a while he still keeps looking around, but when he cannot find anything, he

re-enters the house, resigned to the fact that he will not be able to investigate the galleries.

13. Inside, he once more inspects the white tablet from all sides but finds everything unchanged: on the front side it is still blank, and on the reverse side, facing the astronomical mechanism, there are still the same Latin phrases. As we know, they are of no interest to our Bishop Martin! So he once more walks toward one of the doors — the door of the sun. He opens it and looks at the very distant sun, and since he cannot see anything else, he at least enjoys the sunlight.

14. Thus he spends what he feels to be several hours, and then he begins to talk to himself.

15. (Bishop Martin): "Although the earth is on the whole a madhouse, it is not quite as silly as this so-called celestial world. For what is on earth is real, and stays so, or at least reappears as the same real thing.

16. The stars in the sky do not change ever, and a house remains the same until it is demolished and a new one built in its place. But here, everything is like a silly dream: you see something, and then, when you want to see it again, maybe from another angle, you turn round to it and there is no trace of what you had originally seen from the first position.

17. Take, for instance, this door through which I am looking now into a distance of millions of miles. Where is it when I seek it outside the house? Not a trace of it visible anywhere!

18. Here, immediately beyond the door frame, there is an infinite dark blue empty space in whose depth the dear sun is shining, no larger than a small plate. However, at this same spot, outside the house, there is not a trace of a door, nor the sun for that matter! Whatever can this mean?

19. To understand this, one must evidently have more than a rudimentary knowledge or, perhaps, be an even greater ass than I am, who at least seems to realize that this is nothing but illusion. Thus the scientists on earth would be amazed if they were told that here you can live in houses which are much smaller on the outside than they are on the inside.

20. Oh, what a state of things! And what shall I do now? Stay here? What an awkward situation — alone and nothing to eat!

21. Isn't it peculiar that even as a spirit in this so-called celestial spirit world, one can suffer from hunger and thirst? But this is how it is! I am hungry and thirsty, and have neither to eat nor drink,

and still there is nothing I can do but stay here, for in the little garden there are at least some small berries as food in an emergency.

22. But wait! I just remembered something! Through this sun-door there is only vast empty space. What could happen if I jumped out into it, as there is nothing in any direction?

23. When I put my head out through the door, I do not see the house at all, not a trace of a wall, a roof, or any foundation. There is just nothing there! When I pull my head back inside, I again see my hall, unchanged. Therefore, I couldn't possibly hit my head against anything, even if there were something there, for I am a spirit, and as such should be light enough. So let me jump! Who knows what I may experience on such a journey through the air?

24. No stop! I remember something even better! Through door number one I saw the familiar field. So why should I jump into this empty sun-space when instead I could go for a walk in that field? I might even meet the beautiful lambs! Yes, that is a much better idea. So let me be off to door number one!

25. Here I am, already at door number one! But what has happened to the field? It has vanished and I can see only a dense grey fog. Could it be that this earthly late autumn feature appears sometimes here also in the world of spirits? And why not? There are celestial clouds, so why shouldn't there also be celestial fog? However, I shall not go outside the door, for who knows what or whom I might meet in such a fog?

26. What would happen, I wonder, if I tried a *salto mortale* through the door of Mercury? I might eventually get nearer to that planet and, perhaps, even meet that fair Mercurian who, God forgive me my sins, has roused a real animal passion in me. Oh, oh, just to get a little kiss from her, and some bosom-fingering! What divine delight that would be! So, off to the door of Mercury, which must be next to this one!

27. Here I am. It is the right door, but it is closed. I will open it — but what is this? Instead of the view into the vast sphere of Mercury, I see nothing but a cupboard, well-stocked with food! On the lower shelf I see quite a number of wine bottles. If things are like this, I shall naturally stay here. Farewell, fair Mercurian, farewell endless solar space — I prefer by far this rich table!

28. This really changes my whole attitude! Oh, my beloved Lord Jesus, for this I have to thank You! Now we are again reconciled, my dearest bookseller! Come to me that I may embrace you!

You do not come — but it does not matter, I still love you dearly! And now I shall hold a communion right away, in the name of the Lord!"

55

ABOUT HUNGER AND THIRST IN IMMATURE SPIRITS. — MARTIN IN A TIPSY STATE AFTER HIS MEAL. — THE ADVENTUROUS MARTIN IS SOBERED DOWN BY AN ANGRY JUPITERIAN.

1. After these words, Bishop Martin begins to eat a big piece of bread, with great appetite! If a spirit turns away from Me for a while he is soon plagued by hunger and thirst, and when he gets something to eat again as soon as he begins to repent, he eats and drinks with great eagerness. This eagerness also reveals the inner emptiness of the spirit and that not much can be expected of him for quite a while yet — as will soon be demonstrated by our Bishop Martin.

2. Having eaten the bread and enjoyed a bottle of good wine, he has become very merry and, at the same time, even more sensual. Spirits that have not been reborn out of Me and through Me can become intoxicated, in which state they often are sensually unrestrained, and then they badly misuse their freedom.

3. Having emptied the bottle of wine, our bishop closes the cupboard to protect the food, as he imagines. Then he goes out into the open and says to himself:

4. (Bishop Martin): "Thanks to God that this very hungry stomach has had something to do at last! Now I shall go for a walk in my little garden to get some fresh air.

5. Fresh air after a meal is surely much better than that silly black coffee, and I must admit that the air in this little garden is its best feature.

6. The wine was a real drop from the moon! It was only half a measure, but I feel it now! Not that I am tipsy, but I really feel it!

7. I wish there was a bench in this little garden where I could sit down for a while in case my legs go wobbly — then this garden would indeed be quite enjoyable! But there is nothing of the kind, and the ground does not look too inviting either.

8. I will go to the fence, against which I could lean a bit and at

the same time I could see whether I have any neighbors or not. There is no trace of a landscape here, just a sandy desert with a cloudy sky creating a gloomy and unfriendly atmosphere. So I'll go to the fence and who knows what I might find there?

9. Oh dear, oh dear, I must say I do feel the wine! But, let me proceed to the fence!

10. Ah, here I am! What a beautiful view! One can see simply nothing! This garden with my royal palace seems to be like a ship floating on the waves of infinity, and little chance of any neighbors. So I am now alone — completely alone! This will be my curse, my condemnation.

11. So this is it! I cannot go anywhere beyond this garden! Oh, d---- it! So I am secretly condemned! That was at the bottom of the aphorisms on the white tablet. That is why it said, *'Dies irae, dies illa'* (The day of wrath, that day!). So I shall be here until the Day of Judgment — *requiescam in pace* (may I rest in peace). And then it will be eternal damnation for me! Oh, unfortunate wretch that I am!

12. If I could only tell my beads on and on, and besides one holy lauretanic litany after another, which is most powerful and effective, that might still help me. But I cannot pray and I have the feeling that even if I could, I wouldn't want to. The most I can utter is: 'Lord, have mercy upon me; Christ have mercy upon me; Lord, have mercy upon me!' That is as far as I can go.

13. Why am I staring into this silly nothingness? Back into the house! At least there I can go to the door of the sun from where I maybe could enjoy the beautiful sunlight. Or, wait, it might be better if I went to the door of the moon. Maybe there I can meet the moon philosopher who could possibly tell me what to do to improve my lot somewhat. So, into the house and to the moon-door!

14. Here I am inside the house. It is still unchanged and really looks splendid. I'd better stay in the house all the time now for it is quite pleasant here. But now to the moon-door!

15. Holla, I almost had a fall there! Oh, that wine, it is still in my head! Never mind, there is already the moon-door and it is even open! But — oh, you hopeless chap of a moon — what a great distance from here! Not much chance of talking to the philosopher. Although it is a full moon, it seems farther away from here than from the earth. Nothing to be done here either.

16. I will try Jupiter. Maybe that one is not quite as withdrawn as the shy moon.

17. Here is already the door to the great Jupiter, but it is also closed! I will try to open it. *EPHETHA!* (Open up!). Look, that was easy! Thank God, this Grand Mogul among the planets is quite close and keeps coming closer. O, God be thanked! At last I may be able to reach some respectable human company!

18. Sure enough, the planet is quite close now and somebody is already approaching me. O God, what vast areas! It even looks to me as if my house were standing in the ground of this giant planet.

19. The handsome man, a giant, is standing directly in front of me, but does not seem to notice me. I shall enter into his sphere, then he might be able to see me."

20. Bishop Martin enters the sphere of the Jupiterian, who now sees him and asks immediately:

21. (The Jupiterian): "Who are you that you dare approach me so full of filth, deceit and lechery? All of those infamies are entirely unknown on my great globe. My world is a pure land and would get extremely angry if you stayed on its territory for any length of time. Therefore, kindly withdraw to your filthy abode, where you can gluttonize and whore to your infamous heart's delight! If you stay I shall tear you to pieces!"

22. Bishop Martin darts back into the interior of his house, slams the door behind him, and says to himself: "That chap is all that has been wanting to crown my wretchedness. Farewell, Sir Jupiter, forever! Imagine — tear me to pieces! I shall never ever look out through that door again!"

56

MARTIN'S FUTILE EFFORT TO SLEEP. — HE IS SURPRISED BY A GROUP OF WRETCHED SPIRITS, WHOM HE ASSISTS.

1. (Bishop Martin): "Whatever will I do now? Where can I turn to? Should I go to the doors of Mars, of Venus, or rather to those of Saturn, Uranus, or Miron (Neptune), or maybe to the door of the several small planets? I might be faced with something even worse, and what then? There is no question of resistance on my part, for I lack strength as well as wisdom.

2. I had better stay clear of all the doors in future, so I will now roll myself up in some corner like a hedgehog and try to sleep. Failing that, I will at least lie there throughout all eternity, without moving. I will not eat anything nor speak to anybody, come what may! In short, I shall be dead for everyone, even the fair Mercurian! So, it is goodbye!

3. Since I cannot cease to exist, I'll go to my rest, from which no God shall be able to wake me. There, I see already such a corner where I will lie down and stay forever and ever, Amen!"

4. Bishop Martin walks over to a recess between two columns which help support the gallery. He crawls in, rolls up, and tries to sleep, but of course, it does not work.

5. After he has been lying there for about two hours, as it seems to him, a great uproar can be heard outside the house, like that of a gale, in which human voices seem to be calling for help.

6. (Hearing this, Bishop Martin springs to his feet and says): "Ah, but this is different! I cannot ignore this! In such a case, I cannot continue with my intended eternal rest. I must hurry outside! There is someone in trouble, and I must help."

7. With these words, he rushes outside and notices, just beyond his garden fence, a crowd of apparently hunted spirits seeking help and safety. He rushes to the garden gate, opens it wide, and shouts:

8. (Bishop Martin): "This way, this way, friends and dear brothers — this is a safe place! Here you will be safe from persecution! And should you be hungry and thirsty, we'll find some way out! Just come in, all of you. How many of you are there?"

9. (Says one, nearest to Martin): "We are about a thousand of the most wretched, poor devils. We have escaped from hell and have been wandering about this terrible endless desert for half an eternity, unable to find shelter to hide and rest a little. Believe me, it is a terrible lot to be hunted forever without getting any peace or rest! If you, high-minded spirit, have a corner where we would be safe and have some rest, take us in and we shall be most grateful."

10. (Bishop Martin): "Friends, here is the gate — enter all of you! My house does not seem very large from the outside, but I assure you there will be plenty of room inside."

11. After these words, the hunted stream into the garden, and from there into the house, where they are astonished to find its interior of such splendor and size.

12. The first one embraces our bishop and speaks for all of

them : "Oh, you blessed friend, how wonderful it is here in your house! For billions of earth millennia, it is the first light we have seen. Since we left earth, our eyes have not seen a single ray of light! Oh light, light, how glorious you are! Oh friend, do not send us away, but let us stay always with you."

13. (Bishop Martin): "Why should I send you away when I am myself glad to have so much company? You may stay here forever, so just make yourselves comfortable. I do not possess much myself in this, my heaven, but whatever I have got, I will gladly hand over to you — even if nothing is left for me! God be thanked that at long last I have found company!

14. This is really most enjoyable. I would rather have you than the so-called angels of God, who, in their bliss are capable of forgetting a poor devil for a whole eternity, unable or not willing to consider the feelings of such an unfortunate one. I can tell you this: The Lord alone is good, that is a fact! But all the rest of the celestial rabble can stay away from me forever, for they have an intellectual arrogance which stinks to a straightforward, honest chap like I am, and probably, like all of you are. But, as already mentioned, God, the Lord Jesus, is an exception! He is really good — yes, very good!"

15. (Says another from the thousand): "Yes, yes, you are right — He is really good! Blessed be He, if He exists at all! As for the rest of the celestial rabble, we, too, do not care about them, with the exception of you, dear friend."

16. (Bishop Martin): "Dear friends, heaven is not for me as yet, for I am more or less on the same level as you. But we shall have plenty of time in eternity to discuss our situation, so let us now look for something to eat. Afterwards, we can give vent to our feelings. Some of you come with me to this cupboard, which holds some provisions for the hungry and the thirsty."

57

THE WRETCHED OBTAIN REFRESHMENT. — THEIR GRATITUDE AND LAMENT ABOUT THEIR EXPERIENCES. — SPEECH OF A SAVED SPIRIT, AND MARTIN'S ANSWER.

1. Bishop Martin now opens the door of the cupboard, and to his astonishment finds it full to capacity with bread and wine. "God be thanked," he says to himself, "I was already afraid I could be fooled,

since everything here keeps changing." (Then, aloud, to the party): "There, help yourselves — eat and drink to your hearts' content!"

2. And they all help themselves. They eat and drink their fill but this does not diminish the stock — on the contrary, it visibly increases! Those who have eaten their fill praise the host with great enthusiasm and their features become much brighter and more handsome; only their clothes still look most pitiful.

3. When all have eaten and praised their host, Bishop Martin closes the door to the cupboard, and says: "Listen, all you dear brothers and sisters, do not shower your praises upon me, who is quite an insignificant person. I cannot enjoy your praises as I am not the real giver, only a bad distributor of what the Lord Jesus Himself has given me, although I do not deserve it.

4. So, if you must praise someone, let it be Jesus, the Lord, provided that you have heard of Him. I do not really expect that all of you have, because from what you have told me, you must have been in the spirit world for an inconceivably long time. In that case, you will have to learn about the only God and Lord Jesus!"

5. (Says one of the party): "Friend, you wouldn't be speaking of the Jew Jesus who died a disgraceful death on the cross, together with two robbers and murderers, would you?"

6. (Bishop Martin): "That is exactly the One I mean! He is truly God, and man at the same time. He is the primal source of all things. There is no other God in the whole of infinity — only He!

7. Believe me, it cost me an unspeakable effort to comprehend this. All the archangels would have failed to convince me of this with words. But the Lord Jesus Himself came to me and taught me through acts God alone could have performed — that it was He, the One Lord of Infinity! And now I am as strong in this conviction as I previously was weak in the understanding of this truth.

8. In view of this, I do not think you would find it too difficult to share everything with me: the house, the bread and wine, as well as my convictions."

9. (Say several of the party): "How right you are! Of course we would want to be like you in everything! Not that we had much faith in Jesus during our lives, and even less here in the spirit world, because our lot was hard and there was no trace of clemency. There has not been any mention of a Jesus until now, except that He, too, might waste away somewhere, the same as we, as a poor, deceived devil, deploring that He ever lived and taught on earth.

10. However, if things are the way as you, dear friend, have just told us, it is all right with us! Whoever God may be and whatever His name is, is of no importance to us as long as there is one on whom we can rely.

11. There is but one thing we cannot understand: How could your good Jesus chase us poor devils around without food and drink for such a long time? Really, friend, that is not exactly evidence of love and compassion! Of course, everything is all right now, but we must not think of all the suffering we have been through or we could not possibly love the eternal chaser of souls!

12. It is true that in the world all of us just followed our desires without bothering about His religion. But otherwise we were honest people from the best families. We had a gentleman's education and lived accordingly. A wise God should understand that no man is able to create and educate himself the way he wants it. However, the chasing around has come to an end and, therefore, Jesus shall be forgiven for what He has done to all of us."

13. (Another one steps forward and says): "Basically you are right, for it is better to forgive than to seek vengeance. However, I shall not be in a hurry to forgive completely, for you know how it was during that thousand years. I was jammed between two glowing rocks and my prayers and curses were more numerous than there is sand in the sea. And if you had not made a great effort to save us, I would still be in that unspeakably painful position. An almighty Lord Jesus would not have alleviated this hellish torture in the least.

14. Such a thing is no joke, and you cannot ever forget it. I am not exactly a vengeful spirit, for it would be utter foolishness if a limited spirit rebelled against an almighty God. But you do not forget such a thing. You will understand what I mean by not forgetting."

15. (Bishop Martin): "Yes, of course, you are right. I, too, had such things on my mind, and still do — things which prick me quite considerably. However, the truth is that the Lord Jesus has nothing whatsoever to do with it; it is only he whom it concerns, and probably more likely it is the Lord's celestial officials, who sometimes act in most arbitrary ways.

16. Actually, all this is in the long run justified through wisdom, but woe betide him on whom such wisdom takes effect! Therefore, the Lord must always be excused and highly praised if He interferes with arbitrary actions of such spirits, shaming them in their wisdom.

17. Oh, you wouldn't believe how pig-headed these celestial

angels can be when they are on their own! But when the Lord comes, they immediately draw in their horns and act so sweetly and modestly, making a great show of their meekness.

18. All this I know, and I love the Lord Jesus all the more because of it. If you would do the same, we would get on wonderfully with each other through all eternity. Your motto should be: 'The Lord Jesus alone is loving and kind!' Everything else is simply trash; even Peter and Paul aren't worth a whiff of powder.

19. But one thing you must tell me: When did you leave earth? I can see from our talk that you did not live before Christ, since you seem to know some details about Him, as well as about the Roman church. So it is obvious that you lived in the world *after* Christ. Therefore, if you don't mind, will you tell me when you lived there? The concept of time as we experience it here in the world of spirits is so unreliable, for one hour can feel like a million years to a poor sinner, as I myself have experienced only too clearly."

58

SOME DETAILS ABOUT THE PARTY OF MALE AND FEMALE SERVANTS OF ROME. — A ROMAN-CHINESE MISSIONARY.

1. (Says one of the party): "Dear friend and brother! All of us left earth in the year 1846, after Christ's birth. On earth, we lived in different countries and actually met only here in the spirit world. We were monks of the orders of the Jesuits, Liguorists, Minorites, and Carmelites. We are about eight hundred males; and the two hundred sisters are partly from the order of the Sisters of Charity and partly from the orders of the Teaching Sisters and Ladies of the Sacred Heart.

2. Now, dear friend and brother, you know when we lived on earth and what we were. The rest you can easily imagine: all the foolish things we had to perform for the sake of Rome, which sent us out into the world to do some fishing. And for this dubious honor, we had to give our lives — some in Asia, some in hot Africa and Australia, and others in America. And when we arrived here in the

spirit world, expecting to receive the martyr's crown of eternal glory, the real trouble only began.

3. And I tell you that you are the first human being we have met in this desert after actual, or just experienced, trillions of years. Isn't it terrible to receive such a reward for our martyrdom on earth? Men on earth are great asses, but we were the greatest — there is no doubt about that!

4. Of course, we did not believe any of the things we taught with glib tongues, for our only motive was to catch the goldfish for ourselves and for Rome. But, notwithstanding this, we did preach Christ and converted many heathens to Christianity, for which, in the end, we had to suffer tortures. What a reward we received for this, you can see for yourself: indescribable wretchedness in this world.

5. I had to suffer particularly. I was in China where, thanks to my knowledge of the language, I managed to make many a profitable deal. With the aid of a beautiful Chinese woman, I even gained access to the Emperor's court. There, however, the woman, whom, unfortunately, I had taken into my confidence, denounced me to the supreme authority, citing fraud and other evil designs, including high treason.

6. I was seized and placed between two stone slabs, which the Mandarins then started to heat, and I was slowly fried to death. That is surely the most painful death imaginable, and one would think that with such a death one would have atoned for all one's mortal sins — but listen to this: This torture continued even after my death! Yes, I still had to face those two glowing rocks which I have already mentioned to you.

7. That was the reward I reaped so far for all my efforts on earth; what may still follow, I don't know. You have now a good picture of our nature and our fate. In short, we are poor devils whom you are now helping. If there is a God, may He reward you for it!"

8. (Bishop Martin): "Now I know more about you than I wanted to find out. But it is quite all right — we shall still remain good friends. Now, bring me the nuns, so that I may hear under what circumstances they joined you here."

59

THE ROMAN NUNS' SANCTIMONIOUSNESS. — AS THE WORK, SO THE REWARD!

1. The speaker immediately returns to the door where the sisters are, and leads them to Bishop Martin.

2. (When they are all surrounding Bishop Martin, he asks them): "Dear sisters and ladies, what happened to you and how did you get into such distress? You surely went to confession, communicated, told your beads endlessly — sometimes rather rattling them off than praying.

3. There would have been plenty of other devotional exercises, strict fasting, and the veneration of sacred relics, the font and incense. No doubt you carried out all your various duties indefatigably. How, then, did you come to be in such a wretched state?"

4. (Says one of the Sisters of Charity): "Oh, you dear friend, the good Lord will know that better than we. Believe me, I, and all these sisters of my order, were true martyrs!

5. Day and night we were on our feet, nursing the sick untiringly. Often we did even more than the severe rules of our order demanded. We fasted and prayed constantly and went to confession and communion several times during the week. And if ever thoughts of marriage or sex molested us, we would shout: 'Jesus, Mary and Joseph, protect our chaste bodies from such temptations of Satan!'

6. And if, after doing this three times in succession, it still did not help, we ran to the church. If there, too, we were unable to find help, we castigated our flesh till we drew blood, or we put on the girdle of penance. If all that still did not help, then the confessor had to apply means of exorcism, which, however, could only be used successfully with our younger sisters. We older ones had to have cold baths, or even, sometimes, blood-letting.

7. You see, dear friend, how severe our lives were. Many a watch-dog would not have envied us.

8. We surely were justified in expecting celestial joys for all these hardships and, considering the watch-dog existence we had on earth, surely that would not be asking too much? So we were absolutely convinced that the celestial joys would be ours, as has been promised to all who, for Christ's sake, leave all they have in the

world and choose the narrow, thorny path of the cross for the sake of celestial glory.

9. But just look at the celestial glory we did attain! Don't we look like old hags with our dark grey complexions and our dirty rags? Our figures are like those of mummies, and we are hungry like sharks and thirsty like the Sahara. This is now our heaven for which we hoped with such certainty! What notion is one to get of such a divine justice?

10. On my arrival here from earth, I saw a bad woman — nothing but a harlot. She was carried away to heaven by shining angels — the beast! But not a cat has come to see me so far, much less an angelic being from heaven! Is that justice? Oh, what misery, what misery!

11. I brought many an honest girl, young, rich and beautiful, to my order, but they now curse me for having deceived them. What a bother! For my zeal I may now be called to account by the Eternal Judge!"

12. Here, several younger Sisters of Charity step forward and shout: "Yes, yes, it is all your fault, you old slut, you beast! You did everything to induce us to join your charitable riff-raff order! And when we did not want to take the vows, since we realized we had better chances in the world than in your brothel, you did everything in your power to prevent our withdrawal.

13. And when, eventually, we were coerced into taking the vows in a similar frame of mind to that one of an army recruit, having to swear allegiance, namely: 'You must, or the devil will get you!' — we were treated worse than the poorest of souls in purgatory or even in hell. And we were severely threatened not to let our dear parents know how shamefully we were treated. Only in the confessional to the father confessor were we permitted to complain, because he had to be silent about it anyway.

14. Now we demand the promised heaven from you to which we are more entitled than you are! Where is it? Take us there, or we shall lay violent hands upon you!"

15. The first nun throws herself at Bishop Martin's feet, entreating him to help her.

60

BISHOP MARTIN AS PEACEMAKER. — THE SANCTIMONIOUS FOLLIES OF THE TEACHING SISTERS AND THEIR CONSEQUENCES IN THE BEYOND. — MARTIN'S ADMONITION.

1. (Bishop Martin): "Listen, all you dear sisters, let the Lord Jesus decide this for you. He alone is a just judge! But you forgive each other from all your heart and everything will be all right. This house of mine is a house of peace and love, and not a house of vengeance! Therefore, do compose yourselves and be happy that you have found such good shelter here with me — doubtlessly only thanks to the Lord's compassion. If you manage to change your hatred into love, your appearance is sure to improve considerably.

2. In the world, many walk the wrong path of virtue; why should you have been an exception? Although you did much, it was not done for the sake of the Lord, but only for the sake of heaven. That is not according to the Gospel! You have to do everything in your power and then you shall say: 'Lord, behold, I was an idle servant! O Lord, have mercy upon Your most idle servant!' If you, my dear sisters, will adopt this attitude and not judge or condemn each other, you will surely find favor in the eyes of God.

3. Don't you know what the wise teacher, Paul, says who considers himself only a bad, idle servant, who regards his work as of little merit and only the grace of God essential? He says that a man is not justified by his deeds, but solely by the grace of the Lord. Take this to heart and put your imagined merits at the feet of the Lord. Admit the futility of all that until now you considered your justification for eternal life, then the grace of God will soon become evident to you.

4. I was a bishop in the world, and was convinced that upon my arrival in the beyond heavenly hosts would come to meet me. However, things worked out in quite a different way. So far, I have not yet seen the actual heaven, although I have talked to the Lord on many occasions and have received this house directly from His most holy hands. How do you think you could already be crowned with all glory? Only with patience, meekness, love, and good cheer will everything come right!"

5. The Sisters of Charity are quite appeased and step back, and

Bishop Martin calls the Teaching Sisters, who were just on the point of starting a fight, and he asks them how they came to be in such distress and where they had been living on earth.

6. (One of the Teaching Sisters): "Oh, dearest, highly esteemed and honorable friend, we are not all from one place, but come from France, Switzerland, Wales, and various parts of Australia.

7. We lived most devoted lives. We prayed at least fourteen times each day, for not less than a quarter of an hour; every day we attended holy mass and evensong. On Sundays and holidays we attended at least three masses, a sermon, the afternoon litany, and both benedictions. We went to confession every week, at least three times during Advent and Lent, and received the most holy sacrament daily. We fasted five times a week in honor of the holy five wounds, and on Fridays, in honor of the Blessed Virgin Mary, we gave ourselves seven smart-lashes with a rope or rod, four on the left and three on the right breast.

8. The remainder of the time we used for meditation and the teaching of young girls, in whose hearts we endeavored to promote the desire — if financially feasible — to follow in our footsteps as early as possible, laying all their earthly heritage at God's feet so that they might become pure and worthy brides of Jesus Christ.

9. We were not allowed on the streets unveiled and were strictly prohibited to look at a profane man, not even a priest, but only a holy brother from the Order of St. Francis, a holy Jesuit, a bishop, or maybe also a very pious canon. If we then had any unchaste thoughts, we immediately told the worthy Mother about it, asking her for most severe punishment to rid our chaste hearts of such infernal spook.

10. The worthy Mother, who was extremely holy, gave us her good advice first, and only then the appropriate punishment, dependent on the severity of the unchaste thoughts. For a very small thought, there was one lash on the naked body, three rosaries and a total fast day. For a larger sinful thought, there were seven sharp lashes, until blood was drawn, then twelve rosaries and three total fast days during the week. For a very sinful thought — maybe even about the damnable marriage state as it now exists — there were fifteen lashes with pointed rods, thirty rosaries, nine total fast days over a period of three weeks, and a sharp-pointed cilicium (girdle of penance) over the naked breast or the thighs.

11. In addition to the penance ordered by the dear, worthy

Mother, there were the spiritual penances which were often much worse. We had to get up in the middle of the night and take part in prayers. This was particularly hard in winter, and if we fell ill following these cruel hardships, we were not even allowed to wish for recovery, but only for death, in order to do penance for our sins. These, and other most cruel kinds of self-abnegation, were demanded of us. From this brief but true description, you can see what terribly hard lives we led on earth.

12. Thus we suffered a lot for Christ, usually most patiently, and we obeyed the strict rules of our order without complaint. We signed over to the order all our property, for the good of the order, for the glory of the Blessed Virgin Mary, and for the glory of God. In view of this, we did not think that it was asking too much of God for Him to bestow on us eternal bliss immediately upon our bitter death . However, we not only saw our well-founded hopes melt away like froth, but we also had the following experience.

13. When all of us who are here now arrived almost simultaneously in this spirit world, we were told by some peasants where we were, and we noticed some miserable females, well-known to us, who had also arrived when we did in this spirit world. Of course, we expected a crowd of devils to meet these loose, bad, heretic female souls, in order to draw them into hell as was deserved by them.

14. However, we were amazed to see not devils, but angels descend from heaven, who arrayed these bad, sinful souls in true celestial garments. They gave them shining palm branches and carried them straight up into heaven, without paying any attention whatsoever to us. We cried, we prayed for what seemed to us millions of years, and we implored Mary and God through all His saints and elect — but so far our cries have been in vain. Isn't that just too bad? Haven't we been deceived, in the temporal as well as in the eternal life? Can that be called divine justice?"

15. (Bishop Martin): "Do have some patience! For the time being, you are provided for. And even if your position were not to improve ever, your life now is quite bearable. Do not count too much on your merit! How could you be so stupid in the world to put up with confinement and beatings, and practically allow them to kill you? What good did you do your fellowmen by suffering all that? You were only concerned with saving your own skin and would not have cared if God had condemned all the world, as long as you had won heaven.

158

16. This type of love of your neighbor is of no help whatsoever in this world. Therefore, be patient! Forget about your merit! Consider yourselves bad, idle servants of the Lord, and you, too, will find favor with Him. Step back now and let me see the Ladies of the Sacred Heart."

61

THE LADIES OF THE SACRED HEART SPEAK. – THEIR PHYSICAL ERRORS AND MENTAL FOOLISHNESS. – MARTIN TRIES TO SET THEM RIGHT AND REPRIMANDS THEM.

1. The Teaching Sisters withdraw, grumbling among themselves, and the Ladies of the Sacred Heart step forward and speak as follows: "Your Reverance, we are ladies of the foremost ladies' order in the world, which admits only daughters of the very rich, distinguished and noble families, where they can learn everything that there is to be learned in the world!"

2. (Bishop Martin, to himself): "What a beginning! Just what the Lord wants most to hear! Or does He?"

3. (Ladies of the Sacred Heart): "We learned all the languages, music, dancing, gymnastics, fencing, sometimes also horseback riding; also drawing, painting, and artistic needlework. Besides, of course, all the sciences were taught, like geography, mathematics, physics, astronomy, history, the art of navigation, hydraulics, geometry, trigonometry, stereometry, poetry in the noblest European languages, and a lot of other useful subjects.

4. In short, in our order, all the sciences of the world are taught, all the arts are practiced — naturally, only where required and paid for. The remainder of the time is spent in praying, singing, sometimes also fasting, with a daily mass and confession, and communion three times a week. There is severe penance for offending against the strict rules of the order, and this is observed almost more strictly than the rules themselves."

5. (Bishop Martin, to himself): "Although I was a bishop myself, I have never been able to look behind the secrets of this order to the extent I am now doing! Ah, how that place must have pleased the Lord!"

6. (The Ladies:) "You dear, right reverend friend may see from all this —"

7. (Bishop Martin to himself: "that you are utterly silly geese!")

8. (The Ladies:) „what severe rules our order has and what greatness —"

9. (Bishop Martin to himself: „In folly")

10. (The Ladies:) "in self-abnegation it requires to conscientiously observe all these most severe rules; only real giants —"

11. (Bishop Martin to himself: „of fools")

12. (The Ladies:) "of mental power are capable of adhering to all these strict rules. But we did it most scrupulously like true heroines of heaven, convinced that heaven was assured to us!"

13. (Bishop Martin to himself: "This does require a very strong faith!")

14. (The Ladies): "However, after some millions of earth years, you now find us quite as miserable as when we first arrived here. Your house is the first thing of beauty we have encountered within this world. Say, is this divine justice?"

15. (Bishop Martin, to himself): "More than anywhere else here with you, you silly geese!"

16. (The Ladies): "When we were knocking at a door, above which were the words: 'Gate to Heaven,' instead of being admitted to a well-deserved heaven, a coarse and ill-bred-looking peasant lout said to us: 'Back with you, you foolish virgins! Why did you not fill your lamps with oil beforehand?' "

17. (Bishop Martin, to himself): "Fair enough! Such guests I would almost be entitled to drive from my house!"

18. (The Ladies): "Then, this gate to heaven vanished, and we were suddenly surrounded by numerous small devils, like a crowd of will-o'-the-wisps, frisking around us and teasing us cruelly for an endlessly long time, until quite recently we met the other party in the course of our endless flight.

19. Dearest, most reverend friend, what do you say to all this? What could we do to perhaps improve our condition? Oh, do help us with your advice!"

20. (Bishop Martin, ironically): "Ah, ah, but there the Lord has wronged you badly, since you have lived in strict accordance with the Gospel. Really, I must say that the Lord Jehovah Jesus is most unjust if He has promised you heaven on the strictly evangelical rules of your order, and then does not want to grant it. That is really not

nice of Him to withhold heaven from such gentle and still super-clever dears! Unless — maybe — you secretly committed sodomy? Or did you perhaps, among your order's thousand clever rules, neglect the Christian rule of the love of your neighbor?"

21. (Another lady, pretending to be French, explains in a ridiculously affected language, interspersed with French words, that they had nothing to do with sodomy, but practiced love of their neighbor, and were religious and chaste like flowers. What else could the Lord Jesus Christ want of them?)

22. (Bishop Martin): "For heaven's sake, stop this silly language! You are German! Can't you speak your own language instead of pretending to be what you are not? Do you believe that you will ever get to heaven this way? A silly goose like you will have to wait an extra long time for that! Even spirits from other planets have spoken to me in my language! Your predecessor, who was born in Lyons, addressed me in good German, and you, conceited goose, are pretending to be unable to speak it!"

23. (The Lady): "Oh friend, I did it only to impress you!"

24. (Bishop Martin): "What a silly notion! Just like the one that makes you expect heaven from God for your utter foolishness. Do you think the Lord prepared heaven for foolish geese like you? Oh, there you are quite wrong! Believe me, it will be easier for all the asses and oxen to enter heaven than it will be for you! This you must understand! Withdraw to the farthest corner and teach yourselves humility! Only then may you come and ask whether there might be some dairy-maid's job available for you in the lowest of heavens, which, however, I very much doubt! Go now where I directed you!"

62

DISCUSSION BETWEEN A JESUIT AND BISHOP MARTIN. — ADVICE TO A SISTER OF CHARITY WHO IS AFRAID OF HELL.

1. (A Jesuit steps forward and says): "Noble friend, you do not appear to think much of arts and sciences, considering your dislike of the worthy Ladies of the Sacred Heart. They are the only female

order that indulges in sciences and arts from early morning till late at night, and, consequently, they come closest to our order of the Society of Jesus. Dear brother and friend, you should really treat these ladies with more respect and love."

2. (Bishop Martin): "Why should I treat those silly, conceited females with more respect? I have shown them too much respect already! Actually, they should be sent packing for another million years until they forget their foreign languages, which might do them a lot of good.

3. As I look at them now, I see rage and arrogance in their eyes. They would very much like to dissemble, but that is impossible in the spirit world, and especially such loose spirits are soon seen through and recognized for what they really are. Because I do see through them and find their great folly sickening, I sent them to that distant corner to get rid of their annoying sight.

4. You yourself, and all the others of your silly order, should not take pride in your most unsuitable name. Think it over and tell me what gives you the right to call yourselves Jesuits? Who has given you permission to desecrate that divine name? You will then perhaps understand how shamefully you all have misused this holiest of names and in what way you could atone for this sacrilege.

5. Can any one of you say, 'Jesus, the Lord has appointed us like He did Paul and Peter'? Has any one of you ever seen Jesus or talked to Him, or have you, during your life on earth, thought more highly of the Gospel than of Ignatius of Loyola? You were, in fact, most determined adversaries of Jesus Christ, but still you call yourselves 'Jesu-its'!"

6. (The Jesuit): "Dearest friend, you obviously know little or nothing about this matter. Don't you know what *Omnia ad majorem dei gloriam* (Everything for the greater glory of God) means? On this our name is founded. It is not as if the Lord Jesus Himself appointed us, but we chose this name for His greater glory. I am quite aware that the means as such is not commendable, but that does not matter as long as the end justifies the means."

7. (Bishop Martin): "You also speak like a fool and judge divine things like a blind man might judge colors. Do you think the Great God, Who is forever glorified by countless myriads of unheard-of wonders through the whole of infinity — wonders so sublime and incomprehensible in their divine beauty that their sight would kill you — might gain anything at all in His glory if you call yourself im-

properly 'Jesuit' for His sake, or if you endeavored to achieve seemingly good ends through a thousand different, sometimes most disgraceful, means?

8. Do you believe that Jesus through some monk instituted the shameful Inquisition for His greater glory? Or do you think that Jesus looks favorably upon *autodafés* and other abominations of yours, performed for His greater glory, with quite another, secret, disgraceful end in mind?

9. Or do you think that the Lord Jesus looked favorably on your actions when you made a girl pregnant and then, *ad majorem dei gloriam* had her immured alive in a crypt? Or if, for the greater glory of God, by the foulest of means, you took possession of the property of a thousand widows and orphans, and afterwards showed no pity when you saw them languish in great misery?

10. Do you seriously believe this could be for the greater glory of God, and that the Lord Jesus would look favorably on such a way of glorifying His name? If you really believe this, you are the most pitiful creature in the whole of God's infinity!

11. What would you say if Jesus, the sole eternal Lord and God of heaven and the endless myriads of worlds, would stand here before you and ask how you and all your followers have handled His Word? And who has entitled you to desecrate His most holy name so abominably? What would you, all of you, reply to the almighty, eternal God?"

12. They are all obviously seized with terror, resulting in a benumbed apathy. No one dares say a word to Bishop Martin, for they now take him for an Angel of Judgment.

13. (Only one, a Sister of Charity, approaches Bishop Martin fearfully, and says): "O angel, judging us in the name of God, do not condemn us to hell, but we are quite willing in the name of God to be sent to purgatory. Oh, oh, what a terribly severe judge you are! Do have some pity with us poor sinners!"

14. (Bishop Martin): "Compose yourself, you foolish Sister of Charity! I am no judge, only a poor sinner myself, hoping for the Lord's mercy. However, God be thanked, I now see my great folly and want to show you yours, to help rid yourselves of it and become what the eternal order of the Lord wants you to be. Otherwise, instead of proceeding toward ever-increasing bliss, your misery will keep growing worse all the time.

15. My willingness not to send you away but instead take you

all in and keep you here if you want to stay, proves that I am not judging you. But if you do stay, you must not hold on to your follies, but accept advice from one who has been here much longer and who has surely more experience than you newcomers to this world. Now, calm yourselves and ponder on my words!"

63

BISHOP MARTIN'S DISCUSSION WITH TWO OTHER JESUITS AND TWO LIGUORISTS.

1. (Two other Jesuits and two Liguorists go up to Bishop Martin and say): "Dearest and best friend, we quite agree with the advice you have given to all of us. As matters now have turned out, we have no complaints, and if we could find some minor occupation, we would be quite pleased with our lot and not want for anything better for the whole of eternity. However, if we have to spend eternity without anything to do, we would prefer total extinction to an inactive life."

2. (Bishop Martin): "Friends, can you read what is written on this round, white tablet?"

3. (One of the four says): "Oh yes, it is something quite ominous: *Dies irae, dies illa!* (Day of the wrath, that day!). *Libera nos ab omni malo!* (Deliver us from all evil!). *Memento, homo, quia pulvis es et in pulverem reverteris!* (Remember, man, that you are dust and shall revert to dust!). *Requiescant in pace!* (May they rest in peace!). *Requiem aeternam dona eis, domine, et lux perpetua luceat eis!* (Give them, Lord, eternal rest and may the eternal light shine for them!). *Ex profundis clamavi!* (I cried from the depth!). *Clamor meus ad te veniat!* (May my cries reach You!). *Vitam aeternam dona eis, domine, et sedere in sino Abrahami, et considere ad mensam illius, et comedere cum illo per omnia secula seculorum, amen!* (Give them eternal life, Lord, a place in the lap of Abraham, let them sit at his table and dine with him through all eternities, Amen!).

4. As you see, I can still read, although I feel it to be thousands of millions of years since I have seen any letters. But tell me, what about these old dogmatic phrases? Could it be that they are applied

here in the spirit world? If so, our prospects for the whole, long eternity are not too good! O friend, do tell us how we have to understand this!"

5. (Bishop Martin): "How else should this be understood than as it is written? I assure you, these phrases have no other meaning than what they clearly say with their words. Tell me, have you ever, in the world, put another meaning into these exclamations than the one expressed through their words? If you were satisfied with them in the world, where they brought in money for you and a hidden mental authority, why should they worry you now, when their meaning is practically applied to you? What do you want an occupation for? *Requiescant in pace; ergo requiescamus!* (May they rest in peace; therefore, let us rest!). This rest in eternal peace you have now found — all of you!

6. There is also light here, continuously shining through the nice large windows. My house is like the lap of Abraham, and the large cupboard over there, filled with good bread and wine, is a true table of Abraham, at which all of us will be dining until the Day of Judgment and, if on that day of wrath you will not be condemned, even after it forever. What more do you want?"

7. (One of the Liguorists): "You are right, friend. That is probably what we have to expect. But I still feel that this will be terribly boring. Just imagine, to be forever idle, without having to expect any change! Really, friend, think of the boredom in some decillions of earth years! Oh Lord, no living being would be able to stand that!"

8. (Bishop Martin): "Yes, but what is the use of all your reasoning? Don't you know that it is written that everyone will live according to his belief? Why did we believe all this nonsense if, when it is realized, we do not relish it?

9. If we were stubborn asses in the world, we must now be satisfied with the realization of our foolish beliefs, whether we like it or not. If in the world we had adopted a wiser belief, things would no doubt be much better for us here. But all of us — and I am no exception — were only too happy in the world if we could spread more darkness. Therefore, it should not worry us if here we are buried in our own folly like in a would-be lap of Abraham.

10. Is not the world full of old asses, oxen and blockheads, who are always babbling of enlightenment? Even if they are given enlightenment and better mental food, they ignore it, stay with their old folly, feed on their same old food, and let their eyes feast on

the twilight of their cattle-shed, where they can ruminate the foul contents of their mental stomachs.

11. We, too, were such asses, oxen and blockheads! Therefore, we should not be surprised if the Lord provides most generously for our old bestial natures. Those who used to be pleased by folly, let them stay with what pleases them! Those who enjoyed sleep, may sleep here to their heart's content! Those who liked idleness, let them rest here forever! For those who enjoyed food and drink, there is Abraham's table! Those who liked to occupy themselves with virgins, here have the Sisters of Charity, the Teaching Sisters, and the Ladies of the Sacred Heart! We have everything we need — what are we complaining about?"

12. (They all shrug their shoulders, saying): "You are, of course, right — but our wisdom be damned! We would probably be better off if we could live on earth again as frogs, and croak to our heart's content! But this situation cannot be helped now!"

64

HONEST CONFESSION OF THE MINORITE. — ROME AS THE CULPRIT. — BEGINNING COMPREHENSION AND BETTERMENT OF THE MINORITES.

1. (A Minorite comes forward and says): "Friends, let me say a few words which, should it turn out that they are of no use, might at least help to pass a little bit of time of the eternal rest ahead of us!"

2. (All the spirits): "Very well! We shall be happy to listen to you. Already in the world you were known as a wise, ingratiating orator. Go ahead, and speak as much as you want to!"

3. (The Minorite): "Brothers and friends, in the world all of us had in a way two gospels. On the one hand there was the ancient one by Christ, the Lord, and some of His disciples, and then there was the one of the Roman Catholic Church, claiming to be the only true church, since it believed, and still believes, to have inherited the Holy See from Peter, and to hold the keys for heaven as well as for hell.

4. We took an oath to be faithful to this church to the end of

our days and to believe all it demanded of us — to believe irrespective of whether it was written in the Bible or not! We also vowed to consider everyone a heretic who thought or believed differently, and to condemn him.

5. We kept our oath in all detail, even if sometimes against our better judgment or plain common sense.

6. You are all aware of the fact that we were forbidden by the church to read the Bible, which was considered a deathly sin, except on Sundays, and then only the much condensed Gospels. All the rest only the theologians were allowed to read and comprehend. Instead, there were for us the Church Fathers, the breviary, the legends; also the rules of the order, Ignatius of Loyola, the relics, the images, the masses, the sacraments, the confession, and other things, many of which we can now openly condemn as evil follies.

7. Now we must ask: Can we be blamed for acting contrary to the true Gospel of Christ through the ordinance of the Roman Church, which must have been at least allowed by God? In accordance with all human, and surely also divine, justice, the real culprit must be made responsible. And we should be advised as to what attitude to adopt for our eternal future, and how we can make amends for what we ourselves may have done wrong."

8. (Say the others): "Well said! We have really enjoyed your speech! May the culprit be made responsible! The Holy See should be punished, and everyone who forced us into actions without giving us time to think it over, comprehend what we were doing, and consent to it, or otherwise!

9. We were baptized without our consent, and through this premature baptism, we were forced into the Roman creed, thus making the child in the womb already responsible. Or is it not crazy to have a newborn child, through certain representatives, swear an oath of allegiance without taking into consideration that the child, when grown up, may disagree with this vow, and, consequently, be forced into perjury? Is not that totally antichristian?

10. Christ Himself said that he who believed and was baptized would attain salvation. But how can a person be baptized before he has comprehended and accepted the Christian faith? Is not baptism meant to be a living demonstration that somebody has accepted the Christian faith for his sole guiding principle in life? And what does a new-born child know about faith, the Christian faith? The more you think about it, the more you realize the folly of it.

167

11.   It is maintained that, as a result of baptism, remission of the original sin, as well as all sins committed prior to baptism, is obtained. How utterly foolish that is! Can any intelligent person condemn a child because his parents committed an understandable offense? And God, Whose wisdom is supreme, should keep holding children of more than the thousandth generation responsible for Adam's fall? And as to any sins committed prior to baptism — that is quite ridiculous since a child cannot possibly sin in its mother's womb!

12.   And what sins could a heathen have who has only just been converted to Christianity, which in itself is heathenish enough? His would have to be sins against his pagan laws for, not having comprehended Christian laws, he could not really offend against them. And the remission of a heathen's heathenish sins would only mean confirmation of his paganism. The same would apply to a Jew, for to forgive a Jew in baptism for being a Jew for so long, would be the acme of foolishness!"

13. (The Minorite): "Friends, I fully agree with you! This Roman way of making Christians already in the womb really reminds me now of those ancient fairy tales about people selling themselves to the devil. For the vilest reasons of policy, one is practically sold to the devil already in one's mother's womb, and becomes his prisoner through Rome! And this antichristian, so-called 'First Christian Church' even calls itself the 'Mother Church', and its head 'Vicar of Christ'; consequently, vicar of God!

14.   How peculiar — and still true — that we were all so wrong and did not even notice it that almost from our birth we were more or less of the devil! Baptism should have freed us from the silly original sin to make us children of God. And nice children of God we have been! Instead of away from hell, we were literally baptized into hell!

15.   And to make sure that no one ever truly repented and thought of betterment, auricular confession was invented appeasing all deathly sins, entitling us priests to total absolution. Hereby every sinner was thrown back into his own sink of iniquity, making it impossible for him ever to become a new creature in Christ.

16.   O brothers, brothers, that God allowed these things to happen will forever remain an unsolvable riddle for us! 'Be ye therefore perfect, even as your Father which is in heaven is perfect.' Fine perfection, indeed, when one had to be a stupid blockhead and is

only now, as a spirit, beginning to realize, thanks to the heavenly light, in what error one has lived in the world.

17. We could say a lot more about this and prove without any doubt that the Holy See is the culprit, fully responsible for all our errors. However, what we, at this stage, understand only partly, the Lord Himself sees clearly in the brightest light, and He will have mercy upon us if we forgive from all our heart all those who were, and are still, responsible for all our darkness. That is how I feel about it. What is your opinion?"

18. All the others, with the exception of a few Jesuits, fully agree with the speaker.

65

BISHOP MARTIN ENLIGHTENS THE SPIRITUALLY BLIND JESUITS.

1. Now Bishop Martin takes the Jesuits in hand as they keep scratching their heads and shrugging their shoulders, and he addresses them most bluntly:

2. "Why do you disapprove? Do you know more about these things than your quite sensible companions? I doubt it! But I do know what you are up to and why you have misgivings, and I shall tell you what it is that is still covering your eyes with Moses' three-fold cover.

3. Firstly, there is your original obstinacy, still ruling over your minds and preventing any purer light from entering your hearts. Then there is your false belief that nothing but baptism is needed to be a Christian. The moment somebody has been baptized in the name of the Father, the Son, and the Holy Ghost, according to your erroneous belief, a Christian is ready-made. And finally, in your arrogance and lust for power, you still imagine yourselves to be the Lord's true disciples, filled with the Holy Ghost, and equipped with all power by Him to do as you please.

4. Oh, you fools! Whereby can you prove this? Where in the Scriptures is there a text that justifies your folly? Do you believe the Lord has spoken to you antichristians what He has spoken to Peter and His other disciples when He sent them out to preach the Gospel

to all nations? It says: 'Receive ye the Holy Ghost: Whatsoever thou shalt bind or loose on earth shall be bound or loosed in heaven.'

5. Have you ever been in possession of this Holy Ghost? Can the Holy Ghost ever contradict Itself or change an eternal law? Or can It grow wiser and realize that Its original laws are imperfect and have to be superseded by better ones?

6. Did not the Holy Ghost know at the time of the disciples that at a later time various types of monks would be needed to bring men to heaven? That it would need images, relics, shrines, bells, fonts, incense, vestments, cowls, churches, monasteries, chalices, monstrances, Latin-using ministrants, and a thousand other follies to attain heaven? How blind the Holy Ghost must have been that It did not realize already at the time of the disciples how essential all this was for man's salvation and did not institute it right away!

7. Or would the first Christians, including Peter and Paul, have really been of the devil because they had no churches, bells, Latin masses, requiem, or miraculous images — not even any confession, extreme unction, passing bell, pall, tapers, and so on?

8. Do you really not see the folly of it? Due to our greed and lust for power, and without the least evangelical authority, and contrary to the Word of God and the teachings of the disciples, we created, so to speak, acts of worship, laws, and ceremonies. Don't you understand that this made us sinners against the Holy Ghost — which sins, it is written, will not be forgiven, neither on earth nor in the beyond?

9. If you would for once just superficially compare the pure Word of the Lord with our Roman Catholic nonsense, your eyes would be opened and you would see clearly that Rome is nothing else but Babylon, the mother of harlots, as described in the Revelation and, consequently, we, her priests, are not little angels, but devils in the truest sense of the word.

10. Therefore, dear brothers and sisters, let go all your mundane nonsense, and turn together with me to the one God and Lord, Jesus Christ; and all of you will find salvation!

11. But understand this: Not my poor, though well-meant, advice must determine your decision, but only your own will and the call of your heart !"

12. Now they all agree with Bishop Martin, except the Ladies of the Sacred Heart, who say: "We are not going to accept any new teaching from you which could land us in hell, but we'll remain

170

faithful to our Roman Mother, until God Himself, or at least the blessed Virgin Mary, tells us what to do."

13. (Bishop Martin): "No doubt, you ninnies, the Lord will give you preferential treatment! If you do not want to make the Gospel your guiding principle in eternity, you may stick to your folly forever feeding on the fat of your beloved Roman Mother! And the Lord's wisdom will see to it that you do not get too fat, nor too beautiful! For He has quite an effective superhomeopathic diet for such foolish spirits, which may last for a small eternity, as I know from experience.

14. So let us leave these foolish ladies to their belief and, in the name of the Lord, turn ourselves towards a better light!"

66

EXPANSION OF HEART AND HOUSE. -- THE LORD CALLS BISHOP MARTIN.

1. (Asks the Minorite): "Where is your better light, brother? Whither will you lead us that we might behold it?"

2. (Bishop Martin): "Follow me to the center of this hall, where you will see a truly divine and artistic tellurian and astronomical mechanism. There we shall first have a close look at our earth and then go on to the other planets and, finally, the sun. You will be seeing many things that so far have been riddles to all of you. So, let us go!"

3. They all move to the designated spot, around which they form a close circle. Even the Ladies of the Sacred Heart follow the others furtively to see what is going on and what the better light, referred to by Bishop Martin, will be like.

4. (Bishop Martin notices them and says aloud): "Why are you clever ladies slinking behind like secret agents in the world? There must be no slinking here! If you want to turn to the better light together with us, your brothers and sisters, do it openly and gladly, as we do. Furtive slinking and spying is not tolerated here!"

5. (Hearing this, the Ladies of the Sacred Heart say): "Friend, do not be angry with us! You know that we are foolish and weak and may be misled, as probably you yourself were at the time you entered this world, not taking everything for granted that you were told. Therefore, we beg you to have patience with us. We did not

171

complain when you called us names, and you cannot hold it against us too much if we stand up for our order. Dear friend, you have treated us most harshly, but we suffered it with very little grumbling. We do beg you now to forgive us and not be quite so harsh with us poor sinners."

6. (Bishop Martin): "Ah, this is a much better language than your French. Since you have adopted this attitude, you are now welcome to join us here and see for yourselves what is already here, and what is still going to happen."

7. Now the ladies come forward and are astonished at the sight of the great artistic mechanism. The Jesuits, standing around the earth globe, are most impressed, seeing how true to life this globe has been made and how not the least detail from the real earth is missing. The Minorites and Liguorists are quite as impressed by this globe, whilst the Franciscans are admiring the solar system and the brilliance of the sun which is illuminating all the planets. The Sisters of Charity and the Teaching Sisters are above all impressed by the sun. Everybody is admiring the mechanism and Bishop Martin is eagerly explaining all these celestial curiosities, occasionally making sarcastic remarks about appearances on earth.

8. After this large crowd has spent considerable time with the earth and planet-mechanism, listening to Bishop Martin's explanations, the hall suddenly becomes much brighter, and to the bishop it now appears much larger than before in the temperate light. The others have also noticed it and ask the bishop where the light has come from and what has caused the expansion of the hall.

9. (Bishop Martin): "My dear friends, brothers and sisters, there is nothing strange about this, for here everything keeps changing from its initial type and shape. When you arrived here, did you not notice how small the house looked from the outside, and how large it was inside? Surely that is miraculous, and so is this present manifestation which, incomprehensible as it is to us, is easy enough for the Lord to bring about.

10. I think it means that since you have all become somewhat more enlightened, the Lord is granting us more light. And as our concepts of Him have widened, the Lord has enlarged this safe dwelling so that it may provide ample space for all of us. In this miraculous world, such manifestations are not at all unusual. Here, the Lord's omnipotence, love, and wisdom direct everything depending on the maturity of our hearts.

172

11. But I now see a new, brilliantly shining writing on the round tablet. I have to go and look at what it says!" Bishop Martin goes to the tablet and reads: "Martin, come outside, for I have something important to settle with you. Meanwhile, let the party keep quiet. Come now! So be it!" Bishop Martin, happily gives the others instructions, with which they comply, and then he is ready to follow the call on the tablet.

CHANGE IN THE GARDEN. — BOREM AS GARDENER.

1. Walking through the door of his house, Bishop Martin notices that the garden has expanded considerably and is in a state of full bloom. This makes him very happy. But his bliss is greatly increased by the sight of the Lord's dwelling nearby, towards the east. However, when he looks in all directions, he cannot see anybody awaiting him. This puzzles him, but this time he does not get discouraged nor impatient, but goes into the garden to look for Me, thinking I might be hiding there so as not to be seen by the crowd through some window.

2. (Bishop Martin searches the garden, and when he cannot find Me, says to himself): "This looks to me like a little celestial teasing! But I don't mind; the main thing is that I do my duty. May the Lord Himself, or His deputy, do whatever He pleases, I don't care. Of course, I could go to His house, but then I have not been asked to do so, for the writing on the tablet said: 'Martin, come outside, for I have something important to settle with you.' Now I am outside, and have done my part. If the Lord has called me outside for nothing, that is not my business. I, at least, am here."

3. After these reflections, Bishop Martin strolls about in the big garden until he notices at the far end a gardener planting a number of young trees. Getting closer to the gardener, he recognizes the bookseller, Borem, and says joyfully: " Brother, friend, I have felt deep remorse for having been so rude and unkind to you! Do forgive me and be forever my inseparable guide! For I now fully understand how much I have wronged you and especially how much I have sinned against the kindness of the Lord."

4. (Borem turns around and greets the bishop with these friendly words): "I greet you, my dear brother Martin! It has pleased the Lord very much that you have done good spontaneously. Therefore, the Lord sent me here to tidy up and enlarge your garden, just as you have put your heart in order and expanded it considerably in its love. If you go on working like this in the name of the Lord, you'll advance your spiritual rebirth at a rapid pace.

5. Since you desire it in your heart, I shall now stay with you and help you whenever it is necessary. You have in your house a great task ahead of you which is still going to give a lot of trouble. However, when the fight will have reached its climax, glorious victory will be near.

6. I have now finished with the planting of the young trees. So let us go to those who need our help. They have already been well cultivated by you, similar to this garden, but it will take quite a lot more work before the thousand young trees will be ready to produce fully ripened fruit.

7. Love and patience overcome all difficulties. Therefore, let us now go into the house and begin with our good work in the name of the Lord." Borem and Martin both enter the house.

BOREM'S ENLIGHTENING WORDS ABOUT THE WAY TO BEATITUDE.

1. In the house, one of the Minorites, who already, on a previous occasion, had spoken quite sensibly, comes to meet them, and asks Bishop Martin: "Dear friend and brother, what was there outside that made you rush out like that? We have all been extremely worried, thinking you might have been called to account for us and that something bad might have befallen you. Do tell us — what happened?"

2. (Bishop Martin, smiling): "Dear friends and brothers, do not worry about me. Look here, the Lord has sent me this dear friend and brother for yours and my own sake, to help me guide all of you onto the right path. This is the sole reason why I was called outside.

3. All of you should listen to this friend of the Lord, and follow his advice at all times; then your lot, and maybe mine too, will soon improve quite considerably. For I, too, am still far from being a blessed spirit, but only on the way towards attainment of complete beatitude through the grace of the Lord.

4. Keep striving for this grace, all of you, and it may come to pass that we all may enter upon the path to the realm of Divine Light together."

5. (The Minorite): "Yes, brother, we promise you and your friend to adhere strictly to all the instructions you give us, in order to attain at least a little of the Lord's grace."

6. (Borem): "Yes, dear brothers and sisters, keep to this promise from the bottom of your hearts. Love Jesus Christ, the Crucified, above all else, for He is our one most loving and holy Father. Keep seeking only Him and His love and do not attach your hearts to anything but Him, and you will find yourselves, much sooner than you expected, in the house of His eternal love. But you have to banish from your hearts any material, worldly appendages; otherwise, it would not be possible for you to enter the eternal dwelling of the Most Holy Father. Now, listen carefully to what I am going to tell you.

7. In the world, all of you had two different, but fundamentally false, concepts of God, heaven, and the soul's state and life after physical death. Here, you have already been able to convince yourselves that your earthly belief has not confirmed itself in anything at all. You did not find a purgatory, nor a hell, nor a heaven with winged angels. And, just the same as you did not find all this, you will never find any of the other things you believed in as Roman Catholics.

8. Thus, the prayer aids of your churches and priests, in whom you trusted so implicitly, are of no value whatsoever. Here, no one can come to the Lord through mediated mercy, as the Lord is of the greatest mercy anyhow, and to want to induce the most merciful and loving Father to have mercy, would amount to great and wicked folly.

9. Therefore, to get to God, the Lord of everlasting, unending splendor, everyone here must do his own work. Behold, I am now a great angel of the Lord, and He never calls me other than: 'My brother, how very much I love you!' If I interceded for you for an eternity, it would not make any difference, as everyone must act out

of his own love according to his strength, or he could never attain to true spiritual freedom. God is, of course, omnipotent, but His omnipotence does not make anybody free; on the contrary, we must be freed from it through our free will and our love of God. Otherwise, we would be but machines and automatons of God's omnipotence.

10. This is the reason why God, in His infinite wisdom, has designed ways by which we can attain to this divine freedom. These ways are so far unknown to you, but I shall acquaint you with them. Therefore, be careful to stay on these ways of your own free will and you will reach the destination of every spirit created by God.

11. From now on, you will be allowed every imaginable freedom. You will obtain whatever you wish for. However, this will not be real freedom, but only a test, which must be understood but not misused.

12. Thousands of Eves will proffer you the apple of temptation, but for love of the Lord you may not touch it.

13. You will be defamed and scoffed at, but must never get angry or think of retaliation.

14. You will be persecuted, robbed, and even ill-treated, but your sole defense may be love, although you will have plenty of means of revenge at your disposal.

15. Always keep in mind the Lord and His Gospel and you will lay a strong, unshakeable foundation for your eternal, celestial dwelling.

16. What I am telling you is eternal truth out of God, the Lord of all existence and life. Whoever will not comply with the Word of God in himself actively, cannot enter His Kingdom.

17. Every one must pass through the narrow gate of humility and leave all things to the Lord. We must retain nothing but love and deepest humility. Nothing may offend us. We must never think or say that we are entitled to something. Only to love and humility are we entitled; everything else is the Lord's.

18. As the Lord has humiliated Himself to the lowest possible level, so must we if we want to go where He is.

19. If someone hits you in the face, do not resist but hold out your other cheek for the sake of peace and harmony between you. If someone wants your cloak, let him have your coat as well. If someone compels you to walk with him for an hour, make it *two* hours, to demonstrate the full measure of your love. Bless your enemy and pray for those who curse you. Do not ever requite evil with evil, but

do good to those who hate you — and you will be true children of God.

20. However, as long as you still seek your right anywhere but in the Word of God; as long as you carry a thorn caused by an insult in your hearts; as long as you feel that you have been wronged in one way or another — you are still children of hell, and the Lord's grace is not within you.

21. God's children must be capable of bearing and suffering absolutely everything! Their strength must lie solely in their love of God and of their brothers, whether they be good or evil.

22. As soon as they are firm in this, then they are absolutely free and capable of being admitted into the Kingdom of God.

23. I am aware of the fact that all of you were priests and nuns of the Roman church, which is the least enlightened of all churches. I also know that some of you are secretly still proud of it. But I warn you all not to think back of what you were and did on earth. If you think of the good you did, the Lord will remember all the evil and will judge you according to your works. For, whoever is judged by the Lord, attains death — not life — as judgment is the soul's death in the eternal bondage of its spirit.

24. When the Lord says: 'When ye shall have done all those things which are commanded you, say, We are unprofitable servants,' — how much more you, who have never lived the Gospel, neither concerning yourselves nor your brothers, must confess this.

25. This I have spoken to you in the name of the Lord, passing it on to you faithfully as received from the Lord, without adding or taking away a single word. It is now up to you to act accordingly and from now on you will have no excuse that you had never heard of it if, due to obstinate non-observance of the Lord's will, you fall into judgment.

26. But for those of good will, those who only fall because of their innate weakness, I and this brother are here to help them back on their feet again.

27. So, you see that first of all, to begin with your good will is essential, and only then the action.

28. Therefore, make sure that you have the honest will to do the right thing, and the Lord will not be too particular about the actual work, as the good will can already be considered the work of the spirit.

29. However, woe betide those of you who are secretly of a

cunning and evil will just outwardly pretending to be of good will! I tell you in the name of the Lord's might, which is at this moment blowing through me like a hurricane through a forest, such a one would be instantly driven to hell and thrust into the pit of eternal perdition — like a stone that falls from the sky into the depths of the sea — from where he would not be recovered, but would remain lying in the slime of the bottomless pit of judgment!

30. Now you know what you have to do to enter the Kingdom of the Lord as His true children. Do accordingly, and you shall live!

31. I and your first friend here will be behind you, even if not always visible, to support those who might stumble because of their weakness. But if someone should fall due to his wickedness, he shall not be helped, except that he might be paid off in the same coin. Do not ask about the place where you will be subjected to these tests. They will take place here and there, when least expected, so as not to interfere with your freedom. The Lord be with you and with us! Amen!"

32. (Bishop Martin): "Brother, it is obvious that you have spoken this on the Lord's authority, and every word is absolutely true. Your words have moved me deeply since they have raised some points closely concerning me."

33. (Borem): "So it will not hurt you to heed them! I would not like you as yet to face the fair Mercurian on your own! Do you understand me, brother?"

34. (Bishop Martin): "Of course, you are quite right! You know, I am still a bit of a beast, but I hope this will soon change!"

69

ANOTHER MIRACLE FOR BISHOP MARTIN. — A TEST FOR THE MINORITES AND THE JESUITS.

1. (Bishop Martin): "Now I am curious myself to know how and when this party of a thousand spirits will be tested. It is unlikely to happen inside this house; and in the open every one of them would have to be in a different place. We are only two of us, and I really cannot imagine how this thing can be handled. I would not consider it very difficult to distinguish in a flock of a hundred sheep the one

lost sheep from the ninety-nine just ones; but here, there are a thousand so-to-say completely lost sheep and, therefore, it will mean following a thousand lost sheep. Listen, friend, this will be a most unusual task, quite incomprehensible to me as yet."

2. (Borem): "Friend and brother, do not ask too many questions. Many things that at this stage seem impossible to you, are possible to the Lord. None of these spirits will leave the house, yet still they will, within themselves, be transferred to different areas in all detail corresponding with their inner selves. And as we shall enter their particular sphere, they shall see us and be able to talk to us. As long as we are outside their sphere, they will be unable to see us, whilst we shall have them before us and, by watching the backs of their heads, we shall know what they are doing and how they are complying with the Lord's instructions and if they are walking in His paths.

3. Look, they are already in the spheres of their inner selves where they belong. They are standing in the same spot as before and appear to talk to each other, but they do not since they now can see neither each other nor us.

4. Now they are being arranged in file, which will make it easier for us to survey them. But they are not aware of it, just as someone who is sound asleep would not be aware of being carried with his bed to another room. They are already standing in file and we can see the back of the head of every one of them. Come here to this Minorite and see what he is doing."

5. Bishop Martin steps behind the Minorite and looks through the back of his head, like looking through a magnifying glass. He sees a crowd of Eves. However, the Minorite does not let himself be disconcerted by them, but only teaches them, while his eyes are fixed upon a bright star rising in the eternal east.

6. (Borem): "This one is already saved, and with him quite a crowd of others. But let us continue and see what the Jesuits are doing."

7. They both move behind the file of Jesuits and look at the backs of their heads. And what do they see? About thirty of them are fighting each other for a whole legion of harlots, lusting for their flesh. The stronger ones grab the more voluptuous harlots, leaving the others to the weaker Jesuits. The latter are extremely annoyed about this and begin to withdraw to some distance, with the intention of organizing a revenge party to attack and cruelly punish their

colleagues. And the weaker and less voluptuous harlots herd together against the others, intending to belabor and scratch them with their sharp nails.

8. Bishop Martin watches this scene without a word, astonished, but also secretly annoyed, and does not know what to say.

9. (Borem has noticed this too, and says to Martin): "Brother, what do you think of this sight?"

10. (Bishop Martin): "Oh, my dearest friend and brother, really, I would never have expected this of these hypocritical scoundrels. They are behaving worse than you would expect dogs or monkeys on earth to behave. If I had your power and wisdom, with what I am feeling at present, I would send a million flashes of lightning into this crowd.

11. Oh, you out-and-out scoundrels! Look, brother, there is also the rascal who was burnt to death between two stone slabs in China for treason. Look how he tortures the beautiful Chinese woman — how he tears the poor thing to pieces like a vulture! But this is awful! By God, we must not allow this!"

12. (Borem): "Friend, this is only the beginning. We must not interfere. The situation will soon be reversed. Look, the Chinese woman is escaping and will soon have help. Then she will take terrible revenge on the vengeful Jesuit. Look, she is standing and screaming in front of a grotto, and from it a large crowd of the most atrocious monsters is streaming. They are now spreading and surrounding the group of Jesuits on all sides. They are still unaware of what is in store for them. Now they are all encircled by the monsters. The Chinese woman, her skin torn to shreds, and with a scepter in her hand, approaches the crowd of Jesuits, who are still occupied with the naked harlots. Now watch this, and tell me what you see."

13. (Bishop Martin watches for a short while, then recoils and says, deeply stirred): "How terrible, oh, how terrible! The Chinese woman, in a red-hot fury, steps in front of our Jesuit and seems to say, 'Do you know me, you wretch?' The Jesuit looks angry and obstinate, and says, 'Yes, you wretch! My curse shall be with you for ever!' He orders his colleagues to again grab the woman and tear her to pieces. But at this moment, she shouts, 'Back with you, you cursed seducers of all the world! Your measure is full! Now my vengeance is upon you!' Following her words, I now see a whole legion of huge, atrocious monsters throw themselves on our Jesuits,

and they are tearing them to small pieces! The Chinese woman is taking the head of our Jesuit, the one who had originally attacked her, and flings it into an abyss, from which a blaze is springing up. Now she flings the other remains of him after it. Ah, if that is not real hell, I could not imagine a worse picture to represent it! Shouldn't we, perhaps, intervene in this case?"

14. (Borem): "Oh no! The Lord will handle this Himself! We are much too weak, anyway! But, while they are still standing before us in rank and file, they are not lost for good. Only if some of them should vanish from this file, would it mean that we have nothing further to do with them. But one thing I can tell you: these are not far from hell. Everything you have just seen is taking place in the minds of these spirits, not in reality. However, if a mind has come to be like this, reality is not far off.

15. You have now seen what is in the hearts of these men. Thanks to the Lord, we can watch all this safely, figuratively, and dramatically. Now we know what these beings are like, and we shall see whether they heed all the warnings they have received and change their dispositions and their attitudes, following this demonstration infused into their minds as a sort of counter-vengeance by the Lord Himself.

16. Being torn to pieces by the monsters represents a great humiliation, which should bring them to their senses. Soon we shall see them once more as whole beings, and then we shall find out what impression this demonstration has made upon them.

17. Look, the whole Jesuit crowd is now climbing out of the abyss into which the Chinese woman had flung the one dismembered man!"

18. (Bishop Martin glances at the scene, and says): "True, they are all coming back in one piece again. I wonder what they will do now? Ah, their attitude seems to have improved. Maybe they can be saved after all. Some even appear to commence praying, judging from the expression on their faces. I would rejoice with all my heart if they would all change for the better! "

19. (Borem): "What seems impossible to humans, can be achieved by God. The first test has had more or less favorable results. Now others will follow and we shall then see how they will be passed. I can assure you that the next test will be much harder than the first. Watch now, the second act will be commencing immediately!"

70

SECOND TEST FOR THE JESUITS AND ITS INTERPRETATION BY BOREM.

1. Bishop Martin starts watching again and notices a caravan of pilgrims approaching our Jesuits, carrying with it great treasures and riches.

2. The Jesuits, seeing this, stop the caravan and enquire about its destination and what it is carrying.

3. (The caravan): "We come from earth where we have plundered several monasteries, particularly the rich ones of the Jesuits, who are the greatest robbers and bandits in the world.

4. To rob people of their often hard-earned possessions through double-talk, bigotry, and hypocrisy, as well as false concepts of hell and damnation, is worse than open robbery and theft. Everyone has the right to defend himself against robbers and thieves, but only few are in a position to protect themselves from such Jesuitic or other monastic robberies.

5. Since all their property is illegal, it is only fair that we have plundered those monasteries. Now we are carrying our loot before the throne of God, where we shall cry for vengeance until the Lord grants our request and destroys this evil and deceitful breed with all its roots."

6. Hearing this, the Jesuits start to kindle with rage.

7. (Bishop Martin, who has witnessed all this, says to Borem): "Brother, it really looks bad now for our Jesuits, or at least for the thirty who were already present at the previous test. I notice also the others of this order, but they keep apart from the thirty, and their separate group looks much lighter."

8. (Borem): "Those others are as good as saved; only the thirty are still wavering. Watch now what will happen!"

9. (Bishop Martin watches silently for a while, then he says): "Ah, ah, brother, for the sake of God, we have to do something! They are perfect devils! I would never have thought this of that order!

10. Listen, in case you missed the reaction of the Jesuits: After the caravan had answered the questions of those Jesuits, the latter flew into a red-hot rage and cried:

11. 'You cursed deicides who have profaned the shrine of God! You have delivered yourselves into the hands of just vengeance, for

we are those Jesuits whom you have robbed and against whom you intended to call down God's vengeance. No doubt God has placed us here so that we might hand you over to the terrible depths of hell for your sacrilege. Down to hell with you fiends, to where the most wicked devils are!

12. Come forth, Lucifer, Satan, Leviathan! Take hold of these infamous, heretic and, consequently, cursed fiendish evildoers, torture them and throw them where hell is hottest!'

13. This is really too much, brother, what these men want to do to that poor caravan! I cannot imagine such minds ever repenting!

14. Ah, look, three hideous figures are emerging from the depths. Their horrible, gaping mouths, large enough to swallow whole houses, are emitting fire.

15. At their sight, the caravan is seized by terrible fear. They are putting down the loot before the Jesuits, and are begging for mercy and forgiveness.

16. However, the Jesuits are showing no mercy, and they scream in ever-mounting rage: 'Down with you! There is no mercy for you, nor forgiveness ever! The most horrible torment in ever-burning futile remorse be your lot and your reward for your deeds in eternity! Grab them, you greatest and most evil devils, and requite them eternally for what they have done to us temporally!'

17. The caravan continues to beg for mercy, but in vain, and the three devils are approaching. The Jesuits are gloating over the frightened caravan. Ah, they are truly the most fiendish of devils!

18. The three devils are taking their time, pondering the terrible demand of the Jesuits. But those scoundrels have only one desire – to send their poor victims to hell without mercy or pardon.

19. Look, now the three devils are talking to them, saying that their verdict is too strict and unjust for small sinners like those.

20. However, the Jesuits shout: 'Our judgment is God's judgment and, therefore, just! So away with them — down to the torment!'

21. The devils shout back: 'You are asking too much! God has never passed judgment like that! We shall do as you desire, but mind you, at your own risk if your request does not come from God.'

22. Oh, brother, listen — with a terrible cry the unfortunate caravan is vanishing along with the devils! The Jesuits remain, triumphant! What do you say to this, brother? Aren't they perfect devils?"

23. (Borem): "Do not worry about all this, which is only, as already previously mentioned, an appearance manifesting itself, thanks to God's intervention.

24. The renunciation of evil can often be attained by the evil being ejected from the mind figuratively, showing its true nature. However, it is a sort of false alarm, not a reality.

25. Therefore, you should not take what you see here too much to heart. It is all brought forth thanks to the Lord's profound love and supreme wisdom, and may be compared to the various illnesses of men on earth.

26. Although an evil for the body, the illnesses are of great benefit to the soul, and sometimes even to the body if they cause some bad substance to be eliminated.

27. Thus, these manifestations are nothing but maladies the soul has brought here with it, and they must be expelled with the aid of spiritual medicines, just as the physical ones are expelled through material specifics. Otherwise, the soul could never regain its health, nor its spirit arise.

28. Is it not a fact on earth that while the body is ill, the soul is also ailing and inactive? As soon as the body regains its health, the soul again takes pleasure in activity.

29. A similar process is taking place here. All these Jesuits have very sick souls. Through the power of the Word of God, which is the only and most powerful medicine, the sickness is being forced out of their souls. And when this operation has been successfully completed, it will then be our turn to strengthen the convalescents with the love of the Lord.

30. Now, dear brother, perhaps you understand these manifestations much better, and perhaps they will not shock you so deeply, even if you have to see worse things than these. With every disease, the last morbid matter ejected by the medicines is the worst, as it is the main pathogenic agent. The same applies here.

31. Therefore, do not worry too much at the sight of these basest evils that will now be emerging from the souls of the Jesuits. Watch now the third act commence, which will probably be the last one for these thirty Jesuits."

71

CONVERSION OF ONE OF THE JESUITS. — VENGEANCE OF THE OTHER TWENTY-NINE SPIRITS.

1. Bishop Martin once more watches the back of the head of the Jesuit in front of him, and he sees the thirty look somewhat uneasy, and one of them says:

2. "Brothers, we have won a victory but, looking at this matter more closely, it appears to me that we have dealt with the caravan, now burning in hell, most unjustly and without any authority. Although they grossly abused us, according to the Gospel, we had no right to judge and condemn them.

3. Besides, I now remember the warning we received from the celestial messenger prior to our entering this completely free state of our existence. According to his wise teaching, we were to meet any provocation solely with love, meekness, and humility. On this occasion we have not shown any trace of these qualities. On the contrary, even the greatest devils have surpassed us in meekness and justice, which proves that we are much more wicked than they.

4. What do you think about this, brothers? I admit this is beginning to worry me. Altogether, everything in this spirit world appears fallacious. Our arbitrary act, in no way authorized by God's messenger, now appears to me quite contrary to the order prevailing in this mysterious world. I also have the feeling that someone is whispering to me: 'For this most cruel act, all of you will have to repent in eternity!' Oh, oh, I wish I had not been a witness to this happening!"

5. (This somewhat startles the other twenty-nine Jesuits, but after a short pause, they say): "Basically you are right, but then, how could we have acted differently, being what we are? And whoever has endowed us with rage and all the other negative attributes of our souls, will just have to put up with them!

6. Whoever gave the rattlesnake its deadly venom must have wanted it to be like that, otherwise he would not have made the evil reptile the way it is. Thus also we Jesuits had to be what we are, taught by our order how to give way to emotions of rage and vengeance, and do evil with the best conscience in God's honor. So we

are fully that, what we were meant to be! What more could you, or rather, could God, expect of us?"

7. (Says the one Jesuit): "Yes, you are right! We are meant to be fiends and have perfected our image! What else could you expect? Consequently, we cannot expect to go to heaven, but only to hell! So we may as well continue with our wickedness and malice to speed up our eternal damnation! That is how you see it, and good luck to you on your road! However, I shall now part company with you, for I do not crave the honor of finding myself any moment floating together with you in the hot floods of sulfurous vapor! Be assured, I shall not grudge you that honor, ever!"

8. (Say the other twenty-nine Jesuits, unanimously): "What, you want to forsake your order? You want to turn away from the sublime founder, Ignatius, and his most sacred teaching? What has come over you? Do not forget that all of us have still to face a Day of Judgment, and how will you fare then? If you really do this, your fate shall be worse than that of the caravan!"

9. (The one Jesuit): "Never mind! You please yourselves, but I shall still adhere to my resolution, and may God strengthen me! I do not worry about the Day of Judgment, but I do worry about eternal damnation, of which I am assured of in your company. I do not care about Ignatius or the order, but I shall, in future, follow the advice of God's messenger.

10. As I see it now, the Lord must be utterly disgusted with our whole order, including its founder. All the Lutherans, Calvinists, and the Orthodox, are angels compared with us who, with our rules and institutions, are the worst kind of devils.

11. Do with me as you wish. I shall not revenge myself. I now feel the deepest remorse about the way I treated the poor Chinese woman. But thank God I have been severely punished for it, together with you. However, my participation in the condemnation of the poor caravan is already tormenting me like hell. What would happen if I stayed on with you as your accomplice? No — I am leaving you now, so farewell!"

12. After these words of the one Jesuit, all the others surround him, damning and cursing and mangling him, distributing his skin among themselves. Then they push him out from their midst, pelting him with stones and calling to the devils to come and get him.

13. The devils do come, but not to get the skinless one but only those who called them. These are trying desperately to defend them-

186

selves, screaming for help. Now the skinless one gets to his feet and orders the devils to leave the blind ones alone. And, look, the devils obey him and withdraw from the frantic spirits.

14. Bishop Martin is quite impressed with this scene, and eagerly waits to see what is going to happen next.

72

A GLANCE INTO THE FRAME OF MIND OF THE LADIES OF THE SACRED HEART. — INTRUDERS IN THE CONVENT GARDEN. — ATTACK BY THE VENGEFUL LADIES.

1. (Borem): "Friend and brother, let us thank the Lord's endless wisdom and inconceivable love and compassion in dealing with the party so leniently and promptly, contrary to our expectation. Such tests may sometimes last for many earth-years, even with less evil spirits; but with this party, they took only three earth-days, although the tested ones must have felt it like some decades. However, this is scarcely worth mentioning, considering the reality and that some of the tested are charged with a feeling that their ordeal is lasting through thousands, sometimes even millions, of years.

2. In short, the Lord has shown extraordinary mercy with these thirty Jesuits. They were really standing on the edge of the precipice and were very much closer to hell than to heaven, which is still quite a considerable distance away from them. But the worst is over. They are saved and will now be gradually bettered. This is a great step forward, and praise be to the Lord. For what is impossible for the highest angel, the Lord can still achieve!

3. You would like to see more of this third act, and I see you are still watching the back of that Jesuit's head attentively. But I can tell you that there will be no more to see. This party will now repent and join its better brothers, to be released from this sort of material sphere as soon as we've had a look at the minds of the Ladies of the Sacred Heart.

4. So let us now go to these ladies and watch them the same way we did the Jesuits. There they are! You may choose any of them; you will still see the same thing!"

5. (Bishop Martin): "If so, the nearest will do, and I shall look through the back of her head. There — I can see them already, like the thirty Jesuits, standing all together in a garden with a high wall, against the northern corner of which there is a rather ominous-looking convent building.

6. They seem to be arguing about something, but I cannot yet hear what it is all about. However, I do notice that from time to time they turn darker, then again lighter — similar to snow-clad mountain peaks on earth when the winds drive the clouds and make the mountains appear quite grey at times and then again beautifully shimmering as soon as the rays of the sun get through to them once more. What might be the reason for this manifestation concerning these Ladies of the Sacred Heart?"

7. (Borem): "Dear brother, you have used quite a good metaphor and in your natural picture you can also find the reason for this phenomenon. For here, too, the clouds of misapprehension, driven by the winds of their various earthly passions, are floating across the peaks of these ladies' understanding. And just as on earth bad weather can be expected when the winds start chasing the clouds, so it will be here in this spiritual manifestation.

8. Did you notice that the darkenings are becoming more frequent and lasting? This is a sure sign that the actual test is imminent. When the darkness has become constant, the first act of the bad weather will begin. Watch carefully — for here you will see even more interesting things than you did with the thirty Jesuits."

9. (Bishop Martin): "You are right! With some of them the darkness is already constant. From the others, too, the light is waning, turning all into grey.

10. What a peculiar mixture of darkness and grey! On the darkest ones, already a coloring like that of red-hot iron is gradually creeping upwards. It might originate from the rage within them or even from hell. Oh, dear brother, this looks most ominous!

11. Now I can see two male beings entering the garden from the convent. The Ladies of the Sacred Heart in the middle of the garden, who are already very dark, do not seem to have noticed the approaching intruders as yet.

12. Aha, now something is going to happen! Our ladies have got wind of the fact that there is somebody near them who should not be there. For I see glowing daggers in their hands, pointing in the direction of the intruders, making a not-too-friendly welcome.

13. Now the Mother Superior is making signs for everybody to be silent. I wonder what will happen now? It looks as if she is going to speak. Yes — she is already clearing her throat. It will be most interesting to hear what rubbish she is going to offer the others. Attention — she is already beginning."

14. (The Prioress): "Listen to me, my honorable and highly respectable ladies, our sublime, holy order is in great danger. Two impertinent men, or rather rogues, have sneaked into our divine garden through our holy convent, most likely for unchaste reasons or maybe to spy out details about our possessions, and how best they could rob us. However, we shall make them pay dearly for their impertinence!

15. We are about ninety in number, I estimate. When these scoundrels approach us, we shall call to them: 'Out with you, shameless scamps!' And if they do not leave immediately, we shall all fall upon them and each one of us will thrust her glowing dagger deep into their chests. When they are dead, our caretaker can chop them up and burn them on a pile here in the garden in order to cleanse this holy place after their sacrilege."

16. (Bishop Martin): "I say, what bloodthirsty designs on the part of these dear Ladies of the Sacred Heart of Jesus! Oh, those wicked beasts! This I wouldn't have expected of these true furies of hell! If this is the beginning, I wonder what the further tests will bring? Look, the two men appear good and kind, and I could say of them: 'Behold, two men whose souls are guileless!' And these evil beasts condemn them, even before they have seen or spoken to them."

17. (Borem): "Compose yourself! You know how these things work! Let them do as they wish. When it is time for us to interfere, the tablet will instruct us. But until then, we must be nothing but silent observers of this scene. So go on looking!"

18. (Bishop Martin now continues to watch the scene before him attentively, and after a while, says): "Look, brother, the two men are turning towards the door of the convent as if intending to leave the garden again.

19. However, the ladies, on noticing this, are shouting, quite contrary to their original intention: 'Stop, do not move any further, you ungodly scamps!'

20. The two men seem to ignore this and continue towards the door of the convent. Seeing this, the ladies are turning red-hot with

189

rage, and are dashing screaming after the men to block their exit.

21.   A number of them are surrounding the two men with drawn daggers, and are asking them menacingly: 'What are you doing here, you cursed scoundrels? Admit your evil intentions, your treacherous plan, so that we may torture you all the more without mercy! By your bold and shameless entry into this garden, you have committed sacrilege against God's sanctuary, and thus have spurned the Spirit of God! Death alone can atone for this worst kind of mortal sin, and only eternal damnation can appease Divine Justice! Speak now, you cursed rogues!'

22.   Now the two men speak: 'Listen patiently! We have been sent to you by God to free you from your great folly. However, seeing that there is nothing but rage and glowing revenge in your hearts, it is clear that you are still far from ready for such great mercy, and it will still take a very long time for you to become worthy of it. Have you not heard that whoever judges and condemns, shall himself be judged and damned? We, on our part, shall not reward evil with evil. Therefore, let us go in peace, otherwise you will be in real trouble.'

23.   The ladies now furiously fall upon the two with their daggers. However, the men vanish and the ladies stab each other in their blind fury."

BISHOP MARTIN'S REMARKS AND BOREM'S WISE HINTS CONCERNING THE WAYS OF ETERNAL LOVE. -- THE BURNING LADIES OF THE SACRED HEART.

1. (Bishop Martin, at the sight of this scene, begins to laugh, and says): "Brother, just look at those silly females! Ah, in their blind fury they are tearing each other to pieces with their daggers! What a sight! A charming witches' Sabbath! If they carry on like that there will not be much left of them and our intervention will become quite unnecessary. Never mind, those tatters would not mean a great loss for heaven!

2. Forgive me, dearest brother, if I appear to gloat over the misfortune of those beings, but I just can't help it. Anything is easier for me to bear than females who are stupid and wicked at the same time. They are particularly hard to bear if they, like these here, come near to destroying themselves in their rage and hatred. I do not really wish them ill, but I feel that a bit of hell would not be at all bad for such beasts as these. I do not mean forever, you know, but just for a little bit — like the Roman Catholic purgatory!"

3. (Says Borem): "Do not be overzealous, brother, and make sure you ban all the calling-fire-from-heaven wishes from your heart! Just keep watching what the Lord is doing here, and you will learn from it the only true way in which such dark, ignorant beings may be turned towards the light once more. If the Lord thought the way you do, there would be desperately little hope for such poor beings ever to attain eternal life. But here you can see clearly that the Lord is kinder than the best men or angels.

4. The Lord's ways are strange, their number infinite. And each way the Lord guides a man is an inscrutable wonder, even to the wisest cherub, and holy whatever its manifestation.

5. Looking at all these manifestations from this angle, you will find nothing in future annoying or ridiculous about them. Eventually, you will be convinced how endlessly loving and wise the Lord guides all to the holy goal, and how, by the simplest and apparently most insignificant means, He, at all times, achieves the most sublime purpose. And, where He is helping one, He is simultaneously helping innumerable other beings.

7. O brother, you will understand only gradually how infinitely sublime all this is, which is at the root of these manifestations; how sacred the existence and activity of even a mite which, on earth, you might have seen crawling across a half-parched leaf!

8. Therefore, be glad about all that you see here! For everything is the result of our Heavenly Father's most holy love — without exception! Do you think hell, with all its indescribable horrors, could be the Lord's revenge based on His wrath from eternity? Not by any means! The Lord is the essence of love also in hell, for eternal love knows neither wrath nor vengeance, and thus all its institutions cannot be founded on anything but love.

9. But now go on watching, and look at everything with different eyes and a different mind. You will find it most educational. For the Lord allows all this to happen mainly for your sake in order to

speed up the rebirth of your spirit and the arraying of your soul in celestial garb. So, once more, heed conscientiously all I have told you, and it will be of the greatest advantage to you."

10. Bishop Martin now continues to watch the lady's back of the head, and notices the last two are still fighting, thrusting their daggers into each other's bodies. They then collapse and lie on the ground like dead. Having watched this scene, he says:

11. "Thank God, they have finished each other off! The Lord bless them! It is really miraculous that this is going to aid them towards salvation, as you have just explained. I am really curious to see what will happen now to these amazons, who are now lying on the ground as if they were quite dead.

12. Ah, a new manifestation is commencing! The ladies still seem quite dead, but they are beginning to give off smoke! Here and there even sparks are flying. Dear friend, this is beginning to look rather ominous and I am sure a bit of hell is manifesting itself here.

13. Look, already flames are shooting upwards! It looks like a proper *autodafé*; the poor things are on fire, but except for the smoke, sparks, and flames, nothing is moving on or around them.

14. Look, the flames are increasing in intensity and the dead ladies are already glowing, all the way through. Good for them that they are dead and insensitive! What a peculiar sight and, strangely, nothing seems to be destroyed by the intense flames. Do tell me, dearest brother, what this strange manifestation means?"

15. (Borem): "It serves the best purpose, for what comes from the Lord is always good! Just go on watching and you will soon see for yourself how right I am!"

74

BISHOP MARTIN'S REMARKS ABOUT THE ESSENCE OF EVIL. — BOREM'S EDUCATIONAL WORDS ABOUT THE DIVINE ORDER. — "GOOD" AND "EVIL" AS THE TWO OPPOSITE POLES IN GOD AND CREATION.

1. (Bishop Martin): "Oh, yes, of course you are right! But you must admit that the sinners are God's creatures, just as we are, and

so is the devil! We all come from God. But who will, for that reason, call a sinner or the devil good?

2. As I see it, God has, among His countless creatures, created also free beings. He has acquainted them with His unchanging order and has shown the ways they have to walk to remain within His order. But since they are free beings, they are quite capable of turning their backs on the well-known divine order and act contrary to it. If this happens, the following question then arises:

3. If evil is only thinkable as opposed to the divine goodness, then only an action against the known divine goodness can be called evil. If, however, this action is also good, what then is evil? It must exist, otherwise hell would be the vainest imaginable concept.

4. But if hell is a reality and an action which is contrary to the positive, immutable divine order must be described as evil, then these ladies are evil and ready for hell!

5. Sin and sinners, as adherents of the devil, are, consequently, evil, and their reward, as expressed by the Lord Himself, is hell — as a collecting center for everything evil. The manifestations in connection with these ladies proved that they were evil all the way through. They stabbed each other like furies and now they are on fire! Could that be anything but the image of hell?"

6. (Borem): "Friend, you are still speaking like a short-sighted mortal from the prison of his flesh. Naturally, on the part of a free being, any action which is contrary to the known divine order is sin, and thus evil! But can you determine the bounds between one and the same man's actual free being and that part of it which is under compulsion?

7. Do you know where in the flesh the soul begins and where in the soul the spirit? Do you know exactly where a man's actions under compulsion end and his free actions commence? Do you know how far spirituality and freedom extend into the natural and compulsive being of man?

8. When you filled new wine into a cask and it began to ferment audibly, a pungent smell from the bung hole would knock you back if you put your nose near it. Do you know what it was that caused the wine to ferment? No, you don't! Then the fermentation ended, the new wine had calmed down, cleared and then changed to matured wine. Do you know how this could happen?

9. Soon after a fruit tree had blossomed, you could already see the fruit. If you tasted it before it was ready, you found it sour and

193

unpleasant, contrary to the order of your taste; consequently, it was bad and evil. But how did you find the fruit when it was ripe? Then it suited your taste and was no longer bad and evil.

10. To the senses surely winter must be a sin; for it is not in the order of warm-blooded men and beasts. But what about the fruit-bearing soil of the earth and man's physical strength, if winter did not exist?

11. In the whole of infinity you will always find two poles, both of which are within the order of God although they are complete opposites, like day and night, or yes and no. Tell me — which of them is the evil one? Don't you see that the Lord directs and guides everything on its proper way? Where then could there be a bad way?

12. The Lord knows exactly what free scope He apportions to a being. Within this scope, every being that has a free will may please itself in the practice of its freedom. However, no being is capable of any action outside this scope.

13. A drop of water usually contains countless freely-moving infusoria. Could they live and be active outside that drop of water?

14. Thus, mortals may undermine the moral order of their earth through wars and other evils. Could they impede the change of night and day, or could they hold back the rain and winds, or empty the sea?

15. If you want to talk about the great order of God, you will have to look farther than the narrow space of *your* scope of activity.

16. What is not possible in the drop of water will surely be possible in the sea, which cannot be poisoned by the most poisonous drop. Where an equation cannot be found in the orbit of earth, it will surely be found in the vast orbit of the sun. And should this still be too small, then there are orbits of central suns of endless expansions and depths.

17. If a number is indivisible in another number, does that already mean that there does not exist a number in which it would be divisible? Or, if in music a wrong note is used which is out of harmony with the key of the tune — therefore bad — does it follow that this note should be banned from music altogether?

18. Behold, although God has given every human being on earth a certain order to observe with His 'Thou shalt,' He has also given him all the other things. He knows best how to guide one or the other with a view to attaining to the great goal in due course. There-

fore, He has also demanded us not to judge anybody, just as the greatest angel of heaven, Michael, was not allowed to condemn Satan as he fought with him for the body of Moses.

19. If we want to be wise and true children of God, we must watch what the Lord is doing and adapt our judgment accordingly, for we can move freely only within our own scope. The movement in the countless, infinite scopes of God's order is none of our business, but the Lord's alone wherefore it is written that a person should sweep in front of his own door and not that of his neighbor.

20. Make sure you comprehend this, and then continue to look at the scene. I hope before God the Lord that you will now begin to see things in a different light, and value them accordingly. May the Lord give you the honest will and true insight to this end soon! Now look again — the scene has changed!"

75

BISHOP MARTIN'S FURTHER OBSERVATIONS CONCERNING THE HELLISH STATE OF THE LADIES OF THE SACRED HEART. — BOREM'S EXPLANATIONS.

1. (Bishop Martin watches silently for a while, then says): "Yes, dearest friend, you are right. I begin to realize that the Lord's order is quite different from what I imagined it to be. It is only too true what is written, that the ways of the Lord are unfathomable!

2. But at the same time, it is also unfathomable why my ignorance is so lasting, whilst you, with the least spiritual aid, have become a wise angel of the Lord in such a short time! However, be that as it may, I feel it strongly in my heart that the Lord Jesus has become my only need. And this feeling makes me happy and serene. This is all I want for all eternity! I assure you, dear friend and brother, as long as I have the Lord, nothing else matters.

3. Therefore, I think that since the Lord is doing His best for this stubborn party and we cannot change anything, it is not worth our while to go on watching these scenes, in which I at least can see as good as nothing that is pleasant or beneficial for the spirit. The ladies have come back to life and are now racing around the garden glowing brightly, as if they were true furies or devils. But what good

can this sight give me which I cannot comprehend, nor hardly ever will?

4. If it depended on me, I would much rather go outside and work in that beautiful garden than go on watching these boring scenes!"

5. (Borem): "Listen, dearest brother — what is right for the Lord should also be right for us. For the Lord is guiding both of us too, and He knows best why He is leading us this particular way.

6. Therefore, keep on watching patiently what is to be seen here, and do not worry about the interpretation, which will come to you in due course, clear and comprehensible.

7. Do go on telling me what you see, and I shall explain it to you where necessary. In the name of the Lord, do now as I have advised you to do!"

8. (Bishop Martin): "Of course, you are right! The Lord is guiding us simultaneously, and it is important that we comply with His will conscientiously. So I shall go on watching this spiritual comedy, but allow me to speak without choosing my words!"

9. (Borem): "Speak as you please — that is all I can say. But beware of passing judgment, for that is solely up to the Lord!"

10. (Bishop Martin, quite satisfied, begins to look again at the back of the head of one of the ladies of the Sacred Heart, and says): "Oh dear, oh dear! This is in all earnest a rather savage and evil scene. Those ladies are now quite naked and their flesh is glowing like melting ore. The more it glows, the wilder they run around in confusion.

11. They are not exactly fat, these female salamanders, but they have still retained a rather human appearance. Their figures are not too bad — some have even quite good bosoms, — but their faces are awfully distorted! On earth I have seen similar faces only on monkeys. Ah, how savage and horribly ugly their faces are!

12. Oh dear, look at that one standing near us! Oh Lord, what a face! Her nose is hanging down almost to her belly, her ears resemble those of an elephant, her mouth looks rather like the arse of an old cow, and her neck is full of goiters. The eyes, of irregular shape, resemble a dog's arse, and her hair looks like reptiles. How peculiar — the body would be quite normal but the head, really — I could not imagine anything more abominable!

13. Oh look, another one is approaching and she looks really terrifying! She has the head of a boa constrictor, only her long ass's

196

ears have a somewhat mitigating effect. Those staring eyes and that constant snake's hiss; and with every breath she emits dark brown fumes through her mouth, eyes and nostrils! How disgusting! Here again, her body is quite in order and, except for the glow, could be called well developed. Only her head is so abominable! For God's sake, what unutterable ugliness!

14. Ah, now they are once more running around in confusion like crazy fowls. I wonder what all this means?"

15. (Borem): "I can tell you: nothing very unusual. That they are glowing is due to their furious zeal on behalf of their order. Their activity in running that order expresses itself by their racing around. That these ladies' bodies look quite normal is due to their rather chaste minds, but the peculiar appearance of their heads is due solely to their utter stupidity. When their understanding grows, their heads will improve. However, while they stick to their folly, there is not much hope for any improvement of their heads.

16. Now you know the corresponding cause of such manifestation. But go on looking, for what you have seen so far is only the prelude. The actual drama is still to come."

17. (Bishop Martin): "That will really be something! If the actual drama is yet to commence, I am most anxious to see what it will be like."

76

HEARTLESS ATTITUDE OF THE LADIES OF THE SACRED HEART TOWARDS THEIR PARENTS DESIRING ADMITTANCE. — THE TWO WHITE-ROBED MEN INTERVENE.

1. (Bishop Martin): "Now I see these disgusting tatters of Ladies of the Sacred Heart of Jesus (what a pity about that wonderful name!) hurriedly withdrawing into their convent. What could they be suspecting now? Ah, there I see camped outside the garden a number of very sad and miserable old men and women. I wonder what they want and who they are?"

2. (Borem): "They are the parents of some of these ladies, and

they are seeking help from them, for after much seeking and entreating, they have been told that their blessed daughters are in this celestial convent, constantly praying for their salvation."

3. (Bishop Martin): "Oh what a situation! I am already sorry for those poor, good-natured — but ignorant — parents.

4. Right, there an old man is already ringing at the gate, but no one answers. He rings again and a third time, but in vain.

5. Now the old people start to beg and pray and lament. They even begin to worship those ninnies with loud prayers. This is really going too far! But still not one of the female salamanders is showing herself.

6. Now I can hear loud weeping and sobbing from the old people, and they cry: 'Oh you, our beloved, holy daughters, look mercifully upon your poor parents from your celestial thrones! Let us be your lowest servants! Oh, do grant our request, you holy virgins and brides of God!'

7. Friend, brother, I never expected people — I mean Roman Catholic people — to be that stupid! Although I was a bishop myself and thought the world of some pious looking follies, I would not have put up with anything like this in my diocese. I pity these poor people — or rather, spirits — with all my heart!

8. I am really curious to see what will happen now. None of the objects of worship is visible. Probably they know by now what they look like and are terribly ashamed of letting their parents see them like that. Therefore, all the pleas and prayers will be in vain. Listen to how the poor things are crying and lamenting!

9. Ah, look, a new phenomenon! In the many windows of the convent flashes of lightning are appearing, and it is beginning to thunder, though not very loud. It must be a monastic, theatrical house-thunder, but the lightning looks very much like the real thing.

10. Listen, it sounds as if the thunder were articulating actual words. Indeed, the thunder is now speaking clearly! It says: 'Back with you, cursed spirits, withdraw from this sanctuary of God or the ground will open up and you will be swallowed by hell for having dared set your wicked feet on it! Flee forever from before our holy presence!

11. Ah, how vile they are! Being almost of the devil themselves and ashamed to face their much better parents, they scare them away with this masquerade. And the poor things are now leaving this place, weeping and sobbing.

12.   What a hellish beginning for this drama! I am now anxious to see its further development.

13.   Not far beyond the garden, towards the south, the poor parents have reached a heavily laden fruit tree. They are resting under it, facing the convent — which still seems to be holding false hope and consolation for them, although that shabby, deceptive demonstration should have convinced them that they have nothing to hope for from their presumedly blessed daughters, except maybe a worse demonstration.

14.   I wonder what our ladies are going to do now? Flashes of lightning are still coming from the windows of the convent, and a weak thunder is still audible. The old people under the tree have now discovered the fruit and some of them are beginning to eat and really enjoy it. They are eagerly picking more fruit and passing some to those who do not seem to have the courage to pick their own.

15.   But now I can see something like a megaphone being pushed out one of the convent windows. It is directed towards the tree under which our old people are resting to enjoy the 'celestial' sight of the convent, or maybe for some other reason. I wonder what will develop from this megaphone, which might be a sort of Pandora's box*?

16.   Oh dear, look at that! A great number of owls are emerging from the megaphone, flying straight to the tree, under which our poor, cheated, old people are resting. Those owls are whirring around the tree and shooting down at the people beneath, and those poor old people are getting rather frightened.

17.   Now flames, intermingled with words, are coming from the megaphone, in the direction of the tree. The words appear like glowing serpents; they seem to be carried along by the flames and are full of the most terrifying threats.

18.   This is something quite different — for a change! It is a well-known fact that words can be written down with certain signs called letters. But I did not know that words can also be expressed through such abominable shapes.

19.   Now the old people are rising to their feet and fleeing as fast

---

*Pandora received from Zeus a box from which all human ills escaped; only false hope remained inside. Therefore, the expression "Pandora's box" from which all evils come.

as they can, followed by the owls. They are heading for a stream, which I have only just noticed.

20. There I can see two white-robed men, the same whom the heartless ladies intended to stab to death. These men beckon to the fleeing old people to come to them, whilst the owls, on seeing the men, turn around and hurriedly fly back to the convent, where they shoot like lightning into the megaphone. Also, the serpent-words and flames are quickly withdrawing.

21. The old people are gathering around the two men and they, too, appear to move in the direction of the convent. This is really getting most exciting, and I am curious to know what will happen next."

22. (Borem): "Dearest brother, you must guard your heart against excessive curiosity, which is always associated with some malicious pleasure. Just be a wise observer for the benefit of your own spirit, free from curiosity. As these scenes will contain a hellish element, it is most important that we are very moderate. Now go on watching without curiosity and tell me all you see."

77

THE SOUNDING OF TRUMPETS BY THE TWO WHITE-ROBED MEN, AND THE COLLAPSE OF THE CONVENT. — THE LADIES OF THE SACRED HEART AS GIANT FROGS. — EXPLANATIONS TO THE FRIGHTENED PARENTS.

1. (Bishop Martin once more glances at the back of the head of the lady, and says after a while): "Yes, that is right, the two white-robed men are now really moving towards the convent, accompanied by the old people. The closer they get, the more flashes of lightning are coming from the many windows, but they are not reaching far enough. Also, the thunder inside is only scarcely audible.

2. The party has now reached the wall around the garden. One of the white-robed men quickly opens the gate, and they all enter the garden and draw close to the convent building.

3. There, the two men in white post themselves in front of the group of old people, they pull out long trumpets from under their robes, and are now sounding them with great force. What a strong, majestic sound it is!

4. But what do I see? The convent building is collapsing like the walls of Jericho, and our ladies are crawling out from under the debris, like worms from a swamp, lamenting and cursing. They now look like the giant frogs that are found on earth in Lower Egypt. Only their heads are more like those of boa constrictors than those of frogs. I also notice that they have scorpion tails. The situation now looks rather ominous.

5. The old people are terrified at this sight. The strange frogs have stopped cursing, but are croaking horribly. However, their croaking is quite senseless and has not the least effect, as the two men are now driving them towards the west, whilst the old people follow, greatly astonished.

6. At the site of the convent, there now stands a disgusting, gloomy pool. I find this most frightening! One thing is very strange: I see the frogs and the party behind them as they all hurry towards the west, yet they are still quite as big and clear as before, although they are already at a considerable distance from us."

7. (Borem): "Distances in space have no effect on the eyesight of a spirit. A spirit is independent of space and time. Only the different states of the mind represent true spiritual distances, and influence the eyesight of the spirit, often blinding it completely.

8. If the two men in white were not present at the flight of the frogs, you would not be able to see them at all, for the state of mind of those frogs is too different from ours. But as the minds of the two are closely related to ours, we would still see them the same, even if they were at a great distance from us!

9. We could have a close look at hell also. However, that would not be accomplished through an association of minds, but only through the Lord's miraculous mediation, which you will get to know in due course.

10. Now you know the reason for this appearance, which rightly seems strange, but will become quite clear to you at a later time. Now go on watching the scene before you, which is most educational."

11. Concentrating on the scene once more, Bishop Martin sees how the frogs, already deep in the dark evening, have reached the shore of a vast sea and have stopped. Here they are beginning to croak pitifully, refusing to enter the water. The two white-robed men do not force them in, but give them free choice.

12. (Seeing this, Bishop Martin says): "Look at those ugly frogs!

They do not want to enter the element for which they seem to have been created. I am beginning to suspect the reason why this is so. There must still be something of a better nature in them which does not belong to that element, and which most likely is going to keep them on dry land."

13. (Borem): "That may be so! But go on watching, for the development of the first act will soon be apparent!"

14. (Bishop Martin watches the scene attentively, and says after a while): "Ah, ah, look, how strange! The frogs are now inflating themselves to the frightening size of huge elephants, facing the two white-robed men and the party of old people, who are getting more and more scared. The frogs are still swelling, as if blown up with bellows.

15. They look as if they could attack the whole party, but the two men do not retreat a single step, although the old people seem ready to fly more than run away.

16. Now the two men order silence, and one of them addresses the old people: 'Do not be afraid of these inflated things! It is only the wicked skin that seems so frightening, but the being inside is weaker than that of a mite! We could blow them away with a single breath, these beings whom you worshipped as blessed, but we shall not be as merciless as they — the would-be brides of God — were to us and to you, although we are true Protestants and zealously protest against everything that is not of the Lord.

17. 'And if you want to know exactly who these inflated frogs are, then know that they are your daughters whom your utter foolishness has practically sent to their damnation, driving them into the convent of the Ladies of the Sacred Heart together with considerable fortunes. How do you like them in their celestial garb?'

18. The old people throw up their arms, tear their hair, and scream: 'But for heaven's sake, Jesus, Mary and Joseph, help us! How is this possible? They were said to have led such pure lives and have at all times obeyed the strict rules of the order and their father confessor! And now we find them here in this terrible state! Oh, Jesus, Mary and Joseph, what has become of them?'

19. Says one of the white-robed men: 'Calm yourselves and do not worry about these unworthy ones. We have been sent here by the Lord to seek and recover, in His most holy name, what was lost, and we shall eventually straighten out these frogs. But in order that you may be cured of your folly, you have to be present when we do this,

202

and patiently accept all that might befall you. But first, make sure that you awaken your love of the one God, Lord and Father, Jesus, and the path you will have to follow will be much easier!'

20.   Now the old people are beginning to weep at the misfortune of their supposedly blessed daughters. But the latter are inflating themselves even more so."

78

AN OBSCURE JESUIT STORY: A FATHER CHEATED OUT OF HIS DAUGHTER. — THE STORY IN THE SPIRITUAL LIGHT.

1. (Bishop Martin): "A very old-looking father of one of these ladies comes forward now and addresses the white-robed men in a lamenting voice: 'Oh, you mighty messengers of God, how is it possible that my daughter is also among these unfortunates? As far as I know, my daughter lived in strict obedience of her order's rules, and thus fully in the spirit of the only true church — the Roman Catholic, whose spirit must obviously be the Holy Ghost.

2.   In view of such a life and the assurances of the church, my daughter should have gone straight to heaven. For, in addition to her conscientiously holy life, she was awarded by the Pope himself not just one, but a whole dozen, of plenary indulgences, privileged by the Laurentian Mary, absolving her completely from purgatory. How can it be that here such a life has no value before God?

3.   Yes, I can assure you, upon my life, that my daughter was truly and unmistak ably nominated by heaven as a bride of Christ through a vision received by a most godly and strict-living Jesuit. This pious man admitted humbly to having had the following dream:

4.   Mary and St. Joseph came to him in a celestial light and said, ' Listen you pure brother of the angels. Go to N.N. who has a dear young daughter who has found favor with Jesus, and HE wants to make her His most favored bride. Go on behalf of God, your Lord, and procure this bride for Him, or you will never have a part in the Kingdom of God!'

5. Upon waking, he pondered this dream and after he had had the same dream *three* times, he informed the convent, which then passed it on to the general in Rome. And how surprised the whole convent was when the word came from the general that he had had the same dream, and when he did not believe it, Mary had appeared to him even a fourth time and said sadly:

6. 'Oh, you wretched worm in the dust, since you do not believe, you will be smitten with a severe illness until the dear maiden is in the convent of the Ladies of the Sacred Heart as a bride for my son! As a confirmation of the truth, for three days in succession all the bells in Rome shall ring of their own accord at midnight for an hour!'

7. All this had miraculously taken place, and the general secretly ordered special prayers in all the convents. He had also particularly urged the Jesuit, who had had the dream about my daughter, to keep praying night and day for her to join the convent.

8. I myself did not want to part with her, especially as I was very rich and of high nobility. My daughter was very beautiful, gentle and good, and could have married well. However, eventually I gave in to the pleas of the pious Jesuit, and as my daughter also preferred Christ to any other bridegroom, she took the veil and became a bride of Christ. Oh, you unhappy bride!

9. 'You mighty messengers of the Lord, tell me, poor unhappy father that I am, in what way did my daughter sin that she is now among these unfortunate, truly hellish, beings? Did she have any secret vices, or was she simply a hypocrite? Or is, perhaps, the Roman church a fake? Do tell me why this terrible thing has happened to my daughter!'

10. Says one of the two white-robed men: 'Friend, have you never read the Gospel of the Lord?'

11. Replies the old man: 'Only as a schoolboy, but never after that, for I used to attend mass every Sunday and on all holidays and listened to the sermons. Besides, we laymen were forbidden by the church to read the Bible, and I believe I did the right thing in obeying the church in everything.'

12. Says the messenger again: 'Well, if the church was more important to you than the pure Word of God, you will have to ask the church to account for what has happened to your daughter — not us, who as true Protestants, unlike the Roman church, have never ad-

204

hered to anything but what Christ Himself taught. But in the Gospel there is nothing mentioned about an only true Roman Catholic church, nor about a pope, Jesuits, or Ladies of the Sacred Heart. It simply says: 'Thou shalt love the Lord, thy God, with all thy heart, and with all thy soul, and with all thy mind . . . and thy neighbor as thyself. On these two commandments hang all the laws and all the prophets!'

13. Whoever works only for the sake of the reward is an idle servant and not worthy of the reward, even less of the Lord, Who says: ' He that loveth father or mother, son or daughter, more than Me is not worthy of Me. When ye shall have done all those things which are commanded you, say, we are unprofitable servants.'

14. Behold, those are words of God! Ask yourself whether you knew them and whether you or your spiritually arrogant daughter have ever observed them.'

15. Says the old man: 'If they are really the words of God, which I do not doubt, especially the commandments of love, I am beginning to understand why this has happened to my daughter. However, she is a victim of deception and entitled to forbearance and the Lord's mercy.'

16. Says the messenger again: 'Friend, if the Lord were not better than you and your daughter imagine, both of you would be in hell by now! But, because the Lord is endlessly better and wiser, you are now, instead of in hell, only in a most essential state of correction of your thinking, in a bath of mercy for the healing of your whole being.

17. Let me tell you that the dream of the Jesuit was an invention because of your beautiful and rich daughter. The Lord allowed this to happen in view of the fact that you wanted nothing less than a prince for your daughter. This was all the more wrong of you for, contrary to the Christian teaching that all men are equal, you withheld your daughter from a poor but otherwise righteous man, and even had him punished for his boldness! Such an attitude is accursed before God!

18. In the end it was not a prince who got your daughter, but a sly Jesuit, who deceived both of you! In view of all this, can you call God to account for the unfortunate state your daughter is in now — God Who is the essence of love, humility, and meekness?

19. Besides, my friend, your daughter was arrogant and harsh towards her subordinates, having soon become a prioress of this new

order, because she was the richest. She considered herself a saint in view of her miraculous calling, and even more so because at night a masked Lord Jesus visited her personally, to whom she, as his bride, naturally granted all he asked, after the so-called heavenly veil had been raised. Of course, she did not tell you about this, except that her Jesus demanded that you bequeath your entire great fortune to the holy order, which you also did in your blind faith!

20.   This is how things are with you and your daughter and how they will be with your wife, who is still living on earth. How do you imagine that a human being can expect heaven with such a life next to God's teaching, especially since your daughter knew very soon who her would-be Lord Jesus really was? Is this now clear to you, my dear friend?'

21.   The old man is quite nonplussed, and several others with him. He now feels like cursing Rome, but the two white-robed men forbid him to do so, pointing out to him that the Lord alone may condemn, and that all men must forgive if they want to be forgiven themselves. This pacifies our old man, and I can see that one of the frogs is beginning to shrink. It is probably the aforesaid 'bride of Christ.' Now things are beginning to move in the right direction, brother!"

79

THE OLD MAN'S ANGER CONCERNING ROME AND GOD'S FORBEARANCE. —PARABLES ABOUT THE LORD'S PATIENCE.

1. (Bishop Martin): "The old man once more addresses the messenger, saying: 'I now understand what you have told me and do not doubt that you are right. However, if things are as you describe, I would like to know why the Lord puts up with Rome at all. For in this case, Rome must be an abomination and not a church of the Lord at all.

2.   Where then is Peter, the rock, not to be prevailed over by the gates of hell? Rome claims this for itself, and the Pope, as the so-called deputy of Christ on earth, is allegedly sitting on that rock, constantly inspired by the Holy Ghost. Such a claim must be an

abomination before God! Do explain to me how it is possible that the Lord tolerates this. He must have a thousand ways of controlling such an evil.'

3. Says the messenger: 'That is true, my friend, the Lord can do absolutely anything He wants to. But what would you say of a father of many children if he immediately executed those who disobeyed him? Would not everybody say: What a shame. We have never seen such a devil of a father!

4. What would you say to a ruler who had his subjects immediately put to death for non-compliance with his laws? Wouldn't you cry: Oh, look, what a terrible tyrant, what an inhuman fiend!

5. Such an inhumanly severe father the children might resist quite successfully, and the subjects of such a tyrant could rise in rebellion and kill him.

6. If the Almighty Father were to treat His children like that, what would you think of such action on the part of God?

7. If the Almighty Father would do to His powerless creatures what bloodthirsty villains at one time did to the people in France, would not that be indescribably cruel?

8. The Lord is well aware what a harlot Rome is, just as He knew all about the adulteress, Mary Magdalen, and the woman of Samaria at Jacob's well. But the same forbearance He showed those three women, He is also showing Rome, and He welcomes everyone of her lost sons if he is truly penitent, however much he may have wooed the harlot Rome.

9. As for the rock of Peter, which prevails over the gates of hell, the Lord has referred to this in a number of texts in His Gospel.

10. So, for instance, it says: 'He that believeth on the son hath everlasting life.' — Behold, that is already a rock!

11. It is also written: ' The kingdom of God cometh not with observation . . . it is within you.' — There, too, the true, unconquerable rock of Peter has been erected!

12. And again it is written: 'He that hath my commandments, and keepeth them, he it is that loveth me; and he that loveth me shall be loved of my Father, and I will love him, and will manifest myself to him.' That, too, is Peter, the unconquerable, in the heart of man. That alone is the true, living church of the Lord, if He, through living faith which is love, has come to dwell in the heart of man.

13. Now you know about Peter and where he is. So stop ask-

ing about silly idle things of the world, but seek first the true Kingdom of God within you and its righteousness, and everything else
shall be given you.'

14. The old man now bows deeply before this messenger of the
Lord, and so do all the others. However, the frogs are still frogs; they
only seem to be somewhat less inflated. One of them has become
quite small, and is now approaching the two white-robed men. The
closer it gets, the smaller it becomes. This seems to be a good sign.

15. By the way, I must confess honestly and with gratitude to
the Lord that I have learned a lot from this scene and am now, no
doubt, considerably wiser than before. But the scene is becoming
more interesting and stranger all the time.

16. I must say that the description of the Jesuit in this case is
excellent. It truly requires more than divine patience not to punish
such types who are worse than Sodom and Gomorrah. It is as well
that I am not equipped with the Lord's might at this stage or things
would be really bad for these deceivers of the world! However, the
Lord's will be done!"

80

PARABLE ABOUT THE WHEAT AND THISTLES. — MARTIN'S
LOVE FOR THE LORD IS AWAKING. — CONTINUATION OF
THE SCENE WITH THE LADIES OF THE SACRED HEART.

1. (Borem): "That is right! The Lord's best and wisest will be
done! Apparently, the thistles are inferior to the wheat, which is
more or less the same all over the world. However, if you examine all
the different kinds of thistles, you will find the delicious pineapple,
the medicinal aloe, and the fig-thistle in Africa, rich in sugar content.

2. How foolish it would therefore be to condemn the entire
genus of thistles since nature shows how they can be improved.
Wheat stays wheat, but a thistle, ennobled, can become a pineapple.

3. Thus a Peter, a James, an Andrew, and so on, remained what
they were from the beginning — a pure wheat in the Lord's barn! But

among this wheat there was also a very prickly wild thistle. Its name was Saul. And behold, the Lord made a pineapple out of it, the most delicious fruit on earth.

4. And what the Lord has done then, he is still doing now, and we can only say from the depths of our hearts: 'O Father, Thy most holy will be done!'"

5. (Bishop Martin, moved to tears, says): "Yes, my dear brother, His holiest will be done in eternity! If I had Him here now, I could press Him to my heart in my overwhelming love. Oh, my good Lord Jesus, do come to both of us!"

6. (Borem): "Brother, now you have set your foot on the right path. You have now begun to draw Christ towards you, and salvation is not far off for you. You will soon learn what it means: 'Eye hath not seen, nor ear heard, neither have entered into the heart of man, the things that God hath prepared for them that love Him.' Nothing counts with the Lord but love, and this love for Him you have now awakened in your heart. If you stay in this love and allow it to grow, you will soon find what it will do for you. But now have a look at the tablet and tell me what you see there."

7. Bishop Martin glances quickly at the tablet and is startled when he sees it shine brighter than the sun. In the midst of all the brilliance, he reads the words: 'Brother, have patience for a short while and I shall be with you.' Surprised and overjoyed, he says:

8. (Bishop Martin): "O brother, I feel an ecstasy which I would not have thought possible! What will happen if this continues to grow, this love that I feel for the Lord Jesus constantly growing in my heart?

9. Yes — my love for the Lord Jesus is already overwhelming me, wanting me to be absorbed in Him with all my being!

10. Beloved Jesus, only now do I realize how utterly wise and good You are! And this realization, which so far has only been like a bright dream, has now become a certainty.

11. How I am now looking forward to the coming of the Lord, Who will no doubt help us to straighten out our still rather stubborn looking guests!"

12. (Borem): "Yes, brother, that will happen as soon as these ladies have shed the coarsest parts of their materialistic natures. Therefore, compose yourself now and describe the scene you see, which is going to be even more educational and interesting than before."

13. Bishop Martin once more concentrates on the back of the head of the Lady of the Sacred Heart, and finds that so far nothing has changed since the diversion of the shining tablet and his discussion with Borem.

14. But now the old man turns again to one of the men in white, and Bishop Martin follows attentively what is being discussed. He eventually says:

15. (Bishop Martin): "Now look at this! The old man is quite smart! He begs the two messengers to use their power to free at least his daughter from this abominable state so that he can go to heaven together with her, without any further delay, as he was getting desperately bored. He understood that the two were acting in accordance with the just will of the Lord. However, a feeling of insipidity and utter boredom was getting hold of him and he would like to leave this place as soon as possible.

16. The old man isn't at all stupid! But the two wise men in white seem to disagree with him, and one of them says:

17. 'Friend, patience is the principal rule in life, and this applies here just as it does in the world. Everything has its time, and to the extent that you continue to quicken in your heart's love and true faith in the Lord, your liberation from this desperate plight will be sped up.

18. However, our power cannot assist you in any way, for know that in this world nobody gets to heaven through would-be pious merits, nor through direct or indirect mercy of the Lord, but solely through his own love of the Lord and the consequent grace of the Lord Jesus Christ, Who is the one and only Lord and God of heaven and earth.

19. And mind this: There is no heaven outside of you. If you want to go to heaven, you have to open it up yourself. For true life must be free, and a life under compulsion is not life, but death!

20. If we freed you through our might, you would not be free but condemned; not alive but completely dead. Tell us — would you gain anything through such poor aid?'

21. The old people are now pondering over these words, but do not seem to comprehend their full meaning."

81

VANISHING OF THE FROGS IN THE SEA, AND THE PARENTS' SEARCH. — BOREM'S EXPLANATIONS.

1. (Bishop Martin): "Look, that one frog is now at the feet of the two in white, and is licking them!

2. One of the men says to the frog, pointing to the sea: 'Behold, there is your element!'

3. However, the frog is sitting up, croaking quite distinct words, which seem to say: 'Oh you mighty messengers, I realize that this terrible sea is my element which I have deserved as everlasting punishment. But I still dare to beg you to be merciful and not apply God's just condemnation in all its severity. However, not mine but *your* will be done!'

4. Says the one: 'We two have no will other than that of the Lord, which is eternally unchangeable. We have acquainted you with this will, and it is now up to you to obey. Behold, your element is over there!'

5. Ah, the frog is now beginning to croak pitifully, writhing and twisting and entreating the two to at least allow it to stay on the dry land.

6. Says the one again: 'As long as you are not prepared to walk the prescribed path, you cannot be helped.'

7. Now the frog turns miserably towards the sea and throws itself in. It has vanished — the waters seem to have swallowed it forever. Oh, the poor frog! I must tell you, brother Borem, that I pity that poor frog from the depths of my heart. But since it was the Lord's will, it is good this way. Still, I am very sorry for the frog.

8. Now the old man goes to the shore and says: 'If my poor daughter has not found mercy with the Lord, I do not want it either, and for love of my poor daughter, I shall throw myself into the sea to share her lot of eternal condemnation!'

9. With these words, he too throws himself into the sea, but does not sink since it is not his element. This is strange — he is walking around in the water as if it were dry land, searching for his daughter, lamenting. I wonder what will result from all this?

10. Ah, look — the other frogs also are getting smaller and smaller. They, too, are now licking the feet of the two men in white.

How strange — after having inflated themselves to such giant sizes, they now look like the smallest frogs on earth! They must have an extremely tough skin since it did not burst with that immense inflation.

11. Oh dear, if one of them had burst when they were so big, what an explosion that would have been! That could have driven the sea back for half an eternity. If they could invent something on earth of the elasticity of the skin of these frogs, that would mean the end of rubber.

12. Forgive me, dear brother, for these remarks of mine having a humorous tinge. That is still an old habit of mine. However, this thing, as such, is extremely funny, especially when I think of all the creases the skin of these frogs must be showing after such a shrinking!

13. I know that in the eyes of the Lord and His angels all these manifestations are of utter divine earnestness. But for one like me, they are often very funny. Thus the Lord, doubtlessly, did not laugh when He gave the ass its two long ears, but the likes of me must laugh seeing such a long-eared philosopher, although quite aware that the ass needs its long ears quite as much as the bird its scarcely visible ones.

14. Just as on earth there are many things that appear silly and therefore funny, so it is here, with many manifestations. Not all find them funny, of course, but only beings like myself. In time, if you can speak here of time at all, I shall probably not find them amusing any longer. But in my present state, I just cannot completely ignore the humorous aspect."

15. (Borem): "Never mind, dear brother. I am not morose either, and the Lord even less so. But the type of ridiculing laughter must be banned from heaven altogether, for it — just as excessive curiosity — hides some malicious pleasure.

16. However, in your remark about the elasticity of the skin of these frogs there was no malice, only the wittiness innate in your spirit. Eventually you will smile at your insipid jokes when you realize how meaningless they are. But for now concentrate once more on your little frogs and see what happens to them."

17. (Bishop Martin): "Yes, you are right! I can already see them. They are still licking the feet of the two men. Some are croaking at them, but I cannot understand a thing.

18. Most likely they, too, are asking the two messengers for a

general amnesty, but these do not seem to agree but keep pointing to the sea. The little frogs begin to croak even louder, climbing on the feet of the two men, but in vain. The men threaten them, and now the frogs hop towards the sea and also throw themselves in.

19. All the frogs have vanished. Only the old people are still standing on the shore, staring into the depths, hoping to still get a glimpse of their daughters. However, they cannot see anything, just as the first one, who is still wandering about on the water searching for his daughter. He calls to the others, telling them that the water is as solid as rock.

20. But they do not feel like probing the firmness of the water with their feet and, instead, return to the two men in white. They question them about the fate of their daughters, and whether they are now lost forever.

21. The two men in white do not answer, but walk out onto the sea and far away.

22. The old people are now in despair. Some try to step on the water as urged by the one — and it works. Now they all run out into the sea, intending to follow the two men, but it is not so easy, for the surface of the water seems to be slippery, and they keep tumbling one on top of the other. The first one, the one who wanted to throw himself into the water, makes quite good progress, but not so the others, who keep falling and scarcely manage to move from the one spot.

23. It would be interesting to know what is going to happen to these ladies, or frogs! I do not think they could be in hell since they are actually still standing here, but the Lord will know and see better than I do what non-hellish elements they still possess.

24. Tell me, dear brother, what is the real significance of all this — the frog shape, the sea, the vanishing of the frogs in the sea, the old people who do not sink, and the two messengers who have walked so far away?

25. Although I have watched this happen and have learned some things from it all, I still could not correctly interpret these manifestations. Do be good enough to tell me what they mean.''

26. (Borem): "All — especially female beings who lead spiritual lives with praying and fasting for the sake of heaven, but for whom worldly advantages are still most important — appear in their bare natural substance as amphibia which are capable of living in two elements.

27. The sea represents their natural element which, during their lives on earth, they had more at heart than the spiritual. Therefore, they now have to throw themselves into this element in order to realize the futility of their worldly aspirations. Besides, the sea also represents the accumulation of their great folly, which to recognize they now have to dive to the bottom of it. The serpents' heads of these frogs signify their arrogance and malice and their sly, calculating minds, whilst the scorpion tails denote their duplicity in attacking and wounding those whom they wished ill behind their backs. Is this now clear to you?"

28. (Bishop Martin): "Yes, brother, I understand it. Unfortunately, I have seen a lot of such hypocritical, ultra-papistical machinations on earth, but as a bishop I had to connive at what I saw. And why, you will surely know!"

29. (Borem): "Only too well! But listen! The old people, who were not too clever to start with and most of whom were of noble birth, never had a chance of attaining a light other than a priest-ridden one. In view of this, they accepted all the clerical rules and regulations as truly celestial, and sold their daughters to the clergy, together with considerable dowries. Now these old people are still much too stupid to be able to get to the bottom of their stupidity. That is why they are wandering around on top of it, slipping and falling like an ass on the ice. There is only the one who ist somewhat wiser than the rest. Is this also clear to you now?"

30. (Bishop Martin): "Oh yes, dearest brother, only too clear! And what a dance the nobility is having!"

31. (Borem): "True! But keep on watching this scene attentively. The first act has ended, and the second one is now going to start. And you will be surprised at what you are going to see!"

32. (Bishop Martin): "I am looking forward to it, and I am sure that I shall be able to understand the happenings much better than before. Just one thing, which I asked you before, dear brother, and which you have forgotten to explain to me: The walking away of the two wise men."

33. (Borem): "Oh no, here nothing is ever forgotten! However, the meaning of this and many other manifestations you will have to seek and find for yourself, as you need some practice in purely celestial matters. Try your own interpretation and see how far your wisdom is already reaching."

34. (Bishop Martin): "I see what you mean! Actually, since you

214

have already explained all the other things to me, I feel that this interpretation should not be too difficult. I think about it as follows.

35. The two wise men are like celestial oil, whilst these old, foolish aristocrats are like oily pitch on earth, dirty and smelling. That the oil from heaven cannot bear to be close to the pitch is understandable. What do you think, brother? Am I right?"

36. (Borem): "You are closer to the truth than you can grasp at this stage. However, you will eventually comprehend all the things to the root of which your comprehension cannot penetrate as yet. So do not ponder on this matter any longer, but go on watching the back of the head of the lady. You will soon find the solution to all this."

37. (Bishop Martin): "I am already watching, brother. So far nothing has changed. But . . . oh yes — there is already something new!"

82

SECOND ACT OF THE DRAMA WITH THE LADIES OF THE SACRED HEART. — THE HELLISH STORM ON THE SEA. — CAPTURE OF THE VERMIN IN A BAG. — BOREM'S COMMENTARY.

1. (Bishop Martin): "But what is that? Look — in the far west, dense clouds are rising from the sea, similar to what I have sometimes seen on earth before heavy thunderstorms. The cloud formations are drifting closer and closer, emitting countless flashes of lightning.

2. I also see water-spouts of various sizes moving along, ahead of the dark grey clouds. It looks extremely threatening! Now, also, our old people are noticing the approaching storm and are making every effort to reach the safe shore.

3. How hard they are trying, but their efforts seem in vain. Instead of coming closer to the shore, they are getting farther and farther away from it. This must be an awful ordeal for these old people, both men and women!

4. In the far distance, towards the south, I can still see the two white-robed men, shining like two stars. But they do not seem to pay any attention to this approaching strong gale. I see it coming nearer

and nearer, accompanied by over a thousand water-spouts and numerous flashes of lightning. I also hear terrible thunder, and I see the waves piling up to the height of mountains. Oh dear, oh dear, this does not look too good!

5. But the old people — they are trying so hard, but all in vain! It only shows you how helpless man is against the power of the elements. **Unless he is supported by divine power, he will forever be a nothing.** But I am now most curious to see what is going to happen."

6. (Borem): "Watch carefully and you will soon see what course this gale will take. Do not worry about the old people who are trying in vain to reach the shore before the approaching gale. It does not concern them. The two wise messengers in the south are now the target for revenge, because they did not listen to the pleading of these ladies.

7. This shows already some hellish elements, but only slightly. Having got to the bottom of their folly, they found some residue of their earthly aristocrats' pride and lust for power. This residue **kindled on the flame of their humiliating recollection of how, so they thought, the messengers changed them into frogs and drove them without mercy into the sea of damnation.**

8. The fire kindled by this residue took hold of their whole being, drove them to the brink of the first hell where they found a great many congenial supporters. United with these, they are now moving along in the storm clouds, desirous of taking revenge on the two messengers and on those who sent them. Just watch — the main action will now take place."

9. (Bishop Martin): "Thank you and particularly the Lord for this explanation. However, at the same time, I must confess that I now feel really angry with these ninnies, whilst previously I still felt sort of sorry for them. If I only had the might of those two messengers, these storm-heroines would not fare too well! But I hope the two will know how to defend themselves against these stupid, abominable creatures.

10. Look, the storm is now really swerving in a right-hand turn towards the south. Countless flashes of lightning are aiming in the direction of the two wise men, who are now standing motionless, like the two stars, Castor and Pollux. How mightily the waves are surging and how the storm is raging and roaring!

11. But look at the poor old people! They are now unable to stand upright, only crawl on their hands and feet. It must be real hell

216

for them! Ah, ah, a shred of cloud is now separating itself from the rest and drifting towards the old people. I wonder what will come of that?

12. Just look at that! The shred of cloud is enveloping the first old man who threw himself into the sea, and is carrying him onto the shore. This happened with lightning speed! Now the shred of cloud is drawing together and shrinking into a human shape.

13. Ah, it is one of the ladies — the first one, into the back of whose head I am looking. She is comforting her father, even hugging him, and he is so very happy to hold once more in his arms the daughter he had believed lost forever. I must say it is a most touching sight. Meanwhile, the others are shamelessly storming ahead.

14. I can now see the rearguard of the storm, consisting of a countless army of dragons, crocodiles, and God knows what other vermin! What a noise!

15. What roaring, whistling, and hissing! The sea seems to be seething below the storm clouds, and already begins to glow. Big balls of fire are now visible in the clouds, some already quite close to the messengers, who have now become better visible than before.

16. At last, the two are turning around and threatening the storm which, however, does not yield but seems only to intensify its raging.

17. This looks most peculiar! Look — look, the two appear to be taking to their heels and they are now rapidly soaring towards the old man and his daughter on the shore. They have arrived, thank God, and are greeting the old man and his daughter with the greatest kindness. How wonderful and moving this is. But the storm is now turning in this direction also.

18. This frog- and vermin-storm is most aggressive! I wonder what will come of all this?"

19. (Borem): "Watch carefully! The climax of the second act is imminent. You'll see now some judgment and a fateful development!"

20. (Bishop Martin): "Yes, brother, in this development the crop will probably yield only very little in grain for heaven, but all the more useless chaff for hell. But I had better continue watching this scene attentively.

21. Oh, look, the storm is close to the shore. The old man and his saved daughter are very frightened, but the two wise messengers are comforting them, and I hear them say:

22. 'Do not fear this humbug. It has no real existence! When blindness is raging, the seeing can easily evade it! If a thousand blind warriors armed with swords and spears marched against one sighted, well-armed and experienced warrior, what could they achieve? The one could easily kill all of them.

23. And here in the spirit world, this would even be much easier than on earth, for such low spirits are not only blind, but also deaf. Be assured, the two of us will catch all this storm-vermin in a sack and then we can do with them whatever we please. Watch now what is going to happen!'

24. I am very glad to see that the two wise men are already on the best of terms with the old man and his daughter. But how the two are going to face the fast approaching, raging storm, and even catch it in a sack — that to witness will really be worthwhile!

25. But now the old people, who are still out on the water, are quite enveloped in the storm clouds, and are screaming for help. But no help is coming, except that the force of the storm is pushing them towards the shore, just like a strong wind might carry with it articles scattered on a sheet of ice.

26. Now the old people have reached the shore and the storm is lashing out against the two messengers with countless flashes of lightning. They, however, are holding a big sack open, and one of them says to the storm: 'Listen, you savage monster, either you get into this sack or you will be condemned to hell. You may choose.'

27. There is a mighty thunder-clap, countless flashes of lightning are shooting in all directions from the constantly shrinking mass of storm clouds, and from the center of the cloud formation a horrible monster is poking its ugly head out with yawning jaws, as if ready to swallow the whole earth.

28. It is a terrible sight, but our two messengers do not seem to be frightened at all, and one of them repeats: 'Sack — or hell!'

29. Ah, look, the huge mass of clouds, including the monstrous head, is shrinking into a small coil, about the size of a barrel. It is now rolling towards the opening of the sack, and into it!

30. This does seem funny. The whole storm is in a sack! It is almost like watching a fairy tale from *A Thousand and One Nights*. I wonder what will happen next?

31. The storm is contained in the sack so calmly, almost as if it had never stirred at all. What a burlesque picture! A whole raging

218

storm, with all its terrors, in a sack! Brother, if this too has a wise and deep significance, I'll eat my hat!"

32. (Borem): "But it has a most wise significance! Have you never heard of true penitents in sackcloth and ashes?

33. In view of their utter wickedness, these storm-heroines have been given their judgment by the messengers: They can choose between penitence, that is, entering the sack of their own free will, or being banned by the might of God to the first degree hell, which consists in utter humiliation and abasement of the soul.

34. The first, a freely chosen judgment, may mean life for a soul if pursued with determination unimpeded by false self-respect. The condemnation to hell, however, may mean death for the soul, as this is a judgment passed in case the soul is not prepared to humble itself. But it must be humiliated or other souls might be harmed considerably through the uncontrolled arrogance of one single soul. Whether or how such souls that have been condemned to hell can still attain life and how they are guided from thereon, only the Lord knows, and he to whom the Lord may reveal it in all secrecy.

35. Do you now understand the wise significance of the sack? To go into a sack means to imprison all one's lusts and desires, to rid oneself of them and go forth from the sack as a new creature, pleasing to God. Do you now understand this manifestation which appeared so foolish to you?"

36. (Bishop Martin): "Yes, brother, this is now quite clear to me and another thing too — that I am still a great ass! It is all so clear and logical and I, silly ass that I am, could laugh about this sublime manifestation! Dear brother, you must truly possess more than celestial patience that you do not put *me* in such a sack as well!"

37. (Borem): "Never mind! I can only repeat what I have told you before, that you are close to a great and magnificent goal. Keep cultivating your heart with diligence and watch everything attentively, and you will soon see how close your own redemption is."

BISHOP MARTIN'S LONGING FOR THE LORD. — THE FISHES
IN THE SACK. — SORTING OF THE FISH. — THE CHALICE,
VESSEL OF GRACE, AND OTHER CORRESPONDENCES. —
THE BEGINNING OF MARTIN'S SPIRITUAL REDEMPTION.

1. (Bishop Martin): "May the Lord grant me redemption according to His grace, and thus to all those who are still more or less blind. As long as you are not completely at home in this realm of spirits, you are incapable of the inner, blissful contentment. And you cannot be at home anywhere else but in the house of the Lord, the most holy house of the Father. Therefore, my greatest longing is to be with the Lord as soon as possible. So I will now pay the utmost attention to everything I see, that my redemption may be worked out soon. Therefore, I shall concentrate again on the back of the head of this lady.

2. Ah, the two messengers are dragging the sack towards the shore. What are they going to do now? They wouldn't commit the sack, or rather its contents, to the sea again, would they? The old man and his daughter are helping with the sack, whilst the other old people are timidly awaiting the further development. They do not appear to know what the sack contains.

3. The sack has reached the water and is opened. I wonder what it may reveal? Oh, just look — a great quantity of fish is appearing; there are big and small fishes, some fresh, others rotten and lifeless.

4. Now the two messengers are beginning to separate the fresh fish from the rotten ones, which they throw into the sea. The fresh ones are being placed in a magnificent vessel, which resembles a huge chalice and shines as if made of silver or gold. Wherever are they getting these things from so suddenly, when they hadn't been there before? The moment they are wanted, they are there, as if by magic! But actually, I do understand how such things come into existence. They are needed in the course of the divine order! The Lord wants them, and they are available! Isn't that so, my beloved brother, Borem?"

5. (Borem): "Yes, you are right. You now realize that the Lord is all in all. And, therefore, you find it quite easy to comprehend

from the depth of your being the source of all the many miracles you are witnessing here. Now go on watching!"

6. (Bishop Martin): "Yes, brother, I am concentrating on the scene. I can now see the chalice expanding, together with its stand, but it is not gaining in height, only in girth. The fish in it are swimming about briskly, just as on earth goldfish swim in a glass bowl except that these fish are considerably bigger.

7. They must be the former ladies who were driven into the sea as ugly frogs. However, so far I cannot find an explanation as to why they are appearing this time as fish, or why many rotten and dead ones were thrown back into the sea. I have a very faint notion of the reason why, but I cannot put it into words as yet.

8. Wait — I have a brainwave! Yes, yes, now I have it! The chalice represents the vessel of the Lord's grace and mercy, into which these ladies have now been admitted. And the water in the vessel is living water that will cleanse these ladies who are still in the shape of fish, and give them back their human form. The expanding of the chalice denotes the growing of the Lord's grace and mercy. The fish shape seems to represent the shape of the free, humble penitent and, generally, of all human beings who, of their own free will, are being caught for the Kingdom of God through the Word of God or, rather, are willing to be caught. That is why the Lord Himself called His apostles 'fishermen of men.'

9. And, as concerns the rotten fish thrown back into the sea, the Lord Himself has given a picture of this event in the Gospel, the truest good tidings from heaven. That the fishes in the chalice — at least for the time being — are better off than those in the sea, is obvious. What do you think, dearest brother? Is my interpretation correct?"

10. (Borem): "All our love to the Lord, our God! Rejoice, brother, for the Lord has redeemed your spirit! This was not comprehended by your soul, but solely by your spirit which the Lord has now fully awakened in you. Therefore, you can now understand the heavenly meaning of things. This is the beginning of your redemption, which I have mentioned to you already on several occasions, and at the same time, it is the end of the second act of this great spiritual drama.

11. Your interpretation of what you have witnessed in this scene is correct in every detail, although you have not yet attained complete spiritual vision. But what you are still lacking, the third act

221

will give you — thanks to the boundless grace of the Lord. Therefore, go on watching and you will see the mightiest manifestations and also learn the most miraculous ways in which the Lord guides His children to the great goal of salvation and life. Pay attention — this most important third act is commencing!''

84

BEGINNING OF THE THIRD ACT OF THE CELESTIAL DRAMA. – THE CHALICE OF GRACE WITH BOILING WATER. -- THE INFERNAL RAMPART.

1. (Bishop Martin): "I am already looking with greatest interest at the scene, but so far it is still unchanged. The chalice has grown very large though. It could well be several fathoms in circumference, by earthly standards. And if I see right, it is still growing.

2. The two messengers are standing at the edge of this huge chalice, and the old man and his daughter are looking at it attentively. The other old people, however, are looking at it from a distance, like oxen would stare at a new gate in the world.

3. The fish in the chalice, swimming around briskly in the spacious golden basin, are by now quite big. The heads of some of them look already rather human, while others look still more like fish. I assume they will first turn into some sort of spiritual mermaids, and eventually into actual well-shaped female beings.

4. But what's that I notice? The sea, which previously had looked so ominous, has completely vanished! Instead, on its shore, the still growing chalice is now standing in the middle of a vast plain, measuring maybe a hundred square miles. In the far distance, this plain seems to be surrounded by an exceedingly strong and high rampart; it is clearly noticeable where the plain ends and the rampart begins.

5. The most peculiar thing is that the rampart is getting higher and then again lower in various places. In the places where the rampart is considerably growing in height, I can see that one could easily see through underneath. What an unusual type of rampart! I wonder what that could mean?

6. The chalice remains unchanged, but a good ten thousand feet

from it an immense, completely round hole has now formed on the spot where, I think, the convent once stood and where, after its destruction, the ugly mud hole appeared. Dense smoke is now coming from that hole, but it vanishes again after having risen only a few fathoms above the edge of the hole. What strange preparations for the third act of this drama!

7. But look at the chalice, brother! The water in it is beginning to boil and steam mightily. The poor fishes are lifting their heads over the edge of the chalice, screaming awfully. They all have already human heads, except that some still bear a likeness to sea lions.

8. Ah, the water in the chalice is boiling fiercely and the steam is getting denser. The poor fishes are screaming terribly from the pain. If this boiling continues for a while, there soon will be a great quantity of hot, cooked fish — one of my favorite dishes on earth.

9. Ah, look — the fishes are already getting arms and well-shaped hands, with which they are trying to lift themselves over the edge of the chalice in order to escape the torture. However, their arms do not seem to be very strong as yet for they soon have to let go the edge and fall back into the boiling water.

10. I would like to understand basically what causes the water in this giant chalice to boil like that. The poor fish — they are being whirled around in the fiercer and fiercer boiling water like loose sand whirled by a violently gushing spring! How they writhe and twist, and what a wail of lamentation is coming from that chalice!

11. The two messengers are standing there impassively. Their faces betray no pity. You would think that they enjoyed the scene. No, dear brother, I think that is really overdoing it! Why should these poor souls be tortured so horribly to regain their human shapes? I myself, a sinner of the worst kind, did not have to go through such a refining process. Thank goodness, I am still a human being, even if only in peasant clothes!"

12. (Borem). "Brother, do not forget the word 'appearances'! You are still seeing these ladies lined up before as unharmed. How can you worry about what is going on solely in their inner selves? Although the inner world of a human being is really the true world, man stays human, growing in perfection to the same extent that the inner self is being stirred and activated.

13. You are under the impression that you retained your human shape without being refined like this. I can assure you that you were boiling in the Lord's chalice of grace much fiercer than these ladies.

Were you aware of it at all? When you have been perfected and are shown the activity of mortals on earth, what will you say then, seeing the inner source of life and the countless streams of fire raging through countless channels? So be reasonable, my dear brother!"

14. (Bishop Martin): "Of course, you are right! So let them be boiled and, if necessary, also fried a little bit! To boil and fry in the Lord's love and grace is truly nothing to complain about! Since I have gone through this boiling process, feeling little or nothing of it, the ladies are surely not faring as badly as they make out. Whatever the Lord does is always the best!

15. Now the old people are approaching the two messengers, requesting permission to join their daughters in the chalice, and permission is granted. Also, the first old man and his daughter are jumping into the hot bath. Now they are all in it, and it is terrible to watch how the boiling water is working on this party.

16. Oh, this screaming, lamenting, this desperate wringing of hands and calling for help! No, brother, even if it is only an appearance, if it causes so much pain I'm not for it. The ladies must be feeling something. I notice that they are now beginning to move, while previously they were standing there stiffly and as immobile as if nailed to the spot!"

17. (Borem): "But that is good. Life is returning to them! Is not that something to be glad about?"

18. (Bishop Martin): "If that is the case, I am reassured. However, the sight of this revival is rather unpleasant. This reminds me very much of purgatory."

19. (Borem): "Forget about your purgatory! I can assure you, there is nothing of the kind anywhere, ever! Here you see nothing but the love of God in action which, of course, is a fire of fires. But this fire is not painful. On the contrary, it eases all pain and heals all the wounds inflicted by hell. The souls do suffer pain and cry for help and relief. However, it is not the boiling chalice that causes the pain, only hell which must now relinquish them.

20. Go on watching! Look at the huge rampart surrounding the plain. You will soon realize that this rampart is nothing else but hell, or the devil in the shape of a giant serpent which has positioned itself around the plain so as not to allow these saved souls, its presumed spoil, to escape. All this is still only an appearance, and the plain denotes the worldliness of these saved souls, from which they cannot get away as it is permeated by hell.

21. "Thus it is this rampart that causes all the suffering to those in the chalice. But, before long, this rampart will be destroyed and thrown into the chasm, which is already visible some ten thousand paces north of the chalice of grace. Watch attentively, and you will soon see what preventive measures are being taken."

85

THE IMMINENT CATASTROPHE. — THE OLD SERPENT, THE TWELVE ANGELS OF JUDGMENT AND THE CHASM. — SPLENDID VICTORY AND THE MAGNIFICENT PRIZE.

1. (Bishop Martin): "True, true, of course you are right! Beyond the rampart I can now see twelve great spirits, each with a huge sword in his right hand. But what a sword! With such a sword a spirit could split up the entire earth like an apple! But then, these spirits are big enough to crush the whole world between two of their fingers! Oh dear, oh dear, the rampart is growing more and more furious. Brother, this does look like a last Judgment to me!

2. But now I notice that the water in the chalice has somewhat calmed down and the entire party is lying as if dead under the surface of the still mightily steaming water. There is no sound from the chalice. Only the two messengers are discussing something, but I cannot hear what it is about. One of them is holding a staff in his hand, similar to the one of Aaron's. Now he is raising it. I wonder what will come of this?

3. Ah, look at the rampart! It is coming nearer, growing bigger, and raising its back here and there to astonishing heights. What a terrible sight! Now I can see the abominable head of this infernal monster. O God, how hideous it is; and it is creeping closer all the time!

4. Now it is raising its horrible head, its jaws gaping wide as if to swallow the whole of creation. It is approaching the chalice in a straight line. If it should grab the chalice, this would fit into one of its hollow teeth.

5. Now everything has completely calmed down in the chalice. But the horrible pit at the site of the former convent is emitting

dense smoke, and now I see already fire and flames. The monster is no more than a thousand feet away from the chalice.

6. What is going to happen? The twelve giant spirits are holding their swords raised and their eyes are fixed on the messenger with the staff in his right hand. This one now signals to the monster to retreat, but it does not take any notice, just keeps approaching the chalice.

7. Ah, this does look most ominous! The messenger again signals with the staff, but in vain. What a horrible sight it is now as the monster, unperturbed, creeps up closer and closer to the chalice! The messenger is signalling once more with his staff, but again in vain.

8. Oh, oh, its head has reached the chalice and is trying to upset it with its long double tongue. But the chalice is immovable, and also nothing inside it is stirring.

9. The huge beast is growing more obtusive. Again the messenger raises his staff, signing to the monster to withdraw from the chalice, but it still does not take any notice.

10. Now the messenger dips his staff into the chalice and signs to the twelve mighty spirits. They strike hard, and — look — the monster has been split into twelve parts!

11. Oh dear, what raging, what a frenzy! The separate parts are winding and twisting, bouncing around the vast plain like individual mountains, and gradually rolling nearer to the hideous pit.

12. Ah, and the head — that is worst of all! It is leaping sky-high, sneering at the twelve spirits in such an indescribable rage that it must surely make them shudder.

13. But now one of the messengers drives the head with his staff towards the pit and — God be thanked — into it! Smoke and flames shoot out and, oh, what a crackling noise. It is terrible.

14. Also, the other eleven parts are pushed into the pit by an invisible force, and the crackling and smoke and flames give the impression as if the whole earth were on fire.

15. This thundering noise is so terrible that it makes me almost speechless. One would have to have the tongue of a fiery cherub to be able to describe the horror of this raging coming out of the pit. But let it rage, I am only thankful that this hideous beast is now in infernal confinement. It does not look as if this monster could emerge from there so easily.

16. The two messengers are once more at the edge of the chalice and also the twelve great spirits are approaching it. However, the

closer they get to it, the smaller they become. Isn't that peculiar? They were such colossal giants and now they are scarcely taller than the two white-robed messengers.

17. They have now reached the two messengers. But what do I see now? They are bowing very deeply, particularly before the one who is holding the Aaron staff. That must surely mean that he is an angel from the highest heaven!

18. Now this one speaks to the twelve: 'Brothers, lift up the chalice and carry it over to the gate of hell. Then place the stand above the gate to prevent the evil rising again too easily to drag down this poor party, for whose revival in Me all the powers of heaven had to be used. So be it'"

19. The twelve, now lift the chalice, carefully carrying it over to the pit, where they place the stand on top of it so that no more smoke can come forth. The stand of the chalice seems to seal it hermetically. The whole surroundings look quite friendly already! And I notice something else — the entire party in the water of the chalice is beginning to stir. God be thanked that they are coming alive again!"

86

THE ONE GREAT, EVERLASTING HERO. — THE GLORIOUS REDEMPTION. — PARABLE OF THE SOWING, GROWING, AND REAPING. — THE GREAT HARVEST.

1. (Bishop Martin): "But why would these twelve spirits show that much respect to the one messenger? They have all gone down on their knees and are practically worshipping him. It wouldn't be the Lord Himself, would it? If I could only see his face I would soon know whether it is the Lord or somebody else.

2. The twelve are once more rising to their feet and bowing deeply to the one, but he now shakes hands with all of them, saying in a low, but clearly audible, voice:

3. 'Look, brothers, what a good pasture. I am handing these lambs over to you. Graze and fatten them for My fold as good food which My heart can enjoy. Lift them cautiously from the vessel of

My care and let them feed freely on these vast pastures of My love, grace, and mercy. So be it!'

4. It is the Lord, indeed! In the infinity of heaven, no one but the Lord can speak as this messenger has now spoken. Therefore, I am now convinced that this messenger is the Lord Himself. What do you think, brother?"

5. (Borem): "Yes, brother, it is the Lord. And you could have noticed that long ago, but He confined your eyes to enable your spirit to become all the more active. But now is the time for your eyes to be opened. Now they have been opened, and you now recognize the Lord, which is very good.

6. However, continue to watch the scene before us for a short while longer, so that you will see the complete unravelling of the great tangle, and that you might recognize the Lord's boundless love and mercy. For there is no one like Him, neither in all the heavens nor in all the worlds, nor in all infinity!"

7. (Bishop Martin): "O God, o Lord, You most loving and holy Father! Who could ever conceive Your boundless wisdom and kindness? You, alone, the Holiest of Holy, are a Master of the depths of all being! No cherub could ever conceive Your wisdom completely! Holy, holy, is Your name, and the everlasting order of all things is Your Holy will!

8. You are forever self-sufficient and need nobody's counsel. But Your holy fatherly heart does not want to enjoy the boundless profusion of Your holy perfection alone. So from its most profound ideas, it calls forth beings, shaping them into children of God in the fire of His endless love and in the light of His eternal wisdom, to enable them forever to fully participate in the infinite perfection of this most holy heart of the Father, like independent divine beings.

9. Hear this — all you heavens, you seraphs and cherubs, and all you angels — God, the everlasting Spirit, in all His fullness of divine perfection, forever inconceivable, is our Father, walking among us as if He were not any more than we are! Oh, let us praise Him in our hearts for having so inconceivably lowered Himself to us sinners!

10. O Lord, o Father, from now on nothing else will have room in my heart but You, for You have now become all things to me! There was a time when You were very small in my heart. That was when I was a sinner. Now You have grown infinitely large and, consequently, I am a blessed spirit. But all this, Father, is solely Your work, and I was, am, and shall forever remain, a most idle servant!

228

11. Oh, brother Borem, look, over there, the twelve are now lifting the guests of the holy chalice from the water, and they are so beautiful and sublime that I can only describe them as angels. How magnificent they now look! Look at the joy that is shining from their heavenly eyes, which are now destined to behold God!

12. Rejoice with me, brother, and feel how good the Lord is! Oh, oh, I could waste away with love for the Lord!"

13. (Borem): "That stage of the work where we could not have done anything, and where the Lord Himself always acts directly, is now completed. It is now up to us, as children of God, to carry on with this work within His love and order. Therefore, we now have to be prepared for whatever may emerge.

14. Actually, what the Lord is doing here corresponds with what He is doing on earth. There, men take grains of wheat and sow them into the soil. Such preliminary work was done here, too, when you were teaching and instructing this entire party, aided by me. Thus we sowed God's wheat into the furrows of their turbid hearts.

15. Once the seed is in the soil, no man can do anything at all to make it grow and bear fruit. The Lord alone can do that, through His direct influence on the respective spirits of nature, inspiring them to full activity, resulting in the growth of plants and animals. In this work, only few of those spirits are involved who are at all times the Lord's closest friends and brothers.

16. When this work is completed and the crops are ready, they are once more handed over to men, to be gathered and stored in their barns. And this same work is now awaiting us.

17. First we sowed the seed of the Word of God into their hearts, where it rested like the seed in the soil on earth. During this rest, the Lord commenced His work, and there is nothing we could have done except watch Him at work. Just as on earth, the farmer can only watch his corn grow and ripen for the harvest.

18. This corn here — our brothers and sisters — has now ripened, thanks to the sole efforts of the Lord. Now the time has come for us to harvest it. Therefore, let us take possession of this abundance in the name of the Lord, and let our hearts once again become active.

19. As you know, the harvest always considerably exceeds the sowing; the same will be the case here. Where originally we had to deal with one only, there will now be thirty to one hundred. Rejoice, dear brother, for a rich harvest is awaiting us!"

87

BISHOP MARTIN'S MODESTY, GUIDED BY BOREM'S WISDOM. — MARTIN IN FESTIVE ARRAY. — EXTENSION OF MARTIN'S HOUSE.

1. (Borem): "Now there is another matter. Beneath the Lord's tablet in your house, you will see a chest, as of pure gold. Go and open it, and you will find a robe and a shining hat. Dress in the robe and hat, the true celestial wedding garb, for there will be a dignified reception of the soon-returning guests, in the name of the Lord, Who will bring the recovered souls here Himself. Go and change. It is the will of the Lord!"

2. (Bishop Martin): "Dearest brother, all that you have so far told me was sublime and true, like the Word of God itself. Only this last matter seems suspect of a sort of celestial vanity, which does not bother me at all. Therefore, you must forgive me if I do not obey you in this particular point.

3. I am so happy that at long last my heart is in order — the only thing of importance to the Lord. As for my outer attire, I am quite satisfied with this peasant's smock for all eternity.

4. I really do not care about splendor any longer, be it celestial or earthly. But I now care all the more about love of the Lord, which only my heart can promote and not a splendid robe and hat. Therefore, I remain as I am, a peasant!"

5. (Borem): "You are right, dear brother. Of course the Lord looks only at the heart. And our humility, proven in the true love of the Lord, is every angel's most precious garb. However, it is a requirement of the Lord's order that in His Kingdom every dweller in the heavens has to be arrayed in a garb of rebirth and immortality, corresponding to his inner self. There is no being in all infinity more humble than the Lord Himself, and still you cannot imagine any splendor that does not orginate in Him.

6. Behold the magnificence and vastness of this hall, which is only one of the rooms in your house. Who but the Lord could be the originator and sole builder of such indescribable splendor and majesty?

7. On first entering the house which the Lord gave you, you immediately looked through the twelve doors and saw twelve drops

from the endless sea of the Lord's creations. And you were almost seized with fear by just glancing at such overwhelming magnificence and majesty. What would you say if you had actually seen an angel in all his celestial glory? You could not have looked at him and lived — so endlessly great is his beauty, his glory, magnificence and majesty!

8. From what I have just told you and from many other things I have explained to you, you can see that everything, including proper magnificence and splendor, originates in the Lord. So I do think that you would be doing the right thing to adapt yourself to the Lord's order.

9. Do you know what the Lord said to Peter when he, out of sheer humility, objected to the Lord washing his feet? If you abide with your humble obstinacy, the Lord might say the same to you. Therefore, go and do as I bid you, on behalf of the Lord, and then everything will look different in your house also. However, before donning the new garb, you must first shed the old one to the last shred, and wash your feet with the water from a basin you will find placed in readiness. Only after having done this, open the golden chest, take out the clothes and put them on."

10. (Bishop Martin): "Well, if this is the way it is, I shall have to comply with your orders, in the name of the Lord. I must admit, though, dearest brother, that I do not like the idea very much, because, notwithstanding your wise explanations, I still feel that there is a kind of vanity in it. However, since it is the Lord's regulation, I will follow it in His name. And where do I put my present clothes? Do I put them in the golden chest for an everlasting keepsake?"

11. (Borem): "Do not trouble yourself about that. Somebody else will be seeing to it."

12. Bishop Martin goes to the chest and looks around to see if he is being watched. However, when he finds himself behind a neat protecting screen which conceals him from the many guests in his house, he quickly undresses. He puts the old clothes in a heap before him, and they vanish forthwith. He then scoops some water in his hands from the aforesaid basin and washes his feet. When he has finished this, the golden chest bursts open and our good Martin is already clothed in a purple robe with a border of the most splendid stars. And on his head he has a hat which shines much brighter than the sun.

13. The moment he has been arrayed in these clothes, the interior of his house expands to such an extent that it appears to

Bishop Martin a hundred times larger than before. Simultaneously, the approaches to the galleries open up, which so far had not been possible to find.

14. Noticing all this, Bishop Martin is moved to tears by a feeling of great happiness, and he begins to praise Me openly.

15. As his tears begin to flow freely from emotion, Borem comes to him dressed in a similar attire, and says:

16. (Borem): "Well, brother, how do you like this? Are you feeling any vainer now?"

17. (Bishop Martin): "O brother, only now do I feel how small I am — and how immensely great the Lord is!"

18. (Borem): "Come along now, for everything is prepared to greet you as the owner of this house. Rejoice, for this greeting will be magnificent!"

88

BISHOP MARTIN IS GREETED BY THE HAPPY PARTY. — HIS REFERENCE TO THE LORD AS THE SOLE BENEFACTOR. — THE ONE THING STILL MISSING.

1. Bishop Martin emerges, together with Borem, from behind the rather extensive protective screen, and about fifteen hundred jubilant guests come forward to meet him. They greet him and thank him for looking after them when they first arrived and for his wise teachings which they took with them on their journey of trials.

2. They all express their great joy and even greater love and respect, which makes our Bishop Martin very happy. He is particularly glad to see from their good looks that they are on the best way and have already attained a state of inner refinement.

3. He looks at the party with great pleasure, quite surprised at their good appearance, and only after a while does he say:

4. (Bishop Martin): "My dearest friends, brothers and sisters, I am so very glad for you and also happy about your kindness to me. However, you must not praise and thank me for your salvation and that you now find yourselves in the forecourt to the true Kingdom

of Heaven. All praises and thanks are due to the Lord alone, Whose boundless grace has changed you in such a wonderful way. As for me, just love me as your brother who shares with you the same God and Lord as a Father.

5. Let us love this one and only, truest and holiest Father forever, beyond measure. He alone works all things, and is all things to all men. Therefore, all the honor and glory, thanks and praise , be due to Him alone!

6. I myself, and this dear friend and brother here, have witnessed how the Lord alone guided you, how He removed all the trash from your hearts, and how He fought for your sake a fierce battle against hell.

7. Therefore, let us all open our hearts wide and admit the Lord of Glory! May He come soon into our hearts and dwell there forever!"

8. Hearing such words from their host, the party becomes like transfigured and praises the Lord for giving man such great might and wisdom. Then all the leaders of the party go to Bishop Martin and beg him to be allowed to stay with him as his lowest servants.

9. (Bishop Martin): "Friends, not as my servants, but as my dearest brothers and sisters may you stay here forever and share everything the Lord has provided me with so abundantly. Without you, this boundless splendor and magnificence would be only a burden to me. But together with you I could really enjoy it as it would enable me to give you joy and happiness.

10. Oh, do stay here, all of you, and share my joy in the Lord, Who has prepared for us such a vast and magnificent dwelling in His Kingdom and, as I can now see, also a table with the most delicious bread and wine in an abundance to last forever. And all this without even one of us having deserved it by living a life in accordance with His Word! All the more reason for us to love and praise Him for having given us all this, although we are not worthy of it, nor ever shall be.

11. You can now see how beyond measure His love for us is and, therefore, so should ours be for Him. We now have everything as blessed spirits, except for one thing, which is still missing. And this, my dear brothers and sisters, is the presence of the Lord, visibly, in our midst. So let us beg Him in our hearts to grant us this supreme favor!"

12. (The leaders of the party agree with the bishop, but remark):

"This is our greatest wish, too, but we are still much too unworthy to hope for its realization. Therefore, we are grateful for what He has given us, although we are not worthy of it, and our desire to see the Lord shall at all times be our highest aspiration!"

13. (Bishop Martin): "You are right, dear brothers and sisters. That is what true wisdom demands of us. However, love often over-rules wisdom and does what it wants. In this case, I side with love. I suggest you do the same, and you will not go wrong!"

89

BISHOP MARTIN AND THE BOTANIST IN THE GARDEN. — NEW DESTITUTE ARRIVALS. — THE LONGED-FOR, EXQUI- SITE REWARD.

1. When Bishop Martin is on the point of more praise of love, someone outside calls his name: "Martin!"

2. Hearing this, Bishop Martin asks Borem whether he has any idea who might have called him.

3. (Borem): "Go outside, brother, and see for yourself. Even here it is sometimes like in the world. Except for the Lord, one cannot see everything from one point, but has to go to different places to see and hear, as you will have already noticed on many occasions.

4. Therefore, hurry outside and you will find out who has called you. I do not know the answer to everything as yet, my dearest brother. But again I hear the calling, so better go outside and see who it is."

5. (Bishop Martin): "Yes, I am going. Probably there are some lost spirits again, requiring help."

6. Bishop Martin hurries to the door, opens it, and is surprised at the great magnificence of his garden, which has expanded and im- proved immeasurably since he met Borem planting the trees.

7. As there is nobody waiting for him at the door, Bishop Martin goes into the garden to look for the one who called him. Walking to- wards the east, he comes to an arbor which looks like a large, so-to- speak open, living temple, in the middle of which he sees somebody busy sorting out plants which are lying on an also living altar.

8. (Bishop Martin watches this man for a while, then approaches him and says): "Dearest friend and brother, was it you who called me by my name? If so, let me know in what way my heart can serve you."

9. (The Botanist): "My dear friend and brother, your house has now become very spacious and so has your garden. You have already taken in more than a thousand brothers and sisters, which is most noble of you. However, I think that if there is room for that many, there must also be room for some more.

10. Follow me to the western part of your garden. There you'll find a hundred poor, needing a home. Take them into your house, and me as well, since in a way I belong to them, and you will not regret it."

11. (Bishop Martin): "But, dear friend and brother, what is a hundred? I can assure you, that even if it were ten thousand, I would not let them go but would make every effort to keep them here. Therefore, take me to them right away, so that I may look after them to the best of my ability, with the help of the Lord."

12. (The Botanist): "Oh, friend and brother, you have become like a precious balm to my heart! Let us go immediately, and we shall soon be with them."

13. The two walk towards the west and come across a group of humans, both male and female. All of them are practically naked, emaciated, and covered with boils and sores.

14. (Seeing these wretched beings, Bishop Martin is moved to tears, and says with deep compassion): "Oh, my God, how weak and wretched these poor things look! Come with me to my house, all of you, so that I may help you regain your health and strength! The Lord, our holiest and best Father Jesus, will give me the strength and means to do this."

15. (The Poor): "You are obviously one of God's angels. How kind the Lord must be if already you are so infinitely kind. However, you can see how unclean we are. How could we dare enter your clean dwelling?"

16. (Bishop Martin): "I was much worse than you, and have been purified in this house of love. So I hope to God that you will achieve the same. Come now with me, dear brothers and sisters, and do not be afraid. The weakest may lean on me to help them get to my house. You, too, brother (the botanist), should support some of the weaker ones."

17. (The Botanist): "What joy you give Me, brother, you, My heart, core of My love. One day you shall be rewarded richly for this! You have already a reward, for He Whom you love so much is now with you. I am the Lord, your Brother, your Father!"

18. (Bishop Martin, now fully recognizes Me, throws himself at My feet, and says): "O Lord, o God, o holy Father, how could I praise you adequately? How great your love is and how unfathomably deep Your compassion must be that You show that much mercy to sinners like I was and still am!

19. You holy and good Father, I am now so deeply ashamed that I did not recognize You when staying with Peter in Your everlasting fatherly house; that I did not heed Your words, which were nothing but pure love. Now that my heart recognizes You, I am overwhelmed with love and also shame. Do strengthen me to enable my sinful heart to bear Your holy presence!"

90

JESUS AS LORD, FATHER, AND BROTHER. — PARABLE OF THE SOVEREIGN AND HIS MINISTERS. — RESPECT AND LOVE.

1. (Say I): "Rise, dear brother, and do not constantly think of My majesty, but only that in your love you are My brother. This will make it easier for you to bear My presence. A Lord I am only to those who rebel against My Word and still imagine themselves great in wisdom. To those, however, who have filled their hearts with love, I am not a Lord, but an almighty brother, giving them all that I have like a true father. Therefore, dearest brother, stand up and do not regard Me with such holy awe in future.

2. In the world, if a mighty sovereign goes to his ministers and they throw themselves at his feet out of respect, there is nothing wrong about that, for as long as they are his servants, he is their lord. If, however, those servants love their sovereign above everything and say to him: 'Lord, you are a very kind sovereign! You not only deserve our highest respect, but also all our love. Accept our most loyal services without reward, and since we love you more than our lives, we shall serve you faithfully without regard for our lives. And should you demand a hundred lives of us, we will give them to

you, because you have now become a true sovereign of our hearts!' What would you think, brother, the sovereign would do to such servants?

3. He would be moved by such true love in the innermost core of his being and he would say to them: 'Oh, my dearest friends, since you have erected such a magnificent throne for me in your hearts as well as in your minds, I shall not rule over you through my power and might, but in you through your great love for me! All of you, who have been hallowed through the presence of my grandeur in your hearts, are now carrying the same in your hearts as I do. For that reason, you are now what I myself am and, therefore, my dearest brothers who shall share with me all that I myself possess.'

4. Just as such a wise sovereign would speak to his servants if they took him so much into their hearts, and maybe raise them to the nobility, I speak to all those who carry Me in their hearts as you do. Therefore, to those who love Me like that and are hallowed through My presence in their hearts, I am no longer a Lord, just as I am no Lord to Myself, but a loving brother forever! And what I have, they have too, since through their great love they are carrying Me within themselves!

5. Do you now comprehend, dear brother, what it means if I call you brother as I used to call my twelve disciples brothers? If you comprehend it, rise now and lead these poor to your house, together with Me. But do not reveal Me to your guests too soon. These hundred will not know for some time yet anyway that I am the Lord. They are Chinese who, on earth, were on the point of accepting My Word, although considerably misrepresented, and for that they were put to death, together with the missionary. What they could not attain in the world, they shall have here in the fullest measure. Now you are fully informed, so stand up and take action, together with Me — for from now on, My house and your house will be united and become one house!"

91

BISHOP MARTIN'S LOVE OF THE LORD. — RECEPTION OF THE CHINESE MARTYRS AND THEIR REFRESHMENT.

1. Following My words, Bishop Martin quickly gets to his feet, embraces and kisses Me affectionately, and after this truly childlike demonstration of his love, he says:

2. (Bishop Martin): "Ah, what a relief now that I have been able to somewhat give vent to my mighty love of You, my beloved, holy Father. I could spend a whole eternity pressing You to my heart! However, I will now do as You have suggested and take these Chinese to my house, led by You, of course, for without You, o Lord, it would be impossible to walk a single step! But now to work!"

3. (Bishop Martin turns to the hundred and says): "Now, my dear brothers and sisters, get to your feet and follow me to this house. Let the weakest lean on me, so that we may all go together into my house, where you will get care and tending. The very weakest will be taken care of by my mighty friend here, who will take the lead to the house."

4. "But, friend," say some of the party, "how can we, in such an unclean state, enter your clean house? Don't you know that we have a law which forbids lepers to enter any house? The violation of this law is punishable by death. If the mighty on earth respect this divine law so much, how much more will it be respected here! Therefore, allow us to remain in this garden until we have become clean. And only then allow us to enter your house."

5. (Bishop Martin): "Dear friends, brothers and sisters, do not let those ancient tyrannical laws, which neither you nor your rulers understood, bother you here. For we are not subject to worldly laws, — only God's law counts, and that is the eternal law of love. This law is being imposed on you now and demands of you to follow love unreservedly. Therefore, do now willingly what my love is demanding of you."

6. Following these words, the hundred get to their feet and, hesitantly, follow Me and Martin into the house. Finding themselves in the vast, majestic hall, they cry out in astonishment and fright:

7. (The hundred): "O Lama, Lama, Dalai Lama! This must be the dwelling of the eternal Brahma! Oh, we poor wretches, now we

have been betrayed and are lost forever! For it is written: 'He who enters the holy dwelling of the eternal Brahma in an unclean state, will be seized by the evil Ahriman and tortured everlastingly.' Woe betide us!''

8. (Bishop Martin): "But dear brothers and sisters, what is all this nonsense? I assure you, by my love for you, Brahma is a great deceiver and quite as mortal as you were. Neither he nor your emperor know Lama [God], nor do any of you.

9. I, Martin, a former Christian bishop on earth, in Europe, am the actual owner of this house, forever. And no Brahma will ever have any business here unless he comes like you, seeking help. Therefore, calm yourselves and do not be afraid so unnecessarily. For nobody will ever come to harm in these sacred halls who has not been barred from entering them!''

10. These words obviously reassure the hundred. They are, however, so overwhelmed with the splendor and magnitude of the hall that they forget to thank Martin for his comforting words.

11. At the same time, Borem arrives with bread and wine, which I secretly bless, to refresh the new guests. After both bread and wine have been blessed, Borem says to the guests:

12. (Borem): "Dear friends, brothers and sisters, do be seated and take this refreshment which you so badly need after your long fasting. Our Lord, God and Father is boundlessly loving, kind, meek and patient, and absolves you from all sin which burdens your consciences.

13. Therefore, you should be serene and happy, and enjoy all that is given to you without misgivings or fear. What you will receive here will strengthen you for eternal life and help you to a true cognition of God, which in its essence is the true eternal life. This was expressed by God, the Lord Himself, when He said: 'And this is life eternal, that they [the disciples] might know thee the only true God and Jesus Christ, whom thou hast sent.' "

14. After these reassuring words, the hundred new guests sit down, and Borem distributes the bread and wine. They all reach for it eagerly, expressing their thanks, and eat and drink avidly. This is a good sign, for with the same eagerness with which they are partaking of the bread and wine, they will afterwards accept the even more spiritual Word of God.

92

A HEALING BATH FOR THE HUNDRED LEPERS. — THEY ARE CLOTHED AND EXPRESS THEIR GRATITUDE. — ABOUT THE ESSENCE OF LAMA. — QUESTIONS ABOUT JESUS AND THE LORD'S EXPLANATION.

1. (When, after a while, the hundred are satisfied and refreshed, I speak to them): "My dear friends, rise now from your seats, take off your clothes and enter the bath which you will find between this column and that light but still completely opaque, protective screen. This bath will cleanse you from your leprosy. So be it!"

2. The hundred quickly do as told, and as soon as they are all in the bath, they are clean once more. Their ugly, brownish skin turns smooth and white, and their limbs become shapely and supple.

3. (Noticing this change, the guests are overjoyed and begin to praise us three): "Whoever you three may be — whether you serve Lama or Ahriman — you have done us a very great service, and may your Lord reward you for it in eternity!

4. For an infinitely long time we were so utterly wretched. We searched the entire globe, but found no help whatsoever until, after more than ten thousand years must have passed, we found this friend [meaning Me] in the vicinity of this palace, and we begged him to help us if he could. And he said:

5. 'Yes, I can and will help you! Follow me into this garden and I shall call the owner of the house, who will be only too glad to do what I shall ask of him on your behalf.'

6. He did immediately as he had promised, and all of us are now witnesses to what he has done for us. Therefore, he is mainly to be praised, but you two as well because you did willingly what this, our first friend, asked of you for our sake.

7. But now, dear friends, as you can see, we are completely naked. Since you have done already so much for us, would you do one more thing? Give us something to cover ourselves with. Then we shall be the happiest beings in all infinity!"

8. (Say I to Martin and Borem): "Brothers, open that golden chest, which contains sufficient clothing for our protégés, and is quite adequate for the time being. Eventually, they will be arrayed in

240

the garb of the heavenly Kingdom, in accordance with the degree of perfection of their spirits. So be it!"

9. Bishop Martin and Borem hurriedly open the golden chest and pull from it a hundred blue robes, some heavily pleated, others with fewer pleats. The first they hand to the men, the last to the women. They all don their robes quickly and are delighted to see how well they suit them.

10. (All of them praise Me, saying): "Friend, you are so extremely kind, besides being wise and mighty. We were told on earth that the Great Lama was very good and wise, as long as he did not set eyes on Ahriman, the sight of whom would enrage him to such an extent, that for a thousand years he would vent his wrath on the earth, where Ahriman dwells. After that, he would cover his face for another thousand years, so as not to see his arch enemy. Consequently, he would not take any notice of mankind for a full two thousand years.

11. If all that should be true, we must say that you are much wiser, mightier, and better. We are saying this in defiance of the Lama, wishing to testify to the truth.

12. We did hear on earth of a certain Jesus through messengers from another world, who claimed that he had been the real, incarnate Lama. However, he was slain by Ahriman for having set men against him. If you should know any more about this story, please tell us, for we would like to find out the truth about it.

13. On earth, this interest cost us our lives. But we believe that here there does not exist a death any more. Therefore, it might be useful to hear more about this Jesus-Lama. Provided there is truth to the story, do tell us whether you know about him.

14. Everything seemed to be going well, and we had already learned certain good prayers, but then things went wrong. One of the messengers had gone too far; his mistress betrayed him — all of us and many more — and we had to pay with our lives for having deserted our Lama and for having turned to another god.

15. Probably the evil Ahriman played this trick on us and, therefore, we hope that the Lama will not blame us too much, especially if this Jesus was really an incarnation of him."

16. (Say I): "My dear friends, do still have a little bit of patience and you will find out all that you desire. But now follow us and you will find a big crowd, and among it the messengers who brought this teaching to you; also the Chinese woman who betrayed you and the

messenger who had gone too far. But when you meet them, you must not be angry. You must forgive them for what they did to you and then you will recognize also the Jesus-Lama. So come out from behind that screen and follow us without misgivings and with your best intentions. So be it!''

93

EMBARRASSING SCENE AT THE REUNION OF THE CHINESE. — THE STORY OF THE INFORMER.

1. Now the hundred are happily coming out from behind the protective screen, and are again surprised at the great splendor and size of the hall, in the southern part of which are the other thousand guests, plus a few hundred more who were also redeemed in connection with the salvation of the monks and nuns.

2. The hundred are astonished at the great numbers of guests, many of whom are still in their natural attire. They are also astonished when they recognize the missionaries who had wanted to bring Christianity to them. But when they also catch sight of the Chinese woman among them, who had betrayed the chief missionary and all of them with him, they begin to scowl and then say to Me:

3. (The hundred Chinese): "Listen, dearest friend, we find the sight of this woman rather embarrassing, but since you do not seem to mind, it is all right with us too. It is peculiar that the messenger whom she also betrayed seems to be on the best of terms with her, since we see that they are having quite a friendly discussion. She is beautiful and agreeable — and that is why this messenger loved her in the first place. She was also a popular beauty in the emperor's residence in Peking, and a great favorite of all the people in the city. However, following her despicable betrayal of all of us, she probably lost the respect of the great city's people, and she soon died of a broken heart, so we heard.

4. What surprises us most is that this evident servant of Ahriman, who betrayed the Jesus-Lama through us, has come to these sacred halls. Could it be that the Lama Himself finds pleasure in her beauty, too?"

5. (Say I): "Dear friends, did you not have children too? Weren't some of them good and others rather wicked? Did you throw the wicked ones to the hyenas and tigers, or did you not concentrate more love and care on these wicked children than on the good ones? You all agree with me and say: 'Yes, yes, that is true!'

6. Behold, if you who have never been good yourselves have done only good to your wicked children, how can you think that the eternal, most kind Lama would be harsh with His children if they repented and asked for His mercy?

7. This maiden, in a way, did sin against you in the world. She had loved you all very much before she betrayed the chief messenger and, through him, involuntarily, all of you. Afterwards, she repented deeply of her presumed bad deed.

8. Thus the good Lama is right if He does not condemn forever one of His children which might have done wrong, but comes to Him asking His forgiveness with a truly penitent heart.

9. Therefore, the good Lama need not be in love with a beautiful woman in order to redeem her. It is sufficient for Him to be a good Father to all men and to be known as such. Especially if the latter is the case, a weak daughter of the world will have no difficulty with her salvation.

10. What do you think now, friends? Is the good Lama doing the right thing or not?"

11. (Says one of the hundred): "Yes, in that way the great Lama is acting completely just and right! But look, the fair Chanchah has noticed us and is hurrying towards us. I wonder what it is that she wants to tell us?"

WONDERFUL, GENUINE RECONCILIATION BETWEEN CHAN-CHAH AND THE HUNDRED CHINESE. — THE LORD AND CHANCHAH.

1. Chanchah now falls at the feet of the hundred Chinese, begging their forgiveness for what she had done to them, even if not intentionally.

2. (The hundred reply unanimously): "Fairest Chanchah, if the great, holy Lama forgave you, how could we hold anything against you? Besides, He has forgiven us too, notwithstanding our many and large sacrifices to Ahriman! Therefore, rise to your feet and pinch the lobes of our ears as a mark of our having forgiven each other from the depths of our hearts."

3. Chanchah does as suggested in the sweetest and friendliest manner, and after having gently pinched all the hundred in their ear lobes, she says:

4. (Chanchah): "Your hearts be my most precious gems, and the sight of you a treat for my eyes. My heart be a peaceful resting place for you when love has tired you. My arms be a gentle band for you to unite heart with heart, and may the most precious balm flow from my mouth forever into your lives.

5. On my bosom may you soar to the stars, and my feet carry you over rough roads. And when the sun has set and the earth is lit by no moon nor by the light of the stars — when it is covered by veils of mist, may my eyes illuminate for you the path of your longing, and may my intestines warm you in the frosty nights of life.

6. Thus I will be forever a meek servant to you under all circumstances, because you have granted me forgiveness for my great sin against you."

7. (After this speech by the sweet Chanchah, one of the hundred goes to her, lifts both his hands above her, and lightly touches her head with his forefingers, saying): "Oh, Chanchah, how beautiful you now are! I am telling you this with the roar of a mighty gale and also with the tenderness of a fragrant evening breeze playing with the soft hair of the gazelle! You are more beautiful than the sunrise above the blue mountains adorning the great city of the Middle Kingdom, and more glorious than the chu-yu-lukh [one of the most beautiful flowers grown only in the gardens of the emperor]!

8. Your head surpasses in loveliness that of a golden dove, and your neck is rounder and whiter than a white gazelle's. Your bosom is softer than down, and your feet smaller than those of an antelope. We love you as much as we love the sun, and your sweetness lightens our hearts as gloriously as the light of the full moon lightens the heaving surfaces of the lakes.

9. Thus, from now on also, your wishes shall shine as delightfully in our souls and refresh our hearts, as the stars comfort the

hearts of lost seamen who by day had been unable to take their bearings on the wide ocean and set sail for home."

10. (Then he turns to Me and says): "Is it right, o friend, that we have accepted this our former enemy like one heart into a hundred hearts?"

11. (Say I): "Yes, it is quite right according to your custom. However, since you are no longer in the world, but in the eternal realm of spirits, with different usages and customs, you will have to adapt yourselves to these and follow our example in everything if you want to stay here. But in case you should prefer the customs of your country to those of this house, you would have to join those who will not be reaching this house for quite a while yet."

12. (Chanchah): "Beloved and glorious friend of the poor, we shall be like the finest china clay, which can be formed into the noblest shapes. Your will shall be our life's ambition, and your word the holy word of Lama!"

13. (Say I): "Come here, fair Chanchah, I shall give you a new garb, which shall adorn you more gloriously than the most beautiful sunrise adorns the white peaks of the blue mountains."

14. Chanchah comes to Me eagerly, whilst Martin is already bringing from the golden chest a red robe, decorated with numerous stars. He hands it to Me, and says:

15. (Bishop Martin): "This will really look heavenly on the most beautiful Chanchah. It is a true garb of love! I must admit that I really like this Chinese maiden. Her typically Chinese figure of speech still contains a lot of earthly elements, but it is of truly oriental poetry. I would not have thought that the Chinese possessed such an amount of honest lyrics. However, be that as it may, I like it! On no account must we let these people move on!"

16. (Say I): "You are right — I, too, like them, and especially the heart of this Chanchah. However, they are still going to cause you some trouble. — But now to Chanchah!

17. Here, My sweet daughter, receive this garment. It is the garment of love and wise meekness whithin you. You did betray those who were prepared to accept the truth of the Jesus-Lama, but you became a traitor through the virtue of your country. You only wanted to save the emperor's life and didn't intend to sacrifice your brothers' lives. That was the emperor's doing only. But if he had had your heart in his breast, he would not have done it. Therefore, you

are blameless and pure, like this garment I have for you here. Take it
— it represents My great love for you!"

95

CHANCHA'S DESIRE TO FATHOM THE NATURE OF THE
LORD. — THE LORD'S FORMULA. — CHANCHAH'S GLOWING
LOVE FOR THE LORD.

1. Chanchah receives the garment with reverence, and as soon as
she touches it, it gloriously embellishes her whole being. Standing
there in her celestial attire, she weeps for joy and says: "Oh, friend,
tell me your name that I may write it forever in my heart with glowing letters."

2. (Say I): "Fairest Chanchah, this is already done, and if you
probe your heart you will find that which you now want to hear
from Me. I assure you, your love for Me will reveal everything to
you."

3. (Chanchah ponders My words, astonished, then after a while,
she repeats thoughtfully): " 'Your love for me will reveal everything to you. What you want to do is already done. Probe your heart
and you will find what you want to hear from Me.'

4. How peculiar! Hmm, how can he speak like that? And why
does my heart burn with love for him when he speaks to me? His
voice has such might and magic that I feel he should be capable of
creating and then destroying worlds just by the power of his speech.
His incomparable gentleness, on the other hand, emanates truly
divine sternness. Truly, I have a presentiment of something great!

5. Oh, you holy word, not heard on earth! Holy sound of
speech: 'Your love for me will reveal everything to you.' I wanted to
know only one thing — his name! But he says: 'Everything! Everything!' How much more the 'everything' must comprise!

6. Oh, Lama, you great, holy Lama, how shall I comprehend
this? What a glorious stature, what majesty in the expression of his
eyes! Also, the other two men are of sublime stature, and seem to
be very wise and mighty. However, when I look at this one, my heart
takes fire and burns like the huge torch above the tall tower of the

emperor's castle, illuminating the entire city better than the full moon!

7. (Chanchah addresses Me): Oh, my dear, divine friend! The words you have spoken to me, who but you could interpret them? They have awakened in my heart a profound anticipation and I cannot hide it any longer — a deep and mighty love for you, most glorious one! It is true what you said: 'Your love for me!' Yes, my love for you, glorious one!

8. When I walked on earth through the beautiful, vast gardens of my city, I often listened to the faint sounds with which the swans, gliding gracefully over the surface of a beautiful pond, would greet the setting sun. Although glorious sounds, they could not be compared to the gentle sound of your speech.

9. I often went for early morning walks, taking my wind harp with me. When the gentle morning breeze greeted its strings, it gave such a wonderful sound that it made my heart quiver with joy. That was then, but now — since I have heard the celestial sound of your voice — that sound of the harp would no longer stir Chanchah's heart.

10. How sweet my mother's words used to sound when she called to me: 'Chanchah, my life, come to the heart of your mother who loves you more than her own life.' That call, dear friend, held more harmony than the world could comprehend. And how happy it made the gay Chanchah. The whole world brightened. It became like a celestial garden!

11. But then, dear, glorious friend, I had not yet heard the sound of *your* voice! And when I look at you now, when my quivering heart still hears the celestial sound of your speech like an echo from the heavens, all that former happiness sinks back into the dust. Oh, you glorious one, what will I do if my heart keeps burning for you more and more fiercely?

12. Lama, Lama, you are no doubt great and glorious, and should be loved above all else! But how can poor Chanchah help it if her heart has apprehended this one, who must be your friend, with so much tenderness?

13. And you — most glorious one — won't be angry with me for daring to love you so deeply, will you? For I cannot help it that you have become so sacred to my heart.

14. I was taught in the world that for the good people there was a heaven which was a thousand times more beautiful than Peking,

that great imperial city, and this heaven was more sublime than the majestic blue mountains. But for me, this celestial splendor is empty, and I believe that only a heart can be heaven to another heart forever.

15. In you I have found my heaven of heavens! Oh, if you could only find a little bit of pleasure in me too!" With these words, the sweet maiden throws herself at My feet.

16. (Bishop Martin): "O Lord — I mean 'brother', I almost gave You away — I have never seen such maidenly tenderness. That is surely real love! Compared to this, I feel like a mangy ox! What do you think, brother Borem? There is a lot we could still learn from her!"

17. (Borem, full of respect, says): "Indeed, dear brother Martin, in the presence of the Master of masters, we shall keep learning forever! I do admire this fair Chinese maiden. It will be a long time before we shall be able to compete with the tenderness of her emotions and the typically oriental ardor of her love. It is most enjoyable to hear her words and watch the enhancement of her love. But the greatest happiness for us is to see the direction her still blind love is taking."

96

THE LORD'S WARNING ABOUT HANDLING OF THE IMMATURE. — CHANCHAH'S LOVE FOR THE LORD IN CONFLICT WITH HER LOVE FOR THE LAMA.

1. (Say I): "Be careful with what you say. We three know who we are, but all these are still too weak to bear the truth. I tell you this in confidence, and they cannot hear us, but when we talk aloud in front of them, we are all equal. You know what I mean?"

2. (Bishop Martin): "Oh brother, You beloved brother, we understand! I shall be extremely careful not to say the wrong thing, but please be patient with me in case my tongue should slip a little. Sometimes I imagine myself already quite wise, but whenever You are present, my wisdom seems ridiculous to me. Still, I am happy that, with Your help, there is at least occasionally something wise forthcoming from me."

3. (Say I): "Never mind, dear brother Martin, you may stay as you are, for this is how I like you most, since an appropriate sense of humor coming from the heart should not be lacking even in heaven. But now let us turn our attention once more to Chanchah. Martin and Borem, lift her up from the ground at My feet. For, at this stage, I must not touch her with My hands as yet."

4. The two quickly do as told, and soon Chanchah is standing in our midst, still quite confused and scarcely able to express her emotions in words.

5. (Bishop Martin): "How beautiful she is in her emotion! If this kind of beauty could be seen on earth with such an abundance of feminine charm, I think the sight of it would drive men crazy.

6. I am really surprised at myself that I can now look at such extreme beauty with enjoyment and without the least sensual desire. This, as has been amply proved by the fair Mercurian and the flock of lambs before that, was originally not the case.

7. Although I have enjoyed the touch of this soft, well-rounded arm, it has not stirred my senses in the least. For this I must thank and praise — you-know-Who!"

8. (Martin addresses Chanchah): "How are you feeling now, you fairest tenant of my house which was given to me for eternity by the great, holy, most loving Lama? Do speak again, for we all love you very much and our hearts enjoy your beautiful words."

9. (Chanchah): "Oh, I feel so wonderful, my dearest, heavenly friends, servants of Lama, the Holy! Who would not be happy in your midst? For is not love the most precious possession of the human heart? And if a heart has found love as I have, what else could there be to wish for? What greater bliss could there be than that caused by love? Oh friend, I feel simply wonderful here!

10. But, dearest friends, I will not have to leave you, will I? Of course, I feel I am not worthy of you, notwithstanding this glorious garment, for I have still many faults. But my heart loves you and, I must openly admit, particularly you who did not want to tell me your name. However, because of this boundless love of my heart for all of you — but especially you, the nameless — surely you won't cast me off."

11. (Say I): "Oh no, you shall never ever be separated from us, for behold, all the heavens are founded on love, and love in itself is the heaven of heavens! Whoever possesses such a full measure of love, how could he be banned from what is his very being? Besides, love

such as yours for us, immediately eradicates all defects of the soul, rendering it as pure as if it had only just emanated from the breath of the Lama Himself.

12. Therefore, do not worry ever about whether you will be able to remain here, but think that we shall always keep you with us, as a special little item of love, wherever we might have to go at times in the course of the manifold needs of this realm. You must not take for granted that we shall stay in this house forever, as there are many mansions in the kingdom of the great Lama. But, wherever we might go, you will always be with us."

13. We now love you so much as if you were the only being in the whole of infinity, fully entitled to our fullest measure of love. As we — and mind you, sweet Chanchah, I in particular — love you so much, how could we ever let you go? I assure you that you are now My love forever!"

14. (Chanchah): "O Lama, Lama, how holy and good You must be if already Your servants are so good and kind. But you, my dear friend, if I look at you — oh, I just can't imagine that Lama Himself could be any better than you. Maybe that is the only fault of love: it considers its object the best and most perfect of all. Therefore, I consider you at least as good as the great Lama Himself. I trust He will forgive the poor Chanchah for thinking and feeling like this. For how can I help loving you so boundlessly?"

15. (Say I): "O Chanchah, be assured that your Lama has forgiven you everything long ago! He, too, loves His servants so boundlessly that He can only rejoice if His children, who really are His servants, love each other so immeasurably. Hence, do not fear that your love for Me could be a sin against the great Lama. For that I can vouch with all the treasures of heaven!"

97

CHANCHAH ARDENTLY SEARCHES AFTER THE NAME OF
HER BELOVED FRIEND. — THE LORD'S HINT AS TO THE
BEST FORMULA. — DIFFERENCE BETWEEN THE HOST AND
THE GUEST.

1. (Hearing this, Chanchah says, somewhat embarrassed): "Oh,
glorious friend of my whole being, since you talk about the holy,
eternal Lama with such unbelievable assurance, you must have met
Him often, maybe even spoken with Him as if you were His first
servant. Yes, that must be the answer, or you could not be so indescribably kind and your words could not have such force, as if
they were the words of Lama Himself.

2. Your two friends have also spoken to me, but I did not
notice such force in their words, except when they were talking to
you. In view of this, my heart tells me that you are closer to the
Lama than these two. Am I right?"

3. (Say I): "Ask your heart and your love for Me. That will tell
you everything! But let us now go to the other brothers who, too,
need our care and love. You stay at My side, My dearest Chanchah!"

4. (Chanchah): "It is right and kind that my other brothers and
sisters also are remembered in your hearts. The hosts are always
better off than the guests, for they can give as they please, whilst the
guests may take only what they are given. And they must accept
graciously what they are given and give honor and thanks to the
hosts.

5. A host, if he wants something from his store, need not ask
anybody but may take whatever he wants, whenever he feels like it,
for he does not have to observe rules of courtesy nor thank anybody.
Hence the hosts can count themselves lucky since they can give what
they want, when they want to, whilst the recipients are less fortunate
for they have to take what is given to them.

6. I am now thinking of all these guests here, including myself.
You three very kind and good hosts and masters of this celestial
mansion, irrespective of your boundless kindness, are so much better
off than all these guests, even though they are treated well by you.
However, you will always remain the masters, and these guests will

be dependent upon you for everything. Therefore, they should really be looked after in the best possible way.

7. But you, my dearest friend, do not blame me for my words, will you? I am speaking so bluntly only because I love you so much. My great love for you makes me speak, and then my tongue runs away with me."

8. (Say I): "You sweet balm of My heart, say whatever your heart tells you to. You can never offend us, especially not with such wise words; for I can tell you, My sweet, it is exactly as you have described it. It is much easier to give than it is to receive, and the poorest giver is still better off than the best taker.

9. However, this order can never be changed since everybody cannot possibly be a master. If the Lama made every human being a master with his own house and ample means so that he would not have to ask others for anything at all, what about the love of your brother and your neighbor? What about the love of Lama? This love would simply vanish and still, in the end, the Lama would be the giver and all men necessarily the takers, as it is now and will forever be.

10. But, in order to make it easier for the taker, we hosts are giving such an abundance so that each recipient may take as much of it as his heart may desire.

11. I can even tell you, My dearest Chanchah, that the giving here goes so far that you cannot find a single being in the whole of infinity who does not, at all times, receive a thousand times more than his heart could ever desire. What do you think about it now, My beloved Chanchah? Are the takers still to be pitied under such circumstances?"

12. (Chanchah): "If such is the case then, of course, the takers may even be luckier than the giver, who — forgive me for saying this — must have many worries. He must think how best to replenish his stores to prevent them from running out when constantly so much is being given away.

13. On earth, I have sometimes wondered how it was possible for the Lama to look after so many things — the grass and all the plants, as well as the countless beasts and men. But then my mother said to me: 'Chanchah, how can you think of the Lama in such human terms? Don't you know that He is almighty and omnipresent with His might? Whatever He in His boundless wisdom wills, comes to pass whenever and in whatever way He plans it!'

14. My mother's explanation quite satisfied me, but I would now like to hear from you, a servant of Lama, whether my mother was right.

15. Is it easy for the Lama to care for all infinity, or is it a hard task? If it is easy for Him, then He is quite as well off as all the countless recipients. If, however, He finds it sometimes not at all easy to provide for all the needs of countless myriads, then considering His boundless generosity, one could really feel sorry for Him. Please, do tell me about this, my dearest friend. Do you know the answer?"

THE LORD SPEAKS ABOUT THE NATURE AND ACTIVITY OF LAMA. — THE MIRACLE OF THE TREE. — A WARNING TO TAKE CARE.

1. (Say I): "My sweetest Chanchah, I can tell you in a few words, so listen! Since I know the Lama as well as He knows Himself, I can tell you the following: As concerns the bringing forth and creating of things, you could never imagine how easy that is for Him. As soon as He has conceived an idea, He only has to say, 'Let there be!' and what He has willed is already there. I can give you an example. If I visualize a beautiful, fruit-laden tree here before us, or if you do it — Think of a beautiful fig tree. Have you got it?"

2. (Chanchah): "Yes, yes, I am thinking of one, one like the one that used to grow in my parents' garden."

3. (Say I): "All right! Now watch this! I am thinking of the same tree and, like Lama, I will say to this imagined tree: 'Come into existence!' And behold, here is the fig tree already standing in front of us — full of ripe, delicious fruit!

4. Did you see how easy it was for Me to give you such a living demonstration? It is just as easy for the Lama to create one, or an infinite number of things. But to shape human beings into becoming as free and as perfect as He is Himself, *that* is not easy for the Lama. That requires more than just omnipotence. But, even if it *is* more complicated, to the Lama everything is possible.

5. Now, My dearest Chanchah, do you understand My explana-

253

tion? This fig tree I give you as a present. It will not wither ever, but will always bear rich and good fruit for you."

6. Chanchah is speechless from astonishment, and looks in turn at Me and then again at the fig tree. This miracle has drawn all the guests towards us, and they are all amazed at what they are seeing.

7. (Bishop Martin also looks at the tree, and says in astonishment): "O brother, although I know how easy it is for You to bring forth a tree like this, I still find its sudden appearance most surprising.

8. It must be a wonderful thing to possess a little omnipotence. But then, a spirit like mine is still much too stupid to have such power. And it is as well that I do not possess it, for even You, glorious brother, would be surprised at the silly creations with which I would be filling the infinity of space! Oh Lord, what caricatures there would be forthcoming.

9. Therefore, it is most wise of the Lama to give the ability of omnipotence only to those who possess the highest degree of heavenly wisdom, like Yourself. And that, as far as You are concerned, the giving must be easier than the taking, is beyond doubt. Anyway, as I see it, the taking would not really apply in Your case, since [in a low voice] everything is already Yours."

10. (Say I): "Careful, My dearest brother Martin! Do not forget that there are others present who have not yet reached your spiritual level. Your remarks in the beginning were quite correct, but towards the end, you almost went too far, and that could have been most detrimental to this party for quite a long time. Therefore, watch yourself, be as clever as a serpent and, at the same time, as harmless as a dove. Take an example from Borem, whose attitude is correct and who strictly observes the requirements of heavenly wisdom. Do as he does, and we shall make good progress with these guests."

11. (Bishop Martin): "I thank You for this good advice, and I will follow it conscientiously. But, see how Chanchah is watching You closely, with an expression I have not noticed on her before."

12. (Say I): "That is all right! Let her make her observations for they will lead her spirit closer to Me. She will soon have some questions ready which to answer will keep us busy for quite a while. Look, she is going to speak. You, as the host, had better ask her first how she liked My explanation, and then we shall soon see what follows from it."

13. Bishop Martin immediately follows My advice, and says to

254

Chanchah, who is still too amazed to find the right words: "Fairest Chanchah, tell us how you liked the explanation, and if you find it now quite clear in every respect. You must not be too astonished at this miracle, for such appearances are not infrequent in this world. You will get used to them eventually.

14. I was in the same position in the beginning, and if you only knew what wonderful things I have seen since my arrival, you would surely be amazed.

15. This, my dearest Chanchah, is only just a small miracle and meant to demonstrate the explanations following your previous questions to my brother. Just be patient, eventually there will be even more to see!"

16. (Says Chanchah): "It is easy enough for you, my dear friend, having already got used to such appearances. But it is no wonder if we are confused, for where in the world has anyone ever seen a thing like this?

17. If your words had not been so reassuring and you had not convinced me otherwise, I would have taken your friend and brother, who is at present talking to my countrymen, for the Lama Himself. But since you told me that such miracles are not infrequent in this world, I feel much calmer and love this brother even deeper than before.

18. Although he, according to you, is only your brother, he looks much more divine than you do and has proved this also by his miniature creation. I think a lot of you, too, but am not so sure that you could bring forth anything like that. What do you say about it?"

19. (Says Martin): "Hmm, yes, my dearest Chanchah, if it were of importance — who knows? maybe I could! But if I wanted to produce a miracle just for the purpose of showing off, I would be sure to fail and make a terrible fool of myself. Do you understand what I mean?"

20. (Says Chanchah): "Oh, yes, I see what you mean! But do go on and tell me all you can about this!"

21. (Says Martin): "Hmm, what was I going to say? Ah yes, about working a miracle. You know, fairest Chanchah, actually only the great Lama can work miracles when, where, and how He wants to. We, His servants, can do it only with His permission, to serve a purpose. Thus, my brother here worked this little miracle because it was needed for your instruction. Otherwise he would not have done it. However, the same applies to Lama, Who scarcely ever works a

miracle before our eyes since it would be unnecessary when we already understand His gentlest hints. Is this clear to you, dearest Chanchah?"

BISHOP MARTIN IS EMBARRASSED BY CHANCHAH'S INQUISITIVE QUESTIONS.

1. (Says Chanchah): "Oh yes, I understand all your explanations. However, you just said that you and your brothers understand the great Lama's gentlest hint. Therefore, you must see the great Lama; how else could He give you hints? Or, at least, you must be able to hear Him to receive His hints. If you do see or hear Him, do give me details so that I may be able to form some sort of mental image of Him."

2. (Says Bishop Martin, somewhat embarrassed): "Oh, my dearest, sweetest Chanchah, that is a most awkward question. Even if I answered it, you would not understand. Therefore, it would be better if you did not insist on an answer which, at this stage, could help neither you nor me."

3. (Says Chanchah): "Oh friend, haggling over goods may be the usual thing in your country, but not in China. We Chinese have a firm price for every item we offer for sale, and the one who offers it must also sell it and pay the emperor a sales tax. If the one who offers merchandise for sale cannot sell it, it only proves that its price had been set too high and that the seller wanted to make excessive profit, for which he is duly punished.

4. Thus, people have to watch their speech and must under no circumstances say only half a thing, be it from fear or ignorance. One is punished for either, for it is considered unworthy of a man either to be afraid unnecessarily or to try and pretend to be more than he actually is.

5. I am a strict Chinese and shall not absolve you from supplying any information the course of your speech has given me reason to hope for. It is a rule with us that if a person, through his words,

induces another to ask a question, he must also answer that question. Otherwise, he is considered a braggart, which is as much as a liar, or an incompetent coward, himself ignorant of the subject discussed by him. If you do not want me to think of you as one or the other, give me a complete and exact answer to my question."

6. Bishop Martin is extremely embarrassed and quite at a loss what to do. If he tells her the truth, he must give Me away before the time is right. If he refuses to answer, Chanchah will declare him a liar or a fool and coward in front of all the guests, which would be most disagreeable for him as, secretly, he is rather proud of being the host. So he comes to Me and asks Me what he should do.

THE LORD REPRIMANDS BISHOP MARTIN AND GIVES HIM DIRECTIONS.

1. (Say I): "Did I not tell you to take example by Borem? Why do you have to keep talking when it is not necessary? Now that you have talked yourself into a tight corner, you come to Me that I extract you from it with all honor, but this will not be as easy as you think.

2. Following My necessary miracle and your talk, the Chinese is now considerably stirred up. Her heart senses My nearness and her spirit is awaking more and more. Through your definition as to how you understand even the gentlest hints of Lama, you have kindled a fire in her head as well as in her heart. No wonder that she is now all out for the information she wants! But you have created this situation for yourself and you have to put up with it!

3. I mentioned once before that these Chinese will not be easy to handle, but you were not convinced. Since through your bragging you have now brought about this critical situation prematurely, you will have to fend for yourself like a man and make sure that you straighten out this matter with Chanchah, whilst I will work on the other hundred Chinese. As soon as I have them in order, I will also attend to Chanchah. Go now and do as I tell you!"

4. (Martin scratches his head and says after a while): "Oh, my L-----, ah, my tongue almost slipped again, my brother. If I may act

at my own discretion — naturally under Your secret influence — I think I will soon manage this Chinese without much trouble!''

5. (Say I): ''Please yourself, but you must straighten out this Chinese at all costs!''

6. (Bishop Martin): ''Yes, My L---- — I mean, brother. I shall straighten this matter out with Chanchah. Fortunately, I have now more courage, without which I could not have done too well.''

7. (Says Borem): ''Brother, make sure that your courage does not run out! It will not be easy, and I only hope that you will not be the loser. The Chinese, who have a stoical spirit, are very hard to manage; for every one thing you say, they have a hundred objections. Do you realize that?

8. This Chanchah is an exceptionally pure being, filled with a genuinely oriental, blazing, but still ethereal, charm. Notwithstanding that, she is a Chinese in the fullest sense of the word. Therefore, weigh every word carefully or she will give you a lot of trouble.''

9. (Says Bishop Martin): ''But what shall I do? I am still at a loss as to how to begin. Since I have to do something, I will try my best to straighten her out as demanded by [in a low voice] the Lord.''

CHANCHAH REPEATS HER QUESTION ABOUT THE GREAT LAMA. MARTIN'S EMBARRASSMENT AND LAME EXCUSES. CHANCHAH'S REPLY: "YOU POOR ASS!"

1. (He has scarcely finished, when Chanchah taps him on the shoulder, saying): ''Well, you servant of Lama! How long will you let poor Chanchah wait for a straightforward answer, which is more important to her heart than a thousand lives to her soul?

2. Oh, friend, if I had a thousand hearts and were the most beautiful being under the sun — all those hearts would be yours, and my glorious eyes would keep gazing at you forever, if you give me a true answer. I have only *one* heart, but it shall love you like a *thousand* hearts if you prove to be a true friend and either describe the great Lama to me in words, or even show Him to me. But woe betide you if you deceive my heart which wants to love you so much!

3. It is true I love your most glorious brother with an ardor inconceivable to you. But if you can and will be a true friend, all this ardor will be bestowed upon you. You may depend on my word, which is firmer than rocks of diamond !"

4. Martin is quite confused by these words. He stares at the inconceivably beautiful Chinese, desperately thinking of what to say or do. Only after quite a while has passed does he address her.

5. (Bishop Martin): "Oh, you sweet and most beautiful Chanchah, your beauty confuses me so much that when I look at you, stunned by amazement and love, I cannot find anything to say that would make sense. Therefore, do not expect to make much sense out of me until my eyes have become used to you.

6. It is very well for you to talk and even threaten, for the sight of me would not confuse you. But, peculiar as it may seem, my tongue is so affected by your great beauty that it has become quite lame. Do have some patience with me. Matters will surely improve as I get more used to your beauty."

7. (Says Chanchah): "If that is so, tell me, how was it possible for you to talk to me quite sensibly before, and how is it possible for you to invent a reason why you cannot speak to me now about the thing I want to know?

8. He whose tongue is tied by love, speaks like one intoxicated, stutters, and his words do not make sense. For an embarrassed tongue has no roots to draw incitement from the fountain of wisdom. But the roots of your tongue are full of active moisture. Therefore, justify yourself to my heart like a man and not like a knave. My words to you are as true as my innermost life. How then can you speak to me only out of your skin and not out of your heart?"

9. Bishop Martin is getting more and more embarrassed and cannot think of a single word in his defense. He now actually begins to stutter words and syllables which do not make any sense at all. First Chanchah seems astonished, then she begins to grin indulgently and, after a while, when Martin's stammering is getting too much for her, she says:

10. (Chanchah): "Friend, I am sorry for you. For either you are a sly fox or a silly ass — one thing worse than the other. I would rather think that the latter fits you, which would excuse your outrageous statement that you, too, are a servant of the great Lama. Really, if Lama used such servants, He and His servants would be most deplorable!

11. I did hear some wise words from you earlier, and really believed you were something higher. Your ostentatious headgear and the fact that you called that truly wise man your brother, seemed to prove it. But now I have no more doubts about you. You are, so to speak, a kind ass vegetating here in heaven because on earth you were too stupid to ever commit a sin. And so you are probably a harmless, good-natured soul of an ass which, too, must be respected as one of Lama's creatures. But one cannot expect of you any more than Lama has bestowed upon your nature. Therefore, forgive me, my poor silly ass, for having expected of you human and even heavenly wisdom."

12. Bishop Martin is furious and would love to shout the Chinese down. However, since this has saved him from the embarrassment of her question, he silently swallows her "compliments" and meekly walks away, while Chanchah watches him.

102

BOREM'S GOOD ADVICE ABOUT THE CORRECT INNER ATTITUDE TOWARDS THE LORD AND THE HANDLING OF STOICAL NATURES.

1. (Borem advances and says): "Well, brother Martin, how about your courage? Has it already run out, or is it going to?"

2. (Says Bishop Martin): "Ah, ah, this can really get you down! These Chinese seem to have preserved quite a lot of ancient Asian poetry, but there it ends and that is all the spiritual refinement they possess. In everything else they must surely be the most ignorant people on earth! Compared with those smooth heads, the Kaffirs, Hottentots, Malagasies, Maoris and Australian Aborigines must be real Platos and Socrateses!

3. Can you imagine, dear brother, what the fair Pekinese is taking me for? It is crazy, but listen: she actually takes me for nothing less than a real ass! And this is not in a figurative sense, but in the truest meaning of the word! A genuine ass! That is really going a bit too far!"

4. (Says Borem): "Of course it is going too far to take a host —

and a celestial host at that — for a real ass! But you should not worry about it, for in this way you are relieved of your obligation to her. And for this you may thank the Lord, Who gave the whole matter this turn in your own and in Chanchah's interest. Therefore, keep calm and accept patiently what is coming to you, and in due course, everything will straighten itself out.

5. In future, dear brother, better do not be too impressed with your own importance as a host, and then things will work out much better — even with Chanchah."

6. (Says Bishop Martin): "Yes, you are right! I see now that when the Lord is present, I should never feel as a host. Unfortunately, you sometimes do find deep gratification in being a person of importance. However, I now fully understand that it is best to be a nobody.

7. The silly abuse by that Chinese has once more straightened me out. I have forgiven her ignorance, but you can be sure that in future I shall be wise enough to avoid her. For, having been declared an ass once, I shall not risk skating on thin ice again."

8. (Says Borem): "You are right, brother, but lower your voice, for Chanchah is watching you closely. She is really quite guileless, but she has an extremely strong desire to fathom the many mysteries of her homeland here in the spirit-world. Therefore, she makes every effort to now gain clarity at least vegarding the most important point of her faith.

9. This is the way all those human beings act in this world, in whose countries on earth there is a lot of mystery concerning conditions here. You have to handle them very carefully since they are like half-starved people on earth who must not be allowed to eat their fill right away, but only given food in small doses so as not to endanger their health.

10. It is a fact that humans who have been kept in great darkness on earth develop excessive hunger and thirst for having their countless mysteries revealed to them when they come to this world. These mysteries have greatly nourished their imagination and poetic power and, being to a great extent represented by symbols and metaphors, have taken almost full possession of their innermost being.

11. If in this world they were approached with the pure light right away, it would destroy them completely, as it would tend to dissolve their innermost being. Therefore, you have to treat them with as much care as you would an old, dilapidated house, which you

have to repair slowly and carefully if you do not want it to collapse completely. Of course, a destroyed house can be newly erected to the same plan, but with new materials. However, such is not possible with a human being whose constituent parts must all be preserved or he will cease to exist as one and the same person.

12. I trust this is now clear to you and that you will be very careful. Where these Chinese are concerned, do not do or say anything but what the Lord tells you and everything will run smoothly. If you have a question for the Lord or myself, ask it only in your heart. The answer will also be put into your heart, as is the case with me now. I keep asking the Lord what to do in one or the other situation and the Lord makes it immediately clear to me what I have to do or, if necessary, say aloud.

13. Watch out — the Chinese is approaching you! Do not try to think what you are going to say, but ask the Lord in your heart and He will put the words you have to speak into your heart. Now you are fully instructed, act accordingly and there will be no trouble. However, on no account must you take offense if Chanchah should still address you as a real ass."

THE BLESSED FRUIT OF MARTIN'S HUMILIATION.

1. (Says Bishop Martin, now in his heart): "I thank you with all the love of my heart that you have instructed me in these most important things more clearly than ever before. I am only just beginning to apprehend what it means to be a spiritual man, and to speak and act as such. Now I also understand what a moon-dweller told me, when I was here first under the guidance of the Lord, in reply to my stupid assertions which I was silly enough to try and offer him as heavenly wisdom.

2. Yes, brother, now I begin to see. I see reality where earlier I still believed to be seeing miracles or peculiarities of this world. I thank you, my dear brother, and particularly You, my God, Lord and Father. Yes, now I know also that everything will go well. In

this frame of mind I do not fear a thousand Chinese women and shall know how to handle them."

3. (Says Borem to him secretly): "It is true, brother, but you must still watch yourself, for in the beginning it costs quite an effort to be silent when you are inclined to be talkative, and from habit your tongue can scarcely be checked.

4. Occasionally, for some most likely wise reason, the Lord does not immediately put an answer into our hearts. Then He means us to wait calmly and patiently, in an attitude of love and submission, until it suits Him to put the desired answer into our hearts.

5. Mind this additional advice, dear brother, and you will have no difficulty. But now prepare yourself for the Chinese, who has almost reached you."

6. (Says Bishop Martin in his heart): "She is probably coming with a whole legion of real asses! However, I will bear them as the infinity of space bears the boundless hosts of stars, globes and suns without tiring. In Your name, Lord, may now come what will. My patient back shall carry any given cross with love and meekness. So, in the name of the Lord!"

104

RECONCILIATION BETWEEN THE CHINESE AND MARTIN. ABOUT OFFENDING AND FORGIVING ACCORDING TO CHINESE CUSTOM.

1. (Chanchah now steps in front of Bishop Martin, smiles lovingly, and says in a sweet, trembling voice): "Dearest friend, you walked away without a word when I expressed my rather excusable suspicion about your nature following your inability to answer my question. I now believe that my suspicion has offended you deeply. If that should be the case, do forgive me after punishing me as you see fit. Do forgive me, and I make a sacred promise not to ask you any more questions ever, and never again shall I offend you, neither by glance nor word.

2. It is a customary belief in my country, for which I am not responsible, that men who are not very intelligent are actually animals. When I was under the impression that you were lacking in

intelligence, I took you for an animal. However, I am now convinced that I made a mistake.

3. I immediately regretted my error and wanted to throw myself at your feet. But as I saw you discussing something apparently very important with your brother, I did not want to interfere and waited until you had ended your discussion. This seems to be the case now, and so I am doing what I should have done much earlier. I am falling at your heavenly feet, asking you to punish and then forgive me my sin against you, you glorious and great citizen of the heavens." With these words, she throws herself at Martin's feet.

4. (Martin, deeply moved by the fair supplicant, says): "Oh, you heavenly Chanchah, pray rise immediately. How can you imagine that I would want to punish you, whom I love so much? Do you take me for one of those merciless Chinese? May the great, eternal, holy and true Lama guard me against such a thing! Get to your feet quickly, for I cannot bear to see you like this, my heavenly Chanchah!"

5. (Chanchah gets quickly to her feet and says): "You dear friend, the people in your country must be very much better than those in the great empire on earth into which I was born. With us, an offense cannot be forgiven as simply as you have just demonstrated.

6. If, in our country, you had offended somebody, you had to throw yourself down before him, ask him first for just punishment for the offense, and through that, for forgiveness. In cases of a serious affront, you had to beg to be put to death and, only then, to be forgiven. For they all believe that you can only make up fully for an affront by a physical counter-affront. Only after things have been straightened out like that can the offender ask the offended to also forgive him in his heart.

7. This is the way it is in my country and it will explain to you many things you see in me that may seem contrary to your country's customs. Our laws are very ancient and strict, and woe betide him who might try to mitigate the interpretation of those ancient laws that claim to be still the same that Lama Himself gave to the first human couple.

8. You know, dearest friend, your laws here are mild and kind. Since I shall probably never ever have any more to do with the laws of my country, I need not adhere to them here. Therefore, I will now adhere to your laws and then I shall not ever go wrong. What is your opinion?"

THE HEAVENLY LAW OF LOVE AND ITS BLESSED EFFECT.

1. (Says Bishop Martin): "My beloved Chanchah, I am sure you are quite right. But there is something I have to point out to you, namely, that we citizens of heaven have no actual laws. We live without laws, the freest imaginable life in God, our Lord. To live in God, the Lord, means to live in love forever. Love sets everything free and knows no law but itself. Therefore, we have no other law here but that of love, which is not actually a law but instead, everlasting, perfect freedom for all beings. Do you understand this?"

2. (Says Chanchah): "Yes, I do and am really glad that I can understand such a good doctrine. If love — even while it has to be kept secret — can give such utter happiness to a loving heart, how much happier must be those who are governed by love alone and nothing else. Oh yes, where love is the law, all beings living under it must surely possess the highest degree of beatitude.

3. What use could the sunshine be to a human being if there were no warmth? What use would be gold and gems if their owners had icy hearts of stone? Oh, friend, what you have told me now is most sacred. I am beginning to understand what your very dear friend was hinting at when he said to me: 'Your love for me will reveal everything to you.' Yes, this love has already revealed a lot to me, and my heart tells me that there will be a lot more.

4. I do love all of you with the heat of the midday sun, and particularly him who still owes me his name. You must forgive me for loving your friend and brother so much more than you. I do not know the reason why, for he is not really any handsomer than you or your brother, Borem, nor is his garb any more beautiful. But his large blue eyes hold an indescribable attraction and he has a line around his mouth which gives him a divine expression, so that one could be tempted to take this lovable person for the true image of Lama.

5. If I ask my heart in its love for this one, it tells me: Chanchah, for me it is the great, holy Lama Himself. Who else could talk in such a heavenly way or with one word create a fig tree laden with fruit and then give it as a living token of His love to Chanchah, who loves Him above everything? Who else could have such magnificent,

loving eyes and such a divine mouth? Only my heart's most beloved Lama!

6. You know, dearest friend, it is only my heart that speaks like this, not my mind, although the latter would like to follow the voice of the heart if it were not afraid to commit a sin. For actually, the mind is not a very stern judge where the heart is deeply involved, and is rather inclined to share the heart's enthusiasm.

7. This is now the case with me. My heart worships that glorious one, and my mind would like to do the same if it were the only one, and not so many others all around.

8. However, I shall soon have reached a state where I shall no longer care about all the other minds, but follow only my heart. Maybe that will help me to attain the right goal, since there is not any other law here but that of love. What do you say to that, dear friend?"

9. (Says Bishop Martin): "Sweetest Chanchah, there is not much I can say to that. Just follow your heart and you will not go wrong. Eventually your mind, too, will be enlightened. That is all I can say to you at this stage."

MARTIN IN A DILEMMA THROUGH CHANCHAH'S FURTHER QUESTIONS.

1. (Says Chanchah): "Oh, dearest friend, I love you very much, but cannot ask you many more questions since I made up my mind not to bother you with questions that might not have been weighed carefully enough. But you must forgive me a remark I have to make.

2. I notice from your words and the expression on your face that every time I begin to discuss your heavenly friend and brother with you, you seem to be extremely embarrassed. What may be the reason for such embarrassment?

3. Could you be jealous because my heart prefers him quite considerably to you? Or do you only pretend to be his true friend and brother? Is your heart secretly vexed that this so-far-nameless,

266

glorious one surpasses you so vastly in perfection of the spirit? Or do you, perhaps, resent his manly, divine beauty, his eyes, his mouth, his entire sublime nature, all of which surpass yours, although you display greater splendor?

4. Look, dear friend, these questions are of the greatest importance to me and I crave for answers like a wanderer in a torrid desert craves for a drink of water. Therefore, if you have any love for me in your heart, do give me honest answers to these questions. If you refuse to do this, Chanchah will turn away from you and not ask you any more questions ever!"

5. Bishop Martin, although at a loss of what to say, pretends to ponder her questions so as to be able to supply the right answers. However, inwardly he anxiously waits for Me to put an excellent answer into his heart. But for most wise reasons, I again keep him in suspense.

6. Thus, he has kept Chanchah waiting for quite a while, and she is gradually becoming quite indignant. She is beginning to measure him inquiringly from head to foot with her large eyes, which makes Martin all the more confused and quite unable to find the right reply.

7. Chanchah allows Martin a bit more time to think, as his seemingly wise expression still makes her hope for some answers. But when nothing is forthcoming, she loses patience and says:

8. (Chanchah): "Dear friend and brother, I see now that you either cannot, will not, or most likely *may* not, give me an answer. If you cannot answer, you may be excused, for no one should be asked more than he can give. You will probably understand what I mean, provided you have enough sense for that!

9. If you may not answer, you also may be excused. For then it would be obvious that there is somebody here who has the authority to dictate to you what to say or not to say. In that case, it would be most foolish of me to persist in demanding an answer, for I, as a Chinese, know only too well that laws must be respected.

10. If, however, you do *not want* to give me an answer although you could and are allowed to do so, then you are simply a jealous and wicked man. Then your shining garb would be like the coat of a gentle gazelle hiding a vicious hyena inside. In that case, there would be no excuse for you, and you would deserve my utter contempt.

11. Since you did not answer my previous important questions, I ask you from the depth of my heart, *do* answer at least one or the other of these three points, so that I, as a newcomer to this world

and your house, may know how to behave. But do speak the truth and do answer without fail!''

12. This is much more embarrassing for Martin than were the previous questions. If he were to say, ' I cannot,' he would be lying. If he said, ' I do not want to,' it would not be true either, and besides, he would earn the contempt of his beloved Chanchah. And if he were to say, 'I may not,' he would no doubt be asked *who* did not allow him to speak, and why. Both these questions he would have to answer unless he shamefully took to his heels.

13. At this point, I return to Chanchah from the other party and take over the answering of the above three questions, and thus the vindication of the extremely embarrassed and trusting Martin.

107

THE LORD'S ADVICE TO THE INQUISITIVE NEW CITIZEN OF HEAVEN. THE PARABLE OF THE TIED UP BAG. MARTIN IS REASSURED.

1. As I return to Chanchah from her countrymen, she complains to Me about Bishop Martin's attitude and that she now did not know what to think of him.

2. (Say I to her): "Listen, My dear Chanchah, you are really setting about My brother without thinking that he might have confidential instructions which could tie his tongue for your own good. Therefore, you should in future treat him, who is one of my noblest friends, with more consideration so as not to embarrass him and grieve his heart.

3. Concerning your first six questions, I assure you there is nothing in this friend and brother to justify your suspicions. It is for a very wise reason that he gets embarrassed every time you want to discuss Me with him. However, you would never guess the reason for his embarrassment. Since the true reason of his embarrassment is not at the bottom of your questions, he cannot answer them.

4. As regards your last three questions, he cannot answer them either, because you have not challenged the actual reason for his em-

barrassment at your first three questions, and could not challenge it not knowing the reason yourself. Whatever answer he could have given, be it in the affirmative or negative, it would have been an untruth. This, however, can never be here in the kingdom of heaven; even if someone wanted to speak an untruth, he would be unable to. Therefore, friend Martin, who loves you very much, remained silent and would rather bear your contempt than lie to you, his beloved Chanchah. Was not that most commendable of him?"

5. (Says Chanchah, also somewhat embarrassed): "Oh, glorious friend, if that be the case with our host, I am extremely sorry to have been the cause for, no doubt, hurting him deeply. I do wish I could make up for it.

6. Yes, I am really sorry for this. But then, it might not be all my fault because as you, my glorious, mighty friend, are aware, I am a stranger here and do not know as yet what and how one may ask in this world. But since you have now given me an idea as to how to act, I shall adhere to it in future. Just tell me one thing: Why is it not possible here to obtain an answer at all to an awkward and ill-advised question?"

7. (Say I): "That is quite simple, my dearest Chanchah. Let us assume you gave me a firmly tied up bag with the request to open it up and give you out of it a thousand beautiful gems. I would ask you whether you knew for sure that these gems were inside, but you would say no, you were not sure that they were inside, but you suspected that they were.

8. If I, however, were positive that the bag did not contain the gems, but only hardened dirt, and still opened the bag and handed you the dirt instead of the gems, what would you think of Me if you found out afterwards that I had been quite aware of the bag's contents and only wanted to make you ashamed of your ignorance? Would you not reproach Me for opening the bag knowing what it contained, before telling you the truth about it?

9. The same applies here to a doubtful question. It is like a bag firmly tied, which Martin is expected to untie and hand from it what you demand. If it does not contain what you would like it to, tell Me, what is Martin supposed to do? Should he shame the one he loves so much? What do you think, sweet Chanchah?"

10. (Says Chanchah): "Ah, yes, my glorious friend, when you speak, everything appears so very clear, and I fully understand the truth of your words. But this is not so when friend Martin speaks.

The more he says, the less I understand what he means, and this forces me to try and penetrate deeper and ask more questions to which, however, he has not given me a single definite answer.

11. Had he just answered *one* question definitely, I would not have gone on asking. Or he could at least have shown me, as you have just done, how one has to put questions here to obtain answers, whether one has to ask questions at all, or whether one may not ask questions altogether. Since I was not enlightened on this point, you and Martin must excuse me for having gone too far with my questions, which to our good friend Martin must have been a proper nuisance.

12. Oh, friend, what a peculiar place this is! Wherever you look, there are wonders upon wonders, never suspected on earth. Who, upon seeing such incomprehensible manifestations, would not ask for an explanation from those who are more experienced? Who works all these wonders? If this is heaven, where is Lama Who originated it? Tell me, most beloved friend, are not such questions natural and excusable under such circumstances?"

108

PARABLE OF THE WISE UPBRINGING OF CHILDREN.

1. (Say I): "I agree with you, My dearest Chanchah, that these and numerous other questions are quite excusable. But just as on earth, here, too, everything must take its time.

2. On earth, the children are the ones who are most fond of sweetmeats and are most inquisitive. They seem to be hungry all the time and want to know everything in detail, constantly asking questions. Do you think it would be good for these little ones to overload their stomachs with all the things they crave for? And would it be good to satisfy their curiosity by answering all their questions?

3. Wise parents curb their children and guide them in a natural and modest way towards the fine goal of maturity, whereas foolish parents, those who grant all their children's wishes, make of them apes instead of men. Their overfed flesh becomes oversensuous and

their spirit indolent and, eventually, quite indifferent to all that is sublime, good, and true. You have seen innumerable examples of this in your country on earth, I'm sure.

4. The same applies here, too. No one could benefit from enjoying and understanding everything right away. This must come gradually in accordance with the receptivity of each individual. Guided like this, the youngest children here grow stronger and stronger, and are thus prepared eventually for the conception of the Most High.

5. Thus you, too, together with all the others here, are being guided by the three of us. Therefore, submit patiently to everything and you will soon be able to find complete answers to all your questions yourself. Are you now satisfied?"

109

CHANCHAH'S BASIC QUESTION AND THE LORD'S VERY CRITICAL COUNTER-QUESTION. STORY OF THE MORNING AND EVENING FLOWERS.

1. During My instruction of this dear Chinese, Martin's face has brightened, and in his heart he expresses his deepest gratitude to Me.

2. (But Chanchah says): "Glorious friend of my heart and my life, you are right in every word you say, and still Chanchah cannot help being such an inquisitive child. However, your poor Chanchah will restrain her heart from now on and become like a flower unfolding in the light and warmth of Lama's sun and, nourished by Lama's morning dew, gradually filling its receptacles with the rich seeds of life.

3. Ah, the great, holy Lama must be boundlessly good, wise and mighty, judging from all the things He has so wonderfully made. Oh, if I could only be granted the immeasurable happiness of seeing Him from a distance just once — only for a few moments! Tell me, you glorious one, shall I ever be found worthy of such happiness? If I could only see Him but once — no matter when — I would be satisfied forever and would willingly do whatever is asked of me. But, do give me hope for this one thing."

4. (Say I): "My beloved little one, I can see that Lama is foremost in your heart, which, of course, is very good. However, you

keep telling Me — and so do your eyes — that you love Me too, beyond measure. Now I would like to hear from you which one you love more — Me or your Lama. Ask your heart about it and then tell Me."

5. Here Chanchah becomes most embarrassed and casts down her eyes, while her heart kindles more and more in her love for Me, of which she is only too aware. Therefore, she — who usually has a ready tongue — now can find no answer. After a while, I ask her again to tell Me this, and she says, quite uneasy:

6. (Chanchah): "Oh, you apple of my eye, you altar of my heart, when I was still living on earth with my mother and was but a girl of some thirteen years of age, I asked my mother what one would have to do to love the holy Lama above everything.

7. Then my wise mother said: 'Listen, dearest daughter, plant two flowers of the same kind in the garden — one towards morning, and dedicate it to Lama, and the other one towards evening, and this dedicate to mankind. Tend both equally and see how they will grow and develop. If the evening flower thrives better than the morning flower, it will prove that you love the world more than the holy Lama. If it is the other way round, then your love for Lama is greater than it is for mankind.'

8. I followed my mother's advice without delay, but fearing the Lama's flower might lag behind, I secretly tended it with much more care than the other one. However, notwithstanding all my care, Lama's flower lagged behind.

9. I told my mother everything, and she comforted me, saying: 'Look, my dear child, with this the Lama only wanted to point out to you that you can love Him Who resides in an inaccessible light, solely by loving your fellowmen as you love yourself. For who does not love those whom he sees, how could he love the Lama whom he cannot see?'

10. From then on I watered the evening flower more often than the morning flower and, behold, the latter commenced to thrive much more than the evening flower.

11. And here I am doing exactly the same thing. You are my evening flower, and my heart for Lama is the morning flower. I am tending you to the best of my ability, discerning in you the most perfect spirit of man; and my heart thrives with all its might — but unfortunately not with Lama, but with *you* — yes, with you!

12. You have become a true Lama of my heart! And the great

272

Lama, in due course, will know best what He is going to say to this. I must even admit that my usually most sensitive conscience does not reproach me at all for this. What do you say to this, glorious one?"

13. (Say I): "My beloved Chanchah, you kept Me waiting for some time for an answer in which My heart could rejoice. Therefore, I will now keep you waiting a little bit longer for a good and proper answer. But it will not be long, and you may look forward to a wonderful answer!"

110

PREPARATIONS FOR A CELESTIAL FEAST. MARTIN'S FIRST JOURNEY WITH THE CELESTIAL MAIL.

1. (Meanwhile, I turn to Martin and Borem and say to them quietly): "Friends and brothers, now you have plenty of helpers. Go and place the large table in the center of the hall and set it with plenty of bread and wine. Gather also the fully ripened fruit from this fig tree and put it on the table with the bread and wine. After I have had a few more words with My sweet Chanchah, we shall have a good, invigorating meal together. Go and carry out My wish and will!"

2. The two thank Me in their hearts for this commission and go to fulfill it without delay. Martin summons the now-cleansed members of the various orders, including the nuns, and sets them the task of fetching the bread and wine. He sets the Ladies of the Sacred Heart to bring the figs, after the large table, which came into being without the help of a joiner, has been placed in the correct position.

3. The hundred Chinese are watching this activity with close attention, not knowing as yet what is going to happen. They are most astonished to see the large table, of which there had been no trace a while ago. They have already got used to the fig tree, which had come into existence so suddenly, since they have been looking at it for some time.

4. The numerous earthly parents, too, particularly those of the Ladies of the Sacred Heart, are astonished at the sudden activity in this hall, and watch it with apprehension, not knowing what it all means. The big crowd around the table is blocking their view and they cannot see all the bread, wine, and figs being placed upon it.

5. When the table has been laid, all the helpers return once more to their comfortable seats, while Martin and Borem, accompanied by the Lady of the Sacred Heart who, as a frog, had thrown herself into the sea first – metaphorically – return to Me to tell Me that everything is ready.

6. (But I say to them): "That is all right. But go outside first to the garden fence to see whether there isn't someone else who might take part in this meal. And you, Gella (the Lady of the Sacred Heart), stay here with Me and listen to the wonderful things I am now going to tell my dearest Chanchah. So be it, My brothers!"

7. The two go immediately outside and are not a little surprised at finding the garden in a state of great heavenly abundance and vast expansion.

8. (Says Bishop Martin): "Oh, what distances we shall have to walk, brother, to look along all the fences of this vast garden! It must surely be larger than the largest kingdom on earth. Oh, Lord, how endless and unfathomable this is! This would only be possible in heaven!

9. Oh, look towards the east, that avenue with the most magnificent trees! And can you see its end, brother? I cannot, nor can I see any trace of a fence. No, brother Borem, we haven't a chance of reaching any fence if we walk in the usual way. And to walk around the whole of the enclosure would really be some task!

10. But never mind. To carry out the Lord's will is at all times the greatest joy and, therefore, I am looking forward to a trip around this garden. We shall even have some mountaineering, for towards the south I can see mountains of considerable height. And, oh dear, just look towards the west and north — there are mountain ranges which on earth one could not even have imagined! Ah, those magnificent peaks — are they also inside our garden, brother?"

11. (Says Borem): "Naturally, for this garden keeps expanding, as does our love for the Lord and our brothers and sisters. But you know, brother, for a garden of such celestial expansion as this one, which the Lord has prepared for us with such splendor, there is a special kind of celestial forward movement. This is threefold: firstly, it is a natural movement, with the feet as on earth; secondly, a floating movement of the soul, which has the speed of the winds; and thirdly, there is a sudden, spiritual movement, which is as fast as a flash of lightning and the flight of thoughts.

12. This third kind of movement is used only in an emergency,

and we shall not make use of it here. But we shall use the second kind, which will be quite sufficient for our purpose. The means for using this movement is our firm will. We must only will in the name of the Lord, and we shall find ourselves floating freely in the celestial air, and it will take us wherever we wish to go with the speed of the wind. So will it, and you will succeed."

13. Martin follows Borem's instructions, and immediately they are both floating freely in the celestial air and turning towards the east. Martin is overwhelmed with joy.

111

THE LORD'S RECIPROCAL PARABLE: THE TWO HUMAN PLANTS IN THE GARDEN OF GOD'S LOVE. GOD'S INCARNATION.

1. (Meanwhile, I speak to Chanchah and Gella as follows): "My beloved Chanchah, a while ago you told Me something that was all the more wonderful because it came from the depth of your heart. I promised to tell you something even more wonderful, and I am now here to keep My promise. So listen to Me patiently. You need not expect a lengthy speech, for My speech is always short, and it is My practice to say a lot with only a few words.

2. You gave Me a picture of how you tended your morning and evening flowers, which was very sweet. I shall now submit another morning-and-evening picture to you.

3. Behold, as you planted your flowers, thus also the great, good Lama planted two human beings in the garden of His love: one towards morning for His heart, and then later on, the other one towards evening for His wisdom. He nurtured the first one with all the elements of His deity, so that he might become as glorious as He, the Lama Himself. However, the first man would not thrive, but instead became most arrogant and rebelled against Lama, and still to this day holds Him in contempt, although Lama is prepared to receive him back with open arms and heart at any time.

4. When this first man turned out a failure, Lama soon placed a second one towards evening — that is, in the world — and gave him

His best care. But this one, too, failed through disobedience. Then Lama regretted having created man at all, and thought of destroying such work which had not been a success, like a potter would destroy faulty pottery.

5. But Lama consulted His love, and this stood up for the failures. So He Himself came to the world as a man in order to set an example to all men.

6. However, the divine man was seized by the wicked mortals and put to death, although they could not kill the God in Him. Only very few recognized Him and opened their hearts to His teaching. There are countless men who, although they keep hearing about Him, refuse to believe and accept His teaching, which would make them His children, and who could become like their Eternal Father.

7. What do you think Lama should do with such humans? Should He put up with them any longer?

8. His love for them is so great that He would die for them again a thousand times if it were possible and beneficial. But they still do not want to love Him more than the idle world! They prefer to ignore Him altogether so as to be unimpeded by their consciences in their pursuit of worldly pleasures.

9. Oh, Chanchah, tell Me what do beings like those deserve? Should Lama put up with their defiance much longer, or should He destroy them?"

10. (Says Chanchah): "My beloved friend, what wicked plants of Lama they are! They should be severely punished. But if Lama is so extremely kind, could He really bring Himself to cut down those plants and burn them as the forefathers were warned He would do? I think infinity, as I am now beginning to realize, should have plenty of room to store away weeds like those. If I were the Lama, I would not destroy anything that has life. Don't you agree, my dearest friend?"

11. (Say I): "Of course, My sweet, that is what I think also, and that is what I do! But wait just a little while, for soon our two brothers will return with the strangest guests, and I wonder what you will say to them? So be prepared to see and hear most unusual things!"

112

SATAN AS A MONSTER IN THE HALL. THE INVIGORATING MEAL. GELLA RECOGNIZES THE LORD.

1. After a short while, the door of the hall opens and both Martin and Borem, each with a strong chain in his hand, pull in a hideous-looking monster, attached to the chains and followed by a great number of smaller monsters which are just as hideous-looking.

2. Seeing these terrible guests, Chanchah and Gella are panic-stricken, and Chanchah screams:

3. (Chanchah): "Oh, Lama, Lama, for the sake of Your holy name! Whatever have we done that You now want to destroy us through Ahriman and his scum? Oh, you, my glorious friend, if it is at all possible to you, save us and yourself by maybe destroying them. Oh, how horrible they look and how furious!"

4. (Say I). "Do not be afraid, Chanchah, for the monsters are in our power and cannot harm us in any way. You can see this from the fact that, notwithstanding their size and ferocity, our two brothers have mastered them.

5. So have no fear, but come with Me to meet the monsters, and you will hear how they howl terribly at My approach and see how they writhe and twist. But all that must not frighten you, for I alone am mighty enough to completely destroy countless monsters such as these with but one glance — just like I suddenly called into existence that fig tree. Therefore, follow Me without fear, for at My side you are safe forever, and there is no power that can defy Me!"

6. I now go to Martin and Borem, who have quite a lot of trouble mastering the monster.

7. (Martin says): "Oh, Lord, what fine guests these are and what pleasure they are going to give You! Unfortunately, we did not find anything else, so we brought these with us. But if this isn't Satan himself with his followers, I will be very surprised!"

8. (Say I): "Never mind, I have foreseen this, and it will be of great benefit to all of you . . . for your education and your equanimity. He who wants to apprehend the very highest must not be left in ignorance about the very lowest. Bring the dragon closer to Me!"

9. The two pull the chains with all their might, but to no avail.

10. (Says Martin): "Lord, it is impossible to drag this monster any further."

11. (Say I): "Then leave it where it is. But fasten the chains to the columns of this hall and let it rave there in vain for a while. Meanwhile, we shall have the meal which has been prepared, and we shall strengthen ourselves for this fight."

12. (Says Martin): "Oh, yes, in this undertaking a meal blessed by You will be of the greatest benefit to us. It is as well that our beastly guests are tied up in the background or their sight might ruin our appetites! Also, the air around them does not remind one of roses, but rather of a mixture of sulphur, pitch, and dirt."

13. (Say I): "Good, My brother, now go and invite everybody to the repast that I have prepared for all of you to strengthen you for the everlasting life of the spirit."

14. Martin quickly does as told, calling everybody to the table, where bread, wine, and plenty of the most delicious figs are waiting.

15. They all rise to Martin's call and walk over to the large table quietly and modestly.

16. When all the numerous guests are assembled, they look in My direction, for all of them — except Martin and Borem — still take Me for a messenger of God, and have no idea that I, the Lord Himself, am in their midst. Thus, they now think that I, as a messenger of the Lord, am going to tell them great and important things.

17. (However, I only say): "Eat and drink, My dear children — everyone of you according to his need. The food has been blessed for all who love God and their brothers and sisters as themselves."

18. (Now they all cry): "Praised be our great God in the Father, Son and Holy Ghost. Glory be to Him alone, and praise forever!"

19. Then they all reach for the bread and wine, and the Chinese for the figs; some of them also try the bread and enjoy it more than the figs.

20. Chanchah and Gella, however, are standing by Me, and cannot make up their minds whether to take bread and wine or only the figs.

21. (So I say to them): "My children, eat what you like best. It will all strengthen you for eternal life." Now they both reach for the bread, and Chanchah finds it extremely tasty. Gella agrees, but remarks:

22. (Gella): "I thought that bread of heaven would taste like a consecrated wafer!"

278

23. (But I say to her): "Gella, you are now in heaven at the Lord's table, not on earth at the table of Babel! Therefore, you should think now only of celestial things and not of the things that belong to the earthly Babel, whose lord can be seen there in the background"

24. Gella is startled by these words, and has a feeling as if I might even be the Lord Himself!

25. (But I comfort her, saying): "Gella, even if it were true what you now suspect in the depth of your heart, keep it to yourself for the sake of the others, and think that God, the Lord of all of you, is not inaccessible, but as a most loving Father, bending down to all His children, staying among them like an unpretentious brother. Do you understand this, My little daughter?"

26. (Says Gella): "Oh, my Lord, my God, my Father!"

27. (Chanchah, noticing this, asks Gella immediately): "Oh, sister, whom did you address with those meaningful words? Could it be that Lama is somewhere in our midst? Do tell me so that I may hurry to Him full of awe and love."

28. But I reassure Chanchah that she, too, will soon recognize Lama, and she is quite satisfied.

113

MARTIN IS BEING FORWARD. "WHOSOEVER WILL BE CHIEF AMONG YOU, LET HIM BE THE SERVANT OF ALL."

1. Some of the others, too, have noticed Gella's behavior, also Chanchah's reaction. So they are asking each other who I might be, for although Martin was supposed to be the host here, I am acting as if I were the real host and Martin and Borem only My devoted servants.

2. (Noticing this querying among the guests, Martin walks up to them and says): "Listen, dear brothers and sisters, think of the Word of God. Has not the Lord Himself said: 'Whosoever will be chief among you, let him be the servant of all'? Do you think there would be a different order here in heaven than the one the Lord Himself taught and revealed on earth?

279

3. On the contrary, I assure you that here in this world the Lord's order is adhered to in every detail. Therefore, do not keep wondering who this one might be, or why that is so, but eat and drink, each one according to his needs. And then thank only Jesus, the Lord, for everything. In due course, you will find out all that you have to know."

4. (Say the guests): "Friend, although your words just now were wise enough, thank God we are quite aware of these facts, and you have not helped us with your advice at all. We are also aware that we are allowed to eat of this blessed food as much as we want, and you could have saved yourself the trouble of encouraging us to go on eating. We are convinced that also here in the Kingdom of God, every spirit has his stomach which ought to know how much it can take. Therefore, you could have saved yourself your superfluous zeal!

5. We do know now that in the Kingdom of God the servant of all is the greatest. To be the 'servant of all,' on the other hand, must represent also the highest attainment in love, wisdom, and might. For where there is not enough love, there cannot be enough thirst for action, which would be the main characteristic of a 'servant of all.' Secondly, such a person must be full of the highest wisdom or otherwise he might not be too successful in his service to all. And finally, we are convinced that such a person must be most powerful and mighty.

6. Do you, friend, really imagine yourself to be such a most-humble servant of all? If that were the case, we would be very sorry for you. Of one thing all of us are quite positive, and that is that the Lord alone is capable of such service to all. What do you think about it?"

7. Martin is thunderstruck at these words and quite at a loss what to reply to the wise speakers. One of them, seeing his embarrassment, says to him:

8. (One of the speakers): "Brother, do not worry, but return to your previous place and rely on the one who — to all of us — seems to be a true servant of all. Then you will never be embarrassed again. However, if sometimes you like to take matters into your own hands, thinking that you can manage them on your own, you might find to your embarrassment that your strength is no greater than that of a fly, compared with the colossal strength of a horse. Therefore, return to that strong one. With Him you can achieve great things; without Him, nothing!"

9. (Martin hurriedly returns to Me, saying). "But Lord, what a lesson they have taught me! Nobody has ever silenced me that promptly! There is nothing I could have replied to them. Unfortunately, they are right."

10. (Say I): "Just take an example of Borem. He never does anything without My approval and, consequently, does not hit any opposition, whilst you sometimes like to be prominent, and this gets you into trouble. Yes, My dear Martin, in this world, guests cannot be treated as on earth, for it can happen that those whom one wants to teach, are vastly superior in their wisdom. How many more times will you get yourself embarrassed before you become wise?"

11. (Says Martin): "Oh, Lord, the saying goes that an ass will walk onto ice but once and after that keep off it. I must combine the souls of many asses, each of which has to slip once, or I should be much wiser by now, for the sake of Your most holy name."

12. (Say I): "Well, everything is all right again, but do watch out for My will and you will never be embarrassed. But refresh yourself again with bread and wine to strengthen yourself for the task of dragging that guest over here, together with Borem."

114

ABOUT THE FORM-CHANGING NATURE OF SATAN. A HINT ABOUT MARTIN'S NATURE. THE NEWCOMERS SUSPECT THE LORD TO BE NEAR. CHANCHAH'S HUMBLE ACKNOWLEDGMENT OF GUILT.

1. (Now Chanchah says, quite worried): "Oh, you, my love, will all these guests be able to bear the horrible sight of that monster? And are you sure it cannot harm us? Oh, Lama, Lama, what a frightening scene that will be! See how terribly it is already beginning to writhe. What rage in the expression of those terrible fire-eyes! Oh, friend, whoever will have the courage to look at this monster when it is here before us?"

2. (Say I): "Calm yourself! This guest is capable of adopting any shape that may seem of benefit in a certain situation. However, we

shall control him, so do not be afraid. Everything will go smoothly."

3. (Says Chanchah): "Oh, dearest friend, my love, I have full confidence in you, just as I have in Lama. But I do not have much confidence in brother Martin. He is so forward in his actions, but when the situation becomes serious, he soon retreats as if he were not strong enough to face up to the things he should. Therefore, I think he might do more harm than good in his task of leading the monster up here. Borem is all right; he is a man of wisdom and strength. He can be relied upon. But Martin is and remains impetuous, full of self-assertion but incapable of handling a serious situation."

4. (Say I): "You are not wrong, My dearest, but he still fills his present place here perfectly. In the great order of Lama, also such beings are needed who will tackle a task immediately whether they are equal to it or not. This encourages others to do something too, those who are often much more clever than the one who made the start. The very wise ones are often hypercritical and do not dare touch a thing before they have not logically worked out all the reasons for or against tackling it. And, therefore, there must be Martins too, who possess less wisdom but instead all the more fervid activity, which is often preferable to too much wisdom. Therefore, rest assured about Martin. He will do his job well as long as he does it in accordance with My instructions."

5. (Says Chanchah): "Oh yes, I am sure of that! There is not a doubt in my heart that you are the wisest here. The only thing I do not like with you is the fact that I still do not know who you really are. Recently, when I asked only your name, you told me that my love for you would reveal everything to me. However, notwithstanding my incomprehensibly great love for you, I cannot find out anywhere who you actually are, least of all from my own heart. Oh, my friend, you whom I love above everything, do tell me your name."

6. (Say I): "My dearest, sweetest Chanchah, the name alone would not be of any help to you as long as you are unable to conceive all that it stands for. If you had paid attention to all that I have said, you would be fairly clear about My identity by now. Watch now very carefully what and how I shall speak, how the others will speak to Me, and what happens in response to a word from Me. Then we two shall soon become better acquainted. But now be steady and unflinching, for I have motioned Martin and Borem to lead the raging monster here to us and they are already untying its chains."

7. (Chanchah is now silent, but Gella approaches her and says): "Chanchah, if the unlimited power and might of this friend were known to you as I know it, you would at His side fear a *thousand* monsters like this less than a gnat!"

8. (Chanchah is quite startled by these words, and says): "Sister, what are you saying? Oh, do go on and tell me about him whom I love so deeply. Do you know the glorious one? Oh, speak, speak, quickly! Could it be right what I secretly suspect? Oh, Lama, then Chanchah is either the happiest being in all the heavens or the most unfortunate one in all infinity!

9. For I am a great sinner before Lama, having in my country once betrayed His would-be messengers, who, as a result, lost their lives in the most cruel way . If they were really Lama's messengers, then woe betide me if my suspicion is correct. For could you, sister, imagine any greater grief than to be cast off by him whom one loves so very much? If those whom I betrayed were only evil-doers and imposters and not Lama's messengers — which, of course, I cannot yet decide — then maybe I could bear to face the most righteous judge. Oh, speak, speak, sister — but no, do not speak as yet! Let me enjoy this sweet uncertainty a while longer!"

10. With these words, Chanchah collapses at My feet as if in a swoon. But I strengthen and comfort her.

115

MOVING RECONCILIATION BETWEEN THE JESUIT CHOREL AND CHANCHAH. THE LORD'S JOY AT CHANCHAH'S LOVE.

1. At this moment, that particular Jesuit whom Chanchah had betrayed on earth approaches Me with some of his colleagues, falls at My feet, and says:

2. (The Jesuit): "O Lord, o Father, only now have our hearts recognized You! Forgive us our long-lasting blindness that prevented us from knowing You as You really are — so kind, so gentle, so mild!"

3. (Say I): "Rise, My children, and do not attract attention, for

there are still some who, for the sake of their spiritual freedom, must not fully recognize Me as yet. You will understand that the potter knows best when the pottery is ready to be lifted off the wheel. Stay here with us and bear witness to the evil that dragon, whom Martin and Borem are now bringing here, has done to you. You, Chorel, present yourself to Chanchah, who once betrayed you to the emperor of China, and who is now, thanks to her very great love, here close to Me, a place she is not likely ever to lose."

4. Chorel immediately does as told and approaches Chanchah very friendly. She recognizes him right away, and is startled at seeing her would-be accuser.

5. (But Chorel asks her): "Chanchah, why are you alarmed at seeing me? Did you not do what your conscience bade you? I myself taught you that sin is only what a person does contrary to the voice of his conscience. For the voice of our conscience is the voice of God — or Lama — within us. In the beginning you highly respected me, seeing true messengers of God in me and my companions. But then, with your feminine acuteness, you detected treason in us and achieved with artifice to be let into the secret. Thus it became your duty, as a Chinese, to make known our evil design and save your country from great harm.

6. Although our punishment was terrible, it was not your fault at all, but we ourselves were alone responsible for having reversed the holy purpose of our mission into such wickedness. If we, and particularly I, had remained true to the object of our mission, you would have become one of the most ardent Christians, and many of your countrymen with you. But since we, blinded by the great treasures of your country, betrayed our sacred mission only too soon, we had to lose all — including our worthless lives.

7. In view of this, none of us could possibly accuse you. On the contrary, we should fear your accusation. Therefore, you sweet, trusting Chanchah, have not the least reason to be frightened of us since we, who have every reason, are not frightened of you who might become our accuser. Do forgive us, you beloved of the Most High, so that we may, free from all guilt, approach Him Whose name to pronounce our tongues will be forever unworthy!"

8. (Chanchah is deeply moved at Chorel's confession and says): "Oh, dear friends, there cannot be any guilt in these halls, and if there were, my love for Lama would eradicate it forever. For my heart tells me that my love for Lama is Lama Himself within me.

Friends, this sacred love does not know any guilt. It knows only dear brothers and sisters all around, even if these still persist in their errors. My accusation against you shall be that I love you all and respect you like I do my own life. Have you any objections to this?"

9. Chorel and his companions weep with joy at Chanchah's wonderful words, and Chanchah weeps with them.

10. (But I turn to Chanchah and say): "You most glorious flower of My heart, come and let Me embrace you. Love like yours is most rare and seldom as pure!

11. You, My loveliest, are now boundlessly happy, having won Me like that through your love. But so am I, as the one loved by you and having found in you, a heathen, a love which cannot be matched in Christendom, except for that of a Magdalene and of Mary, the mother of My flesh.

12. Oh, Chanchah, you do not realize as yet how much you have achieved. But your eyes shall be bound for a short while longer so that your bliss will be all the greater. Now prepare yourselves, all of you. The two are pulling the dragon towards us and will be here in a moment."

116

A SCENE WITH SATAN FOR THE INSTRUCTION OF GOD'S CHILDREN. MARTIN'S DISPUTE WITH SATAN. MARTIN IS CORNERED. THE LORD'S ADVICE.

1. (Martin is crying from the distance): "Lord, help us, help us! The beast will harm us. We are not strong enough to manage it."

2. (Say I): "Satan, obey your Lord!"

3. (Roars the dragon): "I shall never obey you! I do not acknowledge any Lord above me!"

4. (Say I): "If you do not obey My fatherly words, you will have to obey My omnipotence, which experience is not new to you. I am calling you once more as Father and Lord: Come here and justify yourself!"

5. (Roars the dragon): "No, no, no, I shall never obey you, for

I alone am the Lord of infinity, and what you are, you are only through me!"

6. (Say I): "Satan, do not defy God, your eternal Creator, any longer, or your everlasting, inexorable judgment will be upon you!"

7. (Roars the dragon again): "I, your Lord, will defy you and your miserable judgment forever. Move me from this spot if you can!"

8. Now I seize him with the might of My will and throw him with all his adherents to the ground in front of Me, holding him down so that he is lying there as if dead.

9. Martin asks him (the dragon) immediately why he has not defied Me now.

10. (But I say): "Let him be until he recovers. Then we shall see what he has to say."

11. (Says Martin): "Oh, Lord, just now I would love to let my tongue run away with me to tell this incredibly stupid being a few truths! If I could only have a go at this foolish, pig-headed monster! Its ridiculously horrible appearance does not frighten me at all. It only makes me laugh — although angrily!"

12. (Say I): "If you are so keen on tackling My arch-enemy, you may as well try your luck. But watch out that you do not get the worst of it! Only his tongue shall be released for this purpose, for if I release him completely he would play with you like a lion plays with a gnat. I assure you that without Me, the entire creation could not withstand him, considering the power he still possesses. However, you may try to master his tongue, which has now been released. You may now start your dispute."

13. (Martin fearlessly walks to within a step of the beast's jaws and begins to attack it with the following questions): "Listen, you most stupid beast in the whole of infinity! What do you hope to gain from God with your constant, ridiculous defiance? Haven't a few eternities sufficed to prove to you that you are the most stupid wretch in all creation? Of an ass, one says that it goes dancing on ice but once. And what about you, you ancient, filthy beast, you deceiver of worlds, men and beasts? Haven't the fires of hell fried your brains long enough, through decillions of years or eternities, provided you know what that means? Answer me, you wretch, if you have an answer at all!"

14. (Says the dragon): "Listen, you forward fool, a lion does not catch gnats! And I, as a primordial spirit, am even in my deepest

misery too generous to enter into a dispute with a nomadic spirit. Besides, I am only too willing to forgive you, who on earth used to be such a good worker for my kingdom. So, no harm meant, my dear Martin!"

15. This answer has infuriated Martin. Such contempt of his person is almost unbearable. He takes a deep breath and says:

16. (Martin): "Oh, you wretched scoundrel, how dare you degrade me, a citizen of heaven, in the presence of God? Don't you know what is written: 'Woe betide him who will lay hands on one of My anoited'? I, as a citizen of heaven, would be one of the anointed, and do you believe, you wretch, that the Lord will let you go unpunished for such wickedness?"

17. (Says the dragon): "Listen, Martin, I, whom on earth, while in my pay, you used to call the prince of falsehood, have calmly told you the plain truth in reply to your infamous abuse of me in my wretchedness. And you, one of God's anointed, a citizen of heaven, blow up like a powder magazine on earth, threatening me with God's revenge if I impugned your anointed person.

18. But tell me, who gave you the right to abuse me in such a way in the presence of God? Am not I, too, from God, only with the difference that I am an infinite part of God, while you are just a particle of dust out of me, recovered by the Lord from the chaff of nothingness and formed into the tiniest human spirit?

19. If you have any respect for God, you have to respect everything that is from Him and not only your own anointed head, which seems to be much more important to you than the Lord. Or have you measured those primordial depths of the Deity in all detail to enable you to face me with the infinite fundamental wisdom and say: 'Why are you as you should not be?'

20. Can you prove to me that I am not what I must be for creational reasons, forever unfathomable to you, to enable you to be the little bit that you are? Or do you know of a potter who makes pots without a wheel? What the wheel is to the potter, the whole world is to God. I am the matter of all the world, thus also its foundation. Therefore, I am the consolidated antithesis, the basis without which no being and evolution could ever manifest itself.

21. From all this, you may gather with your anointed head that, no doubt, I, too, am necessary in the great order of God, and that God, by originally creating me, has surely not placed an absurdity at the root of all being and evolution. Admit that this is so, if

you understand this and are willing to fully respect God! How is it that you, with your anointed head, do not understand that by abusing God's works, you are abusing God Himself, calling Him — in your great stupidity, of course — a bungler?

22. Therefore, my dear Martin, calm down! For many eternities will pass before you will comprehend only a fraction of an atom of that unfathomably deep relationship between me and God. By the way, doesn't it strike you, an anointed citizen of God's heaven, as most peculiar that you have to learn meekness from me, Satan?

23. If you still have to tell me something, Martin, speak up. But speak like a wise man and not like a silly street urchin in the world. Bear in mind that you are standing here before God and His greatest primordial spirit, Whose shape and whose to you forever inconceivable defiance are annoying you because of your ignorance!"

24. (Martin is considerably startled and quite at a loss what to say. He looks in turn at Me and at the dragon, and asks Me secretly): "Lord, what does this mean? How can I answer the dragon? Although inconceivable, deep down he seems to be right.

25. The devil — and to be right. How absurd that is! But what can I say if he is right after all? No, that beats me! The devil — being right!"

26. (Say I): "You were so keen on a dispute with him, so carry on. You must on no account allow the devil to defeat you. So endeavor to fight him to your heart's content. Go on with your dispute and refute his contention."

27. (Says Martin): "Oh, what a refutation that will be! Oh dear, oh dear, I and that one!"

117

MARTIN'S TEMPTATION THROUGH SATAN IN THE SEDUCTIVE SHAPE OF SATANA.

1. (After a while, Martin once more turns to the dragon and says): "Listen, you incorrigible depraver of all life, you mischiefmaker, you ancient hero of spiritual darkness, and merciless bringer of death to all poor souls, even if you speak like a great philosopher,

it is not your will that bids you speak like that but your helplessness, since you were seized by the boundless might of the Lord. I could bet a thousand lives to one that your language would be quite different if you were free!

2. I am fully aware that you came forth out of God as a first and greatest spirit of light and purity. Your power pervaded the expanses of space, and your light shone like an eye of God. And I also know that God created you out of Himself for the supreme resurrection of the freest and most blissful life, but not for the fall, in which you have remained unchanged for eternities in your stubbornness.

3. Tell me, why aren't you on the spiritual level intended for you by the will of God? Why do you keep opposing God's will? Why do you prefer to remain forever in a state of horrible torment instead of turning to the Lord, your God and Father, and enjoying a boundless measure of infinite fatherly love in freedom and supreme power? Speak, if you possess sufficient wisdom to answer my questions."

4. (Says the dragon): "Well, Martin, this way of asking questions is much more sensible than your previous way, and it is a credit to your spirit. You really have touched on matters that deserve a good answer. But prior to answering questions on such profound subjects, I make it a rule to test the interrogator to make sure he is capable of comprehending what I shall tell him.

5. Therefore, I ask of the Lord — if He wishes me to answer you — to grant me full freedom for a short while, in which case I guarantee that neither you nor anyone else will be harmed in any way. If you pass my test, I will answer all your questions. If not, it will mean that you are not ready yet by far for profound wisdom. I may also add that I will test you only if you insist on having your questions answered. Now decide what you want to do."

6. Martin again turns to Me and asks Me what he should do.

7. (Say I): "If somebody starts a job, he must also complete it; this is a foremost rule of all true life. Therefore, you will have to submit to the condition of your opponent. But I tell you, be firm. For this is an extremely cunning spirit, and his tests are clever traps!"

8. (Then, turning to the dragon, I speak): "You are free for a short while. Do not misuse this favor!"

9. The same moment, the dragon's horrible body dissolves and from its dust arises a female being of such supreme beauty that the most beautiful maidens of the sun would be left far behind. A soft-

ness beyond comparison, a nobility of limbs and joints, a tenderness and whiteness of skin — there would be nothing to match this in all of infinity. And the indescribably beautiful body is crowned by a head of such majestic beauty that it beats all the power of imagination.

10. This being of inconceivable beauty looks at Martin in the most friendly manner and says in a very sweet and melodious voice:

11. (Satana): "Well, dear Martin, if you wish it, I shall answer your questions. But first tell me whether you could love me if I loved you more than my life. Could you love me and through your love save me from my great torment of which you are fully aware? Speak, oh speak, Martin!"

12. Martin is overwhelmed and scarcely able to breathe from astonishment. The extreme attraction of this being has made him violently excited. He cannot speak coherently, just stammer and stare. His whole being, in every fiber, is pervaded by glowing love for this — to him — unbearable feminine beauty.

13. (After a long while, during which he has become more and more glowing, Martin cries with all his might): "Oh, heaven, heaven, heaven, who could see and not love you? I love you, love you boundlessly! You most beautiful of all beings, who could be happy having seen you and knowing that you are unhappy and suffer?

14. If I cannot save you, I would rather suffer together with you than be the most blessed spirit in heaven without you! I would give away a thousand lives for just an atom of your being. Oh, you most glorious being, speak, oh speak! What can I do to save you, to win you for myself forever?"

15. (Says the changed dragon): "Oh, glorious Martin, if you love me as you say, give me a passionate kiss. The kiss will save me forever and I shall become the sweetest companion for your everlasting life."

16. (Says Martin, delightedly): "Oh, heaven of heavens, not only one kiss, but you shall have a *trillion* kisses!"

17. He rushes forward to perform his task, but is stunned when this being pushes him back and cries full of contempt:

18. (Satana): "Stand back, lascivious rake, you did not pass your test and, therefore, are not worthy of any answers from me in future. You wretch, how could you forget God and throw yourself into my arms — mine, who am the enemy of all life not in accordance with my own? Oh, you weak creature, you scum of all loathsomeness!"

290

19. Martin collapses in a swoon and the dragon reverts to his previous shape.

118

BOREM RAISES THE FALLEN MARTIN AND GIVES HIM ADVICE. THE LORD ADMONISHES MARTIN. POSSESSION AND POSSESSOR ARE INSEPARABLE IN HEAVEN.

1. (Borem goes to Martin, raises him up, and says): "Dear brother, you are over-zealous! In future, leave the action to the Lord alone! If we only take action where the Lord commands us, we shall never go wrong.

2. To be a match for beings like this one, much more is needed than we are able to comprehend at this stage. Even an angel would not be a match for this being, except with the help of the Lord. For this primordial dragon has a thousand of the most artful means of deceit at his disposal, by which he could inveigle all the heavens if only the Lord would allow it. Considering that none of the citizens of heaven would be at all safe from him without the Lord's intervention, what chance would we have, as newcomers to this kingdom?

3. When Michael, the mightiest of all the angels of heaven, fought with this dragon for the body of Moses, he was conquered, and all he could do was to call the Lord's judgment upon this most wicked of beings, to take its spoil away from it.

4. And if even a Michael had to get the worst of it, what could the two of us achieve? Therefore, do be careful in future whenever it pleases the Lord for good reasons to allow an encounter with such beings, whose essence is wickedness and falsehood.

5. Now rise again and thank the Lord, Who alone saved you from a great evil. For, as far as Satan is concerned, he would have certainly accepted your kiss. Through this, all your heavenly love would have been changed into his hellish kind of love, and with the help of his female shape, which he would not have shed so soon, he would have chained you to himself with more than iron fetters.

6. But at that moment, when you wanted to kiss him, the Lord's judgment took hold of him and threw him back into his evil nature. His boundless arrogance rose to the surface and he knocked

you back, following which he had to assume his dragon shape once more. So it was the Lord Who saved you, and you had better thank Him for the deliverance of your whole weak being.''

7. Now Martin quickly rises to his feet and comes rushing to Me, asking My forgiveness for his great folly and thanking Me from the depth of his heart for his deliverance and the admonitions through Borem.

8. (But I say to him): ''Martin, how much longer will I have to suffer your so-often recurring folly? When will you at last start to act in accordance with your repeated good resolutions? How many more times will I have to make you realize your folly before you have become wise once and for all? Oh, you absurd kind, how much patience is needed to guide you onto the right path?

9. Rise now and make sure you become wiser at long last! It is bad enough if some reality makes you stumble, but to allow yourself to be conquered to the last fiber of life by a mere phantom — what an extreme weakness that requires!''

10. Martin is sobbing from remorse and keeps asking My forgiveness.

11. (Then I bend down to him, raise him, and say): ''Behold, now that I have raised you, you can once more stand before Me as a free being. But how long will you keep yourself erect?

12. Every true citizen of heaven must eventually achieve complete inner freedom and must not fall if, for a while, he has to walk an extremely slippery path. But what would happen with you if I left you completely to yourself? Would you keep your equilibrium and be sure not to fall if you had to walk a slippery path on your own?''

13. (Says Martin contritely): ''Oh, Lord, do not ever let me be completely on my own or I shall be lost. I shall not ever wish for absolute freedom. If I could only be the least one close to You, I would be everlastingly happy. Better give also this house to my dear brother Borem, as I am quite unsuited for such a magnificent property.''

14. (Say I): ''Calm yourself and hold fast to Me in your heart and everything will be all right! However, I cannot take this property away from you and give it to Borem, for that would mean I would be taking your life and giving it away! Here, no one can possess anything which is not forthcoming out of himself, for such a living possession must stay with the possessor, as possessor and possession are inseparable in this world.

15. Only, you must never consider yourself lord of your property and then it will keep growing in magnificence. Although every citizen of heaven is a completely free owner of the works of his spirit, the fruits of his love for Me, I alone am the Lord over every posession, as I am over every spirit.

16. Now you know what things are like here. If you will stand firmly in My love alone in future, your celestial property will not worry you.

17. Also, do not be concerned about Borem, for he has plenty of everything. When you have fully matured, he will make you acquainted with his property. Now go to Borem and join in what he is doing. Meanwhile, I shall have a few words with this guest."

18. Martin does as suggested by Me.

119

THE LORD'S DIALOGUE WITH SATAN. SATAN'S MALICIOUS DEFIANCE. THE LORD'S PARABLE OF THE FOUNDER. SATAN'S ADHERENTS ARE SAVED.

1. (Now I turn to the dragon with the following words): "Satan, how much longer will you keep tempting God, your Lord? How much longer will you abide by your boundless arrogance? What do you hope to achieve against My infinite might which could destroy you at any time? And if it does not wish to do that, it can punish you severely everlastingly.

2. You are aware that this is the final time allowed to you; during this time you can still raise yourself — or fall forever. What do you intend to do? My will is only too well known to you. If it were not, you would be without sin. And since My will is known to you as well as the reward and punishment, say, what are you going to do?

3. Behold, everything is rising against you! All the mountains will be flattened and the valleys filled. All the crowns and thrones on earth which were erected by you, shall be cast in the fiery lake. What will you do? You will not ever be able to defy My might. You will no longer be free to do anything at all! So speak: What are you going to do? Will you raise yourself or will you fall?

4. Below you is the eternal abyss; and here am I — a Father to all who love Me, and here is My table! Choose — and make it quick! So be it!"

5. (Says Satan): "Lord, I know You and I know Your might and my terrible impotence compared with Your boundless, everlasting might. But being aware of this fact, and feeling my impotence deep within my being, I consider it a triumph for my pride to be able to defy You — yes, *defy You everlastingly!* And I also realize that all **Your might has no means of breaking my defiance and conquering my will** — except by my complete annihilation which, however, You could never look upon as a victory over me. For a spiritual victory of life could never be gained by total annihilation of the weaker opponent but only by wise persuasion with the fundamental condition of full freedom for both parties.

6. The basis for such a persuasion, however, must be the unrestricted right to turn to the opposite, if so desired. I am this opposite, and I shall never agree with Your will, justified as it may be. **Even if I understand Your will, I shall never adhere to it because I** want to demonstrate to You that there is another will opposed to Yours which Your omnipotence shall never bend as long as You allow me to exist.

7. It is easy enough to be free within Your will. However, to defy, in greatest torment, You, the Almighty Spirit, well aware of Your everlasting omnipotence, Your wrath and one's own helplessness — that is greater than anything that Your all-seeing eye will ever be able to see!

8. That is also the reason of my first disobedience to You. In it I see the greatest triumph of my impotence against Your omnipotence, for in my impotence I remain forever a victor over Your omnipotence, love and wisdom, as well as Your wrath, and You are unable to bend me, notwithstanding all Your might, strength, love, wisdom, judgment and wrath!

9. It is easy enough to be a Michael, a Gabriel, an Uriel; a celestial pastime to be a seraph or cherub. But it is quite a different thing to be a *Lucifer*, the greatest primordial spirit after You, knowing what infinite bliss Your boundless love offers and, at the same time, **knowing what growing torment Your judgment and wrath offer!** And, still scorning all beatitude and eternal torment, to offer unwavering defiance forever, well aware of one's impotence, without the least hope of ever gaining anything and knowing that one can

294

only eternally lose — such helpless greatness of a creature's will is endlessly greater than the greatness of Your Deity! And this knowledge brings me greater bliss in all my torment than You and all Your spirits and angels could ever experience! Therefore, do not ever ask me how much longer I shall defy You! My answer shall always be the same: Forever! Forever! God will never bend me!"

10. (Say I): "Oh, you blind, ignorant spirit, how profound your death is that you could imagine to be able to defy Me! You have a pleasure in your folly and do not realize that every true or illusory freedom — like the one you imagine to be your own — in the end must be subject to My will. Who has ever counselled with Me or grasped My ways? Are you so sure that it could not be My hidden will that you must be as you are? Do you know whether I did not perhaps destine you to your fall from the very beginning? Can the work ever direct its Creator how and what for he should create it?

11. A founder makes his big crucibles out of fireproof material. They are placed in a furnace and the metal melts in them until it is quite liquid, whereupon it is poured into various molds. When the molds are filled, they are cooled down and not submitted to any more heat. The crucible, however, remains in the fire so that more metal may be melted in it. It is not allowed to cool down until it has become useless, in which case it is discarded forever as useless, burnt-out matter.

12. Am not I a Master-Founder of all works? If so, and if I procure for Myself the tools I want, say, can you defy Me at all? Or can you call it defiance if you are the way you are and cannot be any different from what I want you to be?

13. However, I am not a hard master, but a loving one, even prepared to remove My crucibles from their permanent heat if they so desire and are willing to adapt themselves to the order of My free works. If they are not willing and prefer to remain forever My crucibles, it suits Me all right, for it saves Me getting new ones. But if they remain crucibles, they are what they have to be and never what they want to be. For a tool cannot be any different from the way I want it and shape it.

14. Thus, your would-be defiance, which gives you pleasure, is nothing more than an illusion originating in your great blindness. For just as a pot cannot say to the potter, 'I am as I want to be,' considering that the potter turns and shapes it as he wants it — you cannot tell Me that you are the way you want to be since you have

to be as *I want it!* But I, as Eternal Love itself, allow you in your judgment sufficient freedom to enable you to feel and understand your state of torment so that you can change it if you so desire. If not, you must remain how and what you are, not because you want it this way, but because it is *My will!*

15. If, however, you wish to improve your lot, I shall put another tool in your place to serve Me as you have done. Say now whatever you like, it does not make any difference to Me whether you remain what you are or whether I replace you by another tool!''

16. At this Satan is quite startled and at a loss what to say.

17. (His numerous adherents, however, cry): "Oh, Lord, if this is the position, deliver us from our long-endured torment and replace us by new, useful tools. We have had enough suffering and have become quite brittle in the fire. Therefore, have mercy upon us and reform us, o Lord, according to Your kindness and love!''

18. (Hearing this from his adherents, Satan roars and howls in a rage): "Don't you want to participate in my greatness? Well, then I shall not remain what God wants, but what I myself shall wish to be! Agree with me!''

19. (Cry his adherents): "Fool, could you ever will anything that is not God's will? Is not your would-be free will God's will? Whatever you will, you cannot do it out of yourself but it will, at all times, be God's will within you, your forever unconquerable judge! You may remain under compulsion of the Lord's judgment, but we have been seized by His mercy, which is holding us and we shall follow the better path."

20. (Say I): "Then arise, you wretched beings, and be released! But you, the one, please yourself and stay what you are. Whatever you will now want to do will not be your will but My Divine will — and your will within you shall be forever My judgment within you!

21. However, in addition to this thorough enlightenment, I allow you a short respite to enable you to ponder on the position and state in which you find yourself. If you do want to improve your lot, it will be done. If not, you will stay what you are until the last prisoner in the present period of creation has arisen from the path of the flesh. What will happen to you after that, I alone know in all infinity."

22. At these words, Satan utters a loud cry and rushes out the door, whilst his adherents throw away their dragon armor and stand

there as a thousand completely naked souls of very wretched appearance, asking to be healed and relieved of their considerable pains.

23. I once more summon Martin, Borem, and also Chorel, and tell them to lead these wretched beings to the refreshing bath. The three immediately do as told, and the thousand wretches find relief in their bath.

120

CHANCHAH AWAKES FROM HER DREAMLIKE STATE. THE LORD'S EXPLANATIONS ABOUT THE GREAT HAPPENINGS AND ABOUT HIMSELF.

1. Meanwhile, Chanchah awakes at My side as if from a sleep and remembers all that has taken place before her eyes as if it had been a vivid dream. She immediately starts to tell Me in detail all that she has dreamed and when she has finished, she asks Me whether there was anything in this vision.

2. (But I say to her): "Chanchah, did you not see a while ago how Borem and Martin were trying to drag the strongly-resisting, horrible dragon towards us? And how I, with the might of My will, flung it to the ground here at our feet, when Martin, in full agreement with Borem, asked for My help? You did witness all this with your own eyes, didn't you?"

3. (Says Chanchah): "Yes, glorious one, I did see that. But when the dragon was lying before us, I was seized with such a terror that I lapsed into a kind of stupor and saw all that followed as if I were in a dream. It was quite similar to the state I was in soon after my arrival in this world, when I met Chorel and got involved in a terrible fight with him. When I awoke afterwards, it all seemed like an oppressive dream, just as it does now.

4. The things I see when fully conscious I can understand within the limits of my power of cognition, but the visions during these dream-like states seem to be beyond my soul's scope of cognition. Since I am convinced that You are the wisest and most powerful person in this entire vast mansion, I can but turn to You and ask You to please interpret this my vision for me.

5. In this vision, You acted and spoke as the eternal, most holy

Lama Himself! However, now that I am once again wide awake, I do not notice any change whatsoever in Your appearance as I know it. Therefore, You could be either a messenger of Lama invested with full powers, or even Lama Himself in a justifiable disguise. That is as far as I can judge my vision, and I expect You, my only love, to give me a more detailed and better interpretation. Oh, do not hesitate to refresh my heart with the abundance of Your wisdom."

6. (Say I): "Chanchah, where is the dragon now, and where are his adherents? Now you suddenly begin to wonder, saying in your heart, 'In the name of Lama, the Most Holy, the monster has vanished! And so have his adherents, and Borem, Martin and Chorel. Where are they?'

7. But I tell you: Behold, it was My might that drove the one out through the door with the speed of the flight of the fastest thought. And it bid him go into the swine of the earth to make them, in their crazy lust for power, storm the headland of utter selfishness, and finally throw themselves from there into the sea of delusion, and drown in it.

8. As for his adherents — I took them away from him through the power of the Word and sent them with the three absent friends to the bath of self-realization, humility, and — resulting from it — possibly to betterment.

9. Everything that I am doing here I do of My own power. There is no other power — neither above nor below Me that could bid Me do this or that. But if I say to others, 'Do this or that,' there is no one who could oppose the power of My will.

10. Oh, Chanchah, since you have seen all this from My actions for some time already, how can you still ask whether I am a messenger of Lama or maybe Lama Himself?

11. The simplicity of My outward appearance should not mislead you, for, unlike the princes on earth, Lama has no need for outward splendor, but wants only to shine in the hearts of His children through His fatherly love, wisdom, and might. In your heart I have been shining most brilliantly for a long time now. How is it that you do not recognize Me?

12. Behold, My Chanchah, My daughter, I am your Father, your Lama, and there is no other one ever, except Me. But you must not be afraid for I am and remain forever the same, and all My children should not look upon Me as their God, but at all times only as their loving Father, seeing, loving, and worshipping Me as such.

13. Do not be afraid of Me now that you recognize Me. You will never notice a change in Me, but will enjoy the boundless treasures of My fatherly love and wisdom in ever-growing abundance. Are you satisfied now with this explanation of My nature?''

CHANCHAH'S EXTREME HAPPINESS AND LOVE FOR LAMA. LOVE AND WISDOM. THE LORD AS FATHER AND BROTHER.

1. Chanchah now falls at My feet, weeping and sobbing with utter joy and bliss. When I strengthen her, she rises, gazes at Me with her large eyes and, enraptured, scrutinizes Me from head to foot, unable to tear her eyes away from Me. And only her heart speaks:

2. (Chanchah): "You, You, oh, it is You after all! You are the almighty, holy Lama, the Eternal! You have made the earth, the moon, the sun, and the countless stars, also the mighty sea and the countless living beings in the water, on the land, and in the air. You have *created us human beings!* Oh, Lama, Lama, You great, holy Lama, who could ever praise and worship You enough? Is there a heart worthy of loving You, Most Holy One?

3. But which heart — worthy or unworthy — could help loving You when it sees and recognizes You? Therefore, forgive me, who am most unworthy, for having dared to love You, Holy One! But can poor Chanchah help it if her heart is stronger than her head?

4. Oh, Lama, Lama, I do realize my worthlessness compared to Your greatness. However, my heart now loves You all the more. You would not be angry with me for loving You so inconceivably, would You? Oh, Lama, strengthen my heart or it will be unable to bear this mighty love for You!''

5. And once more Chanchah sinks down at My feet, sobbing with love.

6. (Say I): "Your love is great, Chanchah, and your heart is a most precious pearl. However, you must pull yourself together and not overdraw your strength through glowing too mightily, for then it might become impossible for you to henceforth bear My presence — and that would limit your beatitude considerably.

7. Now look at Gella here beside you, at Martin, Borem, and also at Chorel. They all have known Me already for quite some time and are also full of love for Me. But they are able to bear My presence and, consequently, do and enjoy all that I bid and give them. If they were in the same state as you are in, this would not be so, just as you could not do or enjoy at present anything on a higher level since your overwhelming love is claiming all your strength.

8. I am telling you this, My beloved Chanchah, not because I find your overwhelming love displeasing, for have I not told you on many occasions how very dear you are to Me? And I may still add that no one can love Me enough! However, it must be stressed that love should never be there without wisdom if it is to attain the greatest possible beatitude.

9. For love in itself is an all-consuming fire, and as an elemental fire it cannot be checked by anything but an adequate degree of wisdom. Therefore, you have to temper your love by an appropriate degree of wisdom if you want to enjoy the real bliss of the right love.

10. Do not keep thinking of Me as the most high and almighty Divine Being Whom no one can approach and live, but think of Me as the best and truest Father, in My human nature even as your Brother. Then you will be able to bear Me easily like any other blessed spirit, to be constantly with Me and share in the beatitude of the most blessed who, too, are constantly near Me. They are at all times fully occupied on My behalf in the vast spaces of My infinite creation, and still as close to Me as you are now — and shall forever be. Is what I have told you quite clear to you now, My dearest daughter?"

A HEAVENLY DECLARATION OF LOVE. THE VICTORY OF LOVE. GELLA'S DELIGHT IN CHANCHAH.

1. (Says Chanchah): "Oh, Lama, Lama, where is the heart that recognizes You and is still able to contain its burning love for You, the Most Holy, the Eternal? If I had as many hearts as there are stars in the firmanent, grains of sand in the sea, or blades of grass on the earth, and each heart were a sun of blazing love for You, my most holy Lama, then the burning love of those countless hearts would

still only be like a cool dewdrop compared with a seething sea! For, being Supreme Love Yourself, You could never be loved too much!

2. I am quite aware that You, o Lama, are a Father and even a Brother to Your creatures, because that is how You want it. But is there a heart that can think of You as a Father and Brother only, not keeping in mind the fact that the Father, the Brother, is at the same time also the eternal, most holy, great and almighty Lama? Therefore, I cannot help loving You above everything, and no wisdom could ever temper this love of my heart!

3. If I had a thousand lives and wisdom warned me that I would lose all of them if I did not restrain my love for Lama, my heart would still reply to wisdom: 'Can there be greater bliss than to lose a thousand lives through love for You, o Lama?' This, of course, would not be possible, for how could one ever lose a life for loving You Who represents life supreme?

4. So I shall love You all the more, my Lama, and no wisdom will ever be able to restrain the love of my heart unless You, Most Holy One, should oppose and destroy it. But You would not do this to poor Chanchah, o Lama, Father, would You?"

5. (Say I): "My dearest daughter, one who loves Me as you do is one with Me and has not only one, but *countless* lives that could not ever be lost. Therefore, fear nothing, but go on loving Me with all your strength, and your love will provide the wisdom which will keep widening your heart and enable your love for Me to grow more intense all the time. But now come to My heart and give vent to your love!"

6. At these words, Chanchah utters a cry of delight and throws herself at My heart in a near swoon.

7. (Gella weeps with joy for Chanchah, and says, sobbing): "Oh, you fortunate one, what bliss it must be to breathe at this heart the streams of everlasting, divine love! Ah, what an atmosphere there must be at the primordial source from which all the countless beings, the angels, the suns, worlds, men and beasts, as well as plants, draw their existence, their life, their all! What supreme delight, joy, and bliss!

8. Oh, Chanchah, what bliss you must be enjoying, imeasurable even for an angel!

9. But what are you pondering, my heart — you, too, are quite close to and able to see Him Who is holy, supremely holy. Be still, my heart, the Lord gives everyone a just measure according to his

love and wisdom! Therefore, do not think about the supreme measure of bliss this noble Chinese is enjoying, but rather about your own boundless happiness."

123

SPIRITUAL AWAKENING OF THE OTHER CHINESE AND THE MONKS. THE JEALOUS NUNS AND THEIR HUMILIATION.

1. While Gella is engrossed in her commendable contemplations, all the other Chinese are approaching us. One of them says:

2. (A Chinese): "You, Who obviously have full authority, tell us why our Chanchah loves You so much. Her love for You is such that a man could not even love Lama with a greater love, should He — if at all possible — stand before him visibly!"

3. (Say I): "Have patience, soon Chanchah will tell you everything you have to know at this stage. Do not go into this any further, but let your heart walk ahead of your mind, and it will guide you on to the safest and shortest path to your goal."

4. (Says another one of them): "That sounds fair enough! But will she also be able to tell us the meaning of that monster which You expelled from this house after it had led our good Martin quite a dance, even turning into an enticing woman to trap him? Could he have been an emissary of the devil, or maybe even the devil himself?"

5. (Say I): "Chanchah will tell you about that, too. Just return to your seats where you may look forward to all the answers. So be it!"

6. Following these words, all the Chinese turn back and do as bidden.

7. Also, several of the monks come forward and ask similar questions. They, too, are told to rest a while longer so as to gain more strength for the impending explanations. And they withdraw and wait patiently in happy anticipation.

8. (However, some nuns have put their heads together and are whispering to each other): "Following some hints by our sister, who is now called Gella, we had almost come to believe that this friend of the Chinese, the one who handled the dragon and his adherents so capably, could be either the archangel Michael or even Jesus, the

Lord Himself. However, judging by the way He is going on with that Chinese, who no doubt is more beautiful than we are, and how He is pressing her to His heart and caressing her, He could not possibly be Michael and even less the Lord Jesus.

9. We would consider it a great sin to think — even in passing — that Michael or the Lord Jesus could be playing such an amorous game — and with a heathen at that! And this silly ninny does not even feel embarrassed by our presence! Look at the way she is nestling against His heart, the amorous cat!

10. If He were Michael or the Lord Jesus, He would have come to us also, since we are Christians and have an undisputable prerogative before the heathen. But since He is practically ignoring us and doing homage only to that Chinese, He could not possibly be the Lord Jesus. How silly of our sister, Gella, to stand around there with a face as if she, too, would like to follow Chanchah's example!"

11. (Say I to Gella): "Look, my little daughter, there is room for you, too, as well as Chanchah. So, come also to My heart and give vent to your love!"

12. Gella immediately throws herself at My heart and is blissfully happy.

13. (But the whisperers say): "There you are! Just what we were expecting! If only our host, Martin, would return soon so we could complain to him! Ah, there he is already coming with Borem and Chorel. Let us go to him quickly!"

14. Noticing all the women coming towards him, Martin soon realizes what is wrong with them. He approaches them in the friendliest manner and says:

15. (Bishop Martin): "I know, I know what is worrying you! Better return quietly to your seats, as I am not going to lend you an ear for such complaints! Just note this: Who wants love must first give love himself, for love can be won by nothing else but love. Therefore, you must love the Lord as those two do, and then you'll find a place at His heart. Do you understand this?"

16. (Say the many nuns): "Oh, dear host of this house, don't you see that we cannot do that? We are firm Christians, but that favorite there is a heathen! As for Gella, she was always rather unrestrained, prone to temptation by the devil, and she is sure to take every chance, even in your celestial mansion, to lend a willing ear and heart to such temptations.

17. That man, whom we almost took for the Lord Jesus, or at

least Michael, must be a spirit of a considerably lower grade, otherwise He would not be going on like that with those two loose persons. Therefore . . . . "

18. (Here Martin interrupts them and says): "Never mind, my dears, I had thought you would all be clean by now, having been thoroughly boiled and bathed! However, now some heretofore completely hidden residues of rust and dirt are emerging. In view of this, you will have to go into a bath once more — and a very hot one, too — before you will be fit enough to approach that Holy One!"

19. (Scream the nuns): "What are you saying? We are to have a bath? You, too, are unclean! No wonder the devil is a frequent guest at your house! Did we not see to our horror how you would have kissed the beautiful she-devil had she not pushed you back? If things continue like this, we shall soon know beyond doubt in whose hands we are in this house!"

20. (Says Martin calmly): "Oh yes, into the bath with you! There, behind that white wall, a thousand rare little fishes are swimming around and having a bath. There is also room for you. So go there quietly and join the bathers — or else!"

21. The nuns scream with rage and return to their former places.

124

HINTS FOR THE HEALING OF SOULS. SPIRITUAL METHOD OF NATURAL HEALING. CRISES FOR THE CHINESE SPIRITS. ABOUT THE NATURE OF JEALOUSY.

1. Bishop Martin, with Borem and Chorel, returns to Me. He wants to tell Me that the thousand bathers (the dragon's adherents) — since they are feeling better — are assuming various shapes and are becoming rather unruly, so much so that even Borem does not know what to do with them!

2. (Say I to the three): "The thousand in the bath are quite safe, for they cannot see this house, but only the world of evil within them. This is now becoming more and more active and, therefore, is expessing itself visibly. That is a good sign and you need not worry about them. They will be guided onto the right path.

3. Over there, however, are more than three hundred women suffering from acute jealousy in their hearts, and I am sorry for them. Go and teach them what is right, but do not threaten them again with the bath, brother Martin, if you want to bring those poor souls to Me.

4. Jealousy is a parasite of love, which it undermines. If the parasite on love's tree of life becomes too mighty, it will eventually destroy the whole tree. If the tree is to be saved and strengthened, means must be found to completely rid the tree of these pests.

5. By stirring up jealous minds through threats, you only graft the parasite yourself upon the tree of life, where it will grow rapidly and destroy the tree.

6. In future, when you have to deal with jealous spirits, you must observe this: Look upon jealousy as a product of love and think that where there is jealousy, there also must be love. Appease such jealousy with love, and the result will soon be burning love.

7. I tell you, where no jealousy is evident, there is no love! Or have you ever seen on earth parasitic plants grow on barren trees? You don't see them on willows, pines, spruces, or thousands of other trees like those, but on good fruit trees you'll find them frequently.

8. Thus it is here with these women. They have much love, just as a good fruit tree has a lot of high-quality juice. Endeavor to remove the parasite from their hearts through love and you will achieve with them wonders of the most prolific love. Go now and do as I have advised you, and you will do a good work as an offering to My heart."

125

BOREM AND THE SUFFERING NUNS.

1. The three now approach the poor women in the friendliest manner, and Borem speaks to them:

2. (Borem): "Dear sisters, listen to me patiently. Knowing that your hearts are troubled and that this brother rejected you harshly when you were seeking justice, I shall now see that justice is done to you. Being myself a guest of this house, I was unable to interrupt the

host as he was speaking to you, for in his own house everyone is the chief administrator of justice.

3. But now the Lord of all hosts has entitled me — although myself a guest — to dispense the justice of love to you. Therefore, I will now, to the best of my ability, do justice to you and straighten out in the name of the Lord whatever is troubling or offending your hearts. Do all of you find this satisfactory, dear sisters?"

4. (Say the women unanimously): "Oh, yes, dearest friend, there is no doubt that you are a true friend of God, who means well and recognizes the suffering of our hearts, and we are only too willing to accept your advice. However, we do not want to have anything to do with this Martin. Instead of comforting us in our trouble and showing us the truth if we should have been wrong, he sent us to hell, into the bath with the devils! This was a most unheavenly action on his part, considering that he is, or at least wants to be, a citizen of heaven. We would prefer him to withdraw altogether so that the sight of him will not annoy us."

5. (Says Borem): "Never mind, dear sisters, leave all that to me, and I will straighten things out. Our brother Martin is not an evil spirit, but like myself, a good one of the Lord.

6. We had a lot of trouble and annoyance with those still rather wicked guests in the bath and, tired from the task that rather overtaxed our strength, we were on our way to that mighty friend to get His advice, when you approached us at the worst possible moment. As a result, the easily excitable Martin treated you rather unkindly which, as already explained, is quite excusable.

7. In view of these circumstances, I am sure you will forgive him as he loves you all very much and is delighted to have you as guests in his house. Surely you will forgive him! I would, if you had offended me."

8. (Say the women): "You know, dearest friend, we shall do what you suggest, but mind you, only for *your* sake will we forgive Martin his rudeness. If he should ever treat us like that again, we would not so easily be able to forgive him.

9. He may be a good man, and he is certainly handsome, but what does the outer appearance help if the heart is unripe like a green apple eight weeks after blooming? If Martin would treat us like you do, he would find that we, too, have loving hearts. However, as a tyrannical host, he can be sure to find no love, but instead something quite different.

10. Thank God we now possess celestial beauty, too. All the men who are here in considerable numbers have already looked at us with great appreciation. Not that we pride ourselves on this, knowing that all external beauty is a gift of God, but it hurts our feelings that Martin and that mighty friend of yours don't find us attractive at all.

11. Those two sisters over there are not really any more beautiful than we are, but that friend loves them above everything and devotes almost all His time to them, whilst we are standing here like poor sinners, noticed by nobody, for everybody is looking at those three. How could we not be hurt by all this, especially since in our hearts we had already formed the most sublime conjectures about that friend, which, however, must wither like flowers on earth without the necessary nourishment.

12. The heart, too, needs nourishment if it is to grow strong in love. But how are our hearts ever to grow strong if, instead of being fed, they have to keep fasting?"

13. (Says Borem): "Yes, my dearest sisters, your claim is justified. Just have a little patience and soon your hearts will be fully satisfied. As you know, the good physician heals the sick first and then only calls on the healthy.

14. The same applies here also. As soon as those two patients have fully recovered, that physician will come to you, too. Therefore, have a bit more patience and follow me. I will show you something most wonderful."

15. (Say the women): "That, dear brother, is not necessary, for in this vast hall there are so many wonderful things to see that one could not take one's eyes off them anyway.

16. This magnificent floor, which seems to have been composed of all the different most precious gems in a variety of colors, creating the effect of garlands . . .

17. Those splendid tall columns, carrying the indescribably beautiful galleries — they shine as if made from gleaming rubies, inside which a great number of stars are floating like goldfish in water, thus producing constantly new, most beautiful shapes of light . . .

18. Thus, there are thousands of splendors here for which we have not even a name. In view of all these splendors presenting themselves to us in this hall, we have not the slightest wish to look at any more magnificent and wonderful things.

19. Our eyes are saturated with what they see and need no

more. But it is a different story with our *hearts*. So far, they have not been provided for. What is the use of letting the eyes feast if the heart is suffering? Provide for our hearts first, then our eyes will be easily satisfied."

20. (Says Borem): "Dear sisters, your claim is right and justified, but it has been made before you know what it is that I want to show you. How do you know that what I am going to show you is for the eyes and not for the heart? Could not there be something most wonderful just for the heart?

21. What is more important, the eye or the heart? Cannot the eye be blind and the heart still enjoy the fullness of love? Is there a mortal eye that can see God? No, a mortal eye is blind for that, but a heart can imagine God and love Him. It can even become a living temple for Him, the Lord, wherein He can dwell. So what is more, the eye or the heart?

22. If this is so, how can you, dear sisters, think that here in the Kingdom of the Heart of God I would want to take you where there are wonders for the eye alone?

23. I assure you that here everything is exclusively for the heart. The eye is nothing but a true witness of all that happens to the heart and what one heart offers to another. Thus, the wonder I intend to show you is not for your eyes, but only for your hearts.

24. Since, however, here in the Kingdom of God no one is blind and the vision of every being is quite as strong as the heart, the eye, of course, witnesses all the experiences of the heart. Thus, you, too, will be seeing with your eyes all that happens to your hearts. So follow me!"

25. In response to these words of Borem's, all the women follow Borem, Martin and Chorel to the door leading into the world of the sun.

126

BLASPHEMY OF THE BATHING ADHERENTS OF THE DRAGON. THE LORD'S PACIFYING AND INSTRUCTIVE WORDS.

1. While Borem, Martin and Chorel are taking the women to the sun-door, the thousand bathing guests are becoming most unruly in

their bath. They are beginning to utter terrible blasphemies, loud enough for all the cleansed monks, and even Chanchah and Gella, to hear.

2. The two are coming out of their blessed ecstasy of love and are beginning to listen more attentively. Chanchah is at the point of asking Me what all this means, when a hundred monks hurry towards Me, entreating Me to silence the guests in the bath as this might have a bad effect on the weaker brothers among them.

3. (At this moment also the Chinese with all their wives and the parents of the nuns approach Me, saying): "You mighty messenger of God, don't You hear the adherents of the dragon in the bath threatening God, You, and all of us? If this evil scum from hell is not stopped, the situation here will become quite unbearable for us.

4. Listen to those terrible blasphemies! Those beasts are worse than the dragon himself, which seemed to speak quite sensibily to Martin and also to You. Do make an end to these goings-on, or let us all go outside so that we don't have to listen to such blasphemies of the Most Holy!"

5. (Say I): "It is quite right that your hearts are filled with disgust at such annoying scenes, but it is still necessary for you to watch My reaction and not your own, for otherwise you might set yourselves up for judges. That would then be even worse than all this empty blaspheming by the admittedly still very wicked bathing guests.

6. With blasphemies one can prove nothing but his impotence. One who had any power would act immediately and not waste words that are nothing but an empty noise. One who is impotent but pretends to possess power, only sets himself up for a false judge, thus maliciously interfering with God's exclusive rights. Through his impotence, he desecrates these, whilst in God alone there is and has to be all the might and power and the exclusive right to judge for the sake of the necessary eternal order.

7. Look, dear friends and brothers, you are annoyed by the vile abuse on the part of these bathing guests, and it is only right that in your hearts you find it disgusting. However, in addition to that, I detect in all of you a fire strong enough to finish these bathers off forever. This fire is worse than that senseless, futile abuse.

8. These guests only abuse us knowing quite well that they can never hurt us. They are also aware of God's patience and forbearance. We, however, would destroy them for this, or at least forsake them

forever, because we have the power to do it. Would that be wise? Would it be within the order of God, which never wants to destroy but at all times to preserve? It has to do this, for the Deity would suffer if anything that has emanated from It could be destroyed.

9. "So let them swear and blaspheme. This will eventually come to an end and they will be seized with great remorse. They are still going to be very dear and true brothers to us, or rather sisters, for most of them are female.

10. That they are absolutely helpless you can see from the fact that they cannot move from the bath by even a hair's breadth. It would certainly not be to our credit if we took revenge on them because we have the power and they have not. It would be like a lion degrading himself by becoming a catcher of gnats!

11. I advise you to always look at Me and note what I do, and that should prevent you from being annoyed and feeling in your hearts a desire to judge others. All this concerns Me most of all and still I am calm. Since all this abuse does not concern you in any way, you have all the more reason to be calm.

12. They only abuse God's justice which makes them bathe here and, naturally, this process cannot be quite painless if they are to be helped at all. Every mutation is painful to a certain degree until an integrated being has transmuted to a different order. The pain as such is necessary for if there were no pain, there could be no bliss, and a being that could feel no pain would be incapable of experiencing bliss.

13. These bathers are at present in a mighty process of transmutation, and the pain they must suffer drives their tongues to such abuse. Eventually, as they get nearer to a new, firm order, their pains will diminish and, consequently, their tongues will cease to abuse and begin to form exalting words of remorse, thus building a bridge to love and life.

14. To save you from further annoyance through this idle abuse, follow Me to that door where Borem, Martin, and Chorel are already standing with all the women. The door is still closed to your eyes, but I will open it. You will be afforded a great opportunity to humble your entire being to the innermost fibers of your still rather proud hearts, which is very much needed by all of you. Therefore, follow Me. So be it!"

127

AT THE CLOSED DOOR TO THE SUN. LIGHT IN PROPORTION TO ACTIVITY. HINTS OF CONDUCT FOR THE SPHERE OF WISDOM.

1. The whole party now follows Me to where Bishop Martin, Borem, Chorel, and the women are waiting for Me to open the door of light. There are now about three thousand guests there, but since this door is extremely wide, the guests will have sufficient space to enter the territory of the sun unimpeded and view the wonders of love and light.

2. At the door, Martin immediately asks Me why this door is closed, whilst all the other doors are now open.

3. (But I say to him): "Friend, brother, have you on earth never heard or read about the different births of human beings and animals? Every being, already in the womb, has possession of all its senses, except for the eyesight. It can feel, taste, smell, and even hear. However, its eyes are opened only after its birth. Thus, also, in the spiritual rebirth, the door to the light — or the spiritual eye — is the last one to be opened, for he who wants to see must be well prepared for it.

4. If somebody wants to light up his house at night, he has to make the necessary preparations beforehand. Must he not have a lamp filled with oil and a well-functioning lighter? Even then it requires some action on his part, and some time will pass before the purpose of his actions — the light — is achieved. And only after the light has been lit can he do other useful things in the light, which prior to that would have been out of the question.

5. Considering this, you will easily understand why in this house all the other doors are open and only the sun-door has so far been closed to these guests.

6. I can see that you now want to ask Me why, if this is the case, has this door already been open to you on several occasions. And why had it not been the last one when you entered through it the first and second time. My answer to this is that, firstly, you no longer belong to the level of these guests, who have not yet attained their rebirth and, secondly, as concerns the other doors you entered

after the sun-door, every spirit after his rebirth will want to take up some activity in the light, or in his enlightenment and cognition.

7. You would not think that after receiving the light a permanent state of blissful idleness could set in. Oh, no, on the contrary, the right activity only commences in the light. Prior to receiving the light, every action is aimed only at this goal, but when enlightenment has been achieved, the temple has been opened to the sun, only then will the great activity of the reborn spirit commence.

8. Or have you ever seen on earth schoolboys being given official positions? Of course not! A pupil has to study diligently for quite a while to attain the required knowledge, and only then may he be given a position commensurate with his ability. And, after completing his scientific studies and achieving real enlightenment, it is not likely that he will lie down comfortably and go to sleep instead of working in the light of his new knowledge. Then he will really commence to work properly, for the work he did during his studies was only the means to lighten the darkness of his mind.

9. And, behold, that is another sound reason why there are further doors after the sun-door, especially those leading to the infinite universe. Do you have any more questions?"

10. (Says Martin): "Oh, Lord, You look through my heart like You would look through a drop of water! There is now no other emotion left in me than burning love for You, You boundlessly kind and holy Father! You know that I welcome an activity within the limits of my strength; and surely a higher degree of enlightenment will be of great benefit to me. You know that I have never lacked the will for good works but, unfortunately, most of the time I have lacked the light or the wisdom! In view of this, I am convinced that the full re-opening of this temple will be particularly beneficial to me, although for myself I see the Sun of all suns and the Light of all lights in all fullness in You, and could do forever without any other light!"

11. (Say I): "These words, My dear brother Martin, I prefer considerably to your earlier questions.

12. It is true that I am the Sun of all suns and the Light of all lights. He who has Me, walks and acts in the brightest day! However, since every man out of Me is an individual and a free being, he has also his own light which has to shine within him quite as brightly and freely as the sun in the vast sphere of its planets, as freely as a man's eyes shine and new thoughts come forth from his heart. From

these thoughts arise free ideas and the knowledge of their nature and, eventually, the great knowledge of My Divine Being, My love and wisdom. Therefore, this door will now be opened to these guests that they might come to know themselves and only then Me in all truth! And now it will be time to open this door."

13. (Says Martin): "Oh, Lord, most holy Father, do give me the assurance that when these guests have recognized You fully, You will not leave us again and hide from us and stay away, notwithstanding our searching and calling. Dearest Father, do not ever do that to us!"

14. (Say I): "My beloved son, this should be the least of your worries, ever! For where the children are, there is also the Father, and where the Father is, there are His children. But you know how big My family is and how very numerous the flock of My sheep. Eventually, we shall bring all these together into one house, so that there will be one flock and one shepherd. However, there is still a lot of work to be done toward this end.

15. Note this: There are now many reapers employed on earth and a great sifting is going to take place. I shall require a lot of flesh and much blood will be shed in uprooting all lewdness. I have awakened witnesses on earth, and all that I am telling you here, all that I have already told you, and all that I am still going to tell you is simultaneously being written down on earth and revealed to the flesh. Therefore, do not worry that I might leave you in any way after the opening of this door, but realize that I shall now stay with you, unchanged, forever!

16. There is one more thing, My beloved Martin, this time we shall enter much deeper into the territory of the sun, much deeper than the first time. You will be met by female beings of unimaginable beauty and grace, who will approach you with the greatest love and tenderness, and so will the men. You must treat them with true celestial earnestness, and when you speak, say little and speak wisely. That is the best way for you to win them. You must keep your love for them secret so that they do not notice it. Then you will walk among them safely.

17. In this great world of light, wisdom is foremost, and within it, love is concealed just as the warmth is concealed in the sunlight — invisible, revealing its existence only in its manifold productive effect. Therefore, you must shine in the sun as you will see Me shine, and if you observe this rule conscientiously, your first great expedition will

afford you much bliss. And now go and open the door in My name! So be it!''

128

ON THE LIGHT-ISSUING SUN. THE LORD AS THE LAST ONE. MARTIN AS GUIDE.

1. Martin thanks Me for this commission from the depth of his heart, walks over to the door, and opens it with ease — although in its correspondence it has the height of twelve men and is half as wide again.

2. As the door is standing open, the thousands in front of it give forth a cry of delight intermingled with fright, and they all cover their eyes against the intensity of the light emating from it. Not one of them dares take a step either forward or backward, for most of them are convinced that in this mighty light, the actual Godhead must dwell in the fullness of Its might, power, and wisdom.

3. Even Martin is startled for a moment as the intensity of the light this time seems by far greater than on the two previous occasions he had been there. However, this fact does not worry him too much, and he says:

4. (Martin): ''Brothers and sisters, do not be afraid of what the Lord has intended for our greater bliss. Come, follow me, all of you, for this light is a firm ground on which you can walk as on iron!''

5. Borem and Chorel lead the women out through the door. The women were at first very frightened, but their curiosity overruled their fears and they are beginning to step over the threshold. They are followed by the monks and other guests, namely, the parents of the nuns and of many of the monks. After them follow the Chinese with very careful steps.

6. After they have all passed through the door, I follow with Chanchah and Gella, who, too, at first seem most apprehensive of this dazzling light. But at My side they soon lose their fear, and they enter these new territories of light serenely.

7. Now everybody is standing on the shining ground of the sun, and this not only spiritually, but also bodily. For all the spirits from

My highest heaven can see also the nature of every natural body, inside and out. Being with Me, they see through Me everything, be it in the world of spirits or the material world, exactly as I see it!

8. At first they do not see very clearly as their eyes are dazzled by the glaring light, but gradually matters improve, as is already becoming evident. Some of the guests are beginning to distinguish items and colors on the ground.

9. The women have even noticed some extremely beautiful flowers which they would like to pick, but Borem and Chorel advise against it, as on the sun it is considered a bad omen if some plant is harmed at the wrong time. Here, everything has to be done in the strictest order.

10. After this large party, led by Martin, has walked quite a distance on the ground of the sun, and Martin is beginning to feel a bit uneasy, he orders a halt, comes to Me, and says:

11. (Martin): "O Lord and Father, I have the feeling as if we had already walked more than a thousand miles from my house, and all that we have so far seen is some flowers. How far, and for how long will we have to walk until we reach a certain destination?

12. I must admit honestly that I wouldn't care to spend a lot of time in this much-too-bright world if all you get to see is light and some flowers! It is as well that this gleaming light does not burn and that our spiritual eyes do not get inflamed like the physical ones! Although I am leading, what is the use of it if I do not know whither! Therefore, o Lord, wouldn't You rather lead the way? Then we would reach the right destination much quicker!"

13. (Say I): "My son Martin, just keep walking on the ground of light with patience and perseverance, and we shall reach the destination of our pilgrimage in due course. Don't you know that the sun is a million times larger than the earth? And if you need already on earth a lot of patience and self-denial on a long journey, it must require a lot more patience to travel through the so much vaster territory of the sun. Therefore, take the lead once more and we shall follow you.

14. The reason why I cannot lead here is that none of you must be constrained in your freedom and, besides, if I led the party and the inhabitants of this world of light came to meet us, their enlightened spirit would soon recognize Me and be overwhelmed by excessive awe. If I walk as the last one behind you, this would not happen, for with the sun-dwellers, the first is always paramount. To

them, what follows behind is scarcely noticed, if at all! Therefore, it is the best place for Me.

15. We are still on a very high mountain range. Soon we shall descend into a valley, and there the light will be much softer. There you will see crowds of people, and then you, as well as all the others with you, will be fully occupied. Then you will also understand the true purpose of this journey. But now return to your post and your office as a guide."

16. Martin thanks Me and once more takes the lead of the party, motioning everybody to follow him. They all rise and proceed.

129

MARTIN MEETS PETER AND JOHN. ABOUT THE NATURE OF LOVE AND WISDOM WITH THE SUN-DWELLERS.

1. After Martin has walked for quite a while and is wondering when the valley might appear, Peter and John the Evangelist come to meet him, greeting him in the friendliest manner. He immediately recognizes them, especially Peter, who was his first guide in the spirit-world, and he is overcome with joy to see Peter again for he had missed him for such a long time. After the first joy of the re-union, Martin says:

2. (Bishop Martin): "But friend, brother, you rock of the Word of God, where have you been all this time? Why did you not come to me to the house the Lord has given me? If you had only been there, you would have been amazed at the inconceivable miracles the Lord worked there. However, I am overjoyed that you are with me again. You will now stay with me for a while, won't you?"

3. (Says Peter): "Dearest brother, you know that all of us have but one will, and it is the Lord's will. All that He wills and orders is good. Infinity is vast and filled with His works, but we are His children and are like His arm. Therefore, we have to be here and there — wherever the Lord needs us! Whenever He needs us, we are there in a moment, be it billions of sun-distances, deeper down or higher up, it does not make any difference to us, for we know no distances as far as space is concerned.

4. And so I have had very much to do after I left you, and could not come to you visibly. But now I, as well as our beloved brother, John, have a bit more leisure and so will stay with your party for quite a while. However, the Lord, our Father Jesus, is at all times our principal foundation, and we cannot be without His visible presence for too long, especially at times when He Himself is particularly active, emerging from His patience and forbearance.

5. Oh friend, you cannot imagine all that is going on at present on the different globes, especially on the dear earth. That is also the reason why the Lord is becoming so active, and we shall soon be seeing things of which so far you have no idea. As we shall now descend into the vast valleys of the sun, you will be able to see what a crazy turn things are beginning to take here in the vast lands of the world of light. With this natural forward movement, it will take us still quite some time to reach the first valley, but you will be seeing wonders which at this stage you cannot even imagine, although you are already like me — a dweller in the third heaven.

6. However, you must at all times keep in mind the concept, 'earnestness,' for the sun-dwellers are strange people! Their outer appearance is a reflection of the heavens, but within they are more cunning than foxes. They respect us pure children of God very highly, but if they detect in you the least sensual weakness, you will not easily get rid of them, as their wisdom is greater than you can imagine. But our brother here, he who has had a lot to do with them, will be able to tell you more details."

7. (Says Martin): "Listen, my beloved brother, although your report is most interesting, I am not too anxious to meet these dwellers in the world of light so very soon if they are such queer fellows. That they are inconceivably beautiful, I know, having already had the fortune of seeing some of them from my house. But I did not know that under their beauty they conceal a kind of astute wisdom.

8. The Lord has hinted as to how I should behave, which fully concurs with what you just told me, but about an astute slyness, nothing has been mentioned to me so far. May the Lord strengthen me and you, my dearest brothers. With your help, I hope to be able to deal with their cunning. To be trapped by those smooth, bright beauties of the sun — not on your life!"

9. (Says John): "Brother, in love there is unity, and it is wide open to love! Thus love soon recognizes love. However, the ways of

wisdom are infinite, and most likely no one, except the Lord, will ever fully know them. Therefore, an argument with wisdom should never be started without the Lord. He alone is familiar with all its ways, since all infinite wisdom has issued from Him. That is also why He alone is the path, the truth and life.

10.   You know that the Lord has given me the great gift of profound wisdom. He has given me a revelation of great depth and, because of that, also the peoples of all the suns and authority over countless spirits of profound wisdom, all of whom still draw from my abundance. And even I have been considerably embarrassed by the dwellers on this sun. If, in such moments, the Lord had not come to my assistance, I could have departed in disgrace.

11.   If I, who have had dealings with these sun-people for almost two thousand years, can sometimes be cornered by them, what chance would *you* have, meeting them for the first time?

12.   Look at the splendor of these mountains, at the rocks reaching up into the light-ether like huge diamonds, at the way this highland is adorned with the most glorious flowers, and how gently this path winds along like a gleaming rainbow! And still, all this glory is only a trifle compared to that harmony which a single glance of a sun-dweller in the valley will radiate.

13.   And on top of this, there is the harmony of each word from the purest throats of the glorious orators and singers of this world of light. I assure you, delight and amazement will render you speechless, quite unable to teach those who can silence you with a glance.

14.   If you want to get on with these indescribably beautiful and clear-headed sun-philosophers of both sexes, you have to appear outwardly quite indifferent, but in your heart you must be kindly disposed toward them. Then they will soon recognize in you a citizen of heaven, in possession of great might, and they will respect and love you.

15.   However, also their love differs considerably from ours, who are children of the Lord. It, too, is a kind of sincere affection, provided it is not ruined by wisdom. For, the moment love grows stronger than their light, the greater part of love begins to blaze, and this blazing flame of love unites with the inner light of wisdom and the result, instead of love, is just an increased wisdom, often colder than the south pole on earth.

16.   Therefore, love for the opposite sex, which used to be so

important to you, will not get you anywhere with these sun-women. On the contrary, they are extremely insusceptible in this regard.

17. Look, brother, if you observe strictly these rules, you will find a lot of happiness through these sun-dwellers, but otherwise you will meet with extreme embarrassment, similar to that caused to you by Satana when you wanted to kiss her in the presence of the Lord!"

18. (Says Martin): "But, for heaven's sake, tell me — were you present at that time too?"

19. (Says John): "Of course I was! Your house has vast galleries still unexplored by you, which accommodate a great number of spectators to watch the Lord in His mighty activity. Not I alone, but all the countless citizens of heaven witnessed that scene. Even among the sun-dwellers you will find many who will remind you of that incident should you ever forget yourself in any way."

20. (Martin's face reflects his bewilderment, and after a while, he says): "Oh, what a dreadful business! Now all of you have witnessed that, and so have these fine sun-dwellers! What a situation! But now I don't care. Already on earth the sun has so often made me sweat and now, when I have the good luck to walk on its own ground in my spiritual body, I can expect all the more of it. I can feel it in advance that something is going to happen!"

130

JOHN TESTS MARTIN WITH SOME QUESTIONS. ABOUT INTERCESSION OF THE SAINTS AND CONCERN FOR RELATIVES.

1. (Says John): "Listen, brother Martin, on earth, as far as I know, you used to be a great friend of Mary's, also of Joseph's and other saints. You do not seem to show any interest in them here. Why? You also do not seem concerned about your relatives — your father, mother, brothers, sisters, and many other relatives and friends who preceded you in this world. Tell me, why is this so?

2. They could be unhappy somewhere. Wouldn't you, now a great friend of the Lord, wish to help them if you could, especially if you knew they were unhappy? In the world, you thought a lot of intercession by the saints, but here, a saint yourself and the Lord's

great friend, you do not think of it at all. Tell me, what is the reason for that?''

3. (Says Martin): "Dearest friend and brother, an ox feeds on hay and straw, and an ass is satisfied with an even poorer feed. I was on earth first an ass and then an ox, and my food was as described just now. Tell me, can a spirit grow on such a meager spiritual fare?

4. Only now, thanks to the Lord's love, compassion, and mercy, and His bread of life and genuine wine of true knowledge, have I become a real human being. Should I still have an appetite for the fare of asses and oxen on earth? Should I still make the same mistake as on earth, thinking the blessed citizens of this great celestial spirit-world could be more merciful and loving than the Lord Himself? And He would have to be moved by them to love and mercy? Oh friend, thanks to God I am not quite as stupid as I used to be.

5. What are Mary and Joseph and all the so-called saints? What are my earthly parents, brothers, sisters, and friends compared to the Lord? If I have Him, I do not care about a thousand Marys, Josephs, parents, brothers and sisters, or friends! The Lord looks after them as He has done with me. What more could they need? I think every true citizen of heaven must think like this. If not, he must be more perfect than the Lord Himself.

6. Did not the Lord Himself say clearly who His mother, brothers and sisters were, when He was told that His mother, His brothers and sisters were waiting for Him outside?

7. If He, Who has forever been and will be our Teacher and Master, has taught us these things which, unfortunately, on earth we did not understand, why should we here in heaven seek a better doctrine within ourselves? That would be very stupid, don't you think so, my dearest brother?''

8. (Says John): "Indeed, you have expressed what is in my heart. This is how it is, must be, and will be forever! But if you now met Mary and Joseph, and other persons of consequence, wouldn't you be very happy?''

9. (Says Martin): "Yes, I would be happy, but by no means any happier than when the Lord comes to me. For in Him I have everything and, therefore, He is more to me than anything else. Look, you and brother Peter surely belong to the most important persons who ever lived on earth. I love you both very much, but I respect every good and wise citizen of heaven quite as much as you, since we are all brothers, and there is only *one* Who is the Lord. Am I right?''

320

10. (Says John): "Brother, with such true wisdom you will even get through on the sun! Now I can see that you possess true wisdom and — look — the road is already descending into the valley. Now we shall also meet sun-philosophers!"

131

DESCENT INTO A SUN-VALLEY. HOW SPIRITS SEE. CONDITIONS FOR FAST OR SLOW TRAVEL IN THE SPIRIT-WORLD.

1. Now Martin actually sees how the road winds across the mountain crests down into a vast valley in which, however, he cannot as yet distinguish any objects.

2. Spirits see the things which are still unknown to them, as if at a very great distance, and approach them at the same rate at which their knowledge about these things grows. Thus, also, the descent from high mountains into a deep and wide valley denotes 'the entering into complete meekness and through this into the greatest possible love, without which no spirit can gain full vitality.'

3. Martin, as well as the many guests, are already looking down into the valley. But they are still unable to discern what it contains. Therefore, many of their spokesmen begin to ask questions as to what they will find in the valley. Borem knows very well, but he also knows what he has to say. The Chinese turn to Me and, of course, I am not at a loss as to a suitable answer.

4. (Martin turns to John and says): "Dearest friend, although I can already see the valley quite clearly, what is the use of looking at such a distant valley if one cannot distinguish anything in it? It must still be very far away. The road presents no hardship. On the contrary, we seem to be more floating than walking on our feet! But the valley still does not appear to be any closer. I wonder how much longer it will take us to reach it."

5. (Says John): "Friend, patience is the foundation stone of wisdom. Hold on to this foundation stone in your heart and you will reach the sun-valley much easier and quicker!"

6. (Says Martin): "Friend and brother, I do not lack patience, and never have. However, I know that every spirit is capable of two

or three kinds of movement: a natural, a mental, and also a purely spiritual one with the speed of thought. Why are we in this instance only using the natural kind, the slowest? Wouldn't it be better if we reached our destination sooner through a somewhat faster movement?"

7. (Says John): "But dear brother, now your words are not as wise as before. Why should we reach the valley quicker, since here the hours of our lives are not counted as on earth? Why should we, who live forever, concern ourselves about elements of time? We are not ever pressed for time, but are at home wherever we are, or rather wherever the Lord is.

8. Besides, here in the realm of perfected spirits, the speed of our movement does not depend on our feet anyway, but solely on the perfection of our knowledge. He who desires faster movement, must first learn patience and meekness, from which love and wisdom will arise. When he has gained a full measure of wisdom, he will also gain perfect knowledge in all things, which then will control the movement of the spirit.

9. In view of this, you need not look at your feet, whether their movement is fast or slow. Keep looking at your mind and its knowledge, and the movement will soon be fast enough! Do you understand this?"

132

ABOUT THE UBIQUITY AND SIMULTANEOUS ACTION OF PERFECTED CITIZENS OF HEAVEN. MARTIN'S OBJECTIONS AND THEIR REFUTATION BY JOHN.

1. (Says Martin): "It seems to me as if I do understand, but this matter is not yet perfectly clear to me. I know that the Lord and surely also you, brother Peter, and also Borem, possess this perfect knowledge, and still you do not move any faster than the rest of us. How am I to understand that?"

2. (Says John): "Friend, ours is only an apparent movement, out of love for you and all this crowd. In actual fact, we are already wherever we have or wish to be.

3. While I am speaking with you here, I am simultaneously in countless other suns and worlds, acting there as I am here, in the name of the Lord, fulfilling His holy will as best I can. And the same applies to an even greater extent to the Lord Himself, as well as to Peter and to all perfected citizens of heaven. Do you comprehend it now?"

4. (Says Martin): "My dearest brother, I must admit that this is somewhat beyond me. Your explanation almost gives me the impression of a kind of celestial bragging. Unless out of you, the one John during the earth-time of almost two thousand years, at least a decillion of identical Johns has emerged, this is an absolute impossibility.

5. I, too, am now a spirit, and surely not quite an imperfect one or I would not be with the Lord. But so far I am just the one Martin and am where I am, and could not possibly be simultaneously an identical spirit elsewhere. For while a unit is a unit, a division is unthinkable as it is no longer a unit when it is divided, but a state of division of one and the same being, although each part may be of identical nature. And the value of each individual, identical part out of the former unit, would then be only proportional depending on the total number of parts out of that particular unit.

6. Thus, if the position with you and even the Lord is as you suggest, you are not a complete John, nor is He a complete Lord, as He is with us at present. I can consider you a complete John only when you are once more integrated. Or give me a logical explanation how this could ever be understood in any other way."

7. (Says John): "Oh friend, this is only a very little nut of inner wisdom for you to crack, and it is already choking you. Whatever are you going to do when the children of the sun-dwellers offer you world-sized lumps of diamonds to crush?

8. Behold, you have never seen more than one sun. If its full image had been reflected to you through one or a thousand mirrors, would that have split the sun or lessened its effectiveness?

9. Does not every dewdrop and every eye reflect the image of the sun effectively? And there is still only the one sun with always the same effectiveness.

10. Ponder this for a while, friend, and then we shall continue our progress in this sun-sphere, or it may indeed take us a long time before we reach the valley."

MARTIN'S THOUGHTS ABOUT THE OMNIPRESENCE OF GOD.

1. (Martin opens his eyes in surprise, then begins to ponder the question. After a while, he starts to mumble as if to himself): "Hmm, I am still far behind! Oh depth, inconceivable depth, when shall I comprehend you? Yes, yes, it is true. God is omnipresent! But how is that possible? How can He be omnipresent when I see Him here, acting and speaking in the shape of a man?

2. True, the sun in thousands of mirrors is still one and the same sun. It is only one sun that is reflected from all the mirrors, and one and the same from trillions of dewdrops, trillions of eyes. And its effect only depends on the size of the mirror, the eye or dewdrop reflecting it. How peculiar, and still this is how it is and it cannot be any different.

3. How in a similar way the Lord can be omnipresent is, of course, much harder to comprehend. Is He a sun, too? But where is this sun? I saw only the Lord, the divine man Jesus, and spoke to Him. But I did not see any other sun but the one on which I am now walking.

4. Everything here is light, but I do not know its source. I am sure it comes from the Lord, but then the Lord Himself does not shine. He appears here quite without splendor, even simpler than we. It must be His omnipotent will speaking His eternal "Let there be light!' — in perpetual action, both spiritual and natural. O God, o God, whoever can comprehend Your infinite depth?

5. Now only I realize for the first time that all my knowledge is equal to zero — a vague, empty circle, quite irregular, not even showing a center! O Lord, when shall I be able to comprehend what You are?"

6. After these words, Martin falls silent and becomes absorbed in great and deep thought.

JOHN'S ANSWER TO CHOREL'S QUESTION WHETHER DWEL-
LERS IN THE HEAVENS ARE ABLE TO LOOK AT THE EARTH
AND WATCH THE FURTHER DEVELOPMENT OF ITS HISTORY.

1. (Whilst Martin is engrossed in his thoughts, Chorel approaches
John and Peter, and says): "Dear friends of the Lord, you most enlightened brothers and associates of divine wisdom and love, forgive
me for daring to bother you with a question. I had already asked
Borem this question, but his answer was evasive and I could not
understand him. Therefore, I am now turning to you, hoping for
more depth and clarity than I received from Borem."

2. (Says John): "Brother, you need not ask us at all what you
want to know and understand, for we have known it for quite a
while and shall give you a clear answer right away.

3. You would like to know whether the blessed dwellers in the
heavens will ever be able to see the earth again as it is and to watch
the further development of its history. You have often asked yourself this question on earth:

4. 'Will I be able, after shedding the flesh, to see this beautiful
earth again, with its streams and lakes, its seas, mountains, valleys,
and all the other many splendors? Will I see all the new developments
taking place in its history of rise and fall? Will I perhaps even be able
to exert any influence on it?'

5. To this I answer you: Everything is at the disposal of the
blessed of the Lord. All of us are the Lord's, and so is the earth with
all that is on and in it. Since we are His children, why should our
Father, Who gives us such great things, withhold from us even the
smallest? Should He, Who gives us seas of His love and grace to drink,
deny us a dewdrop?

6. You are now walking on the real true sun, seeing its splendors
— and will soon be seeing much greater ones. If you can see these,
how much more likely is it that you will be able to see those of the
smaller earth? But then, if somebody is residing in a palace affording
him all freedom, comfort, and pleasure he could wish for, would he
still want to have a place in the dwelling of a criminal, in a prison full
of pestilence and death or even wish to watch such a place of death?
Would you like to leave the sun now and descend to the earth?"

7. (Says Chorel): "Oh no, brother, I would not ever want to leave these celestial fields or the most holy presence of the Lord Who is so boundlessly kind, loving, mild, and gentle — not for a trillion of earths! I am quite satisfied with the thought that I could have a look at earth whenever I feel like it, but I shall not likely make use of such ability. I thank you from all my heart, dear brother, for giving me this good explanation. May the Lord bless you for your kindness."

8. (Says John): "All thanks, praise, and honor is due to none but the Lord! Go now back to Borem. I have to look after Martin, for in a moment we shall have reached the valley and its fair inhabitants."

135

SPLENDORS OF THE SUN-WORLD AND ITS INHABITANTS. MARTIN'S APPREHENSION CONCERNING THE WISDOM OF THE SUN-DWELLERS, AND JOHN'S ADVICE.

1. While Chorel is returning to his friend Borem, Martin, still engrossed in his thoughts, notices the vast expanse of the valley strewn with magnificent parks, palaces, and temples. He also notices that from one of the temples a big crowd of extremely beautiful human beings is approaching them. This sight quickly brings him back to reality and he says to John and Peter:

2. (Martin): "At last, as I can see, we have practically reached our destination. How beautiful all this looks, my dear brothers. I find the splendor and beauty of this area breathtaking.

3. And there is a big procession of sun-dwellers already coming to meet us. I can see the ones in front quite clearly. They are infinitely beautiful and so is their attire. Oh, oh, the nearer they get, the greater becomes their beauty! If this continues, I can say already that I will not be able to bear their nearness unless the Lord strengthens me for it.

4. I wonder what turn this battle of wisdom will take? I can rather imagine it, considering my already trembling knees.

5. If these people have good eyes, they must be able to recognize already from a distance what a stupid and sensual chap is com-

ing toward them. No doubt, I and my wisdom will afford them a rare pleasure! I can see the profound wisdom in their eyes, whilst in my eyes there is nothing but a vast amount of stupidity! Oh, what a meeting this will be!

6. Oh, brothers, do step in front of me so these magnificent beings do not catch sight of me suddenly and judge already in advance the full extent of my stupidity!"

7. (Says John): "Never mind, even if you have a rather peculiar experience to begin with, eventually you will get more used to these beings. However, be sure to remain earnest, but in your heart still mild and gentle, and you will get on better with them than you now imagine. Although their wisdom is considerable, like all things created, it has its limits. Therefore, brother, have courage, for you will have to learn to bear these splendors at some time, and it will be easier for you now, when the Lord is guiding all of us so lovingly."

8. (Says Martin): "Of course, you are right, but this matter is no trifle and is desperately serious. Only a short distance separates us now, so in the name of the Lord, maybe things will not look as dark and threatening close by as they look now from this distance.

9. What are these mightily shining hats and garlands these heavenly beautiful virgins, or whatever they may be, are carrying towards us? What are they going to do with them?"

10. (Says John): "They are prizes for the very wisest among us, who will be decorated by them after they have tested us. You are already wearing a hat like theirs, which the Lord gave you, but it makes no difference to them. If they find you worthy of a prize, they will unite your hat with theirs into *one* hat, which, however, will shine much brighter. If they do not consider you worthy of a prize, you will stay as you are now. So pull yourself together so you do not miss out on such a prize!"

11. (Says Martin): "Never mind about that, brother, I have never won a prize anywhere, and am not likely to here! But what about my nature and all this beauty, this charm? That will cause the real trouble, brother! But now I must be earnest and taciturn. They are already quite close . . . here they are!"

THE ENRAPTURED BISHOP MARTIN AND THE THREE FAIR SUN-MAIDENS.

1. (Three maidens of extreme beauty walk toward Martin, stretch out their arms, and say): "You glorious leader of this fairest party, what sublimity are you bringing us from your heaven of heavens? Oh speak, you for whom we have been waiting so long!"

2. Martin bites his tongue and secretly pinches himself as a reminder that he must not too quickly change from his assumed earnestness to extreme affection. So he does not reply to them at all. The three repeat their address even more sweetly, and Martin almost bites off his tongue, but still remains silent.

3. (The three maidens secretly wonder about our Martin's peculiar silence, and then say): "Oh, great one, do you find any fault with us that you do not consider us worthy of a word? Don't you like us? But then we saw how you wanted to kiss the deceptive dragon in your house in the high heavens.

4. You have also been seen on Mercury almost melting away at the sight of a fair Mercurian. Before that, you were seen with a flock of lambs, where you were quite talkative! You were also seen as a mortal on earth and some most peculiar actions of yours were witnessed. There, too, you were most talkative, but you do not deem us, daughters of the sun, worthy of an answer. Do tell us why you are silent.

5. We do know that silence at the right moment is an essential part of wisdom, but your present silence seems to be different. At least tell us why you are silent. Pray do so for our hearts are yearning for your answer."

6. Martin is almost overwhelmed with love for these most beautiful maidens and is thinking hard what to say. He has already realized that they know everything about him and must be quite familiar with his tricks. Therefore, he says secretly to himself:

7. (Martin): "Oh, what a desperate situation! This will be terribly embarrassing. Whatever shall I say to them?

8. Firstly, their inconceivable beauty is becoming more enticing all the time, rendering me dumb. And secondly, they know me anyway, almost better than I have ever known myself.

9. So what and how should I speak to them? O Lord, do not forsake me now! And you, my earnestness, do not forsake me either or I am lost!

10. Ah, this inconceivable beauty! Those eyes, fiery like the sun itself, that hair like the shiniest gold! The softness of the neck, that roundness and indescribable tenderness!

11. And the bosom, oh, I cannot bear it any longer! There is nothing on earth comparable with this!

12. Compared with this, what is the delicacy of the purest dew-drop, the purest cut of a diamond, the most tender cirrus floating around the setting sun carried by a slight evening breeze? Is there a whiteness like that on earth? The purest snow in the midday sun would not even come near it!

13. One could feast one's eyes on it forever! And the arms, the hands, the feet! Martin, turn your eyes away from these much-too-beautiful maidens or you are lost!"

MARTIN IN A TEST MATCH WITH THE THREE SUN-MAIDENS. BETWEEN WISDOM AND LOVE.

1. (While Martin is still indulging in his reveries, the three maidens are beginning to smile, for they have read from his eyes and lips what he is mumbling. Now they speak to him): "Friend, we already know why you do not answer us. You are weak, still very weak, and your innate weakness cripples your wisdom and your tongue. Do you really find us so beautiful and alluring? If so, at least tell us that aloud."

2. (Martin is already at the point of dashing at the first of the three, but he pulls himself together and says): "Yes, glorious ones, you are perfectly beautiful. However, you are too wise, which to a certain degree covers up your beauty and makes it just about bearable for me. I am not too keen on excessive wisdom, and if you want me for your friend, you must talk to me out of love, and not wisdom.

3. You did bring a prize to award me with if you found me to be of great wisdom, but I must tell you that, notwithstanding your

considerable wisdom, you are quite mistaken where I am concerned. I would never accept such a prize, for I know only one prize worth having, and that is Love personified in God the Lord, Whom you know as the Primordial Spirit Who has created all things. This alone is my prize, which I have already accepted forever, and I have no use at all for your wisdom-prize. Therefore, hand it to whomsoever you deem worthy of it, but leave me alone."

4. (Say the three): "Listen, glorious friend, so far we have not tested your wisdom at all, and seeing the spirit in you, this would be futile anyway. It surely would not be wise of us if we wanted to address any other spirit but the one we detected in you! You did mention the prize you already possess and which you are right to value above everything. However, to this we must point out the following:

5. "The primordial, all-creating Spirit is indivisible. No doubt, love is Its essence, but this love comprises also infinite wisdom. Praising this love, can you possibly separate from it wisdom, the light of lights? Don't you think, friend, it might be you who is mistaken with too rash a conclusion? Or how could you want the body alone, rejecting the head? Do explain this to us."

6. (Martin is rather stunned by this, and says to himself): "Just look at this, they have got me already! But now, back to full earnestness! If they only weren't quite as lovable, it would be much easier to deal with them. But considering their sweetness, it really requires extreme composure to be able to speak to them with at least some earnestness.

7. They are waiting for my answer with the most delightful expectancy and sweetest impatience. But what will I tell them? How could I tell them the truth without offending their ears which are used to the harmonies of heaven? Ah, I know what I shall tell them, in the most tactful manner of course, but it will make them think. So, courage, in the name of the Lord!"

138

MARTIN'S REASON FOR REJECTING THE WISDOM-PRIZE. THE PROFOUND WISDOM OF THE SUN-MAIDENS' REPLY.

1. (After this soliloquy, Martin again turns to the three and says): "Oh, you inconceivably glorious daughters of the sun, although you have replied very well to what I have said, you have still made a considerable mistake.

2. You are right if your light tells you that the great Primordial Spirit is indivisible in His love and wisdom. For where there is a body, there also must be a head, or in other words, whoever receives a prize of love must not disregard the prize of wisdom if he wants to be perfect. But your bright, heavenly eyes can surely see that my head is already adorned with a prize looking very much like yours. And since you are so well-informed about all my previous experiences, you must surely know that I was thus adorned by the Lord Himself.

3. This being a fact which you, sweet children, cannot deny, would the Lord have given me a divided prize, namely, the one of love only? However, it does comprise the necessary and justified degree of wisdom. Consequently, this prize given by the great God is not a divided but a *complete* gift, perfectly measured. So, notwithstanding your very wisely put reply, I do not see what good your wisdom-prize could do for me.

4. Since as you can see I have already one head, what would I do with another one? Should I really need another head, I shall be happy, if it is the will of my Lord, to accept it from you, lovable daughters of the sun. But if it is not necessary to have two heads, but only one that is perfect, you will understand that I cannot possibly then accept your prize. Do speak! I am listening!"

5. (Say the three): "Oh, you glorious and sublime one, we are quite aware that with your prize you have been given more than we would ever comprehend. Thus we know very well that your prize is a complete one. But from countless experiences, repeating themselves in one and the same way, we also know that the great God gives every being a perfect and complete life.

6. We also know that no human being is born into the world without a head. It has eyes to see with, ears to hear with, a nose for

smelling, a palate for tasting, and many nerves for various sensations. A newborn child has all this, which surely originates in the Supreme Spirit's wisdom as well as His love, both of which you can discern at a glance.

7. Why then does a newborn child — as a work of the great God's combined love and wisdom — always attains wisdom so much later than love which is the real life? You yourself have already lived for a long time and possess an abundance of love. But if you ask yourself whether your wisdom is as old as your life, you are sure to find a rather conflicting answer.

8. Through our top philosophers, we know that the great God on your earth has said to a certain wise Jew: 'Except a man be born again of the spirit, he cannot enter into the kingdom of God.' Tell us: How can the great God demand of a philosopher who has already lived a long time, rebirth of the spirit, if He has already given a child in the womb everything it needs to take full possession of the eternal Kingdom of God?

9. You can see it everywhere that maturity follows only long after a being has come into existence. Can you prove to us from the history of your earth that a human being has ever come from the womb fully mature? Or do you already know for sure why the Great Spirit has only now, after you have gone through a number of transformations, directed you to this vast world of light, accompanied by these two wisest of spirits? Speak, glorious one, tell us about it as we look to you for a lot of profound wisdom."

139

MARTIN IN A DILEMMA. PETER'S ENCOURAGING WORDS. MARTIN'S GOOD REPLY.

1. (At these words, Martin is quite embarrassed and does not know what to say. He says to himself softly): "Now I am really in a fix! What can I say? They are right in every point and I am an ass and an ox — with a wisdom-hat on my head! And now they are even coming to me with a second hat! Oh, dear brothers, help me from this dilemma."

2. (Says Peter): "Have patience, brother, and accept this trial and things will soon improve. Just keep thinking; you will surely find some answer. But remain earnest and do not give room to argument, but insist on what you maintain. Speak to them like a teacher, and you will soon be able to manage this advance guard. The rearguard will be more troublesome, but then we shall help you as much as is needed. So do not lose heart, everything will work out all right."

3. (Says Martin): "Brothers, I do not feel as if anything worthwhile will be forthcoming from me for I have already emptied my container of wisdom. That wisdom must follow love is now absolutely clear to me. The way these three wonderful beings explained it leaves me no ground for any objections. I must fully agree with them. Or do you have any better idea ?"

4. (Says Peter): "What is right is right, be it on earth or in heaven. But you still should not give in too easily, for your assertions, too, are defensible. Therefore, go on pondering on this for a while and you will find a very good reply."

5. (Martin, after having pondered on this subject for quite some time, has now really found a satisfactory argument, and says): "You wonderful daughters of the great sun, your speech is very wise indeed and well presented, but there is something lacking in it which may not seem important to you, but it is to me.

6. Since you know through your sages that the great Spirit of God has been a teacher on my little earth, and since you are also familiar with the nature of all its beings, I am surprised to find that you do not know what the Lord Jesus, Who is your Primordial Great Spirit, has spoken to us, His children, on other occasions.

7. Once, mothers brought their little children to Him. As this resulted in some crowding, the disciples, who already imagined themselves quite wise, rebuked the mothers in an endeavor to keep them away from the Lord. But when the Lord noticed this, He said to the disciples: 'Suffer the little children to come unto me, and forbid them not: For of such is the kingdom of God. Verily, I say unto you, whosoever shall not receive the kingdom of God as a little child, he shall not enter therein.'

8. Thus the Lord clearly stipulated for those who were already wise, that they must become like children — who have no wisdom as yet — if they want to enter the Kingdom of God. Therefore, I wonder why you value wisdom that high and seem to be convinced that one can win the Kingdom of God only after obtaining your

wisdom-prize? I should think that God's own teaching would be true and more sublime than yours.

9. It is true that the Lord told the wise Nicodemus that he would have to be born again before he could enter the Kingdom of God. However, He was not thinking of your kind of wisdom, which the Jew already possessed, but of the innocence of childhood, which is pure love! And thus I interpret the Lord's words: stick solely to love and leave all wisdom to the Lord. That is also the reason why I am with Him, and God only knows where I would be if the Lord had looked only on my wisdom, which is as good as non-existent.

10. I have also learned that he who would boast with his wisdom before God, commits a sin. But if one's heart, although lacking in wisdom, is filled with love of God, it already holds the highest award of life, helping one to become a child of God. With this award already in its possession, what purpose could yours serve? Therefore, let me tell you once more: I do not need your wisdom-prize since I have had what I need for a long time already.

11. I suggest that all of you strive for my prize, too, and as a result you will be much happier than you are at present, in the light of your wisdom alone, which, notwithstanding your inconceivable beauty, reveals only very little love. Speak now, if there is any more you have to say, but do not count on any further answer from me. For only one thing is needed, and that is love. Everything else is provided by the Lord, as and when required."

140

THE THREE SUN-MAIDENS BEG MARTIN TO TEACH THEM HOW TO LOVE GOD. MARTIN'S CRITICAL BASIC QUESTION. THE LOVE-SICK SUN-MAIDENS AT MARTIN'S HEART.

1. (Following this good reply by Martin, the three bow deeply to him and say): "You glorious son of the Great Spirit, we have now recognized that you are a true son of Him for Whom we do not have a name. As you have defeated us, we are now yours and so is this prize. Allow us to be the lowest in your mansion and teach us how to love the eternal God."

2. (Says Martin, surprised at what he sees): "My house can accommodate many thousands more. So there will be enough room for you too. For my house, which the Lord, my infinitely holy Father, has erected for me forever, is larger than your world. Therefore, if you desire to come to my house, throw away your wisdom-prize, turn to my prize of love, and follow me. But if possible, cover yourselves up a bit more, for to me who am alive in love and not just in wisdom, your attractions are mightier than your words!"

3. (In answer to these words of Martin's, those standing behind the three maidens are coming forward with richly pleated blue garments, in which they dress the three sun-maidens. When they are ready, they say to Martin): "Sublime and glorious son of the Most High, do you now find our attire pleasing to your eyes? Are we now as you wish to see us?"

4. (Says Martin): "That is much better and fit for my house, which is a mansion of the great, holy Father, Who Himself is fully clothed and not half-naked as you were before. You are still infinitely beautiful, but I can bear to look at you, and thus you can stay with me.

5. But now tell me this: Do you know the Great Spirit? Can you picture Him? What would you do if you had to face Him?"

6. (Say the three): "We know, glorious one, that there is a most high, Primordial Spirit of spirits Who has created all things out of His infinite wisdom and omnipotence. However, this Spirit is so holy that we may not ever dare picture Him in any way. Only our highest philosophers are allowed to do that. Therefore, you can imagine how we would feel if, should He adopt any shape, we had to face Him, knowing Who He is. Oh, that would be terrible, the most terrible thing that could ever happen to us!"

7. (Says Martin): "If that is so, why aren't you afraid of us, His children? Look at the fruit pure wisdom bears. That which is the greatest need of our hearts is strictly withheld from yours. And what is our greatest bliss could become your greatest torment.

8. What a difference there is between us and you! Tell me, have you never experienced love in your hearts? Don't you feel something like that now for me, or for one of my two brothers here?"

9. (Say the three): "What do you mean by that? We know that love is a covetousness of the heart, a contracting force which seizes related objects, attracts them and tends to unite with them. However, we do not know what else love is. This force of the heart is only

capable of seizing small things, being small itself! How could it seize an object as big as you are? We can hold you in our highest esteem, but you would be much too big to be seized by our love."

10. (Says Martin): "Ah, your wisdom is already giving out! Do not worry about the size of your heart, which will soon be big enough for a great amount of love. Which of you could embrace me and press me to her heart?"

11. (Say all three joyfully): "Oh, we can do that, and if you, glorious one, will allow it, we shall give you a fiery proof of our ability."

12. (Says Martin): "Go ahead! I give you this permission with the greatest pleasure!"

13. (Now all three embrace Martin, and each of them presses her tender bosom firmly against his, saying): "Ah, how sweet this is! Oh, let us stay here at your heart for a while longer."

14. (Says Martin): "I knew that you had love, and plenty of it! Do stay at my heart for a while. It will teach you best how to love!"

141

THREATENING ATTITUDE OF THE THREE SUN-MEN. MARTIN'S FORCEFUL REPLY. THE SUN-MEN FOLLOW THE ADVICE OF THEIR SPIRITS AND OBEY.

1. The other sun-dwellers, to whose family the three sun-maidens belong, have noticed how they are embracing Martin. This is beginning to worry them, and three men now advance toward Martin and say:

2. (The three sun-men): "High and sublime one, what our eyes are seeing is most unusual here, and not part of our order. Therefore, tell us what it means. Do you intend to take these three daughters from us? What gives you that right? Do you want them for your wives and to impregnate them? This cannot be, for you are not from this world, and besides, you are a spirit which cannot impregnate! Therefore, tell us what this means and what you intend to do with our daughters."

3. (Says Martin to the three men who, too, are extremely beautiful): "Dearest and fairest friends, do not worry about these three daughters, for they are better off with me than with you, who possess only wisdom and very little love. I will teach them to love and they will conceive love. This is the will of the Great God Who, in Himself, is the greatest, highest, and purest love. You, too, should learn it and it would mean progress for you instead of staying permanently in this your world, bodily and spiritually. I will take your daughters into my house, but you I will not accept if you cannot love. When you are able to love, there will be room for you, too."

4. (Say the three men): "There is no order in the meaning of your words. Consequently, no wisdom, and they are incomprehensible to us. Therefore, speak with wisdom when you address us! We do know that you belong to the children of the Great Primordial Spirit, and our top philosophers know you from your own planet. But all this is quite immaterial to us as long as you are not wearing the garment of wisdom. Therefore, we now order you, in the name of the highest wisdom of this world of light, to let these three go immediately, otherwise there will be disastrous consequences for you, as well as for the multitude following you. Unless you obey, we shall call our mightiest spirits to lay hands on you!"

5. (Says Martin): "Ah, ah, my fair and dearest friends, do not excite yourselves! Look at me — among all these many brothers and sisters who are with me here and also share my house, I may be the weakest. However, compared with you, I have enough power to scatter you with just one little thought, like a storm scatters the dust. Therefore, I advise you to take yourselves off with your ridiculous threats or I myself might lay hands on you and your supposedly mighty and very wise spirits. I am going to radiate a sternness that will make you feel as if you had a fever. So you had better go voluntarily or I might take steps forthwith!"

6. The three sun-men stretch their hands upwards, calling to their spirits. These, however, reply from a cloud:

7. (The spirits): "We cannot harm this party in any way, as we feel that it includes the Most Terrible. Either obey this party or flee it as fast and as far away as you can, or you will be in great trouble. All these are almighty, and the Most Almighty is among them! So, obey or flee, but obedience would be preferable for you, for where could you flee to from those whose feet are faster than your thoughts?"

8. (Now Martin speaks again): "Well, my still-lovable and dearest friends, what will you do? What does your wisdom suggest to you now? Are you still going to oppose all of us?"

9. (Say the three): "In such a case, our wisdom says: 'If he whom you want to fight is mightier than you, do not fight. And should he then give you an order, obey him strictly.' In view of the fact that you, with your party, are mightier than we, we are willing to obey you. So tell us what you want of us."

10. (Says Martin): "So, hurry ahead of us all, except your three daughters, who will stay with me, and prepare your house, for we shall be staying with you for a while. What has to be done later on, another One of my party will tell you, for, as already mentioned, I am the lowest among these thousands. So be it!"

11. Following these words of Martin, the three start on their way, crossing shining fields and heading toward a small rise in the valley, on which stands a large temple, which is the dwelling of these sun-people. It is surrounded by some smaller buildings at a lower level, in which the children are raised.

142

THE TWENTY VAIN NUNS' CURIOSITY. — WHOLESOME HUMILIATION THROUGH THE REVEALED BEAUTY OF THE THREE SUN-MAIDENS.

1. As the crowd of sun-dwellers is leaving, the three sun-maidens raise themselves again and are now even fairer than before; from their inconceivably beautiful eyes, love is already shining forth, and their speech is as sweet and harmonious as the singing of cherubs, for they now speak of nothing but love.

2. We, too, begin to continue on our way, and the many women — led by Borem and Chorel, as well as the monks with them — are beginning to push through to the front in order to have a better look at the beauties of the sun. Up till now, they had been too busy looking at all the wonders of this world but, having satisfied their eyes and encouraged by Borem, they now want to see whether the sun-women surpass their own beauty.

3. Through a hint from Me in his heart, Martin knows what is in their minds. He also knows that these nuns, who are extremely proud of their own beauty, will be beaten by the extreme beauty of the three sun-maidens. Therefore, he says to them:

4. (Martin): "Listen to me, fairest daughters, a considerable number of women from my planet will be facing you in a moment to compare their own beauty with yours. However, your beauty far surpasses theirs — to such an extent that this could have a deadly effect on these rather vain women. Therefore, do me the favor of covering your faces with your hair for a short while, then reveal your faces only gradually when I beckon to you."

5. (Say the three): "Oh beloved, are we really that beautiful? Nobody in this world has ever told us that, for here, external beauty is not known, only its order and the wisdom emerging from it. You are the first one who has ever praised our beauty, but we rather thought you were referring to our order and wisdom. Now, however, we realize that you were referring mainly to our looks. Tell us, what is it that makes us look so beautiful to you?"

6. (Says Martin): "Comply with my request first, then I shall explain it all to you eventually."

7. *(Say the three):* "It would be best if you yourself pushed our hair across our faces so that those who are now approaching may not be endangered."

8. Martin is only too willing to perform this task, and has only just finished with the third one when Borem comes to him and says:

9. *(Borem):* "Brother, so far you have done an excellent job! It is true that you have two friends with you who are familiar with all the ways in this world, as well as in countless others, but, that notwithstanding, you have still performed real miracles. However, with these three daughters and the advancing nuns, you will have to be particularly careful or you might witness a terrible upheaval!

10. Don't let them see the sun-maidens' faces at all unless they insist upon it, but it would be preferable if you could deal with them in some other way. As our nuns get to see the faces of these three, they will probably collapse as if struck by a flash of lightning and begin to tear themselves to pieces from grief and shame!"

11. *(Martin, not at all happy at this prospect, says):* "So we have to expect more trouble with these nuns! I have always found them difficult to handle, and even here in heaven these ninnies cannot keep the peace! I would be tempted to show them these three quite

uncovered in their extreme beauty! Let these nuns be humiliated below the level of slaves, and maybe then things will improve with them as a result."

12. *(Says Peter):* "You are right, brother. Those who are so vain and proud of their looks should not be treated with too much consideration. The right way is to commence with gentler measures in an attempt to rid their souls of all residue of worldly vanity. If they fail then, the severest measures would have to be applied. You are right in your thinking, brother Borem. However, Martin is also right. So we will let him handle this as he sees fit."

13. *(John, too, agrees with this, and says to Borem):* "You are right and so is Martin, for, behold, there is no night on the sun, and the North Pole shines quite as brightly as the South Pole. So better go and bring your pious flock, and they shall be well-combed and shorn here."

14. *(Borem goes and returns with Chorel and twenty of the vainest nuns who think highly of their looks. They immediately surround Martin, Peter, Borem, and Chorel, and say to Martin):* "Well, where are your great beauties of the sun, compared to whom we are nothing — as we were told in your house? Show them to us and convince us that you spoke the truth!"

15. *(Says Martin):* "You shall have what you want, you conceited souls. There are already three of them here. How do you like them?"

16. *(Say the nuns):* "We can see nothing but hair and blue pleated garments similar to ours. However, we want to see their faces, their bosoms, and their arms."

17. *(Says Martin):* "If you wish to die from grief and shame, you shall have what you desire. So tell me — yes or no."

18. At these words, the nuns are startled and begin to ask each other what to do; but none of them knows an answer. One of them turns to Chorel and asks his opinion, but he, too, shrugs his shoulders. After pondering for a while, he says:

19. *(Chorel):* "Yes, my beloved sisters, this is quite a problem. If you say 'yes,' you might be in great trouble, judging from Martin's words. If you answer in the negative, your great curiosity will just about ruin you. You see how difficult it is to advise you in this case? I have another suggestion, but you probably won't dare to follow it."

20. *(Say the nuns):* "We will do anything if it can help us! Please, do tell us what you suggest."

340

21. *(Says Chorel):* "Well then, listen: Behind us are the Chinese, and after them follows the Lord, with the two who love Him above everything. Turn to Him! He will tell you what you should do in your best interest. If you then follow His advice, you will be quite safe; otherwise, you can only blame yourselves if you should come to harm. For it is quite obvious that here things cannot be trifled with. That is my advice; but you may please yourselves whether you take it or not!"

22. *(Hearing this, the nuns say):* "Friend, we know all this very well, but in that case it would mean, 'out of the frying pan and into the fire'! We fear the three a thousand times less than the Lord, for the Lord is the Lord, but all these are only His creatures, the same as we — whether of extreme beauty or extreme ugliness, it is quite irrelevant before the Lord. Therefore, we think it would be better to look at the three beautiful sun-maidens than it would be to go to the Lord, thus showing that we fear Him less than those three beings."

23. *(Says Chorel):* "All right, if you do not want to follow my advice, that's fine with me, but you had best know what you are doing; just please yourselves! In any future similar situation, however, you had better save yourselves the trouble of asking for my advice!"

24. *(Now the nuns return to Martin, and say):* "Whatever may happen, we want to see these three sun-maidens in their full beauty."

25. *(Says Martin):* "All right — come closer and open your eyes wide. This will be the end of your stupid vanity!" *(With these words, he turns to the three sun-maidens, and says):* "Now, my dearest daughters, lift up your hair and let these conceited women see your faces."

26. *(Say the three sun-maidens):* "But if it might hurt them, we would rather remain covered up, for we do not want to harm anybody."

27. *(Says Martin):* "This, my glorious, beloved daughters, does not make any difference now. He who is firmly set on having his will — be it good or bad for him — does not suffer any injustice. They have been warned by me, as well as by another brother, but they still insist on seeing you. Therefore, they shall have their wish and it will make them crazy with grief and just about ruin them. So reveal yourselves to these vain fools!"

28. *(Answer the three):* "Sublime friend, you are truly wise, for

your speech is well-founded. We will do as you bid us! Whatever the effect may be, we shall now reveal ourselves."

29. With these words, all three simultaneously push aside their hair, and the brilliance of their extreme beauty has a similar effect on the nuns as if they had been struck by numerous flashes of lightning. They collapse in a heap, and only a few of them moan:

30. *(Some of the nuns):* "Woe betide us ugly creatures! We are lost! Crocodiles, toads, and other abominable vermin would be fairer in relation to us than we in relation to those three! O Lord, strike us with blindness, for it would be better to be blind forever than to have to face such beauty once again!"

143

THE THREE SUN-MAIDENS PITY THE NUNS, WHO ARE IN A SWOON. THEIR REVIVAL THROUGH THE LORD. JOHN AND MARTIN DISCUSS THE LORD WITH THE SUN-MAIDENS.

1. *(After these words, they fall silent and the three sun-maidens say to Martin, Peter, and John):* "Now look what has happened! Why did you want us to reveal our faces if you knew what would happen? Now these poor things are lying before us like dead! Who is going to revive them? If you can, please do it, for we are very sorry for them. Oh, if only we had not revealed ourselves to them."

2. *(Says John):* "Never mind that! What your supreme beauty — in this instance, even enhanced by God, the Lord — has done to these sisters will be good and wholesome for them. It has rid them of a last material burden which weighed heavily on them, one which would have troubled them for a long time yet and would have rendered them incapable of enjoying the supreme bliss of God's heavens. Now they have been relieved of that burden forever with one stroke, and they will rise to better and purer lives, capable of looking at you without resentment and shame, unharmed, like we do. And, being daughters of the most high and holy Father, they will be of great use to you.

3. At present, they are as good as dead, for their false love was taken from them which until now had given them more life than their love of God, the eternal Lord of Glory and all life. But, look,

there from the rear of this crowd, a man is advancing, a father between two daughters. He will in due course revive these nuns who now appear dead, and the Glory of God will reveal itself to your eyes."

4. *(Say the three):* "Glorious friend, you have told us so many comforting things, so do tell us also who that man is who is now approaching us with his two daughters. Is he one of your brothers from the same sacred planet?"

5. *(Says John):* "As you see Him now, He is a brother to all of us. In His visible shape, He is like us from earth, namely, that small world which your philosophers call the 'sacred planet.' However, notwithstanding that, He is the Master and Lord of all of us, for he who is a master, is also a lord, and since this man is our Master in everything, He is also Lord over all things in God's Order."

6. *(Say the three):* "If so, He must be considerably more than you. Maybe similar to our chief sage, whom not only all the people of this vast world have to obey, but all the mountains, waters, beasts, and plants."

7. *(John):* "Yes, yes, similar to that, but even more than that — as you will soon find out!"

8. *(Say the three):* "Do we have to cover ourselves for Him, too?"

9. *(John):* "That is not necessary, for He has known you and your entire world before it came into existence, and before we and your sages existed!"

10. *(At this, the three sun-maidens are quite astonished, and say):* "What are you saying? We have never heard anything like that before, not even from our greatest and wisest sages! They have told us that our world of light is like a mother to all the other worlds, and is the oldest of all. If our vast and almost endless world is the oldest — and this we do not doubt, for we have often witnessed ourselves how it has given birth to smaller worlds — how can a sage from another smaller globe, one which originated from our world in the first place, be older than our sages, and even our whole endless world?

11. Oh, glorious friend, there you must have made a mistake, unless that Master is a primordial, angelic spirit, in which case you might be right. However, this is unlikely since he is not enveloped in an aureole of light like the other angelic spirits, whose brilliance is such that it makes us appear almost dark. Therefore, you must not hold it against us if we think you may have made a mistake."

12. *(Says John):* "My highly esteemed daughters, your sages are good mathematicians, but we are even better ones. There is a great difference between us and you. We are true children of the Most High, whilst you are only His creatures, and can become children of His children only through us. This, too, you have learned from your sages. If so, tell me who would be older: the children or the children's children, which you are?"

13. *(Here, the three are rather startled, and only after a while do they say):* "The wisdom of your question is too profound, and we cannot reply. Maybe our sages can, but we are unable to say, not knowing the depth of their wisdom. Let us drop this subject for the time being, as the One Whom you call Master and Lord is already quite close. We want to give Him a worthy reception. Do tell us how He prefers to be received so that we may be prepared in every respect."

14. *(Says John):* "Concerning this, better ask your second father, Martin, who taught you how to love. He will tell you exactly what to do."

15. Now the three turn to Martin, who says:

16. *(Martin):* "My beloved daughters, with this Master and Lord, nothing counts but pure love. Therefore, meet Him with the greatest possible love, and you will win Him. And when you have won Him, you have won everything, for all things are possible to Him. I am even convinced that He could make of you real children of God."

17. *(Say the three):* "Would we be allowed to love Him the way we love you? Could we embrace Him to our hearts' delight, giving in to this newly-awakened emotion?"

18. *(Martin):* "By all means; for love can never offend Him, even if He said to you: 'Do not touch Me!' Do not let that deter you, but kindle your love for Him all the more. Hold on to Him firmly in your hearts and He will come to you and give you abundantly all that your hearts desire. As soon as He has taken you into His heart, you will experience a bliss which no sage of your world could ever imagine."

19. *(Say the three):* "No doubt those two glorious ones are enjoying such bliss. What a mighty Spirit from heaven He must be that you, as true children of the Most High, accept Him as your Lord and Master! He must surely be the First Son of the Most High — His favorite, His all!"

20. *(Says Martin):* "You are very close to the truth, but you had

better be silent now for He will be here in a moment. Look, even the dead are beginning to stir as He approaches! Isn't He most lovable, dearest daughters?"

21. *(Say the three, enrapt):* "O heavens! How lovely He is! There could be nothing in all infinity to compare with that indescribable gentleness which radiates from His entire being! The closer He comes, the more lovable He appears! Oh, forgive us if we say that even *you,* who are the children of the Most High, compare with Him like empty shadows, and our hearts realize all the clearer that it would be impossible to love any being more than Him.

22. O friend, you, our new spiritual father, we cannot restrain our hearts any more! Our yearning for Him has become too strong for us. Look — He is stopping about ten feet from us and — now, He is beckoning with His finger! Tell us, whom is He beckoning? Look — the mountains of this world bow as He beckons, and there, deep down in the valley, the big water begins to heave. Oh, tell us, for whom is this holy beckoning meant?"

23. *(Says Martin, deeply moved):* "It is meant for you, my beloved little daughters . . . and, besides, most likely it is for your entire world. Therefore, hurry to Him and do as I have taught you."

24. *(Say the three):* "Do take us there, for we lack the courage and strength to do so on our own. Our overwhelming love is almost paralyzing our limbs."

25. Martin, John, and Peter now support the three and lead them gently toward Me.

144

CHANCHAH'S AND GELLA'S ASTONISHMENT AT THE BEAUTY OF THE THREE SUN-MAIDENS. THE LORD'S PRAISE FOR MARTIN AS A FISHERMAN OF MEN. ABOUT THE GIVING AND TAKING HOLD OF GRACE.

1. When the three sun-maidens, escorted by their guides, have reached Me, Chanchah and Gella see their beauty and are quite startled. Chanchah says:

2. *(Chanchah):* "Oh You, my almighty Father, what are these beings? No human heart could ever imagine such inconceivable beauty! O Father, are these also created beings, or are they primordial spirits who from eternity have been purer than the light of the purest star?

3. How terribly ugly I must appear compared with them! When I look at them, I feel — forgive me for such a thought — as if it must be almost impossible for You, o Father, to make the female human shape so endlessly beautiful. Of course, such a thought is silly — just as I am silly at this moment. But that boundless beauty is really almost unbearable for me."

4. After these words, Chanchah is silent. Gella has not yet said anything at all, but only keeps sighing secretly to herself about her imagined great ugliness.

5. *(I, however, leave them for a while to their broken-heartedness with good reason, and say to Martin):* "Well, My beloved brother Martin, you have been quite successful as a fisherman. You caught for Me three nice little fishes from the deep water of the sun, which gives Me great joy. It is obvious that you are more successful with your fishing here than you were on earth! Therefore, I will have to make you a real fisherman in the waters of the sun. You are now becoming quite strong and really useful with My brothers Peter and John, who, at all times, are My chief fishermen in the whole of infinity.

6. This time you have really excelled, and it is the first true joy that you have given Me. For, until now, scarcely any of the fishermen sent to this world of light have succeeded in catching any beings of this world into the net of love. Their wisdom is great, and their beauty has already disabled many a fisherman. You, however, have excelled as a true master, and since you have managed small things so well, I will now set you over greater things."

7. *(Says Martin):* "O Lord, O Father, too much — too much grace! You know that an ox is good for nothing but some beef, and before You, I am but an ox, or even worse! You know what I mean.

8. Without Your particular grace, I would not have done as well in the presence of these three charming daughters of the sun. Even if their wisdom might not have been too much for me, their enticing beauty surely would have!

9. And, what a beauty, from head to foot! But then, You helped me through the two strong brothers and everything worked

out well. But if You had withdrawn from me for only a little while, then it would have been the end of my strength. And how I would have then fared, only You, O Lord, know best!"

10. *(Say I):* "My dear brother, you are right, indeed, for without Me, no one can achieve anything. But, behold, it is like this:

11. The giving of My grace is My work, and it is not withheld from anybody. However, the taking hold of this grace and the acting in accordance with it, is the personal task of every free spirit and, thus, also yours. And that is why I praise you — because you took hold of My grace so well and acted accordingly.

12. I bestow My grace upon many; they know it, and praise Me for it. However, when it comes to acting accordingly, they disregard My grace and remain unchanged in their bad worldly habits. While they are in the flesh, they pamper it and remain sensual to the last moment. After arriving in the spirit-world, they are much worse than on earth, since here they can have everything they want. My grace still keeps flowing to them, but they ignore it, and that is most detrimental to them.

13. You, however, respected My grace as your actions showed, and that is why you deserve My praise — all the more so since here, this acting in accordance with My grace is a thousand times harder to do than on earth. Continue in this direction and your spirit will soon achieve a unique power of freedom."

14. *(Peter and John themselves give witness, saying):* "Truly, we would not have risked to confront the sun-women with love, knowing them and what they can do if they discover only the least trace of weakness in a spirit. But Martin succeeded, and for that be the highest praise to You, Lord, and a glorious crown of valor for Martin."

15. *(Say I):* "So be it! But now, My dear brother Martin, introduce your three little fishes to Me so that I can find out how you have prepared them for Me."

THE LORD AND THE THREE LOVE-RIPE SUN-MAIDENS.

1. *(Now Martin turns to the three sun-maidens and says):* "My beloved daughters, we are now in the right place and you may unburden your hearts as I have taught you and as the fervor of your hearts demands."

2. At these words, the three stretch out their beautiful arms and want to embrace Me.

3. *(But I say to them):* "My beloved little children, do not touch Me as yet, for you are still in your flesh; that would destroy your bodies. You will be able to touch Me without harm when you have left them. I am a perfect Spirit and, therefore, only perfected spirits may touch Me."

4. *(Say the three):* "Is not this brother of yours a spirit too? And yet we were at his heart learning to know love, and it did not harm us at all! If You, You most glorious Master and Lord of Your brothers, are an even more perfect Spirit, it should harm us even less if we vented our love at Your heart, wouldn't it?

5. And what if this should cause us to lose our bodies! Is it not better to love without a body than it is to be excluded from love *with* a body? Oh, look at us and feel how we suffer now that we may not love You as our hearts demand."

6. *(Say I):* "My dearest little children, you may love Me with all your strength; love is not withheld from you. It is only that you must not touch Me, for that would harm you. But, since your love is already so strong that it would almost destroy your bodies, you may touch My feet; My heart would still be too hot for you."

7. *(At these words, the three fall at My feet, clasping them with their tender hands, and saying, in their most gentle and harmonious voices):* "Ah, ah, what infinite sweetness! If only our brothers of many aeons knew how infinitely sweet love is, they would give all their wisdom for a dew-drop of it.

8. Glorious Lord and Master, why is it that we, dwellers in this great, magnificent world, do not know anything about love? Why do we have to keep searching in the impenetrable wisdom of the heavens of the eternal, primordial Spirit, without ever finding out what love, the sweetest love, is?"

DIFFICULT CONDITIONS ON EARTH FOR THOSE WHO WANT TO BECOME CHILDREN OF GOD.

1. *(Say I):* "My dearest little children, behold, man's body has various limbs and sense organs, but the ear cannot have what the eye has, nor the mouth what the nose . . . the head what the heart . . . nor the heart what the feet and hands have. If, however, the whole body is sound, so then are the individual limbs. The eye does not feel unhappy because it cannot hear, nor the ear, because it cannot see.

2. Thus, the head has never complained because it is more distant from the heart than the lungs. For, all the parts of the body, whatever their duty may be, obtain their life and enjoyment from one heart which houses love and life. And thus, you, too, My children, although not being the actual heart in God's great order, share all that issues from the heart of God. Those of you, however, who comprehend love — as you do — will also be accepted by love.

3. While you are still blood, you can become a part of any limb or organ. But once the blood has become the nutrient of a particular part of the body, fusing into a unit with it, such a fused particle of blood can never be carried on to another part.

4. I know that your sages are often full of wonder regarding the great privilege of the small world they usually call the 'Sacred Planet,' whose men — without exception — are children of the Most High. But think of the misery of their temporal lives in that world!

5. From infancy on, they have to put up with frail bodies, with hunger, thirst, excessive cold, and even worse, heat. Their bodies are subject to a thousand painful ailments and, eventually, also a painful death. Man's birth there is also painful and thus is his departure from the world.

6. Until about his twelfth year, man is often barely capable of a mature thought and is frequently shaped into a sensible person by the wielding of a rod. As soon as he has gained some sense, he is burdened with the yoke of numerous hard-to-keep laws, any infringement of which is punished severely, temporally and even eternally.

7. In addition to this, he has to work hard for his livelihood to keep his frail and cumbersome body alive. And, notwithstanding all

that, he is often, to the last moment of his temporal life, uncertain whether some kind of life will await him after the painful death of his body. And, even if he believes there is another life, it is often described to him as terrible and less desirable than everlasting extinction. Despite all these tribulations, he loves his life so much that death appears to him the most terrible thing of all.

8.   Considering what the human beings of your so-called 'Sacred Planet' have to go through in order to become fit for their eventual highest destiny, tell Me, could you envy them when you compare them with yourselves? Or would you like to take this upon yourselves to enable you, maybe, to become what they are not yet from birth and can *never* achieve unless they fulfill all the hard conditions and live in accordance with the severe laws sanctioned directly by the Supreme Divine Spirit?"

THE FAIR SUN-MAIDENS' DEROGATORY CRITICISM OF THE HARDSHIPS FACING THE CHILDREN OF GOD ON EARTH.

1. *(At this description, the three sun-maidens rise to their feet again and say)*: "Most sublime friend and master of great wisdom, if the Great God treats His prospective children like that, we do not think much at all of such a state of filial relationship to God. If finally, perhaps, one in a thousand — after a hard life of self-denial — should attain to this filial relationship and with it the powers of the Most High, it would be nothing compared with all the suffering, especially since he can only become a son of God when he has suffered the greatest hardships patiently all his life.

2. What good is to such a son the greatest possible bliss an almighty God can bestow on him? He would always remember all the suffering he had to go through to attain it, and this would embitter him, surely, forever and spoil his beatitude — all the more so when he finds that thousands of his brothers must languish in some place of punishment whilst he, one out of the countless numbers, has been lucky enough to attain to the goal of his miserable life.

3. However, if he does not remember his former wretchedness and does not bother about his unfortunate brothers, having himself attained to the almost impossible and become a son of God, then he has been cheated out of his life; for, without remembering the past, he cannot possibly claim to have achieved such bliss for himself. And if he does not even know those any longer who failed at his side and became wretched, then we must say that in our world, even a child in its mother's womb is already wiser and more enlightened than such a wretched child of God, to whom this state of filial relationship, except for a dull beatitude, offers nothing but a meaningless name.

4. Under those circumstances, we would not care to become children of God, not even on an equal footing with you, a supreme son of God, assuming that you, too, had to pay for your position with considerable suffering. What we cannot understand is how the wisdom of God could have pleasure in such tortured beings! Truly, such a God and our God have nothing in common.

5. We pity you with all our hearts. Come and stay with us, and you will be much better off than with your God, Who only takes pleasure in the wretched!

6. Your love is sweet, indeed, and is part of the foundation of life. But what good is all this sweetness of life if the spirit is a prisoner forever and has practically no freedom of movement, since he has to stay within the narrow limits of a certain order?

7. We humans in this vast world of ours are truly free. It is wisdom alone that makes us free, and all things are subject only to the wisdom of our guiding spirits. And, since we are free through wisdom and look upon love as nothing but a vegetative force, there are no maladies in our world, neither physical nor moral.

8. We are perfect in shape and perfect in thought, desire, and action. You will not be able to find anything here, neither in the valleys nor on the mountains, that will show the slightest sign of imperfection.

9. Envy, anger, ambition, avarice, lewdness, lust for power, are strange to this world — as far as we know. For true wisdom teaches us equal rights for all. All of us are perfect likenesses of the Most High Spirit, and we honor Him in each other through the proper wisdom He has bestowed on us, which is the only veneration worthy of this Spirit.

10. And you imagine that you will win Him and become His almighty children through love alone! Oh, you wretched and weak

beings, do you, as supposed children, seriously believe that you can win the Supreme Spirit by approaching Him with a somewhat itching heart, offering Him, like a newborn babe, a sweetish teat?

11. Unfortunately, you are mistaken, all of you, and you only show that the concept 'spirit' is quite unknown to you who claim to be, or should be, perfected spirits. You do not know, nor have you ever known yourselves; how, then, can you know the infinite primordial Spirit of spirits, and even be His distinguished children? Come and learn from us, and you will get to know first yourselves and — eventually — the Supreme Spirit!"

148

THE THREE SUN-MAIDENS CONTINUE THEIR CRITICISM.

1. *(The three sun-maidens):* "We did notice that particularly this brother, whom you call Martin, possesses some notable sparks of mystical wisdom which is similar to that of our sages of the high mountain, who also come to us sometimes with things that are beyond our sphere of vision and comprehension, just like their dwellings. But what use is such a high mysticism to him or to you if you completely lack the first principles of practical wisdom?

2. These, however, consist in proper indulgence towards the weak, for where the strong wants to be a victor over the weak, there is no longer any order in wisdom, as every power must seek victory in its enlightened conciousness and not in the humiliating subjugation of one who is obviously the weaker.

3. And that is what we did when we caught sight of you, the considerably weaker ones, on our soil. We did what you wanted so that we might investigate you all the more profoundly; and now we know that you are most unfortunate beings. Therefore, although you are spirits, we invite you to learn from us proper wisdom, which you need badly if you want to eventually gain better thoughts and concepts about the Supreme Spirit.

4. Our pure spirits from the floating seas of light have warned us not to oppose you because of the presence of the 'Most Terrible' in your midst. We did not quite understand that warning, but now we

do! It is clear that they meant you, and what is 'most terrible' is that you foolishly imagine yourself to be farthest advanced, seriously believing that you are the principal son of the Most High, and endeavoring to uphold this illusion in your brothers. And this is, for us, the most terrible thing: someone trying to deceive his weaker brothers!

5. He who is strong need not hide his strength, but he also must not use it against the weak. And whoever is weak should not pretend to be strong, but should show his weakness. Thus the strength of the strong and the weakness of the weak will become one strength in the strong.

6. Ponder these words! They come from children of this magnificent world who are almost minors, but if all of you follow us to the hospitable dwellings of our elders, a much more powerful light shall be given you. It is no obstacle that you imagine yourselves already perfect and think that we could come to harm if we touched you. Oh, do not worry about that!

7. Thanks to the proper wisdom, already as children in mortal bodies of this world, we possess much more spirituality than you ever will! Surely the spiritual does not dwell in the body as such, but only in the actual spirit which never changes, whether it is in a coarser or a finer ethereal body.

8. Furthermore, you spirits should not judge our bodies by the ones you used to have on your so-called 'Sacred Planet,' for they were coarser, heavier, clumsier, and darker than the roughest rocks in this world! You can see for yourselves that our bodies are far more ethereal and closer related to the light than even your spirits, as we see them here. Being at all times permeated with the spirit within them, our bodies unite far greater purity with the right order.

9. Therefore, follow us confidently to our homes and you shall no doubt become purer than you are now. But no force shall be used against your weakness by our considerably greater strength, of which we do not boast, as earlier you did of yours, friend Martin. You spoke ridiculously of a strength in you that would enable you to destroy our big world with ease, even though you were supposedly the weakest of your party; your 'strength' would enable you to destroy our world just as the bud of an ethereal flower can be crushed between thumb and forefinger.

10. Don't you now think that you somewhat overrated your strength? However, we shall not blame you for this, since you were

speaking in your blind zeal, not knowing us at all. Now that you know us better, we hope, you are not likely to think of us in that way again, nor say things like that to us.

11. We shall now walk ahead, and you may follow us if you want to. Be assured that you will be received in the friendliest way into our solid houses, which really exist and were built with our will and our hands — not like your celestial house, built only in a fixed imagination.

12. And so that you, Martin, may see how far our wisdom reaches and that we know you and all the others better than you think, you shall find in the house of our elders a spectacle wherein you shall recognize yourself in all detail from the first beginnings to this moment.

13. You imagine yourself to be far outside your high celestial house, but at this moment, we are inside it and see everything that is happening there. Thus, we were witnesses when you were going to passionately kiss the disguised dragon. However, do not ponder the power of our vision at this stage; in due course, you will find the reason for all this in true wisdom. May you and all your party be guided by your free will. We shall walk ahead!"

14. Following this lengthy speech, the three depart.

149

THE DEPRESSING EFFECT OF THE THREE SUN-MAIDENS' WISDOM ON MARTIN'S TRIUMPH.

1. *(Martin, however, who has been on thorns for quite some time, now turns to Me and says):* "O Lord, O Father, now we have really stirred up a hornets' nest. This surpasses everything I have heard so far!

2. Brother Peter and Brother John, you have praised my courage and victory much too soon in conceding to me a crown of valor. Now it has become evident what a victory I have achieved and how we can relish the three sun-trouts!

3. O Lord, if I now recall my earlier miserable fishing experience, much as I love You, it did me more credit than this one. Your kindness and grace already appointed me a master fisher in the sun's

waters of life, but now I must beg You to again relieve me of this office, for these fishes would surely swallow me up before I could even think of fishing.

4. What a situation! These three have really lectured us thoroughly, and the worst of it is that there aren't many objections we can raise. They are good, noble, gentle, indulgent, and inconceivably sweet and fair. And still I could explode with anger that they have made such a fool of me.

5. And they expect us to follow them! Not I! Just imagine to be taught by them! You, too, Lord, and also Peter and John! What do You say to this, my Lord, my all?"

6. *(Say I):* "Calm yourself! We shall do what they want us to do! Follow them and see what will come of it. The more intricate the comedy, the more satisfactory is its solution. And you, as My leading children, brothers, and friends, have to get acquainted with everything or you will not be suitable for My service. Therefore, let us now follow the three sun-maidens patiently."

7. *(Says Martin):* "Lord, You know that now, as always, I say: 'Your holy will be done!' For I know that You alone are familiar with all the roads that lead us to the goal that You, as God, Father, Lord, as well as Love and Wisdom, have forever set us. And still, I am standing here like an ox facing a new gate, unable at this moment to recognize all the inconsistencies that have gushed from the mouths of these sun-goddesses.

8. I now realize that their words must have been full of inconsistencies, but I am unable to disprove anything they said, for it was factually correct.

9. But You will have seen for Yourself how happy they were at my heart and how they wanted to be taught how to love. They had so much praise for its sweetness that their companions assumed a rather threatening attitude, and even summoned their spirits who, on the other hand, warned them against violence. Then love was everything to the three, but now they describe it as a dumb, vegetative force, practically a thing that is nothing in itself, but only serves the freer beings simply as a sort of unconscious motive for reproduction, most probably consisting in a transient electromagnetic, quite imponderable fluid or influence.

10. How beautiful and lyrical their language was when You beckoned them to come to You! I thought to myself: 'Well, there we are! They must have recognized Him already, or at least have a

strong suspicion as to Who He is.' But how I misjudged them! The way they spoke when they were embracing Your feet and how considerably their speech changed after You had described to them the harsh conditions under which man has to live his life on earth if he wants to become a child of God, and, to be sure, in Your description there was nothing much said about Your boundless love, compassion, and grace.

11. If this is the trend with the sun-dwellers, we shall reap a very poor harvest. I would be more confident trying to achieve some results with Satan than with these three most beautiful sun-goddesses.

12. Their beauty is inconceivable for human imagination, but, on the other hand, they are more cunning than the bathing guests we left behind — Lucifer's adherents who were separated from him. I maintain that a hideous devil is considerably less dangerous than a being of heavenly beauty who posseses so much infernal cunning.

13. However, be that as it may, I — and no doubt all of us — will do as You wish and follow them to their home. But do allow me one thing, O Lord, that I tell them what I think of them when a suitable opportunity presents itself. Their beauty will no longer confuse me. You may look forward to this, you gentle beings of this world. Now you shall get to know the real Martin, so that your great wisdom will appear to you like a mite compared with a mountain! For Your glory, O Lord, and for the sake of Your name, I shall become a lion, and I shall fight with a thousand glowing swords! But, of course, You must not forsake me, for then my great courage would only land me in the soup!''

150

THE LORD'S LOVING AND WISE INSTRUCTIONS TO MARTIN. HINTS ABOUT WHAT IS HAPPENING IN THE HEARTS OF THE THREE SUN-MAIDENS. MARTIN'S VEXATION AND THE LORD'S REASSURING WORDS.

1. *(Say I):* "My dearest Martin, your will and courage are very praiseworthy. However, you should never resolve upon a certain action in the heat of even a justified anger before you clearly under-

stand the reason why you want to fight with a thousand swords like a lion.

2. A while ago I nominated you a master fisher of this world, and that you shall remain. And thus you shall keep the crown of valor proposed by Peter, for you have really handled the situation masterly. Just as My brother Peter has pointed out, it is extremely difficult to accomplish with these beings what you have accomplished, even though it was through My strength within you.

3. Do not think that because I had to restrain these three, they have disavowed the love in their hearts according to their lengthy speech. If that were the case, they would not have asked us to follow them and would not have talked so much anyway, for their wisdom is usually quite laconic.

4. But because their hearts became mightily attached to us, they talked so much and would still have gone on talking if we had raised any objections. But as we did not interrupt them, they had to come to an end eventually. I assure you that they departed from us reluctantly and can scarcely await that we follow them. As you will see, they will, in a moment, come back to us here, where we shall now abide for a while.

5. It would, therefore, be unfair if we judged them by their words, which were prompted only by jealousy — a jealousy which is the result of their newly-awakened love. They noticed that we were rather indifferent to their beauty, and that even with their ardent love they could not ingratiate themselves with us. So they resorted to a good-natured wisdom and intend to be of use to us wherever possible.

6. Ponder this for a while and then tell Me if you agree and whether you think it would be fair to fight them like a lion with a thousand swords."

7. *(Martin, perplexed, thinks this over in all seriousness, and then says):* "Oh, yes, of course, this is how it is! What a beast I am, what an ass and ox combined! Probably the only one in this vast, enlightened and better world!

8. For the sake of Your holy name, where did I have my eyes, my long ears, and my senses, anyway?

9. These sweet, loving hearts — and I wanted to — no, I must not say it for it is too silly! Look, there they are, already returning over a hillock! Oh, you sweet little children, come, oh, come! Your reception will be better this time!

357

10. But how can I now make good my great mistake? Probably they already know in all detail what I have said to You about them. How awkward this will be!"

11. *(Say I):* "Martin, do not go to extremes with your ardor; everything will work out. Think of your instruction as to the attitude you have to adopt here: namely, of love combined with outward earnestness, and you will always be the victor and a master in the art of fishing in these waters of the sun. Now, back to earnestness, for they are already quite close!"

12. *(Says Martin):* "O Lord, do give me a bit more insight and discernment so that in the future I may be a better judge in case the three glorious beings confront me again with their staggering wisdom. Otherwise, I cannot guarantee that I will not blunder once more!"

13. *(Say I):* "Do not worry about that. The way you are, you can be more useful to Me here than Peter and John, whose vision penetrates all the secrets of this world. For he who knows already in advance what fruit his efforts will bear as a result of the order of this world, has less confidence than one who, for lack of such clear vision, will treat these beings rather in accordance with the order of his own world. Therefore, stay the way you are and you will achieve the best possible results.

14. These human beings soon lose interest in a spirit when they find his wisdom to be equal to theirs or — as with Peter and John — far above theirs. In such cases, they become quite sarcastic and rather reserved. However, with spirits like you, they are the friendliest beings you can hope to find, and that is when they can be, so to speak, twisted round one's little finger. Therefore, you will be able to serve Me best the way you are. But now, silent, they are almost here!"

151

THE THREE FAIR MAIDENS ASK THE LORD WHY HE AND HIS COMPANIONS DID NOT COME TO THEIR HOUSES. THE LORD'S WISE ANSWER.

1. *(As the three sun-maidens reach us, still clothed in the same garments they had donned before Martin, they immediately address Me, saying):* "O, Most Sublime, how long will you and your com-

panions keep us waiting before you deem us worthy of entering one of our dwellings, which have been duly prepared for your reception?

2. Thanks to our sages and the spirits of our great world, as well as the spirits of many other worlds visiting us on many occasions, and also from the angels of the Most High Spirit, we know that we, the dwellers in this world, are not only of great physical beauty, but also morally so pure that even the purest angels cannot find fault with us. That they always find us worthy of their visits, enjoy our company in all purity, telling us about all the wonders that are found in the infinite kingdom of the Most High Spirit, Whom you call your God and Father, and new ones that are being created more magnificent and inconceivable, every moment.

3. If all the angels and spirits have such an opinion of us and are not at all reserved, we cannot understand what fault you find with us that you like us so little. We never ask the other spirits to come to us, but they still like to come, because they always find in us what gives them great pleasure. As for you, we implored you to come to us in the purest manner of the wisdom of our greatest sages, but it does not seem to have had much effect on you. Oh, tell us, Most Sublime, what is the true reason for this, and why did you not come to our houses, where thousands are expecting you?"

4. *(Say I):* "It is not your fault morally. I know best what you are like. I know your physical appearance, your pure morals, and your dwellings. However, we are as free as you are, and can please ourselves. Nobody has the right to ask us to account for our actions and say to us: 'Why do you do this, or that?'

5. And with all your wisdom, you should realize that we cannot be attracted by wisdom alone, but only by the proper, living love. We shall follow the desire of your hearts when we are truly loved, but your supposedly great wisdom will not ever make us advance a single step.

6. I am quite aware that you have used your wise words to Me only as a pretense to hide from Me your real love. However, I am not a friend of such pretense, but only appreciate complete honesty of the heart. So, if you want Me and My companions to come to your houses, you must not pretend outwardly to be different from what you are within; for I see through every most secret fiber of your lives. And what I see, all Mine see too, and countless others who are completely Mine forever, just as these here."

152

HUMILIATING EFFECT ON THE OTHER WOMEN OF THE THREE SUN-MAIDENS' PHYSICAL BEAUTY. MARTIN'S STERN WORDS, AND THE LORD'S ADVICE TO THE ANNOYED WOMEN.

1. *(In answer to My words, the three immediately take off their clothes and say):* "Most Sublime One, if so, these garments should not cover our bodies, for they hide the truth and help to cover our hearts and our love, which is not right."

2. *(As they are standing there almost naked, with only loincloths, their beauty once more fully apparent, all the other women present fall to the ground, crying):* "Woe betide us ugliest of beings!"

3. *(Martin is extremely annoyed at the behavior of the women, and says in a loud, stern voice):* "There we are again! There they are, lying on the ground like exhausted frogs! This way heaven, except for the magic and splendor of things, is no better than the earth with its mortal beings. There, perishability causes men to worry about their lives and makes them quite stupid. As a result, they distance themselves so much from true life that in the end they no longer know what life means and whether they are still alive! Least of all, they know whether they will live on, conscious of themselves, after their physical death.

4. Here in heaven, these worries about perishability have ceased to exist, but a thousand other miseries have taken their place, which seem to surpass the first-mentioned by far.

5. To think of all the anxiety these female beings have already caused me! As soon as you think: 'The Lord be praised, now everything is going to be all right!' — some fresh trouble strikes you like a flash of lightning!

6. Oh, you conceited ninnies, you scum of mankind, do you really believe the Lord created you for vanity or as an embellishment for heaven? Do you think you have the right to become almost unbearable burdens to us male beings through your great stupidity? Get to your feet and make sure you behave with more wisdom in the future, or we shall leave you to your own devices; then you may live entirely in your great folly.

7. Because these sun-maidens are so much wiser and more

beautiful than they, to vent their secret rancor these ninnies fall to the ground like stuffed paillasses and scream, hurt by their unbearable vanity, 'Woe betide us ugliest beings!' You fools! Do you expect that out of your stupidity you might become more beautiful than these daughters of wisdom, which is of such a high standard that even we male spirits have to admire it? I assure you, it will take a very long time for you to attain that!

8. If your foolishness keeps progressing at the same rate as it has until now, you will most likely become even uglier than that guest whom I dragged on chains to my house together with brother Borem. So, if you do want to stay with us, stand up immediately!''

9. Upon these words from Martin, all the women get to their feet and turn to Me with the request that I rebuke him for hurting their feelings.

10. *(Say I):* "You have mouths and tongues yourselves, so why not tell him directly what you do not like? Martin has not wronged Me, and it was quite right of him to rouse you with a dressing-down.''

11. *(Say the women):* "So You, too, our Lord, our everything, are against us! Where, then, can we find grace?''

12. *(Say I):* "That you can find in true humility, obedience, and in the right love for Me. Therefore, follow Martin's advice and all will be well. Make friends with these three and love them, then their beauty will no longer disturb you.''

13. After these words, the women begin to relax immediately. Some are already able to bear the sun-maidens' beauty and approach them without much hesitation.

153

REASSURING WORDS FROM THE THREE SUN-CHILDREN. MARTIN AGAIN IN A TEMPTATION. THE EARTH-WOMEN AND SUN-WOMEN IN HARMONY. THE LORD MAKES ARRANGEMENTS TO ENTER THE DWELLINGS OF THE SUN-DAUGHTERS.

1. *(The sun-daughters, following their exposure, have noticed the embarrassment of the numerous women. Therefore, they approach*

them, saying): "Esteemed sisters, shed all that is unworthy of you, and our appearance will not disturb you at all.

2. That it has pleased the Almighty to create us so infinitely beautiful in your eyes is not our fault and, seeing that our beauty is not our work but solely the work of God, it does not make us vain or even proud, which is a bad trait on your earth. Therefore, it would be foolish and wicked of us if we looked down on you because your bodies are less beautiful than ours.

3. You, as well as we, have been made by the power of the Most High Spirit the way His infinite wisdom saw fit. And, considering that we are the works of one and the same Eternal Master, how could we despise each other because of certain characteristics which God bestowed upon us?

4. Therefore, cheer up, dear sisters, and do not look at us with jealous eyes, and then our looks will not worry you at all! Even your men, for whom our attraction must be much greater, can bear to look at us, and we think it must be considerably easier for you who are of the same sex."

5. *(Says Martin to himself):* "But only just, for at this moment you are terribly alluring! The faintest touch of an arm could throw one into ecstasy and extreme lust.

6. Ah, that bosom, those arms and feet, from A to Z! It is unbearable! If they embraced me now, it would be the end of me! They will have to cover themselves up a bit more, for this way their attraction is really quite unbearable!"

7. *(Say the women):* "Glorious daughters of this better, vast globe, on the one hand it is true that in the beginning we were a bit vain and jealous of your great beauty, but on the other hand, we must admit that it is your inconceivable beauty that also overwhelms us, for our eyes are not accustomed to such a sight. Therefore, angelic daughters, we beg you to cover yourselves up again or your appearance will cause us to pine away, notwithstanding the fact that we are, to a certain degree, already blessed spirits and you are still mortal beings of flesh and blood."

8. *(Say the sun-daughters):* "We are only too willing to grant your wish. However, it does not depend on us, but on your masters. Approach them about this, and we shall do whatever they say."

9. *(Say I):* "Stay as you are! This is how you have to serve Me! I know best why, for behold, My three sweet daughters, though born on this earth: No one knows better what his children need than their

father, and I am a true Father of these, and countless other children. Therefore, I know best what is good for them, and I do not want you to be attired any different from what is customary on this earth."

10. *(Say the three):* "Lord, Master and Father of your children, your will be our most sacred commandment! But do come to our dwellings. You will be honored there — should you wish it — also you will be loved with all the ardor of our hearts."

11. *(Say I):* "Yes, My new daughters, now we shall enter your dwellings and see what they are like. Martin, you go ahead with Peter and John. Borem and Chorel shall follow the three with the women and the other brothers, whilst the Chinese, with their wives, shall walk behind Me. You three sun-maidens — now My daughters also — accompany Me with these two sisters whose names are Chanchah and Gella. In this good order, we shall all enter your dwellings."

12. *(Say the three):* "Lord and Master, will the three at the head know where to take this large party?"

13. *(Say I):* "Do not concern yourselves about that! The two accompanying Martin know your dwellings in all detail; for nothing is strange or unknown to My children, and they have all that I have in abundance!"

154

ABOUT TRUE WISDOM AND THE APPARENT WISDOM OF THE SUN-SAGES. THE LAW OF INCEST AMONG THE SUN-DWELLERS, A TRICK OF SATAN'S. THE PURPOSE OF THE LORD'S COMING.

1. The whole party now begins to move, and we proceed slowly.

2. *(While on the way, the three sun-daughters ask Me):* "Good and wisest Lord, Master and Father of your children, why are your two sweet daughters so quiet and do not ask you any questions? Is it because they already know everything and possess great wisdom? Our great sages, too, speak very little, but when they do, one word

from them weighs more than ten thousand words from us! This is probably the case with your two very sweet daughters."

3. *(Say I):* "Yes, you are almost right. However, there is a difference. These two already possess in abundance what your top sages in their most profound mysticism only just suspect, but would scarcely dare to express.

4. For the type of wisdom your sages possess is not real wisdom. It is a sort of secretiveness that does not lead to any knowledge I could truly approve of. On the contrary, some of the laws of your sages are such that would make you quite unsuitable for My Kingdom.

5. You, of course, do not commit a sin if you strictly observe what your laws demand. However, these have already deviated from the original laws and are now as distant from them as heaven is from this world. You still have your original shape and a mighty will, but your so-called principal sages are generally not much good now, although there are a few communities that have still remained faithful to their original laws. And so these two sisters here are very much wiser than your greatest sages.

6. For they are full of love, and during their lives on earth they did not have sexual intercourse with their brothers and fathers, which they considered a major sin and for which I punish severely without mercy in eternity. The earth-dwellers say: 'Cursed be the one who commits incest!' But with you, incest is a law given by your sages. See what great mistakes they make? Therefore, they are not as wise as they think, and the reason for My coming to you is to show them their great absurdity."

7. *(Say the three):* "Sublime Lord and Master of your children, are you also a lord over our sages and our vast, magnificent world, that you want to give us different laws?"

8. *(Say I):* "Yes, My daughters who are still undefiled by incest, Satan has found a way also into this pure world, and has already corrupted many communities. Therefore, I, as the Lord also over this world, have to come Myself to sweep clean its soiled ground. Otherwise, all of you would soon lose your original nobility and, with it, the eternal life of the spirit, the chances for which have already become very weak in many of your communities. If Satan wants to catch a man, he does it by means of a certain arrogance of wisdom and then through unchastity. His designs with you have been extremely clever, but I assure you, nothing can escape My eye!

9. All of you, including your sages, have become very sick; and this is the case in many of your large communities. Your procreation, which originally was purely spiritual, has now become grossly material; it has become an abomination.

10. Among My children on the earth, which you call the 'Sacred Planet,' incest is considered the most wicked crime, and before Me it is the most terrible, so much so that I want one who commits incest punished irrevocably and without mercy, with temporal and eternal death through fire. And this terrible, purely satanic vice has become a law in your world!

11. Do you imagine that I, as the primordial source of all existence and the very essence of order, can condone such a law? That is why I now come to you — to save you or to pass judgment forever. No wonder your spirits exclaimed that the Most Terrible was among this party! However, they were not good spirits, but spirits led astray by Satan himself. I am not the Terrible, but only Love to the innocent. However, to those who have My Word and My Law, yet ignore it, I am the Eternal Judgment!"

155

CHANCHAH'S WISE WORDS. EVIL AND TRUE LAWS. NO TRIUMPH WITHOUT BATTLE. WHY THE LORD COMES TO THE SUN-DAUGHTERS ONLY NOW.

1. These, My words, have startled the sun-daughters, but have encouraged Chanchah, and she begins to speak gently:

2. *(Chanchah):* You most beautiful daughters of this magnificent world who have never seen night nor experienced the harsh change of the seasons, you are most fortunate where your bodies are concerned in not knowing sickness nor ever having witnessed death! Your laws, although worse than our greatest vices, uphold your freedom and so far, also, your immortality. In this way you are free, for you can never infringe your laws, even if you wanted to, as they make such an infringement practically impossible. Why is that so? What must laws be like that they cannot be broken?

3. Thanks to the grace and love of my holy Father, I will show you the reason: The evil Ahriman (Satan), appearing to your sages in the shape of an angel, has pointed out to them various traits and needs of your nature, making them thoroughly familiar with same. He instructed them to make a law of everything any fiber of your being should express a desire for, adding the clause: 'If a person feels like doing something, let him. Should he prefer not to do it, he commits no offense if he does not.'

4. Think for yourselves now, you wise ones, what such laws are worth and what use they could be for you. Or have you ever heard about any punishment for infringement of a law?

5. True laws must be made in such a way that they cost man great self-abnegation until he manages to fulfill them by suppressing the cravings of his nature. If he fulfills them of his own free will, disregarding all material advantages, only then does he rise as a free spirit above his mortal and perishable matter. He then triumphs over his own death, which constitutes part of his nature. And he can then enter the higher order of eternal, spiritual life and become a child of the Supreme Spirit, thanks to His grace.

6. But what triumph can be gained through the empty laws of your supreme wisdom? None, I assure you! For, without a battle there cannot be a triumph! And without a triumph there can be no prize! What, then, is a man who has won no prize? He is more worthless than the simplest plant he tramples underfoot, for the plant will have achieved its purpose in the great gamut of evolution. But the man without a prize has lived in vain. He just lived because he existed, but his life was purposeless and, therefore, could never reach any destination, which is the case with you.

7. After shedding your external frame, you live on as a kind of spirit of light — but also without purpose, just like here in your bodies, the outer appearance of which corresponds to your world. It is true that this world's outermost sphere consists of pure light of great power and magnificence, but within, it is darker than the darkest planet. I assure you, your wisdom is nothing but delusion, and your beauty an empty illusion.

8. That is the reason why the Lord is now coming Himself to give a true light to you children of the sun, and to show you a new path which can lead you in all truth also to us. This is our true wisdom, and if you want to perfect yourselves, it must become effective with you, too. Otherwise, you would be — notwithstanding your

great beauty — the most miserable beings in all the creation of God, my Father."

9. *(The three are really shaken by Chanchah's wisdom and, after a while, they say):* Glorious one, if this is the situation and our laws are really of a nature as described by you, why, then, did not your Lord and Master, the head messenger of the Most High, come sooner to help us? Why did He leave us in our errors for such a long time?"

10. *(Says Chanchah):* "Dearest sisters, the Lord knows best when the fruit is ripe, for He prepared the seed, enclosed in it the living germ with the fruit, and also the time for its ripening. The same is the case with you. You have ripened, but not in truth, only in falsehood. And to prevent you from passing from falsehood into evil, He Himself has come to save you."

THE SUN-DAUGHTERS SUSPECT THE TRUE NATURE OF THE LORD. ARRIVAL AT THE PALACE OF THE SUN-DWELLERS. CHANCHAH'S AND GELLA'S ADMIRING WORDS.

1. *(Say the three sun-daughters, now already close to their dwelling):* "You loveliest sister, you speak about your Lord, Master and Father almost as if he were the Most High Himself and not only His messenger. Since you are so wise, we beg you to explain this to us."

2. *(Says Chanchah):* "Dear sisters, it is not up to me to speak about this, but solely to my Lord and Father. However, we are now quite close to your dwelling and there you will be told all that you want to know. So have patience until then."

3. With this, the three are satisfied and continue on their way. We now reach the enclosure where the first garden begins, which, in terrace-style, is followed by the second or central, and a third or uppermost, magnificent garden.

4. Catching sight of this magnificence and, finally, also of the huge dwelling resembling a temple, Chanchah and Gella are awestruck. After taking deep breaths, they say to the three:

5. *(Chanchah and Gella):* "But for the Lord's sake, is this the type of house you live in? We see nothing but gold and the largest,

most precious gems! And what a daring and superb architecture! To be able to live in such dwellings with the knowledge that you do not have to die as long as you enjoy this life, must be bliss!

6. However, we also realize that it must be extremely difficult in such surroundings to live a life pleasing to God. For where everything is designed to appeal to the senses so mightily, surely no one would think of self-denial or self-abnegation, which is the only means of awakening the immortal spirit and being reunited with one's Creator.

7. O Lord, most loving Father, does this external magnificence please You in any way? Surely Martin's celestial mansion is of great splendor, but compared with this it would seem like a prison cell! And these gardens, these vast and glorious gardens — what an abundance of unbelievable works of art! No, this cannot be just a world; it must be heaven!"

CHANCHAH'S SERIOUS MISGIVINGS AT THE SIGHT OF THIS SPLENDOR. ABOUT THE MAGNIFICENCE OF A HEART GLOWING IN LOVE. VARIOUS CONTRADICTIONS.

1. *(Say the three sun-daughters):* "Dear sisters, if you are already so delighted with this simple exterior, what are you going to say when you see the interior of our dwelling? For all our care and attention is concentrated on the interior of our houses. We believe to do honor to the Great Primordial Spirit by making use of all the talents we have been given in a way we consider worthy of our spirit.

2. We think that every great splendor is fully justified if it is accomplished by us intelligent beings in honor of the Supreme Spirit. For, if the Great Spirit endowed us with such an inclination, which is a law unto our spirit, how could we create the inferior instead of the sublime? Would not that mean that we want to have our spirit different from the way it was made by Him? Therefore, do not take offense at the magnificence of our houses, for they are not the result of vanity, but merely of the wise need of our spirit."

3. *(Says Chanchah):* "So it is the same here as on earth with the so-called Jesuits, whose pupil I used to be — *Omnia ad majorem dei*

gloriam? Is it possible that these wicked monks have found their way even here?

4. Of course, such a house is by far more magnificent than an empire of my country on earth. Oh, you magnificent poor, look at the Lord. His garment will reveal to you the kind of splendor that appeals to Him! It will show you beyond doubt whether He appreciates external magnificence. The magnificence of a heart glowing with love pleases Him above all; everything else is an abomination to Him.

5. If this were not the case, He would have been with you often, just as on my planet He often comes to the poorest and most insignificant, teaching them personally as a loving Father to become His children, and He gives them His grace in all fullness. But He does not come to the great and important who, too, dwell in magnificent palaces, and He does not teach them to make them His children."

6. *(Say the three):* "You may be right, dear sister, but how did you become so pleasing to the Lord — if the Spirit of the Most High should really dwell in Him — since you, as is revealed to us by our inner wisdom, do not come from a poor house on your planet?"

7. *(Says Chanchah):* "That is why on my planet such grace was not bestowed on me. But that I am so close to Him now is only due to my love for Him. For I loved Him with all the ardor of my heart before I knew Him, and before I found out that creatures, too, may love the most holy Creator. And it was this love and not the magnificence of my earthly dwelling that brought me to Him."

8. *(Say the three):* "But we are now with Him, too, even though our house is of great magnificence. How, then, is that possible if He really is what you claim?"

9. *(Says Chanchah):* "Dear sisters, outwardly it appears as if you were with Him, but this is no real, actual nearness. This will soon become clear to you as He speaks to your sages. But we have now reached your dwelling. Martin is already stopping and turning back to obtain advice. Let us now be silent and pay attention to all that will happen."

158

MARTIN'S BLIND ZEAL AGAINST THE CEREMONIES OF THE SUN-DWELLERS. THE LORD'S WISE SPEECH ABOUT TOLERANCE. MARTIN'S DISCUSSION WITH PETER REGARDING THE LORD'S ADMONITIONS.

1. *(Martin has already reached Me, and says):* "O Lord, O Father, this is a magnificence which no spirit from any other world could ever imagine! Even Your most sublime brothers are rubbing their eyes as if scarcely able to bear the brilliance! But, how peculiar it is that no one is coming to meet us.

2. Peter thinks we ought to wait at the entrance until the elders of the house come to meet us with their usual ceremonies, as is the custom in this world. I, however, have had my fill of ceremonies in the world. They make me sick and I think we should not wait for such brilliant follies, but rather enter the house without much knocking. You surely have sufficient power for that!"

3. *(Say I):* "But, My dear Martin, we are not coming as enemies, only as true friends. We want to help and rebuild, not beat and destroy.

4. What glory would there be for us if we destroyed the whole area in a moment? It would not be to the credit of a strong arm to tear off a gnat's head. It is better to restore the head of a gnat than to destroy it. Therefore, we shall here make proper use of our patience and love, and not of our strength.

5. How would you have liked it if I had seized you immediately with My might and thrown you into hell instead of bestowing upon you My patience and love, which you did not deserve at all? Is there any argument you could have brought against it? But I did not do that to you, for I saw no merit in it for Me, the Almighty, to destroy you, the impotent. On the contrary, I gave you My patience and love to save you and to straighten you out. Would it, then, be right of us to act here in a hostile manner?"

6. *(Martin, full of remorse, says):* "O mea culpa, mea culpa, mea maxima culpa!" [*My guilt, my guilt. my immense guilt!*]

7. *(Say I):* "You have been forgiven long ago. But if, in the future, you always kept in mind the true first principle for all our

actions, you will not easily relapse into such folly. We want at all times to preserve and not ever, even for a second, destroy; it is only hell that thirsts for destruction. Comprehend this, and now return to your place!"

8. Martin kisses My feet and quickly returns to the two brothers, Peter and John.

9. *(Peter and John ask him):* "Well, what are we to do? Shall we wait, or shall we enter?"

10. *(Says Martin):* "As you know, fools are always the least patient, because they have no sense. But if they become too foolish, it is good for them to be knocked into shape, as has just happened to me. The Lord has rebuked me, and now I'm once more in order. He has again made a man out of a beast!"

11. *(Says Peter):* "Yes, you are right in what you say. In the world, I, too, received some mighty raps from the Lord, and that was good. Even brother Paul once gave me a knock in the back with his spiritual fist, and that, too, was good! But we still don't know whether to wait and be bored for a while or enter this magnificent house. Tell us this, dear brother Martin."

12. *(Says Martin):* "It seems to me as if you, too, are beginning to pinch me a bit. Of course, we have to wait in accordance with the Lord's will, until those who are going to meet us are through with their ceremonies. You probably know who they are."

13. *(Says Peter):* "But, dear brother, you must not take offense so easily. I am quite aware that a reprimand from the Lord is less agreeable than a caress, but it is just as much an expression of love. Remember when the Lord talked to me and my brothers about His impending suffering and I, in my deep love for Him, warned Him of Jerusalem and said: 'Lord, this shall not be unto Thee'? What was it that the Lord then said to me?"

14. *(Says Martin):* "Oh brother, do not repeat that terrible phrase! I have never been able to understand how the Lord could call you Satan, the chief of hell, after having only a short while before declared you a pillar of His church, against which 'the gates of hell shall not prevail.' That is still a puzzle to me. How do you interpret it?"

15. *(Says Peter):* "When the Lord appointed me a pillar of His church, He was speaking to me out of His wisdom. But when He called me a Satan, He was speaking out of His boundless love for me, because with those words, He forcefully drove out — as if with

one lash — all my worldliness which was the actual Satan within me. Do you now understand that mighty reprimand?"

16. *(Says Martin):* "Not absolutely as yet, but I have a good idea where this is leading. The Lord is love, indeed!"

159

ABOUT MUSIC IN THE SUN-WORLD. PETER'S EARNEST WARNING TO MARTIN TO OVERCOME HIS SENSUOUSNESS.

1. *(Martin):* "But I now hear something like the sound of bells. What can it be? It sounds beautiful! So there is music here, too! I cannot make out any rhythm, but it still sounds beautiful. I wonder what musical instruments they are using."

2. *(Says Peter):* "It is a kind of bell, dear brother, similar to those used by the ancient Egyptians, and today still used by Persians and Hindus. Only here, their sound is much purer than on earth. These bells consist of a kind of disc which is hit with resilient hammers on the occasion of great festivities, or also natural phenomena, which are not unusual here.

3. For lesser occasions, they have little bells with which they give various signals. They also have a kind of harps in the handling of which they are masters. However, you will only hear those when you are already inside the dwelling. Now you know what you were so anxious to find out. But, as they will be coming out any moment, let us be silent and await them."

4. *(Martin asks another question, hurriedly):* "Friend, are we in the right position for their reception?"

5. *(Replies Peter):* "We are neither soldiers nor comedians! What gave you such an idea?"

6. *(Says Martin):* "I beg you, dear brother, do not be annoyed with me or I will really despair. Whenever I open my mouth lately, nothing but nonsense seems to come forth!"

7. *(Says Peter):* "That is almost true, and the reason for it is that you keep talking and asking without having been invited by the Lord to do so. Besides, you still possess a considerable amount of sensu-

ousness, circling and twisting in your soul like small serpents. That still keeps clouding the senses of your spirit to such an extent that you are only able to speak with some wisdom if your slumbering sensuousness is not stirred up anew by some external stimulus.

8. I beg you for the sake of the Lord, do pull yourself together at long last and make a resolution not ever to covet what is unworthy of your spirit. As a result, your spirit will become more and more enlightened and you will at all times speak words of pure wisdom. Otherwise, you will never get away from your foolishness, and the Lord, instead of guiding you to higher levels, will place you on the moon of your earth for a thousand earth years.

9. In a moment a multitude of the most beautiful and alluring women and daughters of the sun will make their appearance, and I now tell you, in the name of the Lord, in all earnestness: This is as far as the Lord intends to guide you to at last rid you of your sensuousness. If you pass this test, it will be most beneficial to you. However, if you fail, you will find yourself suddenly deserted by us, no longer on the sun, but on the most barren grounds of the moon. You have already previously had an encounter with a philosopher of that world.

10. Everything that happened with you and around you since your arrival in the realm of spirits took place mainly for your sake in order to make of you an efficient worker in the Lord's big vineyard. As the Lord has told you Himself, you could become a useful servant for Him, particularly in this world; and that is why He does such great things for you, in order to make of you a true angel. But you, too, have to make some effort, in view of all that the Lord is doing for you, else you will prepare a miserable lot for yourself. At best, you would become just a miserable rag-picker in the true Kingdom of God, with which you have not yet got acquainted.

11. Now you know the meaning of all this. Do pull yourself together once and for all. Be earnest and good, and if you are upset by too much beauty, look to the Lord and you will find peace. You must become so firm that even much greater beauties will be unable to move you, and that only because you are and want to be forever the Lord's. Only then can you be admitted to the true heaven where countless, inconceivable beatitudes are waiting for you, of which you have as yet no idea.

12. So far, your eye has not seen what the Lord has in store for those who love Him truly and faithfully — those who do not, like

you, forget Him almost completely at the sight of a smooth, well-rounded female skin, while the situation is not too bad, and have recourse to Him once more only when they are in a desperate fix through their folly.

13. Look, Martin, this is what you have been like so far and, as you have repeatedly admitted yourself, you have always been more beast than man. But now that we are in sight of the goal, do shed once and for all what is still bestial in you, in the name of the Lord. Put off the old Adam in you completely and put on Christ in the fullness of love. Then you will immediately be admitted into the true, actual, permanent heaven, the New Jerusalem, whose citizens I, John, and countless others have already been for a very long time. Do you understand me, Martin?"

MARTIN'S DEJECTION AND DESPAIR. PETER'S ADMONITION AND ENCOURAGEMENT.

1. *(Says Martin, deep in thought):* "So this is still a test — *my* test! And everything here is for my sake alone! O God, O God, when will these tests end?

2. They will probably go on until I am ripe enough for hell and not for heaven. Most likely, I have to taste so much heavenly joy in order that hell may then seem all the worse to me!

3. How often I have been told: 'Now you are perfected, dear brother Martin!' But if I have achieved perfection, must I still achieve more than perfection for the actual heaven?

4. O God, I wish You had never ever created me; then my non-existence would be so much happier than my existence in constant tests between hell and heaven.

5. At least I know now how I stand, thanks to you, dear brother Peter. However, I tell you that with this revelation, you have also completed all my tests with one stroke. Now you can draw up before me angels or devils — it will all be the same to me! Just as my future existence or non-existence, or heaven or hell, is all the same! For, if those, too, are tests and I am constantly tested, I do not care at all about a future life.

6. And, by God, you mentioned the barren moon to me. Do put me there quickly and forever! I shall be happier there than here with these constant tests, which show me clearly that although you, foremost princes of heaven, are with me together with the Lord, I am being guided to hell instead of to heaven!

7. But be that as it may, as I have already told you, you may now bring to me angels or devils, I do not care! For, from now on, I shall be dumber than a stone."

8. *(Says Peter):* "Brother, let go this thorn, for this is the death that accompanies the unchastity of the flesh. Its name is 'wrath', and that is why the children of the flesh are called 'children of wrath'! But look, they are already stepping outside. Compose yourself — your earnestness will be of benefit to you!"

MARTIN'S EASY VICTORY IN HIS DIALOGUE ON WISDOM WITH THE ARROGANT ELDER OF THE SUN-TEMPLE.

1. Upon these words, the oldest and wisest sage of the third level, clad in a gray pleated robe, comes out of the large vestibule of the temple, surrounded by young men and maidens. In his right hand he carries a staff, like the one of Aaron's, and in his left hand a magic band, stuck to which are various signs of a mystical appearance. When he has advanced to within five feet of the three leaders, he unrolls the band completely and displays it in front of him on the blue, velvety ground. Then he lowers the staff onto the band and says, after a while:

2. *(The elder):* "As the first and oldest man of this everlasting world, which is maintained by me, I adjure you by the boundless strength and might I possess thanks to my infinite wisdom . . . "

3. *(Says Martin to himself):* "What about it? The chap is becoming droll! Just continue on those lines!"

4. *(The elder continues):* ". . . that you tell me faithfully and truly what it is that you want and what has led you to this world. The least trace of an untruth from you, and my unconquerable might will reduce all of you to dust. Now speak!"

5. *(Says Martin):* "All of us simultaneously, or should only one

speak for all? You will have to define this more clearly, for we are not quite as clever as you are, Your Reverence." *(To himself):* "This one suits me fine, for his stupidity draws a veil over the beauty of the maidens. Now I am once more fully reconciled with Peter, John, and the others."

6. *(Says the sage):* "If one speaks, one cannot know what the others are thinking. Therefore, all must speak simultaneously, and very loudly."

7. *(Martin, to himself):* "Normally I am rather stupid, especially compared with these old princes of heaven, but nothing can surpass the stupidity of this sage. With his wisdom I shall deal by myself in a way that in the end he will be helplessly embarrassed by his stupidity. But I had better ask Peter first what I should do here." And Martin turns to Peter for advice.

8. *(Says Peter):* "Dearest brother, it is now your turn to say, with full freedom and truth, whatever you feel like saying."

9. *(Says Martin to the sage):* "You unlimited sage, if your wisdom is so boundless, I cannot understand how you can ask us about the reason for our coming. We, who are much less wise than you, can look through you and know exactly what is behind your supposed supreme wisdom. And so I assume that you likewise can look through us, if you are really so infinitely wise. What do you say to that?"

10. *(Says the sage):* "That I can do if I have before me the large magic band and carry the double staff. However, having for such unimportant guests only brought with me my ordinary equipment, I have to ask for such information. And now you must speak!"

11. *(Says Martin):* "If so, how will you be able to know whether we speak the truth or not?"

12. *(Says the sage):* "To be sure, I have threatened you, and this threat will be carried out if you lie. So, out with the absolute truth, or else!"

13. *(Martin):* "Or else — you are and remain an ass!"

14. *(The sage):* "What is an ass?"

15. *(Martin):* "It is in our world a harmless being of your color. It has very long ears but very little sense."

16. *(The sage):* "What gives you the right to take me for one of those?"

17. *(Martin):* "Will your infinite wisdom allow me a bit of time, for such an important question requires intensive study?"

18. *(The sage):* "What is that you call 'study'? We do not have anything here called 'study'."

19. *(Says Martin):* "Listen, you wisest of the wise, your wisdom cannot be worth much if you do not know what is, at least in the beginning, necessary to acquire wisdom. Study is as much as diligent thinking about the basic concepts and elements that must precede wisdom. Do you now understand what study is?"

20. *(Says the sage):* "No, I do not. For my wisdom is too great and does not comprehend such trifles which are much too insignificant for it. Therefore, express yourself with more grandeur, or I cannot understand you."

21. *(Says Martin):* "Now really, you are not quite as stupid as one would think when seeing and hearing you! So you mean that because your wisdom is so immense, you cannot grasp such trifles. But how, then, could you grasp the considerably small concept of an ass without much explanation?"

22. *(Says the sage):* "Ass is a being, but study is only a concept, and it is always much easier to comprehend a being than a pure concept. Therefore, speak on a grander scale and thus more comprehensible for me."

23. *(Says Martin):* "Friend, I believe the two of us will not be able to understand each other too well, if at all! For, with all your wisdom, you are an extremely stupid human being, without the least trace of any true wisdom.

24. I advise you to step back and let somebody else — one without magic band and staff — speak for you. Maybe he will be more successful, at least like the three daughters of this house, who were the first to meet us and whose words were rather wise, so that I assumed you would be considerably wiser.

25. However, I was mistaken. There may not even be another fellow in this world of yours who is quite as stupid as you! The two of us have now finished with each other and I suggest that you step back and let another speak for you."

26. *(Says the sage):* "That is impossible! For if I descend to these common worms from the height of heights, nobody may speak but I, as the Most High, the Wisest, the Mightiest, the Eternal, the Infinite!"

27. *(Martin):* "Oh dear! Then you may even be the Supreme, Divine Being?"

28. *(The sage):* "Not quite, but also not much less; only He is a bit older, since I am His son!"

29. *(Martin):* "Is that all? Or maybe you can add a bit to it?"

30. *(The sage):* "Of course, there is much more, but that would be quite incomprehensible to you. I cannot tell you anything, for you are a nothing compared with me."

31. *(Says Martin):* "Sure, sure, I believe you! You are really something great, something quite unique! There couldn't be another one like you anywhere on this world! Oh, you, you — !"

32. *(Says the sage):* "Yes, I have no one above me. When I touch the ground with my staff, the whole world shakes, and all beings tremble with fear when I approach them. But I cannot understand why you do not tremble before me, nor your weak companions, considering that I could destroy you in a moment!"

33. *(Martin):* "It is to be hoped that what you do not understand now, you will soon. Not thanks to me, though; but there is somebody present in this party who will tell you why we do not and will not ever tremble in your presence.

34. You have been thoroughly deceived by an evil spirit who once came to you in the guise of an angel and, subsequently, you deceived this entire large community, giving laws that allow its members to do whatever they want, without ever being able to break them — laws that are as good as no laws.

35. I know that you used to be quite a humble sage and a good leader of your large community, until the time when the false spirit of light deceived you, substituting your present extreme stupidity for your original true, divine wisdom."

36. *(Says the sage):* "What you say is factually true, but whether it makes me a fool has still to be proved. I do not feel like one. Therefore, I bid you to go on speaking, but only in a grand way."

37. *(Says Martin):* "Tell me whether you can remember how old you are. Have you always been what you are now, or has there been someone else in this office before you? Maybe your father? Weren't you younger at some time — maybe even a boy? Just tell me this, then it will be much easier for me to answer your question."

38. *(Says the sage):* "I cannot answer your first question, because our big-time recorder was ruined a long time ago. The rope of the large pendulum was torn off by a tempest and we cannot repair it. Therefore, no one here knows how old he is.

39. As to whether I have always been what I am now, or

whether I had some beginning, I can only remember vaguely that I was born at some time, and that I was not always what I am now. I also have a feeling that I had a father who held my office when I was a boy; but, of course, not with the great wisdom I possess. As I have answered your questions, it is now your turn to speak."

40. *(Says Martin):* "Well, I knew that you were neither a god nor the son of a god, but simply a mortal human being like we used to be. And that is good for you and your entire community, for this way you can still be saved. Had you persisted in your stubborn folly, things might have taken a very bad turn for all of you. Why, you will soon see. If you want to become very happy, better throw away your magic band and staff, otherwise it will still not be possible to speak with you sensibly."

41. *(Says the sage):* "You are asking too much! If I put away these essential aids of my strength, might, and wisdom, I would become quite helpless. Who will obey me if I have no might? Who will have confidence in me if I am weak? And who will listen to me if I have no wisdom? You must not ask things of me that are incompatible with my high office."

42. *(Says Martin):* "Friend, we earth-dwellers were given the following assurance by God Himself: 'Whatever you may give up for My sake, you will receive back a hundredfold at the time of judgment!'

43. That will also be the case with you. For all that you do or give up in the name of our Lord, you will be truly rewarded a thousandfold. If you let go what is wretched, you will receive what is noble. For an illusion, you will receive a true existence; for falsehood, truth; for stupidity, wisdom; for weakness, true strength; for impotence, might! Thus, you will receive from God the Lord rich compensation for all the things of your great futility which you may now relinquish.

44. Therefore, comply voluntarily and gladly with my request. I give myself as a hostage to you, and if what I tell you now is not completely true, you may do with me whatever you wish."

45. *(Says the sage):* "All right, I see that you are a truthful spirit and I will do what you ask. But, in return, you should now answer my first question as to who you are and whence you have come, so that I may lead you into this house."

162

ABOUT TRUE FAITH AND SPIRITUAL FREEDOM. THE SPIRITUAL AWAKENING OF THE SAGE.

1. The sage now does as suggested by Martin and throws away the band and the staff. Then Peter walks up to him and says:

2. *(Peter):* "So it is true. You did what brother Martin asked of you in the name of all of us, and this has now made you our new brother. Therefore, it is only fair if we comply with *your* request and tell you who we are and whence we came.

3. It is easy enough to tell you with words what you want to know, but it would not be of much use to you if we did. For you have to believe firmly and without the least doubt in what I tell you. If you lack this faith, whatever I may tell you would be quite useless to you.

4. You are now saying to yourself, 'If proofs will accompany these words, I will and can believe everything!' However, here I must point out to you that in such a case, that would not be faith, but rather pure knowledge, which would benefit your inner being little, or not at all.

5. A knowledge based on proofs is no longer a free knowledge, but a knowledge under compulsion. It does not liberate a spirit, but only imprisons it with each proof that is provided for a certain teaching.

6. The only true faith is the one that is like a voluntary obedience of the heart, where the latter does not ask why, how, when, or by what means! Only such a faith will liberate the spirit, because it is a free, uninhibited acceptance of that which a messenger from heaven has told you, whose authority can only be checked by the love of your heart.

7. If you feel love for the messenger, accept him; if not, let him go. The messenger has the same kind of instruction from God, Who said, and still does: 'Where you will be received, there remain; but where you will *not* be received, shake the dust off your feet and continue on your way.'

8. You can see from this that both — the one who is to receive the message, as well as the messenger himself — must be quite free! The proposition must be free, and so must be its acceptance! If

more is demanded, there is no longer any freedom, but only compulsion, which cannot liberate a spirit.

9. It would be easy, indeed, for God, the Eternal Lord, should He wish it, to teach His mankind by irrefutable proofs that He is, and how and why. He would simply have to place men under compulsion, and then they would be quite incapable of assuming or thinking anything else, because — as is the case with animals — their hearts would be under compulsion. However, the Lord wants completely free men, not robots! And, consequently, their hearts must be free, particularly where the acceptance of the Lord's teaching is concerned. Otherwise, their spirit could never gain freedom.

10. As long as your mind demands a proof in order to accept a teaching or revelation, your spirit is like a prisoner in a dark cell. Being hungry and thirsty, the prisoner clamors for food, which comes to him through proofs like meager crumbs of bread. These, however, will never provide him with the strength he would need to free himself from his shackles.

11. But if the intellect of the heart accepts a teaching freely *without* proofs, the heart reveals its uninhibited strength, which passes into the spirit and liberates it. When the spirit is free, everything else in man is free: love, light, and vision. No proofs for truth are required, for the free spirit itself stands for the clearest and most complete truth.

12. Now ask your heart whether you can believe unconditionally what I tell you. Then I will reveal to you what you want to know. If you cannot do that, my words would be futile, for we have not come to bring judgment, but only to liberate you from the hard yoke of your old servitude."

13. *(Says the sage):* "Sublime friend, you are on a higher level than I. Therefore, speak, and I shall believe you freely, because I want to believe you."

163

PETER GIVES·INFORMATION ABOUT THE PARTY AND THE
PURPOSE OF ITS VISIT. THE SAGE'S DOUBTS REGARDING
GOD'S VISIBLE PRESENCE.

1. *(Says Peter):* "Well then, listen: All of us, as you see us here,
are children of God; that is, in accordance with your concepts,
children of the Most High Spirit. In addition to that, some of us are
also chief servants of the Most High, Who has personally designated
them foundation pillars of His church in the whole of infinity.
Originally, only on earth — namely, the planet which you call sacred;
however, when they had performed their task there with gladness
and devotion, after a painful removal from their bodies, they were
taken to Him into the highest of heavens, there to enjoy all that He
has, thus experiencing the greatest, unlimited beatitude everlastingly.
At the same time, they are able to perform the same service on the
largest possible scale, which on earth they had performed on a small
scale. I, Peter, and that one there, John, are such servants. The others
are more or less beginners in this world and in the service I have just
mentioned.

2. Our purpose in coming here is that in the first instance we
initiate new arrivals in this world into the higher service of love, and
then we want to right some communities of dwellers in this world of
light that have strayed from the right path.

3. However, since the latter task is so difficult that our strength
might not suffice, God, the Lord Himself, is present also, in the fullness of His strength and might. And He is even visible in human
shape, which actually is the divine shape as God has made man in His
image, both outwardly and inwardly. For His beloved children, He
used the original shape of His eternal love.

4. Therefore, there is not a single world in the whole of infinity
where human beings have different shapes from ours. They only
differ sometimes in size, color, and a few more things in their outer
appearance. The basic shape, however, remains the divine at all
times.

5. Therefore, you should not be surprised if you soon see God,
the Supreme Spirit, in a shape and stature like mine. His boundless,
infinite might and greatness does not depend on His stature, but
solely on the greatness of His Spirit within, and this is dwelling for-

ever in an inaccessible holy light and will never be seen or comprehended by any created spirit.

6. Now you know everything! I have omitted nothing that might be essential in the answer to your question. Now tell me faithfully and without hypocrisy — which is most common with you people, particulaly in this community — whether you believe everything that I have just now told you."

7. *(Says the sage):* "Sublime friend, I honestly believe you — everything, except your last statement. For that God, the Supreme, Infinite, Primordial Spirit, should be here among you in your shape and stature, is really hard to believe. You will understand this if you are only a little bit familiar with our most ancient prophecies and revelations. Maybe I shall understand that later, but at this moment, with the conception I have of God, the Supreme Being, it is practically impossible for me.

8. You know that God sends His angels to us on very rare occasions only, who reveal to us top sages the Supreme Godhead, but they always add: 'No one can see God and live!' They claim that this is why He dwells in an unfathomable depth so that no being should lose its life through gazing at the Godhead. What, then, would happen to us if it were really true what you say that God is here among us?

9. No doubt it would be possible to God, but what about His eternal, immutable order, which has so often been revealed to us?"

10. *(Says Peter):* "Friend, just have some patience! You will soon find out that what now seems so impossible to you is quite feasible. But He will come here Himself, and you will comprehend this best through Him."

PETER'S LOGICAL EXPLANATIONS AND THE ELIMINATION OF THE SUN-ELDER'S DOUBTS REGARDING THE VISIBLE PRESENCE OF THE LORD.

1. *(Says the sage):* "Dear friend, it would not be the one walking between the two women, would it — the one behind the three daughters of this house whom we sent to meet you at the spot where you had stopped and did not want or dare to proceed?

2. For us, it would be most improper if even a third-degree sage allowed a woman to guide him. How do you think we would regard it if the Supreme God, from Whom all laws of order must originate, should be guided by women? Provided, of course, that this spirit, or rather, man, who shows no evidence of being somebody special, is such a god."

3. *(Says Peter):* "Friend, have you not during all your life made various items, either for your practical use or just for you pleasure?

4. You say: 'Certainly I have, for both purposes!'

5. Well, since you have made various things, do tell me whether there is one among them of which you would say, 'This work is unworthy of me. I am ashamed of it and it would be against all existing order, and most improper if I looked at it or even touched it'?

6. You say, 'No!' For, if you had such an item, how could you have made it at all if it had been unworthy to look at or touch with your hands? You are quite right. But now listen:

7. If already you, being before God only a most imperfect master of your works, do not find any of them so bad that they are unworthy of you, why, then, should you expect it of God, Who is forever a most perfect Master of all His works?

8. Tell me, which work of God do you find so bad that He should be ashamed of it? Or should He, the Eternal Lord of all His endless works, expect us — His works — to tell Him what would be proper and right in relation to any particular work of His? What do you think about that?"

9. *(Says the sage):* "O friend, I now see clearly that your wisdom is most profound. All your assertions are well-founded and there is nothing one can say against them. I am now seriously beginning to believe that this insignificant-looking man could well comprise the Supreme Divine Being! For, if that was possible on the small Sacred Planet — as we were taught by His angels — why should it be impossible in this large world of light?

10. You see that I can and also do accept this. However, there arises now another terribly· important question: If it is He, the Almighty, the Holiest and Wisest Who is too sublime and holy even for our greatest and deepest thoughts, so that the wisest and purest sage could not ever dare to think His name, how shall we receive Him and find mercy before His eyes?"

11. *(Says Peter):* "Friend, He is already quite close. Look at Him with your sharp eyes and tell me whether He looks so terrible and

frightening. Also tell me whether you think that the three daughters of this house, who keep looking around to Him and seem to be in a very happy mood, show any of your great fear ?"

12. (Says the sage): "O friend, I do not see anything of the kind. He looks gentle and mild, and, as for the three, I have never seen them so exuberantly gay before!"

13. (Says Peter): "Well, since you have noticed that, how can you ask such a question? I tell you, do not fear Him, for whatever He does, He does it out of love, and never wrath and revenge — although wrath and revenge are His, just as love is. Therefore, no one should use them against his fellow-men.

14. For the wrath is God's alone, and revenge is the Judge's, but love is the Father's, and He gives it to His children and seeks it in them. Therefore, He always comes with a father's love for His children, whom, because of His love, He has made in His image, placing in their hearts the wonderful vocation that enables them to become what He Himself is.

15. If this is the eternal truth, would it make sense to fear Him Who is love itself?

16. You are not afraid of me who am mighty and powerful enough to destroy this entire world in a moment with just one thought and create a new one. And since you do not fear me, who has all the might from the Lord but can never be as good as He is, how, then, can you fear Him Whose kindness is infinite?

17. Do not be afraid, but be full of joy that this boundless grace is being bestowed upon your world. And He will be pleased with you and all the others, and He will help you where His help is needed most. But now, friend, get your heart in order, for with a few more steps, He will be in our midst."

18. (Says the sage): "Oh friend, I do not know whether my heart is in order or not. But for the first time I feel a great love for Him.

19. I have been able to overcome my fear with the help of the following suppositions, which seem to me rather wise: As a result of correct thinking, as a creature I cannot possibly be more or become more than a creature. Thus, God can never be less or become less than what He is, namely, God, the most perfect Primordial Being, which is the basis for every other being.

20. Without a Creator, no creature is even thinkable, but the Creator is — without creatures. The Creator is already what He is through His infinite, clearest consciousness, enabling Him to create

when and whatever He wants. The creature can never be anything until the almighty will of the Creator makes it into something.

21. I see in the Creator, as well as in the creature, two necessities, of which the latter appears to depend conditionally on the first. And since this matter cannot be regarded in any different way, I do not see why I, a conditional necessity, should fear the unconditional one.

22. It pacifies my mind to look upon this matter as follows: Our big world has on its surface a lot of things that are so small that their volume, compared with the total volume of our entire world, would be almost like a nothing against infinity.

23. Nevertheless, the small exists alongside the big, unconcerned, and enjoys its existence for the same reason the infinitely big does. Even if, compared with the big, it is a nothing, it is still complete in itself. And further: I can, of course, never become what our most sublime, almighty Creator is; nor can He, notwithstanding His omnipotence, become what I am — a created being.

24. Not that there would be any advantage in this, but it is a peculiar state which can never be entered into by the Creator. And, thus, each of the two necessities has something of its own: The something can, even if apparently, never really be achieved by the opposite party. If I visualize this relation, I also lose the fear that had taken hold of me."

165

JOHN'S DIALOGUE WITH THE SUN-SAGE. THE RELATION BETWEEN CREATOR AND CREATURE.

1. *(Now John speaks):* "Dear friend, I have pondered your words and find that what you have said is in itself correct. However, your two extremes are over-accentuated and you draw too sharp a borderline between them.

2. It is true, indeed, that the Creator can never become a created being, or vice versa, but this neither constitutes a drawback for Him nor an advantage over the creature.

3. For, in the first place, He has no other matter to create the creature from but Himself. In the forming of a creature, He has to use the same substance of which He consists from eternity. And then He has out of Himself to keep it in the created shape whilst the creature has nothing to do for its Creator but to exist.

4. If the creature is as the Creator wants it — namely, within its destined order — it can also attain the perfection of its Creator. It can become a child of God and, so to speak, live in the same house with Him, and enjoy and make use of all His privileges. I would say that under such circumstances, neither the Creator nor the created being would have much of an advantage over the other.

5. Thus, the principle laid down by you is correct only as long as Creator and creature are standing opposite each other in will and actions as a result of the moral freedom of will conferred on the creature. The Creator's precedence can, of course, never be doubted since it is an irrefutable necessity.

6. However, when the created being, through cognizance and the active volition of the Creator's revealed will, breaks down the barrier, absorbs the Creator, becomes completely one with Him, then there remains the question:

7. Where is the Creator, as forever one and the same, more of a Creator: in Himself or in the creature? What would here be older: the creature as a being identical with and in the Creator, or the Creator as an identical being in the creature? For He Himself spoke: 'You are in Me and I in you.'

8. Considering that indisputable fact, I would say, dear friend, that you have somewhat exaggerated your statement and will have to revise it. What do you think about that now?"

9. (Says the sage): "Dear friend, I can see that you are mightily wise. Your assertions cannot be disproved, yet I still think that the productive nature of the Creator remains unchanged, whether He stands alone in isolation or whether, in accordance with His emanating property, He fills His creature like a vessel with His Being to the extent, of course, that the creature is capable of receiving Him.

10. Naturally, the creature will never be able to absorb the infinite fullness of the primordial being of the Godhead, for the infinite can be absorbed only by another infinite, and never by the finite that has gone forth from it.

11. From our world we can see a sun, the size of which — according to our calculations — must surpass ours thousands of

times. However, I have often noticed how even the tiniest dewdrop absorbs the picture of that vast world in its complete shape, only in a size corresponding to its own volume. So there can be no doubt that we created beings are capable in a similar way of absorbing the Creator to the extent that He can be absorbed by us toward our perfection.

12. But then, what a vast difference between the picture of the sun in the dewdrop and the actual sun and, to a much greater extent, between the image of the Creator in His creature and the actual Creator! It would be hard to establish the number of dewdrops required to represent the true volume of that sun reflected in them.

13. In that instance, only two limited objects are comparing with each other. How impossible a comparison would become where the infinite meets the insignificant finite, limited by time and space.

14. The fact cannot be denied that the creative being in the creature is identical with the Creator, and vice versa; but here I must ask: In what proportion? It is essential to take this proportion into consideration because it proves clearly that, notwithstanding all the natural and moral equalities between Creator and creature, there will forever remain a gulf that cannot be bridged completely from either side.

15. In view of this, I stick to my principle insofar that the two opposites can never concur completely to become one. However, I shall welcome a more profound instruction in this matter."

166

MAN'S UNIFICATION WITH GOD. EXAMPLE OF THE SEA AND DROPS OF WATER. THE SLOWNESS OF INTELLECTUAL WISDOM COMPARED WITH WISDOM OF THE HEART.

1. *(Says John):* "Dear friend, although you are very critical in this most important matter, some of your arguments are correct. However, they could lead you so much astray that you would scarcely ever reach the true destination of your existence. Therefore, in the name of the Lord, Who is now stopping for our sake, I shall give you more light on this subject.

2. In order to prove the correctness of your theory, you used a natural metaphor. I shall now use a similar one to prove you wrong and to give you more light than you could ever expect from your immense sun. Although I will not dive quite as deeply into the vast spaces, I am sure the Lord will help me to hit the nail on the head.

3. It is the sea in every world — be it small or large — into which all the streams, rivers, and brooks flow, and which also absorbs the greater part of all raindrops.

4. In every world, the sea is the basis for all the waters, including rain and dew. A world without a sea would be like a human being without blood and, subsequently, without any juices at all, and, therefore, must turn into a mummy or lifeless statue. The sea is as essential to a world as blood is to any living being.

5. Everything in a world that can be called a fluid, originates from the sea, performs certain services, and returns once more to the sea. And the sea dispenses its great abundance in countless tiny globules and drops to the atmosphere which is closely related to it and which envelopes every world. In this atmosphere, which is in constant motion, these minute particles of water are carried all over the world, and in places where they have accumulated, they become visible as mist and, eventually, as they amass, as clouds. In these clouds they unite and form into bigger and heavier drops, which then fall as rain onto the thirsty world, reviving and refreshing it.

6. Now you know what the sea is and what it gives forth.

7. You say: 'But this is already ancient knowledge.'

8. All right, if this is clear to you, then tell me what is actually older — the individual drops of water or the entire sea itself? Naturally, the entire sea was there first before a raindrop could rise from it into the air. However, when it left the sea as a particle of it, was it anything else but the sea itself? And when it has returned to the sea, will you find any difference between it and the sea?

9. You say: 'No, there everything is identical; for where a part of a whole is identical with that whole, both part and whole are the same.'

10. I agree; but when the same relation exists between Creator and creature, how do you explain the barrier you erect between them?"

11. *(The sage is staggered by these words, and says only after a while):* "Wisest friend, I now see clearly that you are right. There is nothing I can say to refute your proof for the identity of the Creator

with His creature. It cannot be any different, for where else should the Creator find the matter for making creatures if not in Himself?

12. And, having been taken out of Him, the matter or substance must be identical with the Creator, even if the time during which the substance of the creature was separated from the Creator is, naturally, not identical with Him. Time is only a fragment of eternity, strictly limited on both sides, whilst the Creator is infinite and must be so, as nothing can come into existence without Him.

13. This question is, therefore, quite clear and could not be made any clearer by more profound proofs. However, this community likes to have detailed calculations for everything, and so it would be most useful to bring this into an equation.

14. I suggest to state the proportions as follows: The Creator as the collectivity of all the individual totalities separated from Him through His will is in the same ratio to the latter as, inversely, the totalities which keep going forth from Him, taken collectively, are to the Creator. Hence, it follows that the total of all the produced individual totalities is equal to the Creator's totality put into them. Or, the oneness of the Creator is completely contained in the oneness of the creature, and vice versa.

15. If the total oneness in the creature equals the oneness of the Creator, then also a separate oneness must be equal to the collective oneness being contained in it in a strictly equal proportion as the whole in the whole. Surely it must be quite useful to state this proportion?"

16. (Says John): "Yes, yes, the proportion is right. However, here I must point out to you that we, children of the Lord, Who is and will forever be our Father, have quite different ways of calculating.

17. All that you work out with your head, we work out with our hearts. And we always obtain the best results, which comprise all imaginable exceptions. But, here comes the chief master mathematician. He will show you quite different calculations!"

18. (Says the sage): "So that is the Lord, the very being of God?"

19. (Says John): "Yes, friend, that is the Lord."

20. (Says the sage): "To be sure, His external appearance does not reveal much glory. But, as He approaches, He awakens a very ardent love in my heart.

21. His appearance is good, very good. But it is practically unimaginable that this so natural-looking man, who may possess the

390

deepest wisdom, is supposed to be the Creator of all infinity and the works it contains.

22. He is quite as limited as the two of us. How, then, can He, simultaneously, permeate and contain the infinite? However, wisdom has unfathomable depths; everything is possible. With this, I only want to express how peculiar I find this. But quiet now, He is bidding silence!"

167

THE LORD AND URON, THE SUN-SAGE. URON'S CONVERSION AND GOOD ANSWER. MARTIN'S APPRECIATION OF URON'S SPEECH.

1. *(Now I advance and speak):* "Uron, tell Me, is the door into this house hard to open, or is it easy? If it is easy, then lead us inside. But if it is hard, let Me test it to see how hard it really is."

2. *(Says Uron, the sage):* "Most sublime friend of all the angels and men, I feel that You are not one Who would seek wisdom from men. For all our wisdom is Your gift anyway, as all our establishments are Your work. And so I think it unnecessary for me to tell You how the door into this house opens. Bid us what to do, and it shall be done!"

3. *(Say I):* "You have answered My question. The door opens easily, so lead us inside. When asking that question, I did not mean the door to this dwelling, for how could that be important to Me Who has the might to suddenly bring into existence myriads of such dwellings and cause them to disappear again?

4. I put the question to your heart, which is the proper door into the house of your being. That door opens easily, and that is where I want you to lead Me. This you have already done in the right way. Now you may lead all of us into this external house, in witness of what constitutes your life, and that all may see that I am a Lord also of this house and this earth."

5. *(Says Uron):* "You are the Lord, here as everywhere! Also this external house belongs to You forever, and nobody else has a right to

be or do in it as he pleases. Therefore, it would be highly presumptuous of me should I lead You, the eternal, true owner of this house, as well as this whole world, into Your rightful property.

6. O Lord, You eternal owner of infinity, since You have come at long last to Your property, do lead us as the only rightful host into this house of Yours!"

7. *(Say I):* "You have spoken well, for it is as you say. But through My angels, I appointed you My administrator, and now I come to settle accounts with you. So I think it should be up to you to lead Me, your Lord, into the property I have entrusted to you."

8. *(Says Uron):* "Certainly, if You were a leaseholder, O Lord. For if somebody who has no other property as yet takes lease of a farm, he must be introduced by the administrator who knows his way around. But You are an owner of this property in the truest sense. Not an atom of what this house contains is unknown to You, nor is my poor administration. There will not be many accounts to settle with me, for I am now quite convinced that my bad housekeeping has forever been known to You in all its unreliable points.

9. Therefore, I once more come to You with the humble request: You sole Lord and Father of this and every other house, do enter Your very own property. And as for me, Your very bad administrator, be merciful and do not punish me according to my evil deserts."

10. With these words, the sage falls at My feet and weeps for the first time in his life. Laughing and weeping are almost unknown to the dwellers in this world with their blunt wisdom.

11. *(However, I call Martin and say):* "Martin, how did you like the speech of this now fully converted sage?"

12. *(Says Martin):* "O Lord, what he said was the full truth, to such an extent that I could not imagine anything more true.

13. If only the Jews had spoken like that when You came to the earth! Then no Judas would have betrayed You, nor would have a Caiaphas and Pilate crucified You. For there, too, You came into what was entirely Yours, but they did not know You as did this stranger here in this world.

14. But no man can undo what has happened. Therefore, O kind Father, do forgive all who do not know what they do and to whom, unfortunately, I also belong."

15. *(Say I):* "You, too, My Martin, have spoken truly. But now take this sage and carry him into the house before Me. So be it!"

THE EFFECT OF URON'S CONVERSION ON THE MEMBERS OF HIS HOUSEHOLD. ENTRANCE INTO THE SUN-DWELLING.

1. Peter, John, and Martin lift the sage from the ground and carry him into the magnificent house. At this, the other sun-dwellers, mainly the members of his household, are startled and say to each other:

2. *(The household members):* "What is this? The immortal, chief sage fallen like dead at the feet of this human spirit? And now three of the strange spirits are carrying him into our house! What will come of all this? Who is this spirit that he has such might as we have never before noticed in any angel?"

3. *(Say some who have followed the carriers):* "Did you not hear a while ago that this spirit is supposed to be the Supreme Spirit of God? We are almost certain of it, but cannot understand how you could have missed out on it.

4. Did you not hear our chief sage talk to Him and acknowledge Him as the sole host and elder of this and every other house?

5. Therefore, search your hearts and think what grace is shown to this house, to this entire world, if its Creator enters it with His most holy feet for the first time visibly to our senses. Hurry ahead and cleanse the luxurious seat of the elder of this house so that the rightful owner may for the first time sit in His rightful place here."

6. Following these words, they all hurry into the house and busy themselves there as suggested by the wiser ones from their midst. And I follow right on their heels, accompanied by Chanchah, Gella, and the three daughters of the house. Behind Me follow Borem and Chorel leading the rest of the party, who cannot open their eyes wide enough to take in all the splendors presenting themselves.

7. They are all full of joy and praise for Me. For, by now, all of them have fully realized that I alone am the Lord. And that they are now in the company of Him Who is the eternal Master of all these splendors, makes them all the happier. In this order we enter the first dwelling on the sun.

URON'S GOOD WELCOME. THE LORD'S GRACIOUS AN-
NOUNCEMENT TO URON. CALLING OF THE SUN-DWELLERS
TO BECOME CHILDREN OF GOD. A SAD TESTIMONY ABOUT
THE HUMANS ON EARTH.

1. When all have entered this magnificent temple, the sage, who
has now regained his composure, comes to Me with humility and
reverence, and says:

2. *(Uron, the sage):* "O You Whom to name nobody dared in this
world! You Who were made known to us endless times by Your archangels as the eternal, Primordial Spirit and almighty Creator of all
the countless beings! You — the first, the most holy, the wisest,
You eternal law and eternal order of all beings and things! Since
You have at long last graciously visited us, do bestow Your grace
upon us unworthy beings and reveal to us Your will and the road
which we have to follow so as to be sure to enjoy Your goodwill
forever!

3. We in this world enjoy great privileges. We are most beautiful
as far as our shape is concerned and sufficiently wise for the requirements of our community. Our work is carried out with our will
rather than with our hands. We have never had to worry about food,
which often is the case in other worlds I am told. Although our flesh
is oversensitive, we do not know sickness of the body and can live as
long as we like. And if we do agree to the transformation demanded
of us by higher spirits, this becomes bliss for us.

4. In short, in the infinite space of Your creations there is not
likely to be another world where natural human beings have a
happier existence than we, thanks to Your grace. But, notwithstanding all that, we still realize that we are infinitely inferior to Your
children.

5. O Lord, look at us who, too, have originated from You like
Your children! Do make it possible for us to attain a spiritual level
closer to theirs!

6. You sublime and most holy Father of Your children, if it is
Your will and not against Your sacred order, do grant my humble
request, which was encouraged by the spiritual need of my people
and the inconceivably mighty love I feel for You. But do not take it

amiss, Father of Your children, that I as a stranger dare knock at the sacred door to Your heart."

7. *(To this, I reply)*: "My son Uron, I have come here because of that very thing you have just spoken of. Mankind on the small earth has forgotten Me completely and turned the earth into a real hell. There are only a few left there who still actively believe and rely on My name. To most of the others, it has become a nuisance. From this, you can see that in the future I shall scarcely be able to raise children for Myself on that faithless earth.

8. My might cannot be used in that process, for it would put them under compulsion, which must never be the case with My children who have to attain supreme freedom; else they will never be able to serve Me as My right hand. But if I do not touch them with My might and instead allow them full freedom, they will turn into true devils and commit acts of the vilest nature with each other so that even the lowest hell could learn from them.

9. They lack faith, love, humility, obedience, and thus, also, faith in Me. But how could they have faith in Me since, as a result of their unbelief, I scarcely exist for them?

10. Therefore, nothing is left to Me but to protect and keep the few righteous and better ones. The others shall have their free will and I shall take My Covenant from them, as a result of which they will soon vanish like shadows from the surface of the earth.

11. In view of this, I am practically unable to obtain any perfected children from that earth. The best are worse than the worst here! And so I shall start here a new nursery for My future children-to-be and sift the other earth to an extent that the few better ones left there will have to travel for days before they find other beings like themselves.

12. As I intend to do this, I must indicate to you the roads on which you may become My children, if you so desire. When the earth has been cleansed, I shall build a spiritual bridge from it to you, across which you shall walk hand in hand with the children of the earth.

13. But now dispatch immediately messengers, and let many of your people assemble here so that I may open to them wide the door of My heart. So be it!"

170

THE PEOPLE OF THE SUN-COMMUNITY ASSEMBLE. MARTIN'S
APPOINTMENT AS PREACHER AND HIS RELUCTANCE. THE
GLORIOUS SINGING AND ITS EFFECT ON MARTIN.

1. At the sage's bidding, messengers hurry in all directions, calling
together many thousands to come and hear the preaching of a new
teaching for the first time in their world.

2. With lightning-speed, the messengers hurry through all sections
of the large community and, like high winds driving clouds before
them, they return with the summoned inhabitants to the dwelling
where, on special occasions, Uron assembles the dwellers from the
heights to preach to them new paths of wisdom.

3. Hearing the call, members of the community now flock to that
particular dwelling. There is a singing and rustling in the air as if from
the wings of eagles, for everyone is most anxious to get to the place
where sublime things are awaiting them.

4. *(Martin, hearing this sound in the air, which near the house has
amplified to such an extent that it sounds like thunder, asks Me):*
"Lord, Father, what is that noise which keeps increasing with every
moment?"

5. *(Say I):* "Do you not know that the power of attraction is
strongest where the magnet is? That noise is made by the fast approach of the humans of this vast earth in anticipation of what
they will find here. They are already surrounding the house. You can
see through the four doors what great multitudes are assembling.
They all come to hear the words of the Lord Who is over life and
death.

6. Here our work will become a bit more strenuous than heretofore. But do not worry about it. The task may be formidable, but the
strength and might we possess is more than sufficient to cope with it.
Or do you think our strength may not suffice, judging by the apprehensive way you are watching the approaching crowds?"

7. *(Says Martin):* "O Lord, to think that would be silly of me! I
am only wondering how these multitudes will be able to hear us.
Although this house is extremely large, it will be impossible to
accommodate all of them, for I can see dense crowds stretching for
miles all around this dwelling. If we step outside, only the closest

ones will be able to hear us, while the others will not even be able to see us. What a formidable task it will be to teach this awesome multitude!"

8. *(Say I):* "You have the wrong idea, My dear Martin. Here things are done in a different way. We shall be talking only to those close at hand — in this case, mainly to Uron. And he will then, after a moment, pass on what we say through special signs, like through a telegraph.

9. But first, it will be your turn. You will begin to preach, and only then will Peter and John and, finally, I Myself. But I warn you, pull yourself together — there will be a violent storm, so make sure you are not interrupted. Now you have to wait a while, and then, when I give you a sign, begin to preach. So be it!"

10. *(Says Martin to himself):* "Yes, O Lord, it is easy for *You* to say, 'So be it!' But I? — that is something quite different! I am now supposed to preach to these millions, who are at least as wise as I, if not wiser! And that in the presence of the Lord and of Peter and the immensely wise John! What a job! And all that during a thunderstorm! I shall make one blunder after another and shall be thoroughly ridiculed! Oh dear!

11. I have already delivered a number of speeches in the presence of the Lord, as well as before Peter and John — some stupid, some a bit wiser. But then the audience did not consist of millions or even trillions, all of them wiser than I. Here, with these multitudes, things look quite different.

12. The whole house is overcrowded so that one can scarcely distinguish the men from the women. Thousands of inconceivably beautiful beings are staring at me with their large, fiery eyes, full of high excitement and, so far, I have not the least idea of what I must say! Oh, they will be amazed at my wisdom, that's for sure!

13. If the Lord now lets me down and does not put every single word into my mouth, I shall be in a worse dilemma than ever before. I keep looking for His sign, but so far — may He be thanked — it has not come. I wish it would never come, but there is no hope for that! The Lord looks already as if He were going to say, 'Martin, be prepared!'

14. But what is that? I hear something like distant harmonies — it is singing, glorious singing. It sounds like organ music with the purest singing voices. Oh, how glorious, how heavenly! Pure, heavenly music, you do not only on earth delight and edify the soul, but

here in heaven, too, you refresh the blessed spirits. More and more forceful chords are alternating with sublime notes.

15. What majesty lies in those sounds! What harmony and purity of sound! O Lord, this music is more glorious than anything else in this world! It has a thoroughly quickening effect on me. Now I feel that I shall be able to preach when the time comes. This music is truly the most glorious hymn a spirit like me has ever heard.

16. How glorious, O Lord! I thank You for this treat. No doubt the hymn is meant for You alone, but it has made me extremely happy and has given me a lot of courage. You have, indeed, countless means for strengthening a timid mind and for giving courage to the fainthearted. So I will now preach about You like a true herald and reveal to them Your hidden greatness, love, might, strength, and holiness. Your Holy name be praised everlastingly!''

171

THE LORD'S ADVICE TO MARTIN. A CURE FOR WRATH. HOW TO HANDLE SATAN. MARTIN'S PRECAUTION BEFORE THE START OF HIS SERMON. THE ADVERSARY'S MIGHTY THREATS. MARTIN'S REASSURING WORDS TO THE FRIGHTENED CROWD. THE LORD'S COMFORTING WORDS.

1. *(Say I):* "All right, dear Martin, the hymn is coming to an end, so get ready! I warn you that things will get rather heated, for we are not safe from a visit by our adversary.

2. Therefore, pull yourself together and do not let wrath overcome you. The wrathful must never be opposed with wrath, but only with gentle earnestness, then you will gain a striking victory over him. Wrath is always anxious to call forth wrath in the opponent in order to destroy him with its imagined superiority. But if wrath does not find an object to seize hold of, it reverts to itself and tears itself to pieces. Therefore, be prepared for anything; be earnest and gentle, and victory will be yours.''

3. *(Says Martin):* "O Lord, should that enemy appear with whom I had dealings already in my house, I do beg You to grant me more

strength. I would love to give that beast a lasting reminder as thanks for all the good it has done to me."

4. *(Say I):* "Not so, My dear Martin, you know that evil repaid with evil has never borne blessed fruit as yet. Therefore, free yourself of such thoughts and act as I have advised you, and then you can be sure of victory. If you oppose the enemy with an act of destruction, he will flee in order to return strengthened, hoping to be better able to harm you.

5. I assure you that he could easily be destroyed if that were not against the established order. So he must be handled and imprisoned in a different way, and the existence of the entire material creation must be sustained by preserving him. Thus the course of action should be to curb him as much as possible, but no one should ever wish to destroy or completely annihilate him.

6. The hymn is now ending, so be prepared. If you follow My advice, you will not lack My help."

7. *(With these words of Mine, the music comes to an end and Uron, the sage, approaches Martin and says):* "I hear that you are going to speak to us first. Everything is ready and you may begin. The people are assembled, those who have to pass on the message have taken up their proper positions, and all ears and eyes are fixed on you. So, if it suits you — or rather the One — you may begin."

8. *(Says Martin):* "Yes, friend, I shall begin in a moment. However, tell me first whether you know all the guests assembled here well enough to assure me that there is no complete stranger among them.

9. If there is no stranger present, I shall speak to you short and straightforward. But if there is an uninvited guest who has sneaked in here like a thief or assassin in order to confuse and excite the minds of the audience during my speech, point him out to me that I may place him here in front of me facing all of you."

10. *(The sage diligently searches the crowd of guests who are standing in a perfect formation, but he cannot detect any stranger, and says to Martin):* "Friend, as far as my eyes reach, I cannot discern anyone strange to me. However, I will give a sign to the crowd to let me know if a stranger is among them."

11. *(Says Martin):* "All right, do that, and I will wait a while longer."

12. The sage immediately sends a question into the distance and receives the following reply from all directions:

13. *(The crowd):* "No, no, no! There is no stranger among us! However, the surface of the large sea close by is considerably disturbed and heaves mightily. It looks most frightening and we are afraid that we may have to flee before the sublime guests have completed their sacred message to us.

14. Whilst we are talking, Uron, we can see the center of a tornado forming not far from us. When it strikes, it will probably force the water up over your highest dwellings. Oh, do beg Him, the Almighty Who is said to be visibly present in your house, to ward off from us this imminent danger and save us from destruction!"

15. The sage, rather embarrassed, informs Martin of this and asks him to beg the Lord to graciously ward off this danger.

16. *(Says Martin):* "Friend, tell everybody immediately not to fear anything, for they will be quite safe. This manifestation is caused by that impotent, evil spirit who once had the audacity to appear as a false angel of light and give new divine laws. These laws, however, were his own and, with their help, he intended to corrupt the people completely. Now we have come to thwart this evil scheme once and for all, and save all of them through the might and strength of Him Who is here in our midst as the eternal, most holy Father among His children. Tell them this without delay!"

17. Uron complies, but after a short while, he receives this reply:

18. *(The crowd):* "Praise and adoration to the Supreme Divine Spirit! This is most reassuring. However, the water is still rising, and it will reach us within ten beats of the pendulum of the large time recorder. Beg the Lord to ward it off or it will be high time for us to flee!"

19. Uron quickly passes this message on to Martin, who says:

20. *(Martin):* "Tell them immediately to be not afraid, notwithstanding the manifestation. They must not flee, even if the water should wash against their feet, for the Lord will allow the adversary to go only so far, then He will seize him with the greatest sternness of His judgment and punish him severely before their eyes."

21. This message is passed on by the sage, and he then receives the following answer:

22. *(The crowd):* "We rely on the word of the Most Holy and will let the water touch our feet. And then we shall rejoice and praise the Divine Spirit for bestowing such unprecedented grace upon us. However, the water is still rising with great rapidity, and the result will be devastating unless the might of God checks it."

23. The sage tells Martin about this reply, and he says, in considerable agitation:

24. *(Martin):* "Listen, friend, this is a miserable reptile that has no respect for God, its eternal Master, for it knows that the Lord is too kind — yes, *too* boundlessly kind! But, although everything about the Lord is of an infinite nature, in this case Satan will have made a miscalculation. This time the Lord's infinite patience will come to an end, and He will know how to restrain that oldest, most wicked evil-doer."

25. *(Say I):* "Do not let this interfere with your task, Martin. I will handle the agitator, but you begin now with your sermon so that we can at last achieve our purpose. Let Satan enjoy himself. I assure you, it will not be for long. To completely reassure you, I can tell you that this time the enemy has made a considerable mistake where My patience is concerned."

26. *(Says Martin):* "O Lord, You best and holiest of Fathers, my poor heart has been relieved, indeed, of a very heavy burden. All my love and deepest adoration is Yours forever!"

172

MARTIN'S SERMON TO THE ASSEMBLED SUN-DWELLERS. HARD LIFE ON EARTH AS CONDITION FOR BECOMING A CHILD OF GOD.

1. *(After these words, Martin faces the congregation and speaks):* "All of you who have assembled on this extraordinary occasion in order to hear words of life from my mouth and, eventually, even from the Lord Himself, must not allow yourselves to be disturbed if a violent storm should threaten us. For God, the supreme, almighty Spirit Himself is visibly present here. It is He with Whom a while ago you saw me talk, although you did not hear us.

2. He, the sole true, eternal Lord and Creator of all infinity, has assured me for your sake that He will punish the evil spirit severely before your eyes should he dare to carry on with his wicked game. Having received such an assurance from the Lord Himself, let

us patiently and without fear await what grace the Lord is going to bestow upon us.

3. I, who am now speaking to you, am not wise out of myself, and everything I shall say to you with the simplest of words, will be of the Lord. Do not expect anything high-sounding or sublime, but, instead, expect all the more truth and spiritual knowledge. I shall give you what I have. So, listen!

4. My dear partners in the grace of my and your God, my Lord and Father and your Lord and now, also, *your* Father. The almighty will of this Father has, since the beginning of time, endowed you in your magnificent world with so many privileges that a comparison with the inhabitants of *my* world would be futile.

5. You are so beautiful in your appearance that we earth-dwellers could not even imagine the purest angel of light to be more beautiful. The duration of your physical lives is not limited, so that every one of you may live as long as he chooses. The difference between your natural life and that of your departed spirits, is, in fact, so small that it does not matter very much whether you live with this body or without it. You can see your departed and speak with them whenever you wish, and you can even associate with us pure spirits as if you had already shed your bodies.

6. All this is vastly different in that harsh world where I and all those who are with me have lived in the flesh. There, the duration of a natural life is undetermined, but very short. If one of you would say, 'I am young,' he would be of very old age on our earth. I know that in this congregation there are many who, according to our earth chronology, are several hundred years old, yet here they are considered young people, whilst on our earth, they would be fabulously old.

7. You also have people here who are already so old that by our chronology they would be older than the entire human race on my little earth — maybe even a thousand times older. What great, important and sacred experiences such men must have accumulated! At the side of such experienced teachers, your spiritual education must have soared high, and your wisdom must have wonderfully deep roots.

8. In our world, one has scarcely realized what life is all about before one must already leave one's wretched flesh in a very painful way, usually not even knowing whether towards eternal life or death. Everything one has worked for must be left behind, be it honors,

402

fame, splendors, virtues, scientific achievements, or wisdom. All this is completely disregarded by the Lord, and when the stealthy angel of death turns up to thrust his sword into one's heart, everything seems to have come to an end.

9. One has to die without a definite prospect for a reward, for faith and hope are all that our handed-down teaching will allow us concerning life after death. There is hardly anybody who has, like you here, already in the flesh a firm conviction regarding eternal life. Just think what a privilege it is for a free man to be a lord over his own life, as is the case with you in this world. He can freely enjoy all that he has achieved as well as the countless other privileges of such a life.

10. You are able to talk to the spirits of your bodily departed brothers and see them as if they had not died at all. In our world, perhaps one in ten thousand knows about life after the physical death and what it may be like. And still we are expected to sacrifice everything for a future life, of which we do not even know whether it exists at all. And those who do believe in it, have not the slightest idea, except for some fables, what it will be like.

11. You will realize what an incalculable privilege it is for a human being to be a lord of his own life from the start."

173

CONTINUATION OF BISHOP MARTIN'S SERMON. DIFFERENT LIVING CONDITIONS ON THE SUN AND ON THE EARTH.

1. *(Bishop Martin):* "Your world is a sun for us, without which we would not have any life at all, because it gives us light and warmth. You who live on it, however, know neither night nor winter.

2. Do you actually know what a sun is? With all your wisdom you, its inhabitants, hardly know what a sun is.

3. You are hardly aware of the privileges of being an inhabitant of a sun. When I was still crawling around like a worm on my wretched planet, I did not know that either. But now I do know it,

and I, as a spirit who has now become a bit wiser, have trouble finding the right words to describe to you what a privilege you enjoy. Compared with you, a dweller on my earth has a miserable existence in all the circumstances of his natural life. Those are only fleeting moments of which he can say that he enjoyed them.

4. The considerable hardness and poorness of the soil on earth compels the poor mortal to earn his livelihood by the sweat of his brow. Men of a weaker nature, who do not relish such labor, resort to begging. Or, if they have enough power, they may rob the more active ones of their produce to use it for themselves.

5. Eventually, such men may hire a great number of like-minded who no longer work, but who live from robberies. They will oppress the industrious workers in many different ways. Using a lot of pretexts that give their actions a tinge of legality, they will demand payment of certain taxes, but will still look down on the workers who pay them as inferior.

6. Gradually, these shirkers become mighty tyrants who rule over the workers and bread producers, and they do with them just as they please. In addition, they give the workers law upon law which, usually, are for the benefit of those who give them. Therefore, any infringement of such laws is punished severely, making the hard life of such a bread producer even more wretched.

7. When the oppression of the workers goes too far, the workers often rebel, band together in great numbers, and march, enraged, against their oppressors — often killing many of them, but usually losing also their own lives.

8. Such furious movements are called 'wars' on earth. Once a war is started, it usually continues until one of the parties involved has been completely annihilated or until the weaker one has realized during the killing that it is useless to war against a more powerful enemy, and so surrenders unconditionally, after which there is once more peace.

9. But what a peace! It is a hellish peace, not a heavenly one! The conquered become slaves and often have to submit to laws that will not only keep their poor, war-mangled bodies in heavy chains, but also keep their minds enslaved.

10. Such a state may last for even thousands of earth years, but the nature of the earth does not change, and night is always soon followed by a miserable day of suffering, a freezing cold winter by a hot summer.

11. Lack of food causes pain in the stomach , which we call hunger. In years with bad harvests, many die from this.

12. Oh friends, compare this life of yours with theirs, and tell me whether your wisdom can find words with which to express how great the privileges are that you enjoy. You say: 'That cannot be called a life, but only a terrible torment! How can men exist like that and still praise their Creator?'

13. Although your question is justified, I assure you that there are very many human beings who love and praise their Creator all the more the worse they have to suffer. What do you think about that?

14. You say: 'Friend, that is impossible! How can a kind Creator give His creatures such a bad deal and then still expect them to praise and love Him? Surely the poor earth-dwellers have never got to know their true Creator. Or, if they do know Him, they are fools to thank Him for such a life, let alone love Him!'

15. Considering your so enormously privileged life, also this question is justified. But what will you say to this: that the Creator has made it quite clear to the humans on my planet that if, notwithstanding the hardships of their lives on earth, they do not love Him above everything, bless their enemies and tormentors, and pray for those who curse them, they have to expect the most severe, everlasting punishment in the fires of hell? And that they must thank God, the Creator, with all their heart for whatever He sends them, be it blessings or suffering? Tell me, what do you think about that?

16. How do you like the fact that on that planet the Lord sends the greatest sufferings to those who love Him with all their hearts? And that those who scorn Him most, usually live in the best circumstances — that is, what you can call 'good' on earth?

17. Speak, friends, and give me your opinion on that, you fortunate beings! You are silent? I will have to tell you more so that you can more easily form an opinion. So listen.

18. I need not stress all the time your wonderful existence in order to give you a very clear picture of the miserable status of my world. You know better than I what your world is like. So I will leave it to your sound wisdom and clear judgment to compare the conditions in my world with those in yours. Since you are already astonished at what I have so far told you, I wonder what you will say to the following?

19. I have mentioned to you before that my world is full of hardship, be it naturally, spiritually, or morally. Its soil can

be worked only with great effort, and before such work can commence, many tools have to be made which are essential for the
achievement of results.

20. In the course of time, the situation of men in my world has
developed in such a way that only a minority still own land. The
vast majority of earth-dwellers does not own anything and has to
slave for the landowners for a meager reward, and often just for a
slender fare.'

21. Many of these propertied men amass a thousand times more
than they and their children could consume in centuries.

22. When the harsh winter comes, the rich have good, solidly-
built homes in which they can get comfortably warm by means of
artificial fires, and in their rooms they have warm and soft beds for
resting.

23. But the great many poor people must live in miserable
dwellings, dress in scanty clothes, and are often hungry and sick.
And, even if there are times when thousands are in a desperate plight
and die of starvation, the rich do not worry. They calmly look on
and say: 'It is as well that the useless beggar-rabble is eliminated and
does not pester us any longer.'

24. The same poverty and food shortage — usually caused by
the rich — is used by them for their further benefit. They practice
usury with the provisions they have amassed, and who does not pay
what they demand, may die of starvation at their doors, yet it does
not soften their hearts at all.

25. Notwithstanding the injustice of this, the Creator does not,
so to speak, do anything about it. Every day is followed by a night;
the rain falls and blesses the fields of the rich more than those of the
poor who did not have the means for preparing their poor soil for the
best results. The fruit trees of the rich usually abound with fruit,
while those of the poor are often almost barren. The rich have
plenty of everything, whereas the poor often must perish in great
misery.

26. As already said, such a revolting and hellish state of affairs
often exists for quite long periods of time, during which the Creator
appears to be completely indifferent. If now and then, maybe as a
result of the tearful pleas of the poor, a judgment is sent upon the
earth which only seems as if it came from Him, again the victims are
mostly the poor and weak. The rich usually get away unscathed, and

while this judgment lasts, some of them become even richer and happier in their material life.

27. In a war, usually the poor have to die on the battlefields for the rich, and that for a very meager pay. But this again safeguards the property of the rich. And those of the poor who, eventually, return from the battlefields, often crippled with the loss of limbs or scarred from their wounds, they have to go begging for a piece of bread. From the doors of the rich they are often driven away like animals with the most disgraceful abuse.

28. And still they are not allowed to wish their tormentors ill, but they must bless and forgive them from the depths of their hearts, or God might punish them with everlasting hell.

29. At all times, the poor and wretched have to suffer most, be it in war, as a judgment of God, or any other judgment, whilst the hardened rich and privileged usually escape unhurt.

30. Notwithstanding this, it is mostly the poor who love the Lord, have faith in Him, and pray to Him as best they can. The lucky rich have more often than not no faith at all. Their hardened hearts hold very little love for God, they pray little or not at all, and often they mock Him and His law.

31. Some gold, good food, and a young, voluptuous female with whom to commit the vilest lechery, they prefer a thousand times to God, Who hardly exists for them, and many thousands of times to those who sweat for them and guard their safety with their own poor lives, day and night, summer and winter.

32. But with all their godlessness, they are happy in their material lives, and it is never the poor, but their counterparts who sometimes rob them of their abundance. However, even when they have had bad luck, the rich are still much better off than the luckiest poor who have never had anything much except misery.

33. Tell me, friends, how do you like the life of human beings on the planet which you call the 'Sacred Planet'?"

174

AGITATING EFFECT OF MARTIN'S SERMON ON THE SUN-DWELLERS. DIALOGUE BETWEEN URON AND MARTIN.

1. *(Here, the sage Uron steps forward and says):* "Friend, I can see that you speak the truth, but what do you hope to achieve by it? Do you want to stir up these people against God? Here, my wisdom is really at an end and I cannot understand you, and God even less! What order is this supposed to be?

2. I know the heavens and hells of many worlds, but no hell is worse than your earth. Therefore, I beg you to speak about something else or you will excite my people against God, Whom so far they have praised and revered above everything."

3. *(Says Martin):* "Friend, every being and thing has been given by the Lord a certain duty to perform, openly or secretly, with the only difference that the things *must*, but we free beings *can* and *want* to perform it. Therefore, whatever the result of my speech may be, I do nothing but the Lord's will. So you may go on listening to me, as I am not quite finished yet."

4. *(Says Uron):* "You may continue with your speech, but the question still remains: Who will profit from your revelation? You can neither lose nor gain anything by telling us purer dwellers in this world about what life is like in yours. And we can surely not gain anything through becoming better acquainted with the wickedness of your world, which has not revealed itself to that extent when regarded by our wisdom. However, your description of the terrible conditions in your world could cause a lot of damage to us which might be irreparable.

5. We have already had a very detailed description from you of the bad conditions in your world, and we can easily imagine that even worse things could happen there. Therefore, I do not see any point in bothering us any longer with these matters which are of little interest to us, because we are quite unable to change the miserable conditions in your world. Besides, we would never wish or agree to adopt the extremely bad order of your world. And so, I think you might now let your brother Peter speak, as he might have something better to tell us.

6. Should it be your intention to accuse God, your Creator and

ours, before us, and let us decide whether He is right or wrong, I would be really sorry for you. What could we impotent creatures achieve against the infinite omnipotence of the Creator, even if we were convinced that He deals unjustly with the inhabitants of your earth? For He is still the sole Lord, and the whole of infinity lies in His hand, and depends on His will.

7. Let us assume that among the countless myriads of worlds He had, indeed, destined one particular world to be a plaything for His whims: who could call Him to account for it? And if you dared do it, could you enforce an answer from Him? He is and remains forever the sole Lord and does what pleases Him. He can bestow His grace upon men or condemn them, irrespective of whether we find it justified or otherwise.

8. Who could prevent Him from destroying this world in a moment if He so willed it? Or, if He sent myriads of terrible spirits to torment us for aeons of time, what could we do toward the prevention of such a judgment?

9. I believe that God, Who is now visibly present among us, is the sole Lord of all the worlds, heavens, and hells. His omnipotence vouches for His likewise infinite wisdom! He will know best why He sometimes allows things to happen which our reason is unlikely ever to comprehend. And I am convinced that if we willingly submit to His will and order, we shall not go wrong. Do you agree with me?"

10. *(Says Martin):* "I do, of course. But, because it is the will of the Lord, I have to go on with my speech. You will have to respect His will in this, too."

11. *(Says Uron):* "If that is so, then go on speaking in His name. We shall listen to you."

175

END OF MARTIN'S SERMON AND A HINT AS TO ITS PURPOSE. CONDITIONS FOR BECOMING A CHILD OF GOD. WORDS OF THANKS AND APPRECIATION FROM THE SAGE.

1. *(Says Martin):* "Despite the very bad living conditions on earth, of which I have just given only a rough outline, I do not mean to say at any time that the Lord is not fair. Nor do I want to maintain that

it is practically impossible to lead a life on earth that is pleasing to Him. I only want to make your minds more receptive, and this can be achieved by pointing out to you the countless advantages of your living conditions. For you who have been born into them are quite unable to judge them unless you are given a comparison with the living conditions in other worlds — especially mine, with which I am only too familiar, having had a lot to do with such things.

2. I have not the least intention of accusing the Lord before you and your wisdom, nor do I want to incite you against Him, which would be unspeakably foolish of me. However, in view of the fact that you, too, have been called to become children of God, and that your wisdom has made it known to you that true children of God can be procreated only in our world, it is essential for you to also know under what conditions a human being can attain to this invaluable and most sublime position of honor.

3. So far, your lives have been nothing but a pastime of God's angels, whose property you were, and this has been totally unsuitable for the attainment of God's sonship, for it is no game, but sacred earnest, and must be striven for in the often most bitter reality of life.

4. Therefore, you shall also be given laws similar to ours, and here, too, the word of God will apply: 'Everyone of you must shoulder his cross and follow Me, or he cannot be where I am, live and act surrounded by My children, who will be My right hand forever, do what I do and live as I live.'

5. For this reason, the Lord Himself came to live in my world as a man, suffered all imaginable hardships of human life on earth, and finally even let blind mankind put His body to death on a cross in the most humiliating and painful manner. And all this only so that the human beings of my world could become gods — if they so desired, of course.

6. But the fact alone that somebody is born in that world where the Lord Himself had assumed the flesh, will not suffice to attain the filial relationship to God; he must voluntarily fulfill all the conditions prescribed by the Lord Himself.

7. All of you have heard my description of the misery on earth which almost gives the impression as if the Lord were not interested in the world which He Himself made the most important and sacred in the whole universe through His incarnation there. But this is not so.

410

8. Men on that earth are free in the fullest sense of the word, and they can do whatever they like: good in accordance with God's law, or evil against it. Nothing draws them toward good or evil; it all depends on their own free will. This is also the reason why the living conditions in that world are so scanty; man's free will must not be influenced and spoilt by them.

9. On the other hand, heavenly things, too, are covered up so as not to force the decision of the free will toward good through seeing clearly what beatitudes are awaiting man in the beyond. Although God's teaching makes it clear to everyone what the consequences will be after either a good or bad life, he can still do whatever he wants, for there is no certainty for him on either side to force his decision.

10. Everything on earth is, therefore, arranged in such a way that man's will is and remains free. For without this free will, it would be impossible to attain to the sonship of God freely without ever being under compulsion.

11. In view of this, it is not hard to understand that most men on my earth err in some way or another. That you, too, if you seriously desire to become children of God, will have to be transferred to quite different living conditions, is quite another thing. How — my successor will be telling you. So listen to him!"

12. *(Says Uron):* "I, and all these assembled here, thank you for your speech and instruction given us through the grace of your and our God and Lord. I found the last part particularly valuable, for it showed me clearly the reason why life in your world is so much harsher than it is in ours. Besides, this has confirmed my previously expressed belief that no intelligent being should doubt the kindness of the Creator.

13. For His infinite omnipotence, with its innumerable works of the most wonderful kind and order, indisputably vouches for His likewise boundless wisdom. And such wisdom can only flow from the great order in the most perfect, everlasting life of the Creator Himself.

14. Where life is based on the highest, purest, and most profound order, in such a perfect life there must dwell a kindness quite beyond the comprehension of even the freest created spirit.

15. I thank you, dear friend, for myself as well as for all the others who are assembled here, and now I am looking forward to what brother Peter will tell us. May the Lord guide his tongue."

176

THE THREATENING FLOOD IS RISING. PETER'S REASSURING WORDS. HIS SIGNIFICANT QUESTION TO THE SUN-DWELLERS: "DO YOU DESIRE TO BECOME CHILDREN OF GOD OR NOT?" URON'S ANSWER.

1. Now a sign is given that the waters of the great sea are already quite close to those in the lowest positions and will be touching their feet any moment. The Almighty Spirit is to help them, or they will be forced to flee.

2. *(Says Peter):* "Friend and brother, tell the people not to lose heart, for the Lord has purposely allowed this danger to arise so that the great glory of God may be demonstrated all the clearer.

3. The water is going to touch their feet, but they will not get wet! The subterranean formation will be forced out, and will distend until it bursts and emits great masses of fire which, however, will dissolve completely as they fall back, and the crust will subside the moment it has burst.

4. Therefore, no one must be afraid, and everyone should ignore the threatening danger completely; then no one will come to harm. Tell them this immediately."

5. Uron, the sage, passes on this message with the help of the already-mentioned signs, and within a few moments, counter signs are coming from all directions. They say that the instructions have been understood by all and that everyone is gratefully and willingly prepared to act accordingly.

6. As the sage tells Peter this, he says:

7. *(Peter):* "So tell them now to give me all their attention, as I am going to tell them very important things."

8. This the sage does, and everybody is tense with expectation.

9. *(Says Peter):* "My friends and brothers, my predecessor described to you the living conditions of the earth-dwellers. I, too, lived there at the time the Lord Himself took on the flesh of man and had to suffer all imaginable hardships, from His childhood on, just like any other member of the poor who did not possess any property.

10. From the true description of living conditions Martin has given you, you can easily judge how much better off in every respect you are in your great world of light. But you will now also under-

stand what is necessary to make a free child of God out of His creature.

11. First of all the question arises: 'Do you or don't you desire to become children of God like us?' You would retain all your privileges, as far as they are not curtailed by a law inviting you to voluntarily renounce them for the sake of the Kingdom of God. Think it over well, and only upon your mature consideration, tell me Yes or No.

12. Think of the advantage of being a child of God, or at least being able to become one, but also think of what must be done to gain such an advantage. However, do take into consideration your present privileges and living conditions which, you must admit, are so vastly different from the others.

13. As a matter of fact, everything that is renounced will be compensated a thousandfold everlastingly in the Kingdom of God! However, the fact of this compensation will not be comprehended as a certainty, but only vaguely to the extent of one's strength of faith.

14. At present, you see before you clearly revealed, the spiritual as well as the natural. With those, however, who in all earnest desire to become children of God, this will no longer be the case. Therefore, consider carefully what you intend to do. You are offered a great thing, but a lot is asked of you to achieve it."

15. *(Says the sage):* "Friend, you are aware that our intelligence is of such a nature that we never have to ponder long over a decision, and we know immediately what we want to do or what we should do. Therefore, I, as well as all the people present, have also in this case no doubts as to what we desire and, naturally, what we are able to do.

16. Every action presupposes the ability to perform it, and surely God Himself will not demand more of any creature than it is capable of doing depending on its nature and strength. Thus, I am convinced that the Lord will not demand also of us any more than we are capable of doing as a result of our natural and spiritual state of development in this world.

17. This guiding principle makes it quite clear that we desire only that which we are able to do, and that is all that counts where the matter of filial relationships to God is concerned. If we are capable of attaining to it, we do desire it; however, if it requires more than our greatest effort, then we cannot desire it, since in such a case it would be unattainable for us.

18. In short, if this is attainable for us under our present living conditions, we do desire it; if not, then, friend, you will understand that we cannot possibly desire it. Now you know our decision! Please yourself, for I believe that also our will is free and must remain so."

177

FURTHER CLARIFICATION BY PETER OF THE QUESTION OF FILIAL RELATIONSHIP TO GOD. HIS CRITICISM OF THE INCEST AMONG THE SUN-DWELLERS.

1. *(Says Peter):* "Dear friend, you have basically misunderstood my explanation. The question runs thus: 'Do you or don't you desire to become children of God like us?' You would retain all your privileges as far as they are not curtailed by laws inviting you to voluntarily renounce them for the sake of the Kingdom of God. (Naturally this applies only to those privileges which are not an essential part of life.) Speaking of retention of your privileges, I, of course, assume that you comprehend this as explained.

2. Believe me, friend, that we in the Kingdom of God are wise enough to know that a sun cannot be turned into an ordinary planet if a once-established order of the entire universe is not to be disturbed. Also, that the nature of sun-dwellers differs considerably from that of the inhabitants of a small planet. Surely we know all that quite as well as you do!

3. However, you have certain laws here which you gave yourselves and which actually cannot be considered laws at all, since they demand nothing but unrestrained liberty in everything. According to these laws, you are even allowed to discard your ancient and wise original laws and replace them with empty new ones. Now the question is: 'Do you consider that kind of liberty as one of the actual privileges of your life?'

4. Angels from heaven have given you directions for matrimony — that is, the proper union between a man and a woman. They have also instructed you in the proper spiritual procreation of children, which you have preserved so far. How is it possible that now

414

fathers sleep with their daughters in a bestial way, whereas they have a commandment forbidding under penalty that a father performs even a spiritual procreation with his daughter?

5. Tell me, do you consider that one of the indispensable privileges of your life on the sun? Give me your opinion."

6. *(Says the sage):* "Oh friend, that is not one of the privileges of our life; on the contrary, it has been most detrimental, both to our natural and to our spiritual lives. In view of this, we can, naturally, renounce such true drawbacks. The 'privileges' I was thinking of mainly consist in our specific nature that makes us to a great extent lords over the nature and substance of our world.

7. One of these privileges is that we can draw from the soil of this earth whatever we want — innumerable and unlimited splendors, as well as all imaginable necessities for the maintenance of our bodies.

8. I am sure that our plea for retention of such privileges will not be a sin in the eyes of the Lord, nor a reason to refuse us acceptance into His sonship.

9. But should He consider such a request a sin, then we would have to insist that we be permitted to stay as we are, rather than exchange this security for something most insecure and difficult to attain.

10. This is how I think about it, friend! If you agree, all of us will accept your proposition; if you do not, we shall refuse it. The Lord cannot ask us to do the impossible, unless He changes us completely, endowing us with properties and abilities as yet totally unknown to us. But no being can oppose the Lord's omnipotence, and this applies also to us."

178

PETER SUGGESTS THANKING AND PETITIONING. URON'S SIGNIFICANT REJECTION OF THE PRAYER TO GOD.

1. *(Says Peter):* "The Lord's omnipotence is His eternal order from which you, as well as all of infinity, have originated. If the Lord now wanted to change you, He would first have to change His entire

order. This He is most unlikely ever to do, considering the fact that He Himself is this order.

2. However, your lives until now can be described as extremely comfortable and carefree; you have to overcome no resistance whatsoever, and nothing ever causes you trouble or costs you an effort. From birth until your voluntary departure from your body, you know of no imperfection worth mentioning, consequently, of no self-denial.

3. You are well aware that you, with your entire world, are the work of a supremely wise Divine Spirit Whom you highly revere. But have you ever prayed to Him for something or thanked Him for any of the great blessings He keeps bestowing upon you so abundantly?

4. Until now you have lived as if completely independent of Him. Would it be asking too much if in the future you condescended to become a little more dependent on Him? Speak again and tell me faithfully what you decide to do."

5. *(Says the sage):* "Friend, we would like that, indeed! Especially as concerns the gratitude we owe Him for so many and great blessings. We shall do our best to express this to the great, holy Giver of innumerable wonderful gifts from the bottom of our hearts. However, as far as petitions are concerned, I cannot agree with that at all, for I look upon every petition as an insult to divine wisdom.

6. For, by praying to the Godhead, I obviously profess to having better insight than God — in a way claiming to know better what I need than the Lord Himself. I think that even a child of God should not presume to do this; other creatures even less.

7. Besides, a prayer appears to me like a polite combat in which the creature endeavors to conquer a certain harshness and kind of stubborn cruelty in the Creator, and thus triumphing over Him.

8. Really, friend, I would rather not exist at all than approach the wisest and kindest almighty Creator with a petition as if I knew better than He what I need, or by praying for others show that I am more merciful than He. What kind of reverence for God, the ever wisest and mightiest spirit, would that be?

9. Therefore, my answer to your proposal is as follows: We want forever to completely depend on Him, as has been the case so far, for it is quite impossible to depend on anyone else. Thus, we shall forever thank Him — from the depths of our being — for every one of His gifts which we acknowledge as infinitely kind. However,

416

we shall not, nor do we want to or can, ask Him for anything, for we are fully convinced that the Lord knows so much better what we need and He does not have to be reminded of it by miserable creatures. Thus, be it far from us to insinuate to Him by means of a prayer that He is a harsh God and has a weakness that can only be brought into the proper order by petitions on the part of His creatures.

10.   Friend, all of us respect God, the Supreme Spirit, too highly and have too sublime an opinion of His perfection, that we could ever forget ourselves to such an extent as to approach with a petition Him Who has made us, without being asked, as perfect as is necessary for us.

11.   We shall always thank Him for the many blessings and gifts, the smallest of which is so great and holy that we shall hardly ever be able to fully appreciate it. However, as already stressed, we shall never offend with a petition against Him, the Most Holy and Perfect One.

12.   You may please yourself, but with all your wisdom you will not likely succeed in convincing us that we should pray to Him, unless the Lord Himself expressly demanded it. Naturally, no creature can ever oppose the will of God. Otherwise, we shall remain free in our actions and do what we consider right before God, men, and angels."

179

PETER TEACHES THE LORD'S PRAYER. WHY A PETITION IS SUPERIOR TO THANKSGIVING. PETER'S IMPORTANT QUESTION TO URON ON BEHALF OF THE LORD.

1. *(Says Peter):* "Friend, when the Lord, the almighty Creator of all the heavens and worlds, took the flesh on my earth, living as a human being among us, He taught all of us to pray, saying:

2.   'But if you pray, then speak: Our Father which art in the heavens, hallowed be Thy most holy name. Thy kingdom of love, truth, and life eternal come to us. Thy most holy will be done

417

always, through all eternities. Give us this day and always our daily bread. Forgive us our sins and weaknesses to the same extent that we forgive our debtors, whatever they may be like. Do not let our weaknesses be assailed by temptations that would defeat us, but deliver us from all evil that might ever befall us. Thine, O Father, is all the power and might and glory forever! Thine be all the praise and honor, all the love and gratitude forever!'

3. Since the Lord Himself taught us to pray like that, it should not be wrong for us as His children to ask Him for what we believe we need.

4. To thank the Creator for all His countless blessings is already a great and holy privilege for us free beings, as we thus acknowledge to God all that we have and receive as free gifts, and not as a judgment. The petition, however, ranks even higher, for it is an expression of our realization that we may not only acknowledge as a free gift what we receive from God, but that we even have a free choice of the gift.

5. To attain complete liberation of our spirit , we not only need to realize what vital necessities we receive from the Lord as free gifts, but even more important is our freedom of choice concerning our needs. This obviously requires more introspection and uninhibited self-cognizance than the realization that everything we are, have, and receive, are free gifts from God the Lord.

6. He who thanks for a gift received, but who does not feel the need for any further gifts he may eventually require, is still very stupid in his sphere of life with a lot of brutish elements. For, also, beasts thank the Giver by their instinctive happy enjoyment of what they receive, although they are unable to recognize Him. However, unable to understand its needs, a beast can also not ask for things. When it is hungry, it looks for food. Having found it and satisfied its hunger, it rests until it becomes hungry again. This rest is a dumb thanks for the food it has found, but while it is resting satisfied, it does not know that it will be hungry again and need further nourishment.

7. With man it is quite different, for he knows what he needs. After having satisfied his hunger, he is quite aware that he will again be needing food. But he also knows the Giver, and, therefore, he should not only thank Him after he has satisfied his hunger, but should combine a petition with his thanks. Thus he acknowledges all the more clearly having received everything from the Creator

418

and that he expects also in the future to receive from Him all that is good and necessary.

8.   At the same time, through such a petition, man stands before his Master just the way He wants him to: as a completely free being who is not only entitled to receive, but also to ask freely and humbly. Surely such a right presupposes considerable self-cognizance, without which no man could attain perfection?

9.   These reasons should suffice for your wisdom to understand that petition is more essential for every free spirit than the most due thanks.

10.   And if my most forcible reasons should still not satisfy you, friend Uron, the fact alone should suffice that the Lord Himself has repeatedly encouraged us to ask for the things we want to receive. But He has only very seldom reminded someone to say thanks.

11.   Thus He gave us a sacred form in which to pray and ask for things. However, I hardly know of any particular form for thanksgiving.

12.   True, the Lord Himself thanked the Godhead, as the Father within Him, on several occasions, and only once reproached the nine cleansed who had not returned with the tenth to praise Him. But, notwithstanding this, He never suggested to us how we should thank, whilst He did that expressly where praying for something is concerned.

13.   Therefore, if the Lord expressly demanded prayers of us much more imperfect earth-dwellers, it is unlikely that He would consider it superfluous with you.

14.   So I am now telling you on behalf of the Lord that you will from now on receive everything that you now have from Him, but only through prayer. Those of you who will not pray, shall receive only little or nothing at all.

15.   For, if you are free, you must also know for yourselves what you need. When you realize this — which will be much easier for you here than it was for us on our earth — then pray, and you will be given what you have asked for.

16.   If you agree to this, answer in the affirmative, and my brother John will take over your guidance. It is up to your free will to choose and decide!"

THE SUN-SAGE'S AFFIRMATIVE ANSWER TO PETER. HIS CRITICISM OF THE LORD'S PROMISES.

1. *(Says Uron, the sage):* "Yes, friend, we are in agreement with the Lord's wishes. For, how could one oppose the almighty will of the Lord, whether what He demands is easy or hard to do? If we do not take this upon ourselves voluntarily for our future benefit, we would have to do it under compulsion, which might prove our ruin. So we by far prefer to do it of our own free will, thus gaining something for our future lives rather than losing.

2. From what you and your predecessor have told us, I realize that we shall have to give back into the hands of the Lord our free, creative will-power with which we have so far cultivated our gardens and, usually, erected our dwellings. But it does not really matter since, no doubt, we can have this ability back completely by way of prayer.

3. We do know by means of our inner discernment, as well as through various spirits from your earth, that the Lord is never very particular where His promises are concerned. Whom He promises wealth, he gives poverty; who has been promised a long life in good health, can reckon on suffering and an early end to his temporal life; the one He wants to give freedom, becomes a prisoner in the world; and those He loves, He has tempted and tormented mightily. Those who stick most faithfully to Him and His Word, have to suffer misery and persecution; and those who love Him above everything, He allows to be crucified — and so on.

4. However, as already said, it does not matter, for He alone is the almighty Master of His works, and He can do with them whatever He pleases. No one may ask Him, 'Lord, why do You do this or that of which we do not approve?' He is the Lord, and that is sufficient for everyone!

5. We know that the Lord promised His kings on earth everlasting sovereignty, but they died like all the others. He promised a certain people a land and reign forever, but, as we heard, this chosen people has no longer a land. Thus, we know that the Lord elected sages who had to reveal His will to the people and what He would do. But when the time came that these revelations had to be ful-

filled, the sages were standing there like fools, for the Lord did not let happen what He had revealed through them. And there are many other such instances.

6. As you see, one cannot take the Lord's promises literally. The same will probably apply to the granting of prayers; for who could ever force Him to it?

7. However, we shall accept your proposition, knowing only too well that a refusal on our part would be extremely foolish. Therefore, the almighty Lord's will be done!''

JOHN'S EXPLANATION OF THE SPIRITUAL MEANING OF THE LORD'S PROMISES. PROPHETIC METAPHOR OF THE NEW HOUSE AND THE NEW CITY AS THE LORD'S NEW PROMISE. REJECTION BY URON AS SENSELESS AND HEARTLESS DRIVEL.

1. *(Says John):* "Friends, and in particular you, brother Uron who is the speaker for all the others, from an earthly point of view, you may be right in what you say, but since the Lord's words and promises must surely be of a deeply spiritual nature and their true meaning concerns only the spirit and not the mortal flesh, it requires, also, a proper spiritual understanding of every divine promise in order to say whether the Lord keeps His promises or not.

2. The Lord always fulfills faithfully what He promises, but only in regard to the spirit and not necessarily to the mortal flesh. I shall now make a promise to you in the Lord's name, and you will then tell me whether and how you understand it. It is as follows:

3. The Lord will erect a new house, and a new city will descend from the heavens alive. And the house, like the city, will consist of many houses.

4. Those who will inhabit the new house and, simultaneously, the many houses of the new city, will be greater than the new house and the city and the many houses of the new city.

5. As they will be moving into the new house of the Lord, it will bow to them and so will the city and the many houses in it.

6. The house, however, will be small on the outside but all the larger on the inside, in order to accommodate the countless dwellers and, also, the city will be like that and all the many houses in it.

7. Happy be those who will move into this house and the city and the many houses in it! For the house and the city and the many houses in it will put on them the garment of the Lord's sonship!

8. They will at all times draw strength from the house, the city, and the many houses in the city. But he who will not dwell in that house, that city, and the many houses of the city, will be weak, and this weakness will grow and destroy him.

9. Well, friend Uron, there you have the Lord's promise which shall be fulfilled for you faithfully. But now tell me whether and how you have comprehended this purely divine and true promise?

10. However, I must tell you beforehand that you will be waiting in vain for a literal fulfillment, just as once on my earth a prophet by the name of Jonah waited in vain for the destruction of the big city of Nineveh, as predicted by the Lord. Now tell me what you think of this promise."

11. *(Says Uron after some consideration):* "Friend, from a rational point of view I can tell you about that purely divine type of promise only that it is senseless and heartless drivel. Consequently, it cannot be acceptable to our enlightened judgment.

12. May I make this quite clear? Whoever wants to make any promise or give a commandment to me and this entire people, should use words that represent their true sense — clearly and straightforwardly! However, in this world, we can never accept a promise which in all its parts amounts to unnatural, irregular nonsense.

13. For, if we are already compelled to relinquish our present privileges in order to attain the filial relationship to God, which so far we have actually never sought or desired, we want at least to be given clearly expressed promises and conditions. We want words that clearly say what we have to expect, but not words with which we are promised *white*, and then are given *black*!

14. That is surely only a fair demand! So speak in accordance with it, and we shall have no trouble in coming to an agreement. But do not come to me again with a new house built by the Lord which is supposed to be smaller than its dwellers and its interior larger than its exterior, the same as the city with its many houses! Those contradictions would disgust any one of our listeners!

15. The Lord, as the purest Supreme Spirit, has still created also the impure nature. Therefore, let Him speak with spirits in a spiritual language, but with us human beings in a natural language. Since He has created nature to be purely natural, He should also be able to speak naturally and comprehensibly.

16. The Lord, of course, has the indisputable right to speak the way He pleases, but I believe that we, too, have a right to say: 'Lord, we cannot understand this. It appears to us like nonsense, therefore, do speak with us the way You know that we can understand You.

17. Do not always hide behind clouds, but enter Your property openly. There is no need for You to be embarrassed before us, Your work, since we cannot be any different from what You want us to be.

18. You know best what language You have taught us and what we are capable of understanding. So speak in a spiritual and celestial way with Your spirits and children from the heavens, but in a natural way with us.

19. However, if You insist on speaking with us only in spiritual and transcendental metaphors, do give us first the ability to grasp them; otherwise, Your speech is neither of benefit to us nor of credit to You. What one does not understand, be it from God, a spirit, or a man, one cannot appreciate   ; and what one cannot appreciate, how can one respect it?

20. I have surely expressed myself very clearly, and now it is your turn to speak. I shall listen to you and follow you with this great people and all its descendants.''

21. *(Says John):* "You are demanding things which are quite impossible, and are even in complete contradiction to your pure, natural wisdom. How can you expect purely spiritual things to be expressed naturally? Or, if you insist on a natural language, is not that as natural as possible if I describe to you the Lord's purely spiritual and celestial promise by natural pictures which contain the spiritual and celestial, just the same as your natural body comprises your actual spiritual life?

22. What would be the benefit of a purely material word for your spirit? Would not that resemble a hollow fruit which looks on the outside as if it were something, but which has nothing inside to refresh and invigorate you?

23. Thus, I do not give you hollow words and promises from the Lord, but they are filled from the innermost core right to the

outermost shell. And the gift of comprehension will follow in due course. Tell me, what more do you want?"

24. *(Says Uron):* "Yes, friend, if the right understanding of this language will follow, I have no further objections. But tell me, what will one have to do in order to achieve this understanding?

25. What is the explanation of the new house and the city which shall descend from the heavens, and the many houses in it? Why is it alive? How can the many dwellers be bigger than the houses, or a house, or the whole city? How will the house, the city, and the many houses in it bow before their dwellers? And how will the house, the city, and the many houses in it, be smaller on the outside than on the inside?

26. All these things are most peculiar and absolutely incomprehensible to our wisdom. Give us the understanding and we shall accept even more than that, be it first, for the same reasons, quite incomprehensible to our wisdom."

182

JOHN'S INTERPRETATION OF THE PROPHETIC PICTURE. AWAKENING UNDERSTANDING AND FAITH OF THE SUN-SAGE, URON.

1. *(Says John):* "Well, listen then: The new house is the Lord's new revelation to you which He is now building in your hearts. The living city descending from the heavens is the Lord and we, His children, full of life everlasting. You are expected to go into this revelation brought to you and to make it your true life's dwelling. Then this teaching will bow and submit to you.

2. And if you will live actively in accordance with this revelation, your wisdom will grow beyond that one which we are now giving you. As a result, you will find in these few words, whose outer casing is, indeed, small, an internal contents of wisdom so infinitely great that you will hardly ever be able to fully comprehend it! And countless descendants will be dwelling in this wisdom, yet not ever reaching its outer limits.

3. Just as man has a physical house in which he lives after he has furnished it as best he can, so God's teaching is an eternal dwelling for the human spirit, in which it will live and be active forever.

4. Then the City of God and the many houses in it are identical with the one house, for he who dwells in such a house or is active in the minor wisdom of the limited Word of God, will thus enter the City of God. This means, he will enter into the fullness of divine wisdom and partake in everything that the Lord has in His house, His eternal city, and the many dwellings in it.

5. I think you now have understood me better, friend. So tell me whether you agree and whether you find this matter more acceptable now."

6. *(Says Uron, the sage):* "Yes, of course, now it looks quite different! This time I knew already with the first interpretation of the house what the idea behind all this was. I can see that these are profound correspondences, but they are conceivable. Therefore, you may continue to reveal God's will to us, and we shall accept it without any opposition."

7. *(Says John):* "Friend, I have already told you all that I had to, but now He Himself is coming! His Word will really transform you and give you true freedom. Pay good attention, for every word that He speaks represents eternal life and supreme wisdom. So listen to Him!"

183

THE SUN-DWELLERS' RECEPTION OF THE LORD. HIS WORDS TO THE SUN-SAGE. MEEKNESS, THE MEANS OF REDEMPTION FROM THE STATE OF A CREATURE. LIGHT BURDEN OF THE NEW RULES OF LIFE.

1. Now I step forward, still surrounded by Chanchah, Gella, and the three sun-daughters, who have together had a lively discussion about this world. As I appear, the sage and all the people in and outside the dwelling, prostrate themselves before Me and praise Me out loud.

2. *(The sun community):* "Hail and glory to You, the Inscrutable, the Eternal, the Infinite! Accept our deepest gratitude for this in-

conceivably great grace that You have honored us little worms of this sun, a mere particle of dust, with Your visible presence!

3. There is quite an unseemly desire stirring in our hearts, namely, that it would be utter bliss if from now on You would stay with us forever. But all we can do is give vent to this yearning in our hearts before You, the Most Holy.

4. O You, Whose feet are too holy to tread this unworthy ground, You will surely forgive us this unreasonable desire. But if You, Most Holy, deem us worthy to speak to us a few words of life, we beg You from the depths of our hearts to bestow this grace upon us. However, Your most holy will be done!"

5. *(To this most humble address, I reply):* "Rise, My dear children, and listen to Me, the eternal Father of Infinity, Who is your Father and the Father of myriads of your brothers and sisters who have come forth from Me to dwell in the infinite spaces and witness that I am their Father from eternity."

6. *(Says Uron, the sage):* "O Lord, Lord, our eyes are much too unworthy to gaze upon Your inconceivably holy countenance! Therefore, allow us to remain in this position, which, I think, is much more appropriate for worms like us before the infinite, almighty Creator."

7. *(Say I):* "Dear little children, meekness is the foremost and greatest virtue of every human heart, but it must not be exaggerated, just like any other rule of life.

8. That I am the Creator and you the created beings is a necessity for both sides, and it is a fact that cannot possibly be changed, even not for Me. If I want created beings, I have to create them the way I want them, and no creature can be asked beforehand whether and under what conditions it wants to be created. It depends on Me alone how I want a creature to be.

9. Therefore, since the creature is a necessity of My will, and since, on the other hand, My will as the basis for a creature's coming into existence and being, also, a necessity for the creature — in this particular point, neither the Creator nor the creature have any special advantage one over the other. Just as I, the Creator, am a necessity for the created being, the latter is a necessity as a point of support of My will.

10. However, the situation changes considerably when the Creator wants His creatures to become free beings of independent strength and power similar to Himself. For then, the creature enters

quite a different sphere of life. Through the free, living, powerful Word, the Creator provides the created being with a power of its own. By diligently and actively tending this, the created being can develop it to full maturity within itself and thus become a free being of independent power.

11. Only then does true meekness arise, being the sole means by which the created being can completely extricate itself from the compulsion exercised by the Creator. Then it is able to stand before Me, the Creator, as an independently living, mighty being, as if it were My second self. However, this essential meekness must still not be exaggerated, but must be just as I, a Master of all life, demand it; otherwise, it would not achieve its purpose.

12. Therefore, rise now, all of you, and look at Me. Only then shall I be able to give you the true words of life."

13. Following My words, they all rise to their feet, and Uron, the sage, speaks as follows:

14. *(Uron):* "Brothers and sisters, we have now all risen to our feet and are facing the Lord. Bear in mind Who He is before Whom we are now standing, and comprehend it in the depths of your hearts!

15. He is the Lord, the most holy, primordial Spirit of God, the almighty Creator of the infinite heavens, of all the angels, the worlds, human, and all other beings. He, the Most Holy, the Most Sublime, told us to rise before Him, and we did this with the greatest awe.

16. He promised us further words of life, and we have every reason to look forward to them, knowing that from Him, the very origin of life, we could not possibly expect anything but words of life.

17. So rejoice with me, for the Lord will speak to us words of life, words of freedom, almighty words toward a complete transformation from our state of created beings under compulsion. Therefore, open your ears and your hearts wide so that you do not miss any one of such most holy words as have never been heard in this world.

18. O Lord, Most Holy One, our hearts are prepared! We now beg You for the promised words, full of life and divine might and power, if it is Your holy will, which shall be praised forever!"

19. *(Say I):* "My beloved Uron, verily, verily, your heart gives My heart great joy! Therefore, you and your people shall receive

great joy for your hearts. This joy will remain with you forever and no one will be able to take it from you.

20. Of this you may be assured if you will adopt My teaching as well as the teaching of these, My children and messengers. This will be all the easier for you, as in the wisdom of My justice, you surpass anyway all the other peoples by far.

21. My teaching is easy enough to follow, for I, as the Creator, know best what all of you need, and what, considering your nature, would be easiest for you to observe in order to achieve your deliverance. So do not be afraid of the new burden I am going to put onto your shoulders. I assure you, it will be light and gentle enough!

22. The teaching I now give you is in short, as follows: Love Me, your Lord, God, and Father, with all your strength and, also, love each other.

23. Everyone of you should endeavor in My name to be of service to the other. No one should think himself better than his brother or sister. Thus, it will be easy for you to become My beloved children, and remain so forever.

24. Preserve also your former moral purity. Far be it from you to indulge in the lust of the flesh to which you were led by the deceit of an evil spirit only recently. Procreate in the ancient, proper, spiritual way, which was implanted in your will and not in your flesh.

25. Carnal procreation through natural cohabitation would also be possible for you, and you could thus beget children of the flesh and children of the world. But what good would it do you? You would only breed for yourselves thieves, robbers, and murderers, who would soon become more powerful than you and make you slaves of their evil desires. Therefore, take all care to protect your flesh from such evil and do not touch your daughters through whom you would be bringing true devils into the world. If you observe this, it will be quite easy for you to attain to My sonship.

26. But should you continue to lust in your flesh and that of your daughters, you would soon lose your power of spiritual procreation. Instead of your present light, etheric body, you would receive a coarse, heavy, ugly body, plagued by diseases, in which the immortal spirit would be able to move only with great effort. In addition, you would have to suffer death, which as yet you have not experienced at all.

27. Therefore, do keep to your former moral purity, and prac-

tice from now on spiritual procreation. For what the living spirit begets, remains life, which does not know death, whilst what the dead flesh begets, stays dead and has great difficulty in gaining life, for the root of the flesh is death.

28. As unlikely as a living branch grafted upon a withered stick will bring forth life will this be the case with a living spirit in the dead flesh.

29. Your will, too, would be weakened so that you could not depend on it alone to tend your gardens and till the soil. In that case, you would have to be satisfied with those plants only that grow from seeds and you would not be able, as at present, to constantly reap ripe food from the soil of your earth, but would have to wait anxiously and often impatiently for the time when one or the other fruit had ripened.

30. It would be similar with the building of your dwellings. The building materials would then be hard, heavy and brittle, and you would be unable to make them pliable, light and durable by the power of your will.

31. Thus, it now makes you happy that you are able to make visible contact with your departed brothers — that you can see them, speak with them, and even caress them. If you continued to live in your errors, all this would become impossible for you.

32. However, if you live in accordance with My teaching in the future, you will not only retain all your great privileges, but you will gain additional ones, the advantages of which will be so great that you, at this stage, could not comprehend them at all.

33. I have now told you all that you have to do. It is now up to you to accept it and act accordingly.

34. Ask your hearts and tell Me honestly what you intend to do. I give you complete freedom of decision, and I will not even look into your minds so that you can make that decision without the least interference.''

184

THE SAGE'S GOOD ANSWER.

1. *(Says the sage):* "O Lord, what You demand from us is indescribably mild, gentle and kind. We need no time to think it over, but can accept it immediately with grateful hearts.

2. O You most holy benefactor, we shall never be able to thank You enough for Your boundless kindness and grace, for Your inconceivable love in showing us such a very simple path by which we — Your creatures — can attain the supreme heavenly honor: to become Your free children! And we are even invited to think it over!

3. O Lord, Father, You eternal, Holy Spirit, if I had a thousand lives and had to surrender them in order to attain the lowest degree of Your sonship, I would truly surrender them joyfully, even if the loss of each life would cause me great torment and pain. And I am still expected to think it over whether I — and these people — will accept such great gifts of Your grace or not!

4. Most Holy Father, I shall say neither 'yes' nor 'no' with my mouth, but do graciously look into our unworthy hearts and see 'yes' written there a thousand times more fiery than is that ominous swelling of the sea over there which will soon be ripe to burst!

5. O Lord, O Father, we shall fulfill everything that You demand of us with more precision than that with which the small worlds orbit around our big earth, now sanctified by You forever!

6. We pray to Your most holy, fatherly heart not to leave us for good, but from now on to come visibly to us whenever it suits You.

7. Our love for You is now burning fiercely and our hearts would be deeply grieved if we could never see You again, most holy Father, nor hear Your fatherly voice utter such edifying words as these which have suddenly quickened our troubled hearts to an extent that we can find no words to describe Your truly divine grace.

8. Therefore, O Lord, let Your fatherly heart grant this our prayer. Your most holy will be praised forever!"

9. *(Say I):* "My children, what you are asking for has been taken into consideration already long ago. The Creator remains invisible and unfathomable only to His creatures, for they are under compulsion in the Creator's power and can never stand before Him, see Him,

or hear His voice. But it is quite different with the children whom I, as the Creator and now also the Father, have liberated through My word and teaching. Provided their hearts are within the order of My teaching, they can see Me and speak to Me whenever they want.

10. If that is not the case and their hearts are inclined toward sensuousness, if material things and vain worldly worries fill them, inactivating My word and teaching, then I can, of course, no longer be seen or heard. In such a case, the prospective child of My grace, love, and mercy, has once more donned the garb of a created being under compulsion, which it is free to do.

11. Therefore, let all of you stay in My teaching from now on! Keep your hearts in your original moral purity so that My fatherly love may dwell in them and create there a new life which is a truly free and independent one. Then you will never have to complain: 'Lord, Father, where are You? Why can't we see You or hear Your fatherly voice?'

12. Verily I say to you: All those who are active in accordance with My teaching are the ones who truly love Me. And, because of that, I shall always be among them, either visibly or audibly, teaching and educating them Myself toward becoming My children.

13. But now bring us as much food and drink as you can, for we all want to satisfy our hunger. You shall see that I will eat and drink like all of you, blessing you as well as all the brothers and sisters who are with us. So go and do as I have bidden you!"

185

THE SAGE EXPRESSES HIS JOY AND GRATITUDE. THE IN-UNDATED ORCHARDS. SATAN'S EXPULSION THROUGH PETER AND MARTIN.

1. *(Following these words from Me, the sage says, full of happy excitement):* "O Lord, O Father, full of love, kindness, glory, might, power, and holiness, this gives us the best guarantee that You will never leave us. For he who eats with us makes it clear that he will

stay with us. And so will You, as You have promised us earlier. Praise and glory to You forever, and our deepest gratitude!"

2. Now they all hurry outside to fetch plenty of select food from the gardens to display before Me.

3. But, as they step outside, a great disappointment awaits them, for the water that was forced out by the immense fiery swelling is now covering all the rich orchards. They are, therefore, unable to gather anything at all from the usual abundance of the large gardens, and they return to Me quite depressed, whereupon the sage speaks:

4. *(The sage):* "O Lord, forgive us! As You can see, the evil fiery bubble has flooded our orchards with dirty seawater so that we cannot get anything at all from them. Do drive away this evil flood, and then we shall be able to immediately comply with Your wishes."

5. *(Now I call Martin and Peter, and say):* "My brother Peter, and you, too, Martin: Go outside, fight the flood, and destroy the evil fiery bubble so that these here are not delayed in carrying out My wishes. Should the evil one disregard your first summons, command him in My name for a second and third time. If he still remains obstinate, then make stern use of the celestial power you possess. So be it!"

6. Peter and Martin bow to Me and hurry outside, together with the sage. Out there, Martin is amazed at the spectacle presenting itself, and says:

7. *(Martin):* "Ah, that low and infamous scoundrel! Tell me, brother Peter, will this semi-eternal arch-beast never cease to do evil and commit infamies?

8. You shrug your shoulders, brother, as if to say: 'The Lord alone knows that.' Yes, yes, you are right, but if that scoundrel will not obey us immediately, it will have to pay dearly for its stubbornness. The celestial power bestowed upon us by the Lord will teach it where in the future not to play its evil tricks. Shall we call out together, brother, or will you do it alone? Or shall I do it for both of us in the name of the Lord?"

9. *(Says Peter):* "You do it in the name of the Lord for both of us."

10. *(Says Martin):* "All right, I shall try! And now listen, you evil flood and you infamous fire-bubble, but mostly you ancient, most wicked Satan: Return instantly to the order laid down by the Lord or you have to expect a just and very severe divine judgment! Amen! Three times: Amen! Amen! Amen!"

432

11. This call is answered by a shrill burst of laughter and these words:

12. *(Satan):* "You wretched blowfly of a bishop! You who are ten thousand times less than nothing want to command me to withdraw! Neither God, nor all His heavens, will get me to retreat — much less you, wretched nonentity!

13. But from pure magnanimity I am warning you, and the rest of the blowfly rabble, to find some holes to hide, or else you will get a taste of the very warm dish which in a moment will be cooked in my big pot.

14. Not that I want to take revenge on you nonentities, for a mighty lion does not catch flies. What I am doing here is necessary for the preservation of my creation. But so that you nothings may not perish, flee from here and do not ever again dare to threaten me! Do not push my great patience to extremes, for woe betide you if it comes to an end!"

15. Martin is furious at Satan's insolence and cannot think in a hurry what to reply.

16. *(Peter, however, admonishes him and says):* "You must on no account be angry, for that is exactly what he wants you to be. That one must be handled in quite a different way. Look, I shall get him to withdraw immediately, and that very calmly! I shall only say to him gently: 'Satana, the Lord Jesus Christ be with you, too!' And look, already the flood is retreating, the fire-bubble is shrinking to a nothing, and he is silent and must obey my celestial power, even though he does so furiously!"

17. *(Says Martin):* "I would not have thought that that monster would give in so soon. Is that the effect of the celestial power? I imagined that to be quite different. I thank you, brother, for this truly heavenly-wise lesson. It has made me considerably wiser.

18. Look, the water has completely retreated, and there is also no trace left of the fiery swelling. Praise and glory to the Lord forever! I think now that that evil scoundrel of a Satana, or a Satan, will not so soon dare approach us again."

19. *(Says Peter):* "Never mind that, he has already been taught worse lessons than this, but in no time he was back with some new trick. It will not be long before he will cause us more trouble. However, if nothing else will drive him away, we shall just have to resort to the power from the heavens again, and the victory will be ours. Remember this well, brother, and act accordingly next time!"

20. *(Then Peter turns to the sage, who is still standing before them quite amazed, and says to him):* "Your gardens are free again. Now you may do the Lord's bidding."

21. The sage bows deeply and then hurries to the orchards to fetch food and drink.

186

WHAT IS PURE JOY TO THE CHILDREN IS A JOY ALSO TO THE HEAVENLY FATHER. A HOLY SECRET. ABOUT CHILD-LIKE SIMPLICITY.

1. Peter and Martin now return to Me at the sun-dwelling, and Martin is on the point of telling Me naively all that has happened.

2. *(Peter, however, says to him secretly):* "Brother, what is it that you want to tell the Lord that He has not known from eternity? Don't you know that the Lord is, and has forever been, omniscient?"

3. *(Martin slaps his forehead and says):* O brother, and particularly You, O Lord, do forgive me when from time to time I still relapse into a sort of earthly stupidity.

4. Naturally, You, O Lord, are omniscient and need not be told about anything at all. However, there is still in me this doubtlessly foolish earthly urge to tell You, like some friend on earth, about everything as if You did not know it already.

5. However, I am rather certain that You, Lord, will not hold this earthly foolishness against me. I shall do my best to avoid it in the future."

6. *(Say I):* "My dear son Martin, it is not quite as wrong as you imagine. For all My children like to talk — and with Me more than anything.

7. If I did not allow My children to tell Me things because I am omniscient, there would never be a word exchanged between us. But as I do not ever want to spoil a joy for them, they are welcome to tell Me about all their experiences.

8. I assure you by the faithfulness and love of My fatherly heart, that only what gives joy to My children gives also joy to Me.

The supreme bliss of My whole being is not due to My divinity, My wisdom and omnipotence, nor My omniscience, but solely to My great love for My true children who love Me, like all of you now with Me.

9. Believe Me, I was incomparably happier on the cross than when I began to create heaven and earth through My almighty Word. For, as the Creator, I was in the center of My forever inaccessible godhead as the inexorable judge, whilst on the cross I was already an affable, most loving Father, surrounded by a number of children who loved Me above everything, at least as the son of the supreme Father, not yet having fully recognized the Father in Me, because the crucified son, that is, the body of the Father, was still impeding them.

10. Verily, I assure you that a heart that loves Me truly, gives Me more than all the heavens and worlds with all their splendor. I am willing to leave ninety-nine heavens to seek just one heart that can love Me.

11. Would not a mother immediately leave a great party with music and all kinds of entertainment to hurry to her newborn child if she heard it cry and knew it was in danger of falling ill? Of the guests in her house, she has a right to expect gratitude and respect, but in the bosom of her child a heart is beating with the seed of love for its mother's heart.

12. This mother, too, would leave ninety-nine of the most splendid parties to hurry to the side of her child because of that love to come, since a tiny spark of true love ranks higher than a thousand worlds of great magnificence.

13. Now, if already a mortal mother would do this, how much more would I, Who am everything to My children — father and mother, a father in My heart, and a mother in My patience, meekness, and boundless kindness?"

14. Therefore, My dear children, do not hesitate to tell Me all that you see or hear. Give vent to the love of your hearts, for I enjoy the wonders of My creation only if you enjoy them.

15. Does not the mother know already what her little child is babbling to her? And still the first cry of 'mother' from the mouth of her darling, indistinct as it may be, will give her a thousand times more joy than the most clever speech of a sage.

16. What are the boldest thoughts about worlds, suns, peoples, and angels, compared with the call: 'Dearest Mother!' from the heart

of a child where love is sprouting? Thus it is also true with Me. What else can compare with it in significance if a loving child who has only just awakened from its inevitable preliminary slumber of judgment, calls Me truly and of its own accord: 'Dear Father'?

17. Therefore, My dear son Martin, do not let yourself be disconcerted in the future, but follow the call of your heart, and this applies to all of you. Your childlike simplicity rates much higher with Me than the supreme wisdom of a cherub. I gave an indication of this already on earth when I said to My disciples that from the beginning of this world, not one born by a woman was greater than John the Baptist, but that in the future, the lowest one in My Kingdom of Love would be greater than he.

18. But now our hosts have laid the tables and the sage is already coming to invite us to the meal. So let us listen to him attentively to see how he will present his invitation. And then we shall sit down at the large table in the exact order as arranged by him. So be it, My children!"

187

THE LORD'S LOVE-FEAST AT THE SUN-DWELLERS' TABLE.
THE RIGHT PLACE FOR THE LORD.

1. *(The sage bows deeply to the Lord, and says with the greatest possible reverence):* "O Lord, God, Father of Your children, and most holy, almighty Creator of Your infinite works, we have done our best to comply with Your will. All kinds of food and drink have been procured and the large table is laden with them. And now Your most holy will be done!"

2. *(Say I):* "That is fine! But it is now up to you, as the head of this entire community, to determine — together with the actual host — the seating order for us."

3. *(Say the sage and the owner of the house simultaneously):* "O Lord, how could we, who are just worms before You, presume to tell You where to sit? O Lord, such presumption on our part should

strike us dead forever! Everything is Yours, and the spot where You are, the foremost, the highest, and holiest anyway! And we — no, we cannot say it again!

4. O Lord, we beg of You just this one thing: that You make known to us Your most holy will in everything! We shall then receive it into our hearts as a treasure and make every effort to fulfill it faithfully.

5. Therefore, do graciously withdraw this instruction that we must determine the seating order for You and Your sublime children at the large table."

6. *(Say I):* "What you now say is good and right, and it was your love for Me that made you say it. However, if you acknowledge My will as a treasure of your hearts, you must accept the instructions given to you and the owner of this house, and comply with them. Otherwise, it is with you just a matter of saying the right thing about My will, but when I want you to do something, you think that you offend Me if you do what I ask of you. Therefore, do what I want, and you will eventually understand why I want you to do it."

7. Now the sage and the house-owner bow deeply and ponder anxiously how to handle this and where to place Me, for here one place is like the other. The so-called host's place and the prominent place of the sage are considered unsuitable by both of them, for by placing Me in one of their seats, they would only honor themselves. They ponder over this matter for a while, but cannot find a good solution.

8. At last the sage turns to Martin for his advice.

9. *(Martin shrugs his shoulders, and says):* "Well, friend, this is not easy to decide. Is there no seat dedicated to love?"

10. *(The two are quite surprised, and say):* "Friend, we have never had anything like that. What can we do about it?"

11. *(Says Martin):* "You had better arrange for such a seat now, for it might be your solution."

12. *(Ask the two):* "But what must such a seat be like?"

13. *(Says Martin):* "Go to the three daughters of the house who are now with the Lord. They will soon prepare such a seat."

14. The two sages do as suggested and put their question to the three sun-daughters.

15. *(The three sun-daughters press their hands against their hearts and say):* "Look, dearest fathers, this is the right place for the Lord of Glory. Do not try to figure it out with your heads, but draw Him

with your hearts, and then the first place you come to will be the right one."

16. Only now do the two understand what I want of them. They come to Me, bow deeply, then raise their heads again, and say:

17. *(The two sages):* "O Lord, God, Father! Praise be to You, our gratitude, and all our love! With the help of dear brother Martin and our dear daughters, we have at last recognized Your most holy will and have fulfilled it to the best of our ability.

18. O Lord, God, Father, here in our hearts we have for You, and also for all the other brothers and sisters, the best and, doubtlessly, proper place of rest. So come, You kindest, holiest, and most loving Father, with all those whom You love, and take full possession of it for all eternity.

19. For now we realize that this table with all the material dishes is nothing but an external symbol of what we are to prepare in our hearts for You, most holy and loving Father.

20. The table of our inner life is, of course, not by far as richly laden as this external one with the dishes that are to Your taste. But we beg You, O holy Father, to bless it for us so that it may become richer through deeds of love, humility, and meekness. Then we, too, will be able to receive You, O holy Father, with a true, eternal, and active hosanna!

21. Your name, which is Your almighty, holy will, be praised by us and all infinity forever!"

22. *(Say I):* "So it is right, My beloved, new children! If you remain the way you are now, everything that has been promised to you will be fulfilled in every detail. And now, let us sit down to a meal at this external table.

23. I shall bless the dishes for you and share this love-feast with you. And all who take part in it will receive Me into their hearts, and have thus embodied within them everlasting life, enlightenment, and truth.

24. So let us now all sit down to the meal. However, no one should look for a particular place to sit; instead, the first place that comes will be the best and right one for each. For, only what is within you is important; all the external things are quite immaterial. So let it be as I have said!"

25. They all now move towards the table and wait until I have taken a seat. Having chosen the nearest one, with the five maidens beside Me, then John, Peter, Martin, Borem, Chorel, and all the

others who have come with Me, the sun-dwellers respectfully take their seats on the opposite side, with Uron and Shonel (the house owner) directly across from Me.

26. In all, about 3,000 are seated at the table. I bless the foods and the beverage made from them, and invite them all to eat and drink. I eat and drink with all those who have come with Me, and the sun-dwellers eat and drink with us and rejoice in their hearts to see Me take part in the meal.

188

ABOUT THE EVERLASTING BLESSING AT THE LORD'S TABLE. SUDDEN TRANSMUTATION OF THE THREE SUN-DAUGHTERS. HINT ABOUT THE POWER OF LOVE AND ITS WONDERS.

1. The meal has soon come to an end and everybody is refreshed and praises the wonderful taste of the dishes. When all the food has been eaten, I am humbly asked by the two sages:

2. *(Uron and Shonel):* "O dear Father, should it be Your holy will, we would like to procure more food for the table."

3. *(Say I):* "That would be quite unnecessary, for once one has dined at My table, he is appeased with everlasting life. If he only absorbs Me once, he possesses Me fully for all eternity.

4. But now, My children, there is something else we have to attend to. It will be a dish, too, but a *spiritual* and not a material one.

5. These three daughters, who were the first to meet and also to recognize Me through the glowing love in their hearts, and who have since successfully passed a severe test, I will adopt as My children. However, I shall do this only if you agree, for you shall not lose the privilege to live on your earth as long as you wish. Therefore, let Me know your wishes, whether it is agreeable to you that I shorten their lives in this world and adopt them."

6. *(Say Uron and Shonel):* "Lord, You beloved, holy Father, since Your forever holy will is our life and has given us form and substance, and since we are all Yours and not our own, how, then, can we make known our will, whether it is agreeable to us or not?

7. O Lord, with all our hearts we agree with what You want to do, for now Your most holy will is our love and our life. You have originally given us these three beloved daughters, and so they are Yours, not ours, and You can take them whenever You want to. Your holy will be praised forever!"

8. *(Say I):* "Dearest children, your words please Me, for they come from your hearts, not from your mouths. And so the three, as you see them here at My side, are now no longer in their mortal, but already in purely spiritual bodies. They were transmuted in that moment when in your hearts you agreed truly and joyfully. Do you notice in them any difference between their previous and present states?"

9. *(Say Uron and Shonel):* "O Father, we do not notice any difference at all! How did this happen, and how are we to understand it? Our departed spirits look much lighter and more ethereal, whilst these three look as if they still had their physical bodies. Besides, our departed always leave their dead bodies behind, which are then taken to a certain place where they soon fully disintegrate. But the three have not left their bodies behind. How is that possible?"

10. *(Say I):* "Mind this, My children: If someone's love for Me is as ardent and mighty as the love of these three, he will be transmuted already in his body through that ardent love. His flesh is dissolved and purified by the fire of his spirit and becomes part of his spirit's own life and essence, without the body having to be completely separated from the essence of the spirit.

11. If you will follow the example of these three in your love for Me, your transmutation will be the same, and thus it will be for all those who love Me enough to leave everything for the sake of that love!"

12. *(Says Martin):* "O Lord and dearest Father Jesus, it would be wonderful if that could happen, also, on our little earth. But probably the bodies of my brothers on earth are too coarse in their material substance for such a transmutation."

13. *(Say I):* "Martin, the earth is not what the sun is, nor is the sun what the earth is. However, I am the same in heaven, on the sun, and on the earth, and thus, also, the right love in its power and effect is the same everywhere.

14. There are sufficient examples of such transmutation, also, on the earth — in ancient as well as in recent times. But this effect must be preceded by the necessary cause! Too little warmth does not

even melt wax, so how could it be expected to melt metal? Is that clear to you?"

15. *(Says Martin):* "O Lord, that is quite clear to me, for I myself was such a wax or metal. My warmth did not even suffice to somewhat soften the wax and, of course, could not possibly melt the hard metal of my matter. And there are most likely many brothers living on earth whose matter may be not only like metal, but even as hard as diamonds. There is obviously not much chance for such matter to be transmuted like that of these three heavenly daughters."

16. *(Say I):* "This is not the time to go into that, Martin. However, you should know that many things are possible to Me which seem impossible to you. I assure you, miracles take place even in the grave, unnoticed by the mortal eyes of man.

17. But now, no more about that. We have something quite different to do. An important task is waiting for us, for our enemy has once more been up to something!"

189

MARTIN SUGGESTS HOW TO RENDER SATAN HARMLESS. THE LORD'S HINT ABOUT PERMITTING SATAN'S EVIL DEEDS. MARTIN IS GIVEN AUTHORITY TO BAN SATAN.

1. *(Says Martin):* "Is that evildoer still not resting? O Lord, if I had just a spark of Your omnipotence I would attach him forever to some other globe. As long as that evil being is not fettered forever, matters will not improve on the poor globes.

2. Probably Your material creation, O Lord, has already been in existence for some decillions of earth years, or even sun years.

3. And through all those unimaginable aeons, and even prior to that, Satan has existed just as evil as at present. All the endless tribulations and punishments have failed to better him at all and, also in the future, nothing is going to change him for the better.

4. In view of these facts, I think he should be banned forever to some uninhabited globe so that the rest of creation can be left in peace.

5. For if You, O Lord, allow him a certain — even if most

restricted — freedom, matters will never improve in the whole of infinity, and we shall always have our hands full with him.

6. Naturally, You, O Lord, see the whole situation much clearer than we do and know why You have so much patience and forbearance with Satan. I have only described this matter from my point of view, and that is what I would do about it. I realize that You will be doing what is right in the light of Your everlasting love and wisdom."

7. *(Say I):* "My dear son Martin, you speak as your wisdom teaches you, and another one would speak differently again; but he who sees into the depths of My order will speak as I do.

8. What does it matter if this being destroys something, since we can make it whole again? Did you not go through his school on earth, and were you not completely destroyed? And behold, you have been restored for all eternity.

9. Tell Me, does it still worry you how you fared when you were in your state of destruction? You say no, it does not worry you at all. Well, the same will be the case with trillions of others of your kind.

10. Very many are, of course, sick and suffer a lot, but we are able to help them. And when healed, would they still suffer because of their former illness? That is most unlikely, for one whose health has been restored, soon forgets what it was like to be sick, and then he does not often show much pity for the others who are sick and suffering.

11. And that is how it is now with you. You have been healed forever and no longer know pain, fear, and terror, as does he who is still very sick.

12. Therefore, we healthy and mighty spirits must have a lot of patience with the extremely sick Satan, and that all the more so because he must serve us through his sickness.

13. Or do you really think that Satan, who is under compulsion, can do unimpeded as he pleases? There you are very wrong!

14. Satan can do only as much as he is permitted to do. Although his designs are very wicked, he cannot carry them out without My permission. And why I occasionally allow him to carry out his evil designs is still beyond your comprehension at this stage. But when you have gained more experience through the activity of love in all the heavens, many things will become clear to you which, at present, you cannot comprehend.

15. However, I will not divert you from your opinion. If you want to ban Satan in order to gain everlasting peace for all infinity, I do not mind. I shall also endow you with sufficient might so that you can master him the way you imagine it. You shall find your will fully realized, but in the end you yourself will release Satan from the fetters in which you now want to bind him. Now, do whatever you wish; I have already bestowed upon you the necessary power and might."

16. *(Says Martin):* "O Lord, as long as I have the power and You agree, I shall be able to manage that scoundrel. But, at least one brother should be with me."

17. *(Say I):* "Not only one, but Peter, John, Borem, Chorel, Uron, and Shonel shall accompany you, and that right away. For, on the central belt of the sun, opposite our feet, so to speak, on the lower half of the sun, Satan has been responsible for considerable devastation and is still carrying on with it in a great fury and pain, laboring hard. Do with him what you think right. So be it!"

18. *(Says Martin):* "I thank You, O Lord and Father, and with Your help we shall succeed! Now brothers, let us be on our way at once or that scoundrel might destroy half the sun before we reach him."

19. *(Says Peter):* "Brother, if we travel fast, we are already at our destination without having moved a foot, for in spirit motion 'here and there' is instantaneous."

190

MARTIN AND HIS COMPANIONS AT THE SITE OF DEVASTATION. SATAN IS CONDEMNED BY MARTIN. MARTIN PITIES THE WEEPING SATAN AND RELEASES HIM.

1. When Martin looks around to all sides, he no longer sees the house or the Lord; there is no one except his above-mentioned companions. He sees a scene of destruction. Smoke and columns of fire are rising from the devastated ground. Here and there, huge craters of thunderous fire have formed, out of which, from time to time,

earth-sized glowing masses are thrown into the endless space. Many of them fall back with a thunderous noise, driving water into the vast, glowing craters and causing mighty explosions of steam. And all this is effected with enough force to shoot a world like this earth for millions of miles into space.

2. *(Seeing this force from the fire-crater play with world-sized masses like the wind on earth with snowflakes, Martin says in astonishment):* "Brothers, this is beyond the comprehension of a poor human spirit! What an inconceivable manifestation of strength! Tell me, is all this the work of the archfiend, Satan?"

3. *(Says Peter):* "It is, to be sure! We certainly are not helping him, nor are others of our kind. So we can only assume that he alone is responsible."

4. *(Says Martin):* "But where is he that we might go there and make an end to his activity?"

5. *(Says Peter):* "You need not worry about that, brother. He himself will honor you with his presence! Look, there he is already rising above that immense crater, glowing like liquid ore flowing from a furnace. Prepare yourself for his reception, but make sure he does not get too close to you or you might find it a bit too warm!"

6. *(Says Martin):* "Very well, brother, he will not proceed too far."

7. *(Here, Martin addresses Satan with mighty words of judgment):* "The might of the Lord within me shall keep you banned forever on that sea of fire, for the sake of gaining everlasting peace for all created beings! And to make it quite impossible for you to inspire any evil schemes, some world-sized mountains, as hard as diamonds, will cover you hermetically. So be it in the name of the Lord!"

8. *(Martin has scarcely spoken these words, when they are already fulfilled. But, after a short while, Martin asks John):* "Brother, you had the revelation which, in your time, you wrote down for the world and which was inspired by the Spirit of the Lord. Tell me now whether what I have done to this evildoer is right or otherwise."

9. *(Says John):* "Ask your own heart and through it, the order of God. You, too, are as old as this one whom you have now banned, and until the Lord took you in hand, you were nothing but evil. If the Lord did to you what you have now done to this evil spirit that was created simultaneously with you, would you be happy about it?"

10. *(Says Martin):* "O brother, that would be the most terrible

444

thing that could happen to me. Tell me, is he also feeling pain in this state?''

11. *(Says John):* ''I assure you, the most terrible, indescribable pain! Is it now a relief to you that this one is thus tormented?''

12. *(Says Martin):* ''O brothers, no, no, he must not suffer pain! He is only meant to be inactive. Away with this cover and the heat!''

13. What Martin has ordered happens immediately, and Satan rises painfully on the still-steaming cinders of what had been the fiery crater, and weeps pitiably.

14. *(Seeing this, Martin says):* ''Brothers, notwithstanding his wickedness from time immemorial, I am now extremely sorry for the poor devil. How would it be if we now called him to us and suggested ways by which he could improve his lot? He certainly does not lack intelligence, only the will. And wouldn't it be possible to bend this will with the help of his own intelligence? What do you think about it, dear brothers?''

15. *(Says John):* ''You are quite right, for this is also the Lord's immutable will. But you will soon convince yourself that there is no other way to handle him than that of the long, continued judgment — which consists in the external, material creation. This weakens him more and more and, aware of his weakness and impotence, he must submit to a lot of things that he would never submit to while still in full possession of his strength, free and unjudged.

16. However, you may try your luck to convince yourself as to the state of his intelligence and will. Call him, and he will be here right away.''

191

MARTIN SUMMONS SATAN. SATAN TRIES TO JUSTIFY HIMSELF.

1. Martin does as suggested by John, and with the might of his will, he summons Satan, who immediately stands before him in the shape of a wretched man covered with countless burns, and he asks Martin:

2. *(Satan):* "What else do you want with me? Isn't enough that you have made me already so wretched, as you can see from may appearance? Do you want to make me even more wretched? What have I done to you? Aren't you as happy as a spirit could possibly be, and that forever? Do you hope to increase your bliss by condemning me to the greatest torment? Oh, you weak spirit, how distant you still are from perfection and comprehension of God's eternal order!

3. You look upon me as the most evil of all beings and, thus, by heavenly standards, the most cursed and detestable one. But I ask you: When did I ever abuse you as you did me? What harm have I ever done to you? You infringed God's laws on earth quite independently and did not need my enticement at all. If I had led you astray, the Lord would have made me responsible on your arrival in the spirit world, not you.

4. When, with the help of the Lord, you caught the fish from the sea of your own wickedness and thus destroying your sins, you also removed the so-called dragon, thinking that it was I. But there you were quite wrong! You yourself were that dragon in the entirety of your gross sensuousness, not I!

5. I am within you, too, of course, for I am your innermost being, except for your spirit. As once on your earth the Lord made the woman from Adam's rib, thus you and all creation have been taken out of me. However, I do not care about all that which has been taken out of me, and I do not judge it. Anyway, the Word of God is implanted through the Spirit of God in every human being, judging it constantly. If this is so, why do you keep condemning me and why are you filled with such unquenchable hatred toward me?

6. Maybe you are still angry that in my transformation I pushed you back in the presence of the Lord when you wanted to kiss me! If I had not done that, you would have been lost in the sink of your gross sensuousness. But since I did push you back, humiliating you and thus doing you the greatest possible service, do I now deserve such treatment from you?

7. As for these earthquakes which I called forth on the sun, they are necessary, or this globe would have become useless for its future destination, like an animal that keeps eating but cannot rid its body of the coarse, useless excrements. How long could it live in such a case and still be of service?

8. Like you, also I am a servant of God — although under compulsion and with a very limited freedom. I must do what I do! And

446

if I commit the least offense anywhere in the whole of infinity, I am punished severely. Of all servants, I am the lowest and most wretched one, condemned by the Creator. I can do nothing but what I have to do under compulsion, although I am in possession of the most perfect intelligence and would often rather act differently. This makes me even more miserable.

9. How would you like to be in my place and be used by the Creator for the same purpose? How would you like it if some Martin did to you what you have just done to me? I have said enough; now it is your turn to speak!"

192

MARTIN'S CLEVER REPLY TO SATAN. SATAN'S ARROGANT ANSWER TO MARTIN'S PROPOSITION.

1. *(Says Martin):* "You poor wretch, as I have listened to you patiently before all these dear friends and witnesses, I now expect you to listen patiently to me. I tell you in the name of the Lord that we have actually come to either help you or to judge you forever.

2. You spoke a lot about your most unfortunate position in which you have been for aeons of great cycles of creation, but since I am not a credulous type, I tell you honestly that I do not believe even a third of what you have said.

3. That you are miserable — sometimes even inconceivably wretched — I well believe. As for the reasons for your great misery, I do not believe them at all! I am too well acquainted with the Lord's endless kindness, love, patience, meekness, and His inconceivable affability to us, His created beings. How, then, could I believe that He created you for the worst misery in all infinity, when there is not a being anywhere who could accuse Him of such terrible harshness?

4. When I arrived in this world, I was most miserable, and I suffered hunger and thirst and was plagued by the most terrible boredom which turned minutes into millennia. But all that was only meant to arouse me and prepare me for the kingdom of the eternal glory of God. In this kingdom, I realize more and more how all

these apparent states of misery were nothing but an expression of the Lord's great love, and only served to purify me and make it possible for me to absorb that love of the Father in its fullness.

5. Things would have improved much quicker for me if I had shed my bishop's arrogance sooner. I could have easily done it, as I now realize, but I was stubborn and held on to it, for it stimulated me and my extreme sensuousness. And, as a result, I had to suffer – not due to the Lord's will, but solely to my own. For that I shall not ever hold you responsible, and even less the Lord's will.

6. Thus, I am firmly convinced that none but you yourself is responsible for your misery. If at this moment you were prepared to return to the Lord as a truly repentant son to your holy, eternal Father, I am willing to be in your stead the most wretched being in all infinity if He did not come immediately to meet you with loving embrace to welcome you as His beloved son with the greatest festivities in all the heavens.

7. Do that, my poorest brother, and your misery will come to an end in a moment! I also ask your forgiveness for often being harsh and making you responsible for all my sins. I now take the full responsibility and shall be your everlasting friend if you will accept my proposition and act accordingly.

8. I admit my unworthiness to make such a proposition to you, the first and greatest spirit from God, knowing that even now in your judgment, you possess endlessly more wisdom and strength than I, a sheer nothing compared with you, will ever be able to comprehend. But, because I respect you so much in your greatness as God's first created, I wish, like all the heavens, that you would at last return to God, your Father.

9. Eternities have passed during which you used all means at the disposal of your profound wisdom and immense might to outdo the eternal, almighty God; however, you not only failed, but your efforts only made you more miserable, weaker, and poorer. You gained nothing but ever-increasing, consuming wrath against God.

10. Doubtlessly you have had countless propositions like mine and probably better ones, but they were fruitless because of your incomprehensible obstinacy. But, never has a more insignificant messenger stood before you with this plea; therefore, make an exception this time and turn back with me!"

11. *(Says Satan):* "You have now really spoken very nicely, and I, therefore, forgive you all your rudeness and harshness towards me.

However, as concerns your plea, which is only too familiar to me by now, I shall only be able to answer that when in all the infinite spaces neither a sun nor a hard earth will be holding my being in fetters.

12. My ego is the immense universe, and this is under judgment. How can I free myself from the judgment in my entirety? What you see here before you is only the innermost living core of my — for your understanding — endless being. If you can give me back what I have lost, then I shall follow you immediately."

13. *(Martin stares at Satan for a while, then says earnestly):* "Yes, all of it for sure, you poor, first-created of God, so follow me!"

14. *(Says Satan):* "What guarantee can you give me for the truth of your promise?"

15. *(Says Martin):* "The endless love of God, your Father! Isn't that sufficient for you?"

16. *(Says Satan):* "Friend Martin, you mean well in accordance with your limited notions, and your guarantee is good and acceptable for spirits who, like you, are transient and limited. But whether this guarantee can suffice me who am an infinite spirit like God — even if from God — that is quite a different question.

17. It would be easy enough to find food for a gnat, not so easy for an elephant, and much harder for the huge leviathan who needs mountain-size morsels to satisfy its hunger.

18. Thus, God's for you boundless love is more than sufficient to satisfy finite beings forever. But for an infinite spirit who is equal to God, it could only suffice if it had to satisfy him exclusively.

19. But to satisfy an infinite number of beings, each of which will eventually need an infinite amount of love, there, even the boundless love of the Godhead must have its limits, for how could it maintain two infinities out of its one infinity? That would be simply impossible!

20. I even now need still a lot, physically and morally, throughout the universe which is a hard prison for me. How much more I would need after having regained my freedom.

21. I assure you, and all those present here. For your sake I do not return; for when I do, all of you will perish. I alone know how great God is, what He possesses, and what He can give. I realize that it is impossible for Him to keep me and you simultaneously. Therefore, I prefer to remain in this miserable state so that you, as my

449

children, can enjoy the glory that is due to me alone, but which I sincerely do not begrudge you.

22. I do realize that God is endlessly kind; but it is that endless kindness that makes Him too extravagant. If out of love for you, my children, I would not check Him or limit Him in His extravagant magnanimity, He soon might have to return to the earth to find a livelihood among His callous creatures.

23. So you see that God's endless love cannot serve me as an acceptable guarantee. You will have to give me another more suitable than that!"

193

MARTIN'S FURTHER GOOD PROPOSITION FOR THE SALVATION OF SATAN. SATAN'S OBJECTIONS. THE ORDER OF CREATION BEFORE AND AFTER THE LORD'S INCARNATION.

1. *(Says Martin):* "My very poor friend, you have given us logical reasons why God's infinite love cannot suffice you, yourself an infinite spirit. However, things would improve for you quite inconceivably if you would demand a bit less and were satisfied with what each of us has — so enormously more than you have at present in your wretchedness. And, in that case, God's infinite love should be a sufficiently powerful guarantee for your conversion.

2. Actually, you are at present as good as nothing; you possess nothing, and have to suffer a lot. But if you agreed to my proposition, you would at least become what we are and would not need more than we. Would not that be better for you than your present state?

3. You say that you are making an immense sacrifice out of love for us, your actual children, which, however, none of us could ever demand of you. Could you not rather make a sacrifice inasmuch as waiving the condition for your conversion that you get back everything and instead be satisfied with only as much as everyone of us has? It would not make any difference to the endless generosity of God, nor would it reduce the contents of the Father's great storehouse.

4. What do you say to that? I think it could be a possibility."

450

5. *(Says Satan):* "My dear Martin, you speak in accordance with your natural, limited understanding, but since you do it in a nice way, I can have the necessary patience with you. But think about what is possible and what would be absolutely impossible. How could I become smaller than I am? Do you still not understand that the entire infinite universe is filled with nothing but my indivisible being?

6. Or would you, in order to reduce your requirements, have your feet, hands, one limb after another, amputated? Without feet you would need a much shorter garment; without hands, you could save the sleeves; and even your stomach would need less food with fewer limbs to maintain. This calculation would be quite correct, but, tell me, whether you would find it satisfactory?"

7. *(Says Martin):* "Poor friend, that will not be necessary for you as it wouldn't be for me, where the Lord is concerned. Since even a human being must leave behind its body, which for a while represented its whole being, you, too, could let go your material substance and like us be satisfied with the spiritual alone. For then the Lord would surely make the wisest and best arrangements for your large universe-body, just as He does for our small physical bodies. We are completely happy with this noble spiritual body; why couldn't you be too?"

8. *(Says Satan):* "Dear friend, you keep talking from the viewpoint of your limited understanding. That is because you are incapable of lifting your eyes as I do, above and beyond the universe, which is my being. Your will is good and so is your heart. But your wisdom is no more than a shining dot in infinity.

9. Do you not understand that every being must have a basis, a support, to enable it to come into existence and continue? Every force, to be able to express itself as such, must have a counterforce. Two forces rising against each other find resistance in each other and, thus, express themselves by polar counteraction. Only through such a conflicting manifestation of two forces can something be called into being.

10. God is the positive, highest force, whilst I, as the negative, lowest force, am quite as infinite as God's highest. God would be quite as incapable of expressing Himself without me, as I would be without Him.

11. If I now followed your advice to return to the Godhead and as a result merged with it into one positive force, tell me, would not

all existing creation out of God, as well as that out of me, disintegrate into nothing? And wouldn't it revert to its origin within us as a mere idea, relinquishing substance, being, and consciousness?

12. Speak now and convince me that there are other ways for the continuance of all things. Then I shall follow you!"

13. *(Says Martin):* "My wisdom is not yet profound enough for that, you know, and I believe also my brothers here will not yet have lifted their eyes above and beyond infinity. However, I have my strong doubts that the Lord has to rely on you for supporting His already existing creation.

14. I believe that prior to His incarnation the old earth and the old heaven were founded on you, and that was when you were the negative pole. However, when the Lord Himself took the flesh, He discarded you as a polarity and, instead, set up a much better one within Himself — worthier of Him and more durable for all eternities. Thus, He once more firmly cemented His creation together which, due to your weakness, was threatening to fall apart. In this way, as it were, the old passed and was replaced by something completely new.

15. You may have been a necessity before the incarnation, but since then, you are neither more nor less than any other spirit, and in no way are you necessary to keep things going. I think you should now realize this fact and do as I have proposed."

16. *(Says Satan, now somewhat more annoyed):* "Friend, you are once more getting a bit pert; however, your limited wisdom is your excuse.

17. Look, you shortsighted spirit, who was it who helped the Godhead to establish a new creation? Was not I the one who had to persecute Him, who tempted Him, and finally even had to help in killing His flesh to enable Him to absorb my negative polar substance of pain and suffering into His positive divine nature?

18. That nature in God is now what you call His endless love, which, as I have already mentioned, may suffice you finite beings, but not me who am endless and infinite. And now less than ever, since there are still so many myriads of suns and earths firmly established which are my substance.

19. Only when all matter has been dissolved as a negative polarity and has merged into God, will my opposition become quite unnecessary, and then, as a spirit stripped of all my substance, I shall be able to do what you are now asking of me.

452

20. Then I shall become smaller than I am now; I shall not need any more to keep me than you do, and I shall be quite unable to ever again endanger your beatitude. But, at this stage, it would be most detrimental to all of you if I now turned back and followed you to the Lord. I, therefore, will have to abide in my present state for a few more aeons of earth-years before I shall be able to do as you desire without endangering all of you.

21. Oh friend, oh son, the endless sweetness of the heavens is only too well known to me, and so is the terrible harshness of my present state! But what can I do?

22. A fully grown oak tree can no longer be bent, and even less I, as the original 'oak' of all creation. But eventually it should become possible that your kind wish is fulfilled.

23. You should now rather look towards the earth, where things are in a very bad state; that would be of more benefit to you than endeavoring to achieve the still quite impossible! What do you think about that, my dear son, Martin?"

MARTIN'S REPEATED EFFORT TO MAKE SATAN UNDERSTAND THE ABSURDITY OF HIS OBSTINACY.

1. *(Says Martin):* "Poor friend, it may all be as you describe to me with kind patience. However, like all blind persons, I am rather sceptical -- or maybe more ignorant than sceptical. Therefore, I simply cannot understand why all creation should be unable to exist without you. All the more so, since through your conversion to God, you would not cease to exist, but on the contrary, you would become endlessly more perfect in your being.

2. The Lord has given me the realization that you must be preserved at all costs because, according to the divine order, the preservation of the natural worlds and beings depends on you. However, what do the transient substances matter?

3. Once you have been won as perfected — which depends entirely on your will -- all matter will have become quite superfluous anyway. Since matter is nothing else but your obstinacy under judgment, with your conversion and perfection it would immediately

disintegrate in accordance with the Lord's wish, and be perfected in its purely spiritual substance which, at present, your judged obstinacy is holding imprisoned and gagged within matter.

4. However, our spiritual substance, as well as the new earth and new heaven, have really nothing to do with you, for the polarities for their eternal existence are to be found in the Lord alone in the form of love and wisdom or goodness and truth.

5. You are right in advising us to concentrate our attention on the earth, which is, indeed, in a bad state. But I maintain, my poor friend and brother, that the moment you turn back, not only the earth, but all creation, will regain its original divine purity and perfection. All evil will cease, and all that has still to walk the hard path of the flesh and matter under judgment, will be perfected in the moment of your conversion.

6. For, what else is the path of the flesh if not a laborious separation from you and a troublesome rise from your state of judgment. When the judgment has ended for you, there would not be any need for matter or the difficult way of the cross for the flesh.

7. I am convinced to have spoken the full truth with my best intention and will. Follow my advice and you will see that the result will be quite different from what you now imagine."

SATAN REPLIES TO MARTIN AND REPROACHES HIM WITH ARROGANCE.

1. *(Says Satan):* "Friend, at least you present your shortsightedness concerning me in a nice and calm manner; otherwise, your understanding of these things and circumstances is still extremely backward.

2. I now see that you have not really understood a word of what I told you. Therefore, it would be futile to endeavor to reveal to you the deeper relation between God and me in more detail. You would comprehend it even less than what I have told you so far.

3. So I think we should part in peace and each attend to his own important business. For, without understanding each other, our

futile discussions will never bring results. I do understand what you want, but you do not and you cannot understand what is possible and what is not.

4. But, because of your very nice attitude, I shall tell you something that you will find very useful. You, like all your world, regard me as the basis for all principal evil originating in my extreme arrogance. If self-confidence, the awareness of your existence, self-determination of your power, and the activity resulting from it, deserve this insulting term, I accept it. But what is that within you, friend Martin, if you want to accomplish my conversion in order to be praised by the Lord and make for yourself the greatest name in all the heavens?

5. With your tongue, you have gained a victory over the dwellers in this world, and the Lord has highly praised you for it. He has treated you with distinction before all your brothers of equal or even greater merit, and now, by winning a victory over me, you probably want to attaint for yourself the greatest fame in heaven. You want to hear yourself praised thus: 'Look, what myriads of the mightiest spirits and even God Himself have failed to achieve, there, the weak Martin has gloriously succeeded!'

6. Do you think, Martin, that such an aspiration is anything but the greatest hidden arrogance, compared with which mine is nothing? Abandon this from deep within you, and only then we might be able to continue our discussion. For, in my true shape, I am light, and we can only talk with each other effectively if you are quite pure. So go and cleanse yourself of all impurity and then return to talk to me, the original light from eternity!"

MARTIN, JOHN, AND SATAN. MARTIN'S HONESTY AND JOHN'S WISDOM AND FIRMNESS. SATAN'S SPIRIT OF CONTRADICTION AND CRITICISM OF JOHN. JOHN'S ANSWER.

1. *(These words from Satan have startled Martin considerably, all the more so because he really feels a bit guilty. When his mind has somewhat calmed down, he turns to John and says):* "Dear brother

whom the Lord has filled with wisdom like none other, what do you think about this? Should I believe Satan in this one point? I do have an innermost feeling that he is not quite wrong."

2. *(Says John):* "Leave this matter now alone, for where we have never been able to achieve anything, also your efforts will be in vain. Bid him to keep peace in the name of the Lord, and let us then go home to the Father. Let Him do with Satan as He pleases, and that will be best."

3. *(Says Satan):* "And just because you have given my Martin such advice, I will not be told by him to keep my peace. I will do him the honor of going with him before the Lord, in order to discuss this matter — which none of you understands — with the Lord Himself. Now, go home and I shall follow you of my own free will."

4. *(Says John):* "Unfortunately, we know your intentions and that you are never more dangerous than when you don the garb of highmindedness. Therefore, if you have the courage, you will have to find your own way to the Lord. We are not commissioned to take you, the Lord's greatest enemy, with us.

5. It would be quite different, of course, if you had followed Martin's sound advice and returned to the Father as a repentant, prodigal son. In that case, all of us would have welcomed you as a companion. But you are of no use to us the way you are.

6. However, if you want to see the Lord, you know the road to Him only too well. But, as you now are, you can never ever walk in our company. So be it, in the name of our and your God and Lord!"

7. *(Upon these words, Satan scowls and says):* "If the Lord will send me messengers like you again, I swear by all that is sacred to me that I will not turn back in eternities — even if the Lord judged me with the fire of all the central suns.

8. Martin might achieve something with me, but John, Peter, and Paul, not ever! Mind these words, you hard, merciless lout of a disciple of Christ! Do you think I am scared or intimidated by you and your words because you are John, the scribbler of the Gospel and the Revelation? You are quite mistaken if you do!

9. A blowfly created by me has much more worth to me than a thousand prophets like you! You should be ashamed of your hard-heartedness towards those who are the same Creator's work, even though miserable and wretched!

10. The Lord Himself has characterized you most appropriately

when, in His great parable of the prodigal son, He said: 'When the father gave a great feast for the poor prodigal son who had returned home, and the other sons and children heard about it, they came and said angrily: You have never given a feast for us who have always been faithful. But when this depraved son returns, he who had hurt you so much that heaven and earth shook from horror, you give him your signet ring and prepare a feast for him!'

11. I need not remind you of the father's reply to this complaint, for you will remain unchanged — hard-hearted and merciless like all the rest of your rabble.

12. Martin, however, is an exception, although, since influenced by you, he was rather rude for a while. But he improved, and the talk with him was the first blissful moment for my heart since unimaginable aeons. Therefore, I shall always hold him in high esteem, and if ever anyone could achieve something with me, it would be Martin. You others can save yourselves the trouble forever! Go now, and I will stay here!"

13. *(Says John):* "You have wronged me very much, because it was I who reproved Martin and caused him to set you free after he had, through his might, banned you forever to that steaming crater of fire and even covered you up with glowing mountains. Considering what I did then for you, how can I be a hard and merciless lout?"

14. *(Says Satan):* "Friend, do not talk to me of your charity! What Martin did was done out of thoughtlessness. And, upon realizing that it was wrong, he immediately righted his thoughtless action. But you are the way you are, and you will never change your outlook — be it right or wrong! Because of this, I hate and despise you more than my worst suffering and torment. To you, Martin, my respect, but to the rest of you, my everlasting and deepest contempt! Now go away or I shall cause an uproar as has not been seen in all infinity as yet!"

15. *(Says John):* "We are not here to take orders from you, but to stop your evil activity. Therefore, we shall leave when it is the Lord's will, not when it suits you! If you wish to cause an uproar, you may try, and you will soon find that our power over you is greater than yours over us.

16. Since you ordered us to leave here immediately, we could give you quite a different order in the name of the Lord. But we do not want to repay evil with evil, and we advise you to keep quiet if you do not wish or are unable to follow Martin's call. This is the final

short period of time you have left for your conversion. If you do not make use of it, you shall be under the most severe judgment forever.

17. You referred to the parable of the prodigal son in order to accuse us of hardness of heart. However, I assure you that the prodigal son will return also without you, namely, in the many devout brothers who will be standing before God with one mind, like one man. But you shall be cast into the everlasting fire of God's judgment like the rich spendthrift if you do not follow Martin's call very soon."

18. *(Says Satan):* "The Lord may do as He pleases, but so will I. I shall prove to Him and all of you that the Lord can scatter all infinity with His might like chaff, but my heart and will shall forever defy His omnipotence and wisdom with the hardest, invincible defiance. Now do what you want and I shall do what I want!"

19. *(Says Martin):* "Oh brother, as I can now see, all our efforts are in vain, so let us go. I now realize beyond doubt that nothing more can be achieved with this Satan."

20. *(Says John):* "Dear Martin, if he had not ordered us to go home, we would already have done so. But his will must never determine our actions; therefore, we shall delay our departure for a while. If we left now just because he told us to, he would have achieved a triumph over us, and if that happened, we would be in trouble. So we will, and must, wait for a while and tidy up this area. So be it!"

197

SATAN'S FURY. MARTIN'S FEAR AND JOHN'S SERENITY. CHILDREN OF GOD ARE INDEPENDENT OF SATAN.

1. When Satan notices that the party does not leave as bid by him, he becomes furious deep within, and this state of fury renders also his external appearance most frightening.

2. *(Noticing this, Martin says to John and his other companions):* "Friends, things obviously do not look good with the prodigal son. A terrible secret fury is flashing from his eyes, he is frowning, and the distorted corners of his mouth forebode his intention of taking terrible revenge.

3. Haven't you been a bit too harsh with him, brother John? I must admit that notwithstanding the power of the Lord within me, I am getting rather afraid, although I am sure that he cannot harm us in any way. Look at the faces of Uron and Shonel, they are as scared as can be. For the sake of the Lord, how will this end?"

4. *(Says John):* "Things do look most threatening! But you must not be afraid of him. Fear of him is a sort of subordination of our might under his power. That, too, would be a triumph over us on his part, which we must never allow. If we did, his evil polarity would draw us to such an extent that it would be extremely difficult for us to free ourselves from his power.

5. He treated you in a most humane way, making you considerable promises. However, he did this not with a view to fulfilling them because of your civility, but only in order to trap you as an inexperienced newcomer to this realm.

6. However, I saw through his nice scheme and prevented it, and as a result he is now so furious that he would crush us in his rage if he felt equal to our might. But, knowing only too well how weak and impotent he is compared with us, he has become so terribly furious.

7. We must take no notice of it and he will soon show a different face."

8. *(At this moment, Satan stamps his foot with such a force on the ground that the earth shakes in a wide radius, and then he says threateningly to John):* "You wretch! Have you not found enough satisfaction in my misery? If I am nothing and of no value in the infinite creation, destroy me altogether with your might, if you dare! But watch out that with my destruction you do not destroy yourself as well!

9. But I can see only too clearly how, for your own sake, you are anxious to preserve me. You are a wretched coward, terribly scared of me because you would not find my work as enjoyable as that of the soft heavens. You are afraid of my triumph over you, and so you tell the others not to fear me.

10. "Oh, you simpleton, which fear is worse: vain fear of me or the fear of my triumph over you? Don't you see that such a fear is a greatest triumph for me. Tell me, am I not right?"

11. *(Says John):* "A thousand times, no! There is a vast difference between fear of a behavior through which one might become as absurd as you, and a silly fear of your individual spirit. The first one could be most detrimental to a pure spirit, whilst the latter

could not possibly affect a spirit who is strong in the Lord, and it could not harm weaker spirits because they are always surrounded by mighty guardian spirits.

12. Therefore, I warned Martin mainly of such a giving-in to your will, the result of which would be your triumph over us, and this could endanger even me. But I did not warn him for fear of you yourself, because you have no power to oppose us, except that of falsehood and persuasiveness.

13. That in your stupidity and pride you are of the opinion I must be afraid of you and dare not destroy you for fear that with you I might destroy myself, is one of your mighty errors, Satan. My preservation, as well as that of any of us, is quite as independent of you as is the Lord's, for we now live forever in the Lord, and the Lord through His fatherly love in us.

14. In view of this, you will understand that I could destroy you completely without the least harm to my own existence. That I refrain from doing so is not due to my love for you, nor my fear of you, but solely to the Lord's endless love and patience, which also dwell in my heart.

15. If it depended on me alone, the whole of infinity would have peace from you, for I, John, would have made an end of you long ago. I assume that you understand my very blunt words!"

16. (Says Satan): "Indeed, I do! But, unfortunately, I have again found to my disgust that you, the so-called pure heavenly spirits, have the most impure and unworthy notions and ideas of God!"

17. (Says John): "Why so? Tell me. That seems to be quite a novel trap of yours. We would like to hear your argument."

18. (Says Satan): "You ask why so. Does that sound peculiar and new to your so-called heavenly pure ears? Wait just a moment and I will give you a light that will keep you wondering forever. But if you want an explanation, be good enough to first answer briefly the question I will now put to you.

19. I give you in advance the most sacred assurance that if you are able to accuse me of an untruth, I shall forever submit freely to anything you might demand of me. If not, I stay as I am, and you and your companions may leave here unharmed and unmolested by me so that you can gain in your heavenly homeland a purer and worthier concept of God."

20. (Says John): "Well then, ask! But do not come again with

your old only-too-familiar questions, for then our discussion will soon have to come to an end."

21. *(Says Satan):* "All right, this will mean to be or not to be. I shall see how far you will get with your wisdom! The question is: 'Is God ubiquitous or not?' "

198

DISPUTE BETWEEN JOHN AND SATAN ABOUT GOD'S UBI-QUITY AND THE ORIGIN OF EVIL. SATAN AS SUCH A TRIUMPH OF THE CREATOR'S. JOHN'S PROOF OF THE TRUE DELIVERANCE FROM EVIL.

1. *(John replies):* "Certainly! God is infinite in His divine essence and will, therefore also ubiquitous. However, as the personified God and true Father of His children, He dwells only among His children in the heaven of heavens."

2. *(Says Satan):* "All right, so you irrevocably acknowledge the ubiquity of God. Then be also good enough to tell me whether God is supremely wise and good and, consequently, all-knowing and all-seeing. And does He, thanks to His supreme wisdom and infinite goodness, always choose the best and most suitable means to achieve His purpose?"

3. *(Says John):* "Certainly! For God Whose essence is the purest love, can never be anything but supremely good and wise. I already know what you are aiming at, but go on asking. I shall answer every one of your questions."

4. *(Satan continues):* "Has God created all things in the whole of infinity, or is there any other god who has mixed what you call evil and bad in between the works created by your good God? Or is it possible that the one good God could have created both good and evil?"

5. *(Says John):* "In the beginning of all existence was the Word, and the Word was with God, and the Word was God, and all things were made by Him. This Word Itself became flesh and dwelt among the created flesh, but the darkness did not comprehend It.

6. The Lord Himself came to His own into His property, but His own did not recognize the light, the learned of the world did not recognize the Word, nor the children their eternal, holy Father. For you alone kept all minds captive so as to prevent them at all costs from knowing Him Who from eternity has been, is, and will be, all in all.

7. Since God is the sole Creator of all things and there is no-where any other god besides Him, it is obvious that whatever originates from Him cannot be anything else but good and perfect.

8. He created all spirits as pure and good as He is Himself. How-ever, He gave the spirits absolute freedom of the will He had instilled into them, enabling them to do whatever they chose. And, in order to teach them how to use these gifts, He gave them simultaneously with the free will laws sanctified by Him, which they were free to observe or not.

9. And they all observed these laws, except for one. This one, who was also the first created and endowed with the greatest light of knowledge, rejected God's laws with his free will and opposed them, disregarding the consequences.

10. Thus, this spirit, with his free will instilled into him by God, reversed the divine order within him; he became opposed to those spirits who had not misused their free will and in himself evil and bad. And then, compelled by his own adverse nature, he had to leave the company of the other spirits and keep at a distance until such time when he will turn back voluntarily and re-enter the order the Lord has given to all spirits without exception, namely, the order of love.

11. To God and all of us who are now pure celestial spirits, you, the spirit who became opposed to God's order, are not evil since you cannot ever harm us. Evil and bad you are only against yourself, for while you remain in your opposition, you harm no one but yourself.

12. You tried to set a trap for me, assuming that I would be compelled to say that God had created also evil, considering that you, as an evil spirit, are God's creature too. But, as far as thinking is con-cerned, I am an eternity ahead of you, well aware of the cunning of your wisdom. Therefore, I can only advise you to save yourself the trouble of any further questions with a view to trapping me, for in rivalry with me, you will not ever have a chance to win.

13. I can see it in your mischievous eyes that you would have liked to prove to me at the end of your questions that we have the

most impure concept of God, quite unworthy of Him, and that we ourselves would have had to admit the existence of either two Gods — one good and the other evil — or a God of hybrid character and, consequently, a bungler of His works. However, this is not so, but exactly as I have just described to you.

14. "God would, indeed, be imperfect if He had not endowed His created spirits with a completely free will, but instead only with a will under compulsion. However, as for that, you yourself provide the best counter-evidence. The fact that you, although under severe judgment, are in a position to oppose the Creator as long as it suits you, proves only too clearly how free and perfect God has created all spirits, including you. You, too, can with perfect freedom act in accordance with the Lord's will, like all of us.

15. I assure you that there is no other spirit in all the heavens who demonstrates God's infinite perfection more clearly than you! You are, so to speak, the Lord's greatest masterpiece and, therefore, cannot be bungled work where the Lord is concerned.

16. This makes it quite clear that you could never trap me with your absurd opposition, for whatever you know, I have known for a long time. And that is another proof of God's endless perfection, that I — a spirit freed from your substance — am capable of resisting you mightily in all your intentions.

17. What do you say now? Do you have any more tricky questions ready? Then out with them, and I shall answer everyone of them properly!"

18. This has startled and considerably embarrassed Satan, for he cannot think of what to reply to the mighty John.

199

JOHN'S INVITATION TO SATAN TO POSE FURTHER QUESTIONS. SATAN'S MEGALOMANIA AND ARROGANT ANSWER. JOHN ORDERS SATAN TO LEAVE THE SUN. SATAN BEGS FOR LENIENCY.

1. As Satan does not pose further questions and the expression on his face looks more foolish and perplexed than evil, John continues:

2. *(John):* "What about it, Satan? Have you no further questions? Just now I would simply love to practically bury you in answers! However, you are silent, and so I must assume that you have just about come to an end with your wisdom and that your paternal inheritance, which you gained by force, has been wasted to the last coin! What have you to say to that?"

3. *(After a while, Satan replies shrilly):* "There you are quite wrong! Rest assured, my wisdom is still quite infinite. I could still pose an infinite question, but how could you — a finite spirit — ever be able to answer it? Realizing that it would be quite impossible to expect satisfaction from you, I prefer to be silent. A dewdrop may quench the thirst of a gnat, but it would scarcely suffice a central sun! You might be able to understand more or less what I am hinting at with this parable."

4. *(Says John):* "Oh yes, it does not give me a headache at all, but it tells me even more than you think. I see from it that when your imagined wisdom comes to an end, you have immediate recourse to your old, deceitful arrogance only to satisfy yourself. But that will not do any longer!

5. Measure me and then yourself and you will easily convince yourself as to the range of infinity for each of us. I think that an infinity that can be measured is not worth very much, and this also applies to your infinity as well as mine. I assure you that he who considers himself infinite, has no idea what infinity really is. Or he may be a complete fool and quite incapable of comprehending it in all its aspects.

6. You were foolishly talking about an infinite question. Would you ever come to an end with it? Now then, if your question would never come to an end, when is the equally infinite answer supposed to begin? You must realize that such bombastic words from you are nothing but the most absurd twaddle! Or can't you really see that?"

7. *(Says Satan):* "I see everything if I want to. But some things I simply refuse to see because it does not suit me, a lord of glory. Do you understand my language?"

8. *(Says John):* "Of course I do, for it is an old — and to all of us — a most familiar language. However, we do not intend to listen to that language, but order you now, in the name of the Lord, to leave this world with your central substance and return to the earth, to the place assigned to you. If there you will keep the peace, there shall be no further suffering for you. However, if you are restless and mis-

chievous, it will be solely your own fault should you get a taste of
the severity of the Lord's wrath!"

9. *(Says Satan):* "Dear friends, don't do that to me! I loathe the
earth like a nauseous carrion. Allow me to stay here. I promise you
to stay forever quiet like a stone. But do not expel me from here!"

200

SATAN IS ENTANGLED IN CONTRADICTIONS. SATAN, THE CORRUPTER AND SEDUCER. A NEW PEACE COVENANT BETWEEN JOHN AND SATAN.

1. *(Says John):* "Listen, you say that you loathe the earth like
a nauseous carrion. That is most peculiar since it is none but you
who, with your profound wisdom and outstanding skill, made the
earth into what it is now. How, then, can you find the masterpiece of
your own wisdom so nauseous?

2. Thanks to the Lord's grace, I, too, have called into existence
many things, but I have never had any reason to be ashamed of those
works, let alone loathe them.

3. The same applies to my numerous heavenly brothers and
sisters, but none of us have ever boasted with supreme divine wisdom
and might like you. The only thing we ever praise is the Lord's grace.
All our works are pleasant before Him and magnificent in every
respect, and we have every reason to rejoice in them. But how is it
possible that your exceedingly wise creations are loathsome to you?"

4. *(Says Satan):* "Is the earth my work? Isn't it written: 'In the
beginning God created the heaven and the earth'? How, then, can the
earth be my work?"

5. *(Says John):* "Well, well, how you keep changing your state-
ments! You have repeatedly maintained not only to be the real
creator of the earth and the whole of infinity, but that all that is
actually you, your substance.

6. Thus, I can well remember that great time of times when you
had the nerve to lead the Lord, your God and Creator, to the summit

465

of a high mountain and say to Him: 'Behold, all that is mine! I shall give you all the kingdoms of the world if you will fall down and worship me'! If at that time you called the earth yours, how can it now be the Lord's? Tell me, when did you lie, then or now?"

7. *(Says Satan):* "I beg you not to shame me so mightily. I admit that I have lied — then as well as now — to a certain degree, but only because it is part of my nature. I also admit that it is largely my fault that the earth is now so loathsome. But do spare me now these reproaches and let the matter drop. In the future you will never again have reason to be angry with me poor devil."

8. *(Says John):* "What guarantee will you give that we can believe you?"

9. *(Says Satan):* "You know that of old it was always claimed that there is no truth in me. If so, what could serve as a guarantee for you? Your will shall be my judgment if I go back on my word. That is the only guarantee I can give you."

10. *(Says John):* "Not mine, but the Lord's will shall be your judgment; so stay here as requested."

11. *(Now John summons all those present and says to them):* "Brothers, you realize that a covenant between two parties, of whom one is honest but the other suspected of dishonesty, requires witnesses so that the covenant can become legal. You have heard and seen all that has taken place here, and you know for what purpose. The Lord sent you here as witnesses, just as Martin and I had to come because of the Word and conciliation, as well as to bear witness. Therefore, all of you shall remain forever a living testimony of what you have seen and heard here. And your testimony shall be true everlastingly before the Lord and all His heavens and His children!"

12. *(Say the witnesses unanimously):* "Yes, as sure as our lives are out of God!"

13. *(Says John to Satan):* "Our covenant has now been ratified and sanctioned by eternally true witnesses. Therefore, keep your promise. But woe betide you — *three* times woe - if you don't keep your promise, as you have shown on all previous occasions!"

14. *(Says Satan):* "Why all the fuss? Show me a place where I can stay and I assure you that if you return in a decillion of sun years, you will find me exactly as you left me."

15. *(Says John):* "All right, so be it! Over there, between the two mountains, you can see a plot of grass as green as hope. Go there and rest in the name of the Lord Jesus, the Anointed from eternity!"

466

16. At the name of Jesus, Satan dashes off with lightning speed and settles with a great howl in the indicated place. But all the envoys return home.

HAPPY HOMECOMING TO SHONEL'S HOUSE. THE LORD'S LAUDATORY WORDS OF WELCOME, DIRECTED MAINLY TO MARTIN. HIS GREAT PROMISE: FROM JUDGMENT TO SALVATION.

1. The return trip is quite as fast as the first trip, and in a moment the messengers are back with Me in the house of Shonel.

2. Upon their return, they come to Me full of joy, love, and gratitude for the strength, might, love, and great patience bestowed upon them.

3. Martin is the first to throw himself at My feet in his burning love, and he begins to praise Me fervently.

4. *(But I lift him up, and say):* "My beloved son and brother, you have handled this most difficult business very well and have been an extremely good pioneer for My brother John. Well done, My Martin!

5. In the beginning you were a bit too ardent, making exaggerated use of My power bestowed upon you, but when you were warned by brother John, you acted in complete accordance with My most just order, conducting yourself so well that you achieved something with Satan that so far no one has ever succeeded in achieving quite without judgment.

6. So far, practically all messengers could only achieve something with Satan through a most severe and temporary judgment, since they were unable to hold their own against the shrewdness of his words. However, with *your* words, you got him into such a state that in his dispute with John he had to surrender voluntarily, which has never happened before! He is free now, and although he could move away, he is still resting in the designated place, which is good.

7. He has, of course, still many legions doing evil in his name – which will be felt on earth, but only for a short time. Then the spring will begin to dry up and, consequently, the evil will weaken, al-

though it will not cease altogether. But then, the end of all evil will not be far away.

8. The judgment of all evil will come through our love, which will captivate everything, and nothing will be able to resist it! Love's judgment, however, will be a constant one, forever unchangeable. It will not oppress like a heavy burden, but will simply hold captive all that does not want to be liberated.

9. Before this judgment commences, however, we shall once more dispatch messengers to all stellar worlds, with invitations to the Great Feast. Everyone they come across will be invited, and happy will be those who don't decline it, for their joys will be without end!"

THE CONQUERORS' REWARD. CELESTIAL MATRIMONY AS SUPREME PERFECTION OF THE DIVINE ORDER. ABOUT THE NATURE OF WOMEN. MARTIN'S GOOD CHOICE AND SUBMISSION TO THE LORD'S WILL. A HINT ABOUT CELESTIAL MATRIMONY. MARTIN'S CELESTIAL MISSION AS A PERFECTED SPIRIT.

1. *(Say I):* "And now there is something else, My dear children. Martin, Borem, and Chorel, come closer to Me! You have managed to get through all the hard trials and have emerged as victors from many a fierce battle. Thus you have fully qualified yourselves for My Kingdom of all the heavens.

2. You have now become skilled workers in My vineyard and are entitled to a proper reward, which you shall now receive. I know and read it clearly in your hearts that I am your highest reward and that you never ever wish for another one. But it is just this attitude of your hearts that renders you worthy and capable of receiving every other reward.

3. My order requires for your supreme perfection that in the future you shall live and work within the celestial matrimony. Therefore, each of you must have a wife so as to be perfect in every respect, to strengthen your wisdom for eternity and to receive the light which issues from the flame of love within your hearts.

4. A wife is like a spiritual vessel for the reception and preservation of the light from your hearts. At the same time, she is a servant in the heart's kitchen of life, feeding the sacred fire of life in the hearth which I have erected in your hearts. And, therefore, each of you shall now take a wife with whom to completely unite forever. Martin, I think you will not be opposed to this?"

5. *(Says Martin, overwhelmed with happiness):* "O Lord, You know my nature best! What You will give me will make me endlessly happy, be it Chanchah or Gella or, if possible, one of the sun-daughters. Oh, that would be supreme bliss!"

6. *(Say I):* "That is up to you. You are free and may choose freely!"

7. *(Says Martin):* "O Lord, only Your will be done!"

8. *(Say I):* "Well then, take the one next to you."

9. *(Martin, turning happily round, catches sight of Marelisael, the first and most beautiful of the three sun-daughters. He leads her to Me and asks):* "Lord, is this the right one?"

10. *(Say I):* "Yes, it is!" And I bless him for eternity. Thus Martin is now perfected.

11. In supreme bliss, he kisses his celestial wife and realizes that in this way his love has forever been united with wisdom. They now both praise Me from one heart and one mouth, for thus the segregated Adam becomes an integrated man again in heaven, although in the form of separate, individually blissful beings.

12. After Martin, Borem is given Surahil, the second of the three sun-daughters, and Chorel is given Hanial, the third. And both Borem and Chorel are boundlessly happy.

13. *(Martin, who can hardly contain himself for bliss and supreme delight, says):* "O Lord, You best and most holy Father, now I could exclaim, like Peter once did on Mount Tabor: 'Lord, it is good for us to be here!' However, only Your will be done!"

14. *(Say I):* "My dear, now perfected Martin, have you never, when on earth, heard the old saying: 'He who has love, will take the bride home'? This will be the case, also, with you. Since we have now brought order into this large house, we shall again return home.

15. The road that we shall take will in the future remain open to My new children of this big world of light, and it shall take them into your house and Mine. And all those, whom you have taken into your house, shall remain yours and Mine forever. For, what is Mine is now, also, yours, and what is yours is, also, Mine forever.

16. Therefore, you will forever remain the guardian angel of this house and its community, in Me as I in you. But it will not only be the community of this earth; the twelve doors of your house will lead you to the communities of countless other earths where you will find beatitudes beyond measure.

17. And now another word to the new children of this earth, but that shall come from you!"

203

MARTIN, THE NEW GUARDIAN ANGEL'S ADDRESS TO HIS SUN COMMUNITY. URON'S GOOD REPLY. HIS REQUEST TO THE LORD, AND THE LORD'S "AMEN."

1. *(Martin thanks Me for this commission from the depths of his being, then turns to Uron and Shonel, and says):* "Dearest friends and brothers, you have now seen with your own eyes and heard with your own ears what the Lord Himself has done and said. When you realized that a petition is more essential than a thanksgiving, you requested that the Lord and all of us remain in your midst permanently. The Lord has granted your request and is willing to give you whatever your great love for Him and us should desire. But all this can, of course, happen only in accordance with His eternal order.

2. Although we shall not stay here in person, a sure way will be open to you by which you will always be able to reach us, and we you - visibly.

3. Abide from now on with the teaching the Lord Himself has given you, and then the road from you to Him will be surprisingly short. But if in time you will observe His words and teaching less than now that you are filled with His Word, then that road would gradually become longer and more laborious. But the Lord Himself and your great love for Him will prevent this.

4. My house and the Lord's house are not *two* houses, but only *one* – a house of love. You know where to find it, and you are at all times welcome to visit us there. There you will always find the Lord in our midst as the forever holiest and best Father among His children who love Him above all else. So be it, in the name of the Lord!"

5. *(Says Uron):* "All our love to God the Lord, and to you through Him! Hallowed be His name everlastingly!

6. Our dear daughters, given to you by the Lord and us, shall be our heart within you and the tongue of our deepest gratitude in your mouth. May the hymn of praise, which we shall keep offering to the Lord and you in Him, sound in purest harmony as far as the rays of our world reach into the infinite spaces!"

7. *(Turning to Me, the Lord):* "And You, inconceivably holy Father, think of us, Your new children; keep us and all our descendants and our large community forever in Your grace and love! But do remember, also, all those other communities and peoples of this immense earth, inhabiting lands and areas still completely unknown to us. May Your will do for them what it has done for us, according to Your love and infinite wisdom!"

8. *(Say I):* "Amen, I say to you! They shall be assembled around Me from all the regions of My endless creations, and I shall give each one his due in abundance. My love, My grace, and My mercy be with you!"

204

HOMECOMING OF THE CELESTIAL PARTY. AN ACT OF MERCY. VISIT TO THE GALLERIES IN MARTIN'S HOUSE. THE ROAD TO THE CITY OF GOD. GLORIOUS ENCOUNTER AND WELCOME.

1. In a moment we are back in Martin's house. There, we are met by the now-completely cleansed bathing guests, who throw themselves at My feet begging for grace and mercy, which they receive in the fullest measure.

2. Martin, with all his guests, friends, and brothers, is led by Me for the first time to the galleries of his house. Here, a door is open towards morning and a glorious road leads to the holy City of God.

3. At this door, Martin is met by all the other disciples, with Mary, Joseph, David, Moses, Abraham, Noah, Enoch, Adam and Eve, and also all the other patriarchs and prophets, who all greet him with great friendliness as a new citizen of My City.

471

4. Martin's eyes are now fully opened, and his true bliss commences only here.

5. This far, I wanted to show you My guidance of Bishop Martin in the beyond. If I wanted to take you further, you would hardly be able to comprehend things, and we would then never come to an end.

* * *

CONTENTS

473

477

481

485

The Great Gospel of John

Received through the Inner Word
by Jakob Lorber

Lorber's greatest and best known work, written during the years 1851 to 1864, ist the Great Gospel of John in 10 volumes. It begins with an explanation of the Biblical gospel according to St. John an then gives a detailed account of the three teaching years of Jesus, revealing 'to a matured humanity many secrets of creation and divine guidance.

To make this work accessible to more people, The Great Gospel of John was condensed by the German publishers to about a third of its volume and is available in a set of 6 books now being translated into English.

This literature will speak for itself to the reader with an open mind, who has the honest desire to learn the truth, possesses humility and perseverance in his studies. Here the truth seeker finds answers to all the questions that have forever puzzled mankind. He sees the great panorama of creation and God's plan with mankind unfold, begins to understand the purpose of man's existence on earth, of life and death, of God's love and guidance and this knowledge gives him a feeling of security and frees him from his manifold fears.

6 Volumes, No. 2381-2386

Lorber Verlag, D 7120 Bietigheim-Bissingen
Germany